THE AMERICAN SOUTH
A Reader and Guide

Edited by

Daniel Letwin

EDINBURGH
University Press

For Nicholas and Timothy
whose past has only just begun

© selection and editorial matter Daniel Letwin, 2011, 2013
© in the individual contributions is retained by the authors

First published in 2011 by
Edinburgh University Press Ltd
22 George Square, Edinburgh EH8 9LF
www.euppublishing.com

This paperback edition 2013

Typeset in 9.5pt on 12.5pt Sabon by
Servis Filmsetting Ltd, Stockport, Cheshire, and
printed and bound in the United States of America

A CIP record for this book is available from the British
Library

ISBN 978 0 7486 1996 2 (hardback)
ISBN 978 0 7486 1997 9 (paperback)

The right of the contributors to be identified as authors
of this work has been asserted in accordance with the
Copyright, Designs and Patents Act 1988.

CONTENTS

NOTES ON THE CHAPTER AUTHORS

Eric Arnesen is Professor of History at The George Washington University.

John B. Boles is the William Pettus Hobby Professor of History at Rice University and editor of the *Journal of Southern History*.

Victoria Bynum is Professor of History at Texas State University-San Marcos.

Adam Fairclough is the Raymond and Beverly Sackler Professor of American History at Leiden University.

Kari Frederickson is Associate Professor of History and Director of the Summersell Center for the Study of the South at the University of Alabama.

Lorri Glover is the John Francis Bannon, S. J., Professor of History at Saint Louis University.

Paul Harvey is Professor of History at the University of Colorado-Colorado Springs.

Alex Lichtenstein is Associate Professor of History at Florida International University.

Kate Masur is Assistant Professor of History at Northwestern University.

Adam Rothman is Associate Professor of History at Georgetown University.

Anne Sarah Rubin is Associate Professor of History at the University of Maryland-Baltimore County.

Stephanie J. Shaw is Associate Professor of History at Ohio State University.

Frank Towers is Associate Professor of History at the University of Calgary.

Stephen Tuck is University Lecturer in American History at Pembroke College, University of Oxford.

Clive Webb is Reader in North American History and Head of the History Department at the University of Sussex.

INTRODUCTION

The South has always been one of the more captivating themes of the American experience. For generations, students of the nation's past have been drawn to the region's distinctive qualities, to its singular aura of poignancy, even mystery. The South's enduring hold on the popular imagination – above and below the Mason–Dixon Line, within and beyond the United States – comes across in countless movies and novels, documentaries and art exhibits, musical releases and best-selling biographies. College courses in southern history fill regularly to capacity.

Part of this abiding fascination with the South has lain in the mythologies draped so copiously around it. Seldom anywhere has the gulf between caricature and historical reality been so pronounced. Yet, in some ways, the latter has always been more intriguing than the former. Beneath Dixie's proverbial "way of life" lies a world of remarkable diversity: a region ranging in *ethnicity* from Native Americans to peoples arriving or descended from Europe and Africa; ranging in *geography* from the Mississippi Delta to the Appalachians, the port towns to the upcountry, the Black Belt to the timberlands; ranging in *occupation* from indentured servants to planters, yeomen to slaves, industrial workers to maids, artisans to intellectuals, urban professionals to sharecroppers. And, behind the image of a fixed "southern culture" stands a thicket of paradox and contradiction. The South, after all, has been noted at once for its refinement and its coarseness, for its traditionalism and its quest for modernity, for its entrenched hierarchies and its chronic social conflict, for its elaborate codes of honor and its elaborate schemes of corruption, for its rigid segregation and its abundance of interracial contact, for its infatuation with violence and its innovations in non-violence, for its ideals of "southern womanhood" and the grittier realities of most women's lives.

It should come as little surprise, then, that the South persists as one of the liveliest fields of American historical scholarship. The historiography covers a myriad of topics, spanning from the region's colonial beginnings to its uncertain entry into the twenty-first century. Leading points of study and debate include: the origins and development of southern slavery; the role of the South in the American Revolution; the South's emergence as a distinctive region within the new nation; the evolving ideals, and realities, of southern "womanhood"; power relations between the planter elite and the "common folk," slave and free; the roots, experience, and outcome of the Confederate rebellion; the coming of emancipation, and subsequent struggles over the meanings of freedom; the origins of the New South; Gilded Age revolts among southern farmers and workers; the rise of Jim Crow; Progressivism and traditionalism in the twentieth-century South; Dixie's transformative passage through the eras of the New Deal, the Second World War, and the Cold War; the civil rights movement; and recent trends in politics, economy, demography, and popular culture.

Weaving through these many strands of inquiry is a series of deep, underlying questions:

When did the idea of the "South" as a region unto itself first crystallize, and how has the notion altered over time? What has it meant to be a "southerner"? How have conceptions of "southern-ness" varied within the South, or between the South and other regions? How exceptional, in the end, has the South actually been?

What kinds of circumstances and outlooks have southerners shared broadly in common? Which (if any) generalizations can hold up against the region's enormous diversity of perspective, experience, and background? How in particular have persisting divisions of gender, race, class, religion, and local setting cut through the unifying aspects of southern society?

What, finally, has been the interplay of image and reality in representations of the southern past? How has the telling of the region's history reflected or, at times, *affected*, the course of contemporary southern society?

The American South: A Reader and Guide surveys key themes and issues in the historiography of the American South. Drawing together selections of major works in the field – introduced by some of today's leading historians of the region – this volume illuminates not only essential problems in the history of the South itself but also vital controversies over how that history should be interpreted.

The fifteen chapters that make up *The American South* cover the history of the region from its colonial beginnings to the present. Each chapter has been prepared by a historian with special expertise in the topic at hand. At the heart of every chapter is a set of three or four works of scholarship, selected by the chapter author for their significance to the topic in question. Preceding these selections is an introductory essay, surveying the central issues and developments of the chapter topic, setting up the various perspectives and approaches contained in the readings to follow, and suggesting some of the vital questions they raise.

"The past isn't dead," the novelist William Faulkner once quipped; "it isn't even past." In few settings have the stakes of historical interpretation been greater – or the rendering of the past more hotly contested – than in the American South. In reviewing the opening essays and scholarly selections found in these chapters, the reader is encouraged to consider how each generation of southern historical scholarship has been shaped by the passions and assumptions of its own time. There is no saying what future researchers will have to say about southern history, or how their insights will reflect contemporary sensibilities. But so long as Faulkner's maxim holds true – so long as the past remains "not past," but very much alive – we may be sure that creative scholarship and vigorous debate will continue to enrich the field.

A good number of people had a hand in the production of *The American South*. Thanks first are due to the excellent team at Edinburgh University Press. Special mention goes to Nicola Ramsey, who first commissioned this volume, and has provided sound and patient guidance along the way; James Dale, who ably assumed Ms. Ramsey's role while the latter was on leave; Neil Curtis, for his skillful work in copyediting the typescript; and Eddie Clark, who oversaw the final stages of production.

I wish also to recognize the chapter authors for their stellar efforts in choosing the selections and contextualizing them with original essays of their own. Recruited for their command of the literature, their contributions to the field, and their readiness to challenge and engage a broad readership within the classroom and beyond, these authors did not disappoint. Collaborating with such insightful and devoted scholars has made the work of editing this volume a pleasure.

I

John B. Boles

THINKING ABOUT THE SOUTH

To study the South is to take up a series of age-old questions – challenging, often paradoxical, always intriguing. What, to begin with, has it meant to be a "southerner"? When did the concept of the South as a coherent region first take hold, and how have its distinctive qualities been identified, and contested, in the generations to follow? What have been the central themes of southern history? How exceptional, in the end, has the American South been? How have its evolving patterns of demography and geography, culture and class, gender and race, politics and economy, compared with the wider patterns of national and world development? The opening essay by John B. Boles, and the selections that follow, offer a variety of perspectives, old and recent, on these kinds of questions.

John B. Boles, the William Pettus Hobby Professor of History at Rice University, is one of today's most influential historians of the American South. While specializing in the social, cultural, and religious dimensions of the antebellum South, he has written broadly on the history of the region from its colonial beginnings to the present day. Among the numerous books he has authored or edited are: *The Great Revival, 1787–1805: The Origins of the Southern Evangelical Mind* (1972); *Black Southerners, 1619–1869* (1983); *Interpreting Southern History: Historiographical Essays in Honor of Sanford W. Higginbotham* (co-edited with Evelyn Thomas Nolan, 1987); *Masters and Slaves in the House of the Lord: Race and Religion in the American South, 1740–1870* (1988); *The Irony of Southern Religion* (1994); *A Companion to the American South* (ed., 2002); *Shapers of Southern History: Autobiographical Reflections* (2004); and *The South through Time: A History of an American Region* (1994, 1997, 2004). He has been editor of one of the nation's foremost historical journals – the *Journal of Southern History* – since 1983.

Most people have some sense that the American South is different from the rest of the nation. Whether that idea is based on personal experience, novels, movies, or even a knowledge of history, the difference is harder to define than to feel. Most people think they know the South – and southern-ness – when they see it. But with the passage of time onlookers have seen the South differently, and different people at the same time notice various aspects of the region. So what do we mean when we think about the American South?

Around 1750 observers saw the southern colonies from Maryland to Georgia not as a unity but rather as several subregions having diverse agricultural economies, with South Carolina and Georgia's rice cultivation giving them an identification different from tobacco-growing Maryland and Virginia. North Carolina partook of some of the characteristics of its northern and southern neighbors but was less involved in either staple crop. In many ways North Carolina was more like the so-called backcountry, where farmers emphasized subsistence agriculture, grains, and livestock. But the entire nation was primarily agricultural in 1750, and slavery existed in every colony – although it formed the basis of the economies only of the colonies from Maryland southward. Still, travelers would probably not have seen slavery per se as a marker of the South. Indeed, the colonies were often spoken of as northern, middle, and southern, with Pennsylvania grouped with New Jersey, Delaware, Maryland, and Virginia. Even at the time of the American Revolution, when South Carolina and Georgia began to stress their distinctiveness because of their special dependence on slavery, the writers of the Constitution tended to differentiate states mainly in terms of their size and the extent of their western landholdings.

Only the most perceptive early observers, such as Thomas Jefferson, perceived subtle cultural or social differences between the regions which, Jefferson reasoned, were based on climate. In a 1785 letter to the Marquis de Chastellux, Jefferson detailed his "idea of the characters of the several states." Then, in two parallel columns, Jefferson listed his observations about the inhabitants of the northern and southern portions of the new nation. Persons in the North, he wrote, were "cool, sober, laborious, persevering, independant [sic], jealous of their own liberties and just to those of others, interested, chicaning, and superstitious and hypocritical in their religion." Southerners, by contrast, were "fiery, Voluptuary, indolent, unsteady, independant [sic], zealous for their own liberties but trampling on those of others, generous, candid, without attachment or pretentions to any religion but that of the heart." This well-known letter, however accurate or inaccurate its observations may have been, represents perhaps the first recorded effort to spell out the cultural differences between North and South.[1]

Over time, climate came to loom ever larger as a defining characteristic of the South. Perhaps the most famous and all-encompassing attribution to climate came from historian Ulrich B. Phillips who opened his seminal 1929 history of the Old South with a remarkable proposition: "Let us begin by discussing the

weather, for that has been the chief agency in making the South distinctive."
He followed that attention-grabbing sentence with a six-line summary of the
entire history of the antebellum South, a marvel of historical compression. The
region's distinct climate, he asserted,

> fostered the cultivation of the staple crops, which promoted the plan-
> tation system, which brought the importation of negroes [sic], which
> not only gave rise to chattel slavery but created a lasting race problem.
> These led to controversy and regional rivalry for power, which produced
> apprehensive reactions and culminated in a stroke for independence.[2]

From climate to Civil War in less than a paragraph! Although climate remains
a significant part of the region's image – stereotypes portray southerners as
people who walk, talk, and think slowly because of the omnipresent summer
heat and humidity – most scholars who have emphasized the role of climate
have seen it as only one of several factors shaping the South, its economy, and
its people. And in truth, since the advent of air conditioning, climate has lost
favor as a major causative agent in the South.

Just as Jefferson was offering his thoughts on the role of climate to the
Marquis de Chastellux, the northern states were beginning the process of
ending slavery within their boundaries. Increasingly after 1780, slavery was
confined to the southern states, where it had long been essential to the agricultural economy as it had never been in the more northern colonies. By the
early nineteenth century, slavery came to be perceived as a southern institution
and, as the number of enslaved Africans and African Americans climbed, the
South's racial codes and customs hardened. Slavery came to be the shaping
agent for the southern economy and society, and it was the primary reason for
the Civil War. After the demise of slavery, most southern whites sought other
means to control the black population, and as race relations in some ways
became harsher after the era of Reconstruction, whites developed political and
legal institutions as well as personal practices to maintain white domination.

Writing within the context of a racially divided South in 1928, historian
Phillips – who had in 1919 authored a pioneering if flawed history of American
slavery – saw race or, more properly, racism as the central theme of southern history. His contention that the "white folk . . . with a common resolve
indomitably maintained . . . that [the South] shall be and remain a white man's
country," seemed for several decades to accurately, if sadly, define the region.
While few today would argue that race was the sole factor shaping the South's
culture and tortured history, fewer still would discount its central importance.
A number of historians have shown the influence of white racial attitudes
throughout the course of southern history. From the way racism toward blacks
helped provide the flux that welded together a cross-class white folks democracy in eighteenth-century Virginia, to its role in justifying southern secession
in 1861, to its no less powerful role in politically unifying whites in George

Wallace's America of a century later, race had a long run as the chief ingredient in southern distinctiveness.

For too much of its history the South suffered from self-inflicted wounds, such as racism, violence, general intolerance, and irrational politics. Outsiders have often been quick to note these shortcomings. At the height of the Civil Rights era, historian Howard Zinn ungenerously portrayed the region as the receptacle for the concentrated essence of all the nation's vices.[3] But even southerners who cared deeply about the region, such as North Carolina journalist W. J. Cash, saw much to criticize and little hope for improvement. Cash concluded his evocative 1941 classic, *The Mind of the South*, with these heartfelt words:

> Proud, brave, honorable by its lights, courteous, personally generous, loyal, swift to act, often too swift, but signally effective, sometimes terrible, in its action – such was the South at its best. And such at its best it remains today, despite the great falling away in some of its virtues. Violence, intolerance, aversion and suspicion toward new ideas, an incapacity for analysis, an inclination to act from feeling rather than from thought, an exaggerated individualism and a too narrow concept of social responsibility, attachment to fictions and false values, above all too great attachment to racial values and a tendency to justify cruelty and injustice in the name of those values, sentimentality and a lack of realism – these have been its characteristic vices in the past. And, despite changes for the better, they remain its characteristic vices today.
>
> In the coming days, and probably soon, it is likely to have to prove its capacity for adjustment far beyond what has been true in the past. And in that time I shall hope, as its loyal son, that its virtues will tower over and conquer its faults and have the making of the Southern world to come. But of the future I shall venture no definite prophecies.[4]

By 2009, more than six decades later, great change has occurred in the South, more than Cash could have imagined, but we are aware that race still plays an influential role in American life. Yet it seemed for a while in the early 1950s that the South (and wider nation) might be moving beyond the malignant grasp of racial bigotry. In a momentous move, President Harry Truman in 1948 had initiated the desegregation of the nation's armed forces. Then, in 1954, the Supreme Court, in its *Brown* v. *Board of Education of Topeka* decision, had declared that segregated schools were prima facie unconstitutional. The Court did not provide an effective mechanism to achieve desegregation, however, and neither the Congress nor President Dwight D. Eisenhower provided sufficient moral leadership to effect dramatic change quickly. There was no rush to justice. Nevertheless, perceptive observers understood that the ground had moved underneath the hitherto impregnable foundations of segregation. Desegregation seemed to be, as the cliché put it, an idea whose time had come, and hopeful South-watchers began to ponder what would be the effect of a fundamental transformation of race relations.

At this time, historian David Potter, who had won a Pulitzer Prize for a book in 1954 that suggested that economic abundance had been essential to the making of the American character,[5] brought his incisive analysis to the long-lasting puzzle of the southern character. A native of the region, Potter drew on history and on personal experience to consider what made southerners *southerners*, even if they were unaware of their apparent peculiarity. When expatriate southerners met one another in such places as New Haven or San Francisco, they often felt not only slightly out of place, but also something of an attraction for one another. Potter, with perhaps just a tinge of romanticism for his natal home, posited that the essence of southern character or distinctiveness was neither an artifact of climate nor a residue of racism but rather a reflection of an older folk culture, a more personal relationship one to another and an almost instinctual identification with place. In the face of the increasing anonymity of modern urban life, where every suburb seemed the same, southerners held on to a personalism that resisted urban ways and retained a strong connection with their homeplace. "Where are you from?" a southerner is quick to ask when meeting someone, and interpersonal relations with a southerner are often so open and friendly that nonsoutherners read southern behavior as not genuine. So bone deep was this folk culture, Potter suggested, that southern distinctiveness would be little affected by racial or economic changes. And, in a real sense, he adds, black southerners may possess this distinguishing characteristic more fully than whites. Ironically, despite the South's long history of racial discrimination, there was perhaps reason to believe that the personalism that marked relations between persons might triumph over the worst aspects of the region's heritage. One can almost see the popular television series *The Waltons* emerging from this perspective, and it is difficult to imagine the effectiveness of Jimmy Carter's 1976 campaign without the emergence of this regional characteristic.

Several years before David Potter offered his solution to the riddle of southern-ness – what he called a "sphinx on the American land" – another gifted historian sought to unlock the puzzle. C. Vann Woodward had long been convinced of the significance of change in the South over time, and in perhaps the most important book ever written on the region's history, *Origins of the New South, 1877–1913*, he had argued that the South that emerged from the Civil War and Reconstruction era was fundamentally different from that which had come before. Other influential observers (such as W. J. Cash) had argued for the essential continuity of southern history; Woodward, by contrast, saw transformative change with the passage of time. From this perspective, Woodward presented a series of lectures at the University of Virginia that were published in 1955 as *The Strange Career of Jim Crow*, a book of extraordinary influence, not just on academic historians but upon an entire generation of educated southerners. Woodward gracefully argued that the first two decades after the Civil War were a time of what might be called racial experimentation, as dominant whites and insistent freedpeople attempted to negotiate mutually acceptable racial relations. Yet in the final decades of the nineteenth century and the opening decade of the twentieth, racial practices hardened, more restrictive laws were passed, and almost total segregation resulted. But Woodward's overarching point was that racial practices were not immutable; they had evolved in the past, and if they had once changed for the worse, they could also change for the better. This was a message of hope for many progressive white (not to mention black) southerners who had been reared to believe that segregation had always existed and was dictated by nature if not by God.[6]

By the mid-1950s, then, racial change was afoot. It was also clear that, as a result of a number of factors – including the aftereffects of heavy wartime spending in the South both at military bases and at defense-related industries – the South's almost century-long plague of poverty (President Roosevelt had called the South "the Nation's No. 1 Economic Problem" in 1938) was coming to an end. Sharecroppers and farmers were leaving the fields, and southern cities were booming. Woodward saw all this change, the economic portion of which he summed up in the phrase "the Bulldozer Revolution," and wondered what it meant for the future of southern identity.[7] In the past the South had been commonly defined, as we have seen, by its devotion to white supremacy and its warm climate. Commentators such as W. J. Cash had pointed to the South's nearness to a frontier stage of development (with its attendant violence) as a shaping factor, while others had talked about the South's poverty, rurality, and backwardness. But, if these markers for southern identity were increasingly inapplicable, did that mean that the South's vaunted distinctiveness was also dissipating? No, answers Woodward in his essay on southern identity, for the essence of southern-ness is not to be found in such discrete factors as race or climate or poverty, so much as in the entire southern encounter with history, an experience so at variance with that of the United States as a whole as to indelibly embed the southern identity in the character of its longtime people. In a nation that had known only success, the South had met failure and defeat. In a nation that had long been a marvel of prosperity, the South had long known poverty. And in a nation that had considered itself morally innocent, free from the evils of the Old World, the South had committed the sins of slavery, rebellion, finally segregation. In its fundamental historical heritage, the South was set apart from the rest of the nation, and in that separateness inhered its distinctiveness.

However persuasive Woodward's analysis may have been in 1958, does it still persuade? The American nation shortly afterwards discovered poverty in its midst so extensive that a president saw fit to declare a war on it; the nation failed in Vietnam, and in the Watergate event it lost much of what remained of its innocence. Has history then so brought the nation (read the North) and the South together in the half century since Woodward wrote that we could imagine the end of *southern* history? Would the loss of the traditional distinguishing factors create (or has it created) a recognition of identity loss, and a compensatory desire to rediscover reasons for maintaining, or even refashioning, that identity? After all, it was the Census Bureau's announcement of the end of the frontier in 1890 that inspired Frederick Jackson Turner to formulate his famous thesis that the existence of the frontier had been essential to the development of American character and institutions. At a time when some southerners have written of the death of Dixie and argued for the end of southern distinctiveness, others have apparently decided to pick and choose ingredients from their heritage, discarding older images that suggested hate or reflected poverty, disease, ignorance, and close-mindedness and highlighting positive values such as personalism, religion, a devotion to place and kin, good manners, and so on. But even if popular magazines try to prescribe what southern living should be, one can only question the genuineness of such traits when used, with the artificiality of costume jewelry, to define a people or region. Wearing a gimme cap or chewing tobacco or affecting a stereotypical good ol' boy or southern belle image does not really a folk culture make. Those who act as though southern-ness is an accessory one can simply add to one's wardrobe must also be cautious not to mistake small-town or rural values per se for something uniquely southern – that is, to exaggerate southern identifiers. Peter Bogdanovich's famous 1971 movie, *The Last Picture Show*, based on a Larry McMurtry novel, seemed as true to the memory of a Kansas small-town viewer as it did to a small-town Texas viewer.

The specifics of the place in which one grows up, along with the surrounding and supporting people and institutions – that is, the community – no doubt shape people's identity without their always being aware of the process. They simply are who they are, unselfconsciously, with little recognition of their being an example of "a southerner" while they are on their native ground. There is nothing fake or constructed about such southern-ness; it is, quite naturally, who one is. But when such persons are suddenly surrounded by people of a significantly different upbringing – whether they are in New York, California, or France – they instantly realize their distinguishing regional identity. Displaced southerners, for example, usually find they ache for the kinds of cooking they grew up eating when that food is no longer readily available; after all, gastronomic preference is for people everywhere a deep-seated marker of ethnic identity. Contrast highlights difference. And, of course, it works in the other direction, too: when New Yorkers, for example, or midwesterners, find themselves in the southern states, they are instantly and strongly aware of the difference and consider the South somehow exotic. (Nonsoutherners almost always note southern accents as a surefire indicator of southern-ness, despite the variety of southern ways of talking.) One might expect that, as southerners become better educated, more urban, more affluent, and more cosmopolitan, they would subtly lose their southern-ness. But as historical sociologist John Shelton Reed has pointed out, it is just such modern southerners who are more likely to find themselves outside the geographical South and interacting with nonsoutherners from around the world – thereby discovering, sometimes to their surprise, the resilience, and resonance, of their hitherto little noticed *southern-ness*.[8]

Polling data on a range of issues show that black and white southerners share more values with each other than either group does with its racial counterparts in the rest of the nation. Such is the shaping power of place and community. Unlike white southerners, though, black southerners do not have a tradition of seeking, in U. B. Phillips's phrase, "a central theme of southern history," nor do they lament, as have white southerners for a least a half century, the supposed demise of the South as a culturally distinct region. But, for more than three decades, more blacks have been moving back to the South than leaving it – a dramatic shift from the half century between 1910 and 1960, when a net total of almost 4.5 million blacks left the South. Many of these returning blacks have written about what calls them back to a region that had mistreated African Americans so long and so severely. They repeatedly speak of the sense of place, the role of kinfolk, the remembrance of the church, the taste of the food, the smell of the flowers – using exactly the same language white southerners employ to explain why they identify with the South. As black novelist and poet Margaret Walker put it, she "had the feel of the South in my blood."[9] The South today remains a profoundly biracial society and culture.

Ironically, overcoming the older southern characteristics of white racism, poverty, and backwardness has not weakened, but rather strengthened and broadened, southern identity. And this identity, while comparative in certain contexts, does not – as historian James C. Cobb emphasizes – have to be *invidiously* comparative. That is, one can recognize one's difference from others without disparaging the "other" or unduly valorizing one's own behavior or values. This, of course, is an attribute of our increasingly globalized world: one recognizes one's regionalism or nationalism, comes to terms with it, and, without total acceptance or rejection of one's identity, sees positive traits in other cultures.

Southerners themselves have often been insufficiently aware of the extent to which they are – and have always been – fundamentally American. After all, George Washington, Thomas Jefferson, and John Marshall were indispensable in the founding of the nation. Even at the apex of southern separateness – the moment of secession in 1861 – southerners saw themselves following in the tradition of America's founding fathers. Certainly southerners in the twentieth century tended to be proud Americans – even knee-jerk, uncritical Americans. And, however southerners appraise their distinctiveness, commentators from abroad perceive the South as primarily American. As David Potter once observed, robust regional loyalties may, in fact, be necessary for strong national attachments to develop.[10] Contemporary southerners' almost stereotypical patriotism proves that southerners today are, in the grand scheme of things, primarily American.

A modern southerner can also be a citizen of the world without renouncing his or her southern-ness. As C. Vann Woodward suggested in a famous 1953 essay, the very fact that the South has experienced a history rather unlike that of the larger nation – a history instead more consonant with that of the rest of the world – should give southerners a special rapport with people from around the globe.[11] The international popularity of Presidents Jimmy Carter and Bill Clinton – which often exceeded their domestic approval – suggests the validity of this insight. Even the more salient role of religion in the South may help create bridges to other cultures, for much of the world is less secular than are Europe and the United States. For example, it was Jimmy Carter's evident religious faith that facilitated his unusual accord in 1978 with Israeli prime minister Menachem Begin and Egyptian president Anwar Sadat. And, of course, southern music and literature have found an enormous international following. The authenticity of down-home southern culture may mean less a proclivity for provincialism than a potential for internationalism. If southerners white and black can learn to come to terms with each other, with their region's complicated and conflicted history, and with its ambiguous place in the nation, the South might yet offer lessons for the nation in its relations with all the peoples of the world.

Notes

1. Thomas Jefferson to the Marquis de Chastellux, 2 September 1785, in Julian P. Boyd, ed., *The Papers of Thomas Jefferson*, Vol. 8 (Princeton: Princeton University Press, 1953), p. 468.

2. Ulrich B. Phillips, *Life and Labor in the Old South* (Boston: Little, Brown and Company, 1929), p. 3.

3. Howard Zinn, *The Southern Mystique* (New York: Alfred A. Knopf, 1964).

4. W. J. Cash, *The Mind of the South* (New York: Alfred A. Knopf, 1941), pp. 439–40.

5. David M. Potter, *People of Plenty: Economic Abundance and the American Character* (Chicago: University of Chicago Press, 1954).

6. See C. Vann Woodward, *Origins of the New South, 1877–1913* (Baton Rouge: Louisiana State University Press, 1951); Cash, *Mind of the South*; and Woodward, *The Strange Career of Jim Crow* (New York: Oxford University Press, 1955).

7. C. Vann Woodward, "The Search for Southern Identity," in Woodward, *The Burden of Southern History* (3rd ed., Baton Rouge: Louisiana State University Press, 1993), pp. 3–26 (quotation on p. 6).

8. This is the argument of John Shelton Reed, *The Enduring South: Subcultural Persistence in Mass Society* (Lexington: Lexington Books, 1972) and, especially, Reed, *Southerners: The Social Psychology of Sectionalism* (Chapel Hill: University of North Carolina Press, 1983).

9. For a survey of recent black responses to the South, see Chapter 10, "Blackness and Southern-ness: African Americans Look South Toward Home," of James C. Cobb's *Away Down South: A History of Southern Identity* (New York: Oxford University Press, 2005), pp. 261–87 (quotation on p. 267).

10. David M. Potter, "The Historian's Use of Nationalism and Vice Versa," in Alexander V. Riasonovsky and Barnes Riznic, eds., *Generalizations in Historical Writing* (Philadelphia: University of Pennsylvania Press, 1963), reprinted in Potter, *The South and the Sectional Conflict* (Baton Rouge: Louisiana State University Press, 1968), pp. 34–83.

11. See the influential essay by Woodward, "The Irony of Southern History," *Journal of Southern History*, 19 (February 1953), pp. 3–19, conveniently reprinted in Woodward, *Burden of Southern History*, pp. 187–212. This essay was originally Woodward's presidential address in 1952 to the Southern Historical Association.

* * *

FURTHER READING

Boles, John B., *The South Through Time: A History of an American Region* (3rd ed. Upper Saddle River: Pearson Prentice-Hall, 2004).

Boles, John B., ed., *A Companion to the American South* (Malden and Oxford: Blackwell Publishers, 2002).

Boles, John B. and Evelyn Thomas Nolen, eds., *Interpreting Southern History: Historiographical Essays in Honor of Sanford W. Higginbotham* (Baton Rouge: Louisiana State University Press, 1987).

Brundage, W. Fitzhugh, *The Southern Past: A Clash of Race and Memory* (Cambridge, MA: Belknap Press of Harvard University Press, 2005).

Brundage, W. Fitzhugh, ed., *Where These Memories Grow: History, Memory, and Southern Identity* (Chapel Hill: University of North Carolina Press, 2000).

Franklin, John Hope and Alfred A. Moss, Jr., *From Slavery to Freedom: A History of African Americans* (7th ed., New York: McGraw Hill, 1994).

Gray, Richard, *Writing the South: Ideas of an American Region* (Cambridge: Cambridge University Press, 1986).

Hobson, Fred C., *Tell About the South: The Southern Rage to Explain* (Baton Rouge: Louisiana State University Press, 1983).

Kirby, Jack Temple, *Mockingbird Song: Ecological Landscapes of the South* (Chapel Hill: University of North Carolina Press, 2006).

Kirby, Jack Temple, *Media-Made Dixie: The South in the American Imagination* (Rev. ed. Athens: University of Georgia Press, 1986).

Reed, John Shelton, *The Enduring South: Subcultural Persistence in Mass Society* (Lexington: Lexington Books, 1972).

Wilson, Charles Reagan and William Ferris, eds., *Encyclopedia of Southern Culture* (Chapel Hill: University of North Carolina Press, 1989).

* * *

Ulrich B. Phillips

The Central Theme of Southern History[†]

An Ohio River ferryman has a stock remark when approaching the right bank: "We are nearing the American shore." A thousand times has he said it with a gratifying repercussion from among his passengers; for its implications are a little startling. The northern shore is American without question; the southern is American with a difference. Kentucky had by slender pretense a star in the Confederate flag; for a time she was officially neutral; for all time her citizens have been self-consciously Kentuckians, a distinctive people. They are Southerners in main sentiment, and so are Marylanders and Missourians.

Southernism did not arise from any selectiveness of migration, for the sort of people who went to Virginia, Maryland, or Carolina, were not as a group different from those who went to Pennsylvania or the West Indies. It does not lie in religion or language. It was not created by one-crop tillage, nor did agriculture in the large tend to produce a Southern scheme of life and thought. The Mohawk valley was for decades as rural as that of the Roanoke; wheat is as dominant in Dakota as cotton has ever been in Alabama; tobacco is as much a staple along the Ontario shore of Lake Erie as in the Kentucky pennyroyal; and the growing of rice and cotton in California has not prevented Los Angeles from being in a sense the capital of Iowa. On the other hand the rise of mill towns in the Carolina Piedmont and the growth of manufacturing at Richmond and Birmingham have not made these Northern. It may be admitted, however, that Miami, Palm Beach, and Coral Gables are Southern only in latitude. They were vacant wastes until Flagler, Fifth Avenue, and the realtors discovered and subdivided them.

The South has never had a focus. New York has plied as much of its trade as Baltimore or New Orleans; and White Sulphur Springs did not quite eclipse all other mountain and coast resorts for vacation patronage. The lack of a metropolis was lamented in 1857 by an advocate of Southern independence, as an essential for shaping and radiating a coherent philosophy to fit the prevailing conditions of life. But without a consolidating press or pulpit or other definite apparatus the South has maintained a considerable solidarity through thick and thin, through peace and war and peace again. What is its essence? Not state rights – Calhoun himself was for years a nationalist, and some advocates of independence hoped for a complete merging of the several states into a unitary Southern republic; not free trade – sugar and hemp growers have ever been protectionists; not slavery – in the eighteenth century this was of continental legality, and in the twentieth it is legal nowhere; not Democracy – there were many Federalists in Washington's day and many Whigs in Clay's; not party predominance by any name, for Virginia, Georgia, and Mississippi were "doubtful states" from Jackson's time to Buchanan's. It is not

---

[†]Ulrich B. Phillips, "The Central Theme of Southern History," in *American Historical Review*, 34 (October 1928), pp. 30–1.

the land of cotton alone or of plantations alone; and it has not always been the land of "Dixie," for before its ecstatic adoption in 1861 that spine-tingling tune was a mere "walk around" of Christie's minstrels. Yet it is a land with a unity despite its diversity, with a people having common joys and common sorrows, and, above all, as to the white folk a people with a common resolve indomitably maintained – that it shall be and remain a white man's country. The consciousness of a function in these premises, whether expressed with the frenzy of a demagogue or maintained with a patrician's quietude, is the cardinal test of a Southerner and the central theme of Southern history.

ৡ ৡ ৡ

David M. Potter

The Enigma of the South[†]

Among the many flourishing branches of American historical study during the last half-century, one of the most robust has been the history of the South. Fifty years ago, there was already one large body of literature on the Southern Confederacy, especially in its military aspects, and another on the local history of various Southern states, but the history of the South as a region – of the whole vast area below the Potomac, viewed as a single entity for the whole time from the settlement of Jamestown to the present – is largely a product of the last five decades. Today, a multi-volume history, a number of college textbooks, a quarterly journal, and a substantial library of monographic studies all serve as measures of the extent of the development in this field.

Anyone who seeks an explanation for this interest in Southern history must take account of several factors. To begin with, the study of American regions is a general phenomenon, embracing not only the South but also New England, the Middle West, and the great physiographic provinces beyond the Mississippi. In a nation as vast and as diverse as ours, there is really no level higher than the regional level at which one can come to grips with the concrete realities of the land. But apart from this regional aspect, the Southern theme has held an unusual appeal for the people of the South because of their peculiarly strong and sentimental loyalty to Dixie as their native land, and for Americans outside the South because of the exotic quality of the place and because it bears the aura of a Lost Cause. Union generals, for some reason, have never held the romantic interest that attached to Stonewall Jackson, Jeb Stuart, George Pickett, Bedford Forrest, and, of course, Robert E. Lee. Today, the predilection of Yankee children for caps, flags, and toys displaying

---

[†]David M. Potter, "The Enigma of the South," in Potter, *The South and the Sectional Conflict* (Baton Rouge: Louisiana State University Press, 1968 [originally published in *Yale Review*, 51 {Autumn 1961}, pp. 142–51]), pp. 3–4, 15–16.

the Rebel insignia bears further witness to the enduring truth that lost causes have a fascination even for those who did not lose them.

But it seems unlikely that either the South as an American region, or the South as Dixieland, or the South as a Lost Cause could hold so much scholarly and popular attention in focus if the South were not also an enigma. To writers for more than half a century the South has been a kind of sphinx on the American land.

[. . .]

On the face of it, it seems a matter of observation and not of theory to say that the culture of the folk survived in the South long after it succumbed to the onslaught of urban-industrial culture elsewhere. It was an aspect of this culture that the relation between the land and the people remained more direct and more primal in the South than in other parts of the country. (This may be more true for the Negroes than for the whites, but then there is also a question whether the Negroes may not have embodied the distinctive qualities of the Southern character even more than the whites.) Even in the most exploitative economic situations, this culture retained a personalism in the relations of man to man which the industrial culture lacks. Even for those whose lives were narrowest, it offered a relationship of man to nature in which there was a certain fulfillment of personality. Every culture is, among other things, a system of relationships among an aggregate of people, and as cultures differ, the systems of relationship vary. In the folk culture of the South, it may be that the relation of people to one another imparted a distinctive texture as well as a distinctive tempo to their lives.

An explanation of the South in terms of a folk culture would not have the ideological implications which have made the explanation in terms of agrarianism so tempting and at the same time so treacherous. But on the other hand, it would not be inconsistent with some of the realities of Southern society, such as biracialism and hierarchy, whereas agrarianism is inconsistent with these realities. The enigma remains, and the historian must still ask what distinctive quality it was in the life of the South for which Southerners have felt such a persistent, haunting nostalgia and to which even the Yankee has responded with a poignant impulse. We must now doubt that this nostalgia was the yearning of men for an ideal agrarian utopia which never existed in reality. But if it was not that, was it perhaps the yearning of men in a mass culture for the life of a folk culture which did really exist? This folk culture, we know, was far from being ideal or utopian, and was in fact full of inequality and wrong, but if the nostalgia persists was it because even the inequality and wrong were parts of a life that still had a relatedness and meaning which our more bountiful life in the mass culture seems to lack?

C. Vann Woodward

The Search for Southern Identity[†]

The time is coming, if indeed it has not already arrived, when the Southerner will begin to ask himself whether there is really any longer very much point in calling himself a Southerner. Or if he does, he might well wonder occasionally whether it is worth while insisting on the point. So long as he remains at home where everybody knows him the matter hardly becomes an issue. But when he ventures among strangers, particularly up North, how often does he yield to the impulse to suppress the identifying idiom, to avoid the awkward subject, and to blend inconspicuously into the national pattern – to act the role of the standard American? Has the Southern heritage become an old hunting jacket that one slips on comfortably while at home but discards when he ventures abroad in favor of some more conventional or modish garb? Or is it perhaps an attic full of ancestral wardrobes useful only in connection with costume balls and play acting – staged primarily in Washington, DC?

[. . .]

The Southerner may not have been very happy about many of those old monuments of regional distinctiveness that are now disappearing. He may, in fact, have deplored the existence of some – the one-horse farmer, one-crop agriculture, one-party politics, the sharecropper, the poll tax, the white primary, the Jim Crow car, the lynching bee. It would take a blind sentimentalist to mourn their passing. But until the day before yesterday there they stood, indisputable proof that the South was different. Now that they are vanished or on their way toward vanishing, we are suddenly aware of the vacant place they have left in the landscape and of our habit of depending upon them in final resort as landmarks of regional identification. To establish identity by reference to our faults was always simplest, for whatever their reservations about our virtues, our critics were never reluctant to concede us our vices and shortcomings.

It is not that the present South has any conspicuous lack of faults, but that its faults are growing less conspicuous and therefore less useful for purposes of regional identification. They are increasingly the faults of other parts of the country, standard American faults, shall we say. Many of them have only recently been acquired – could, in fact, only recently be afforded. For the great changes that are altering the cultural landscape of the South almost beyond recognition are not simply negative changes, the disappearance of the familiar. There are also positive changes, the appearance of the strikingly new.

[†]C. Vann Woodward, "The Search for Southern Identity," in Woodward, *The Burden of Southern History* (3rd edition, Baton Rouge: Louisiana State University Press, 1993 [originally published in *Virginia Quarterly Review*, 34 [Summer 1958], pp. 321–38]), pp. 3, 15–21, 25.

The symbol of innovation is inescapable. The roar and groan and dust of it greet one on the outskirts of every Southern city. That symbol is the bulldozer, and for lack of a better name this might be called the Bulldozer Revolution. The great machine with the lowered blade symbolizes the revolution in several respects: in its favorite area of operation, the area where city meets country; in its relentless speed; in its supreme disregard for obstacles, its heedless methods; in what it demolishes and in what it builds. It is the advance agent of the metropolis. It encroaches upon rural life to expand urban life. It demolishes the old to make way for the new.

It is not the amount of change that is impressive about the Bulldozer Revolution so much as the speed and concentration with which it has come and with which it continues.

[. . .]

It is the conclusion of two Southern sociologists, John M. Maclachlan and Joe S. Floyd, Jr., that the present drive toward uniformity "with national demographic, economic, and cultural norms might well hasten the day when the South, once perhaps the most distinctively 'different' American region, will have become in most such matters virtually indistinguishable from the other urban-industrial areas of the nation."

The threat of becoming "indistinguishable," of being submerged under a national steamroller, has haunted the mind of the South for a long time. Some have seen it as a menace to regional identity and the survival of a Southern heritage.

[. . .]

While the myths of Southern distinctiveness have been waning, national myths have been waxing in power and appeal. National myths, American myths have proved far more sacrosanct and inviolate than Southern myths. Millions of European immigrants of diverse cultural backgrounds have sought and found identity in them. The powerful urge among minority groups to abandon or disguise their distinguishing cultural traits and conform as quickly as possible to some national norm is one of the most familiar features in the sociology of American nationalism. European ethnic and national groups with traditions far more ancient and distinctive than those of the South have eagerly divested themselves of their cultural heritage in order to conform.

[. . .]

The same urge to conformity that operates upon ethnic or national minorities to persuade them to reject identification with their native heritage or that of their forebears operates to a degree upon the Southerner as well. Since the cultural landscape of his native region is being altered almost beyond recognition by a cyclone of social change, the Southerner may come to feel as uprooted as the immigrant.

Bereft of his myths, his peculiar institutions, even his familiar regional vices, he may well reject or forget his regional identification as completely as the immigrant.

Is there nothing about the South that is immune from the disintegrating effect of nationalism and the pressure for conformity? Is there not something that has not changed? There is only one thing that I can think of, and that is its history. By that I do not mean a Southern brand of Shintoism, the worship of ancestors. Nor do I mean written history and its interpretation, popular and mythical, or professional and scholarly, which have changed often and will change again. I mean rather the collective experience of the Southern people. It is in just this respect that the South remains the most distinctive region of the country. In their unique historic experience as Americans the Southerners should not only be able to find the basis for continuity of their heritage but also make contributions that balance and complement the experience of the rest of the nation.

At this point the risks of our enterprise multiply. They are the risks of spawning new myths in place of the old. Awareness of them demands that we redouble precautions and look more cautiously than ever at generalizations.

To start with a safe one, it can be assumed that one of the most conspicuous traits of American life has been its economic abundance. From early colonial days the fabulous riches of America have been compared with the scarcity and want of less favored lands.

[. . .]

The South at times has shared this national experience and, in very recent years, has enjoyed more than a taste of it. But the history of the South includes a long and quite un-American experience with poverty. So recently as 1938, in fact, the South was characterized by the President as "The Nation's Economic Problem No. 1." And the problem was poverty, not plenty. It was a poverty emphasized by wide regional discrepancies in living standard, per capita wealth, per capita income, and the good things that money buys, such as education, health, protection, and the many luxuries that go to make up the celebrated American Standard of Living. This striking differential was no temporary misfortune of the great depression but a continuous and conspicuous feature of Southern experience since the early years of the Civil War.

[. . .]

A closely related corollary of the uniquely American experience of abundance is the equally unique American experience of success. During the Second World War Professor Arthur M. Schlesinger made an interesting attempt to define the national character, which he brought to a close with the conclusion that the American character "is bottomed upon the profound conviction that nothing in the world is beyond its power to accomplish." In this he gave expression to one of the great American legends, the legend of success and invincibility. It is a legend with a foundation in fact, for much can be adduced from the American record to support it and explain why it has flourished. If the history of the United States is lacking in some of the elements of variety and contrast demanded of any good story, it is in part because of the very monotonous repetition of successes. Almost every major collective effort, even those thwarted temporarily, succeeded in the end. American history *is* a success story. Why should such a nation not have a "profound conviction that nothing in the world is beyond its power to accomplish"? Even the hazards of war – including the prospect of war against an unknown enemy with untried weapons – proves no exception to the rule. The advanced science and weaponry of the Russian challenger are too recent to have registered their impact on the legend. The American people have never known the chastening experience of being on the losing side of a war. They have, until very recently, solved every major problem they have confronted – or had it solved for them by a smiling fortune. Success and victory are still national habits of mind.

This is but one among several American legends in which the South can participate only vicariously or in part. Again the Southern heritage is distinctive. For Southern history, unlike American, includes large components of frustration, failure, and defeat. It includes not only an overwhelming military defeat but long decades of defeat in the provinces of economic, social, and political life. Such a heritage affords the Southern people no basis for the delusion that there is nothing whatever that is beyond their power to accomplish. They have had it forcibly and repeatedly borne in upon them that this is not the case. Since their experience in this respect is more common among the general run of mankind than that of their fellow Americans, it would seem to be a part of their heritage worth cherishing.

American opulence and American success have combined to foster and encourage another legend of early origin, the legend of American innocence. According to his legend, Americans achieved a sort of regeneration of sunful man by coming out of the wicked Old World and removing to an untarnished new one. By doing so they shook off the wretched evils of feudalism and broke free from tyranny, monarchism, aristocracy, and privilege – all those institutions which, in the hopeful philosophy of the Enlightenment, accounted for all, or nearly all, the evil in the world. The absence of these Old World ills in America, as well as the freedom from much of the injustice and oppression associated with them, encouraged a singular moral complacency in the American mind. The self-image implanted in Americans was one of innocence as compared with less fortunate people of the Old World. They were a chosen people and their land a Utopia on the make.

[. . .]

How much room was there in the tortured conscience of the South for this national self-image of innocence and moral complacency? Southerners have repeated the American rhetoric of self admiration and sung the perfection of American institutions ever since the Declaration of Independence. But for half that time they lived intimately with a great social evil and the other half with its aftermath. It was an evil that was even condemned and abandoned by the Old World, to which America's moral superiority was supposedly an article of faith. Much of the South's intellectual energy went into a desperate effort to convince the world that its peculiar evil was actually a "positive good," but it failed even to convince itself. It writhed in the torments of its own conscience until it plunged into catastrophe to escape. The South's preoccupation was with guilt, not with innocence, with the reality of evil, not with the dream of perfection. Its experience in this respect, as in several others, was on the whole a thoroughly un-American one.

An age-long experience with human bondage and its evils and later with emancipation and its shortcomings did not dispose the South very favorably toward such popular American ideas as the doctrine of human perfectibility, the belief that every evil has a cure, and the notion that every human problem has a solution. For these reasons the utopian schemes and the gospel of progress that flourished above the Mason and Dixon Line never found very wide acceptance below the Potomac during the nineteenth century. In that most optimistic of centuries in the most optimistic part of the world, the South remained basically pessimistic in its social outlook and its moral philosophy. The experience of evil and the experience of tragedy are parts of the Southern heritage that are as difficult to reconcile with the American legend of innocence and social felicity as the experience of poverty and defeat are to reconcile with the legends of abundance and success.

[. . .]

The South was American a long time before it was Southern in any self-conscious or distinctive way. It remains more American by far than anything else, and has all along. After all, it fell the lot of one Southerner from Virginia to define America. The definition he wrote in 1776 voiced aspirations that were rooted in his native region before the nation was born. The modern Southerner should be secure enough in his national identity to escape the compulsion of less secure minorities to embrace uncritically all the myths of nationalism. He should be secure enough also not to deny a regional heritage because it is at variance with national myth. It is a heritage that should prove of enduring worth to him as well as to his country.

❧ ❧ ❧

James C. Cobb

Away Down South[†]

For all the contemporary statistical data documenting regional convergence and the physical evidence afforded by skyscrapers, suburban sprawl, and gridlocked

---

[†]James C. Cobb, *Away Down South: A History of Southern Identity* (New York: Oxford University Press, 2005), pp. 336–9.

expressways, I have yet to encounter anyone who has moved into or out of the South and did not sense that, for better or worse, living here was different from living in other parts of the country. In one aspect or another, I have spent the last thirty-five years pondering the question of southern exceptionalism. Over the last decade or so, however, both in the course of researching and writing this book and of trying to pay some attention to events in the contemporary globalizing world, I have seen human beings driven again and again to extremes of both savagery and superficiality by a desire not simply to *be* different but to be *acknowledged* as such by others. This leads me to believe that continuing to focus on why the South is not like the rest of America may actually prevent southern historians from fully understanding why the South is like it is (or was like it was) and southerners themselves from knowing who they really are and, perhaps, even from becoming everything they could really be.

At the risk of sounding every bit as heretical as Hazel Motes, who championed the church without Jesus in Flannery O'Connor's *Wise Blood*, I believe the lessons of both the distant and the recent southern pasts underscore the need to consider a conception of identity without distinctiveness or at least one that emphasizes the importance of being "oneself or itself" over not being "another." Certainly, in trying to understand some of those who have struggled most thoughtfully with the idea of southern identity, nothing is so clear as the importance of their own personal connections with a particular place, family, and community to their sense not only of what it meant to be southern but, more critically, their sense of who they were as individuals. Ellen Glasgow became both herself and a southerner in Richmond; William Faulkner in Lafayette County, Mississippi; Harry Crews in Alma, Georgia; Alex Haley in Henning, Tennessee; and Randall Kenan in Chinquapin, North Carolina, all of them influenced by unwitting role models who probably spent little, if any, time worrying about whether they were like other southerners or unlike everybody else. These authors may have taught us a great deal about the South as a region, but Faulkner was surely correct, after all, when he concluded that ultimately "it is himself that every Southerner writes about."

Finally, as I suggested at the outset, our historical survey definitely points to the need to rethink the association of identity with "remaining the same one . . . under varying aspects and conditions." On the contrary, as Ayers has pointed out, "the very story of the South is a story of unresolved identity, unsettled and restless, unsure and defensive." As the most adept chronicler and analyst of the continuity of southern white identity, W. J. Cash enjoyed, albeit posthumously, a phenomenal surge in credibility in the midst of the often appalling response of many white southerners to the civil rights movement. By the same token, however, Cash's characterizations have seemed increasingly out of sync with events and trends in recent decades as it has become ever more obvious that many of the traits he had identified as regional were a lot more national than he and many others had realized. Certainly, Cash's model of a monolithic and static southern mind rooted in dogged resistance to change has proven inadequate to explain the experience of most southerners, white or black, in the post-Jim Crow, post-North era. Writing at the end of the longest period of relative continuity in the region's history, he did not perceive that what he saw as the southern white mind, which he believed had already persisted for roughly a century, could actually be only a stage in an ongoing process of interaction with – and ultimate adaptation to – the forces of change. In fact, this interaction had already fostered a more flexible, sensitive, and self-critical spirit that was emerging even as he undertook a book about what Daniel Singal called "a permanent mind impervious to the forces of historical change."

Cash's concerns about white southerners' behavioral and emotional pathologies, especially their exaggerated emphasis on racial values, seemed to be borne out in the ugly, violent, and utterly shameful short term. Yet, their ultimate, relatively rapid and low-key accommodation to the integration of schools and other public venues and facilities suggested that their "capacity for adjustment" was greater over the long haul than he had anticipated, just as the eagerness of many black southerners to claim the post-civil rights era South as home also came as a surprise to many observers. Ultimately, instead of destroying the "southern way of life," the overthrow of Jim Crow seemed to result in a broader, biracial effort to keep it alive, although often on dramatically different terms. Resolving some of these differences or at least learning to respect them may well be crucial to determining whether the label of "southerner" continues to have legitimate meaning and, more important, whether the South finally becomes a place where southerners can truly come to know themselves and each other.

Those of us who care about how things turn out "away down South" can certainly take heart in George Tindall's suggestion that "to change is not necessarily to lose one's identity, to change sometimes is to find it." Yet, as we have surely seen, identity is not a matter of simply deciding either to be different or remain the same. Its sources are not just internally but externally contingent as well. Just as the demise of the North against which they defined themselves left many southerners, whites especially, hard-pressed to explain who and why they are, allowing the newest New South simply to fade uncontested into a "No South" would have similar, and only marginally less severe, consequences for many others throughout the nation at large. Certainly, if its history is any guide, the southern identity of the future will reflect not just what southerners themselves have chosen to make it but what other Americans need or want it to be as well.

2

Lorri Glover

ORIGINS OF THE OLD SOUTH:
THE COLONIAL ERA

The colonial period – spanning from the initial settlement of
Jamestown, Virginia in 1607 through the American Revolution
of the 1770s – comprises a sizable portion of the southern past.
Historians of the colonial South pursue a variety of questions.
How did the colonial settlement of the American South fit into
the broader formation of the transatlantic World – that is, the
complex encounter among Europe, Africa, and the Americas? In
what ways did the cultures of red, black, and white southerners
draw upon their pre-colonial traditions in North America, Africa,
Britain, and other parts of Europe; in what ways, upon the more
immediate circumstances of the region? How pervasive, and rigid,
were hierarchies of gender, race, and class in the colonial South?

Of all these questions (and others besides), none has stirred such
abiding interest as those surrounding the origins of black slavery,
and its eventual emergence as the salient system of labor in the
colonial South. What explains this outcome? In what measures
did it reflect material considerations, and in what measures deep-
rooted cultural prejudice? How did dynamics of class and gender
enter into this process? In what ways were African Americans able
to shape their own destinies, as the colonial South hardened into
a slave society? How, finally, can we explain the emergence in the
colonial South of two conflicting traditions: the system of slavery
on the one hand, and the ideology of "liberty" on the other?
These questions make up the focus of the readings assembled for
this chapter.

Lorri Glover is the John Francis Bannon, S. J., Professor
of History at Saint Louis University, where she specializes in
colonial American history, with a particular interest in the social
structure of the early South. Over a series of research projects,
she has explored the interplay of kinship, gender identities, and

broader patterns of politics and economy in the colonial South. Her published works include: *All Our Relations: Blood Ties and Emotional Bonds among the Early South Carolina Gentry* (2000); *Southern Manhood: Perspectives on Masculinity in the Old South* (co-edited with Craig Thompson Friend, 2004); *Southern Sons: Becoming Men in the New Nation* (2007); and *The Shipwreck that Saved Jamestown: The Sea Venture Castaways and the Fate of America* (co-authored with Dan Smith, 2008). She is currently working on a book about the familial experiences of the leaders of the American Revolution.

The study of the colonial American South is extraordinarily rich and complex. Unfolding over two centuries, extending over a vast territory, and encompassing a myriad of peoples, the field inspires a sweeping range of questions. How did different Native American nations, such as the Powhatans, Catawba, and Creeks, respond to contact with Europeans? What diverse motivations lay behind the colonization of the southern seaboard provinces – Virginia, Maryland, Carolina, and Georgia? How did these mainland colonies fit into, and how were they shaped by, the broader Atlantic world? These are but a few of the questions that occupy historians who study southern colonies. But no issue has drawn greater attention or stirred more debate than the origins of racial slavery in the region. Why and how did African slavery become the dominant labor system in the South? What were the consequences? What was the connection between racism and slavery? How was a life of bondage experienced? Answering such questions about slavery has been seen by many historians as essential to understanding the South, so this chapter focuses on the development of southern slavery in the place were it all started: colonial Virginia.

In point of fact, the American South, distinctive in terms of economy, culture, and the self-consciousness of the region's inhabitants, took shape only after the founding of the American republic. Historians often disagree over exactly when and why the qualities that distinguished the South from the rest of the young nation first emerged. But on one point there is general agreement: racial slavery was pivotal in creating the Old South. Slavery exerted a profound influence over southern politics, law, family life, economy, and religion. More than any other single factor, slavery set the South apart from the rest of the United States.

And so, to explore the colonial origins of the Old South is at once crucial and counterfactual. On the one hand, historians can better understand the defining characteristics of the Old South – racial slavery, plantation agriculture, and the cultural conservatism of the ruling gentry class – by tracing the earliest origins of that southern culture back into the colonial past. At the same time, there was no "South" to speak of in colonial America.[1]

What became by the early nineteenth century the American South's "peculiar institution" operated throughout British America; indeed, racial slavery thrived in much of the British Empire well into the nineteenth century. More broadly, the whole enterprise of New World colonization depended in no small measure on the forced exploitation of African labor: in colonial Latin America; in the British, Dutch, French, and Spanish Caribbean settlements; and all along the North American seaboard. Among the British provinces, only Georgia forbade slavery (and there only briefly). In British America, Rhode Island merchants ran a robust slave trade, Puritan households often included bondspersons, and slaves made up more than one-sixth of the population of early eighteenth-century Philadelphia. When the British seized New Netherland from the Dutch in 1664 and renamed both the colony and the principal city after the Duke of York, slaves constituted 20 percent of New York City's population, and 5 percent of the entire colony – figures comparable to those of Virginia at the time.[2]

Beyond the fact that their racial values and labor systems were not appreciably different from those of their neighbors to the north, the early British settlers in Virginia and other southward colonies did not see themselves as "southern" in any way. Colonists' identities centered on their connections to the imperial center or to their own province: white residents of Virginia thought of themselves as Britons or Virginians, but never as *southerners*. Colonial Virginians also shared little in common with their neighbors in Carolina and Georgia – colonized more than sixty and a hundred years after Virginia, respectively – and certainly they felt no stronger connection to Georgians and Carolinians than to New Yorkers or Pennsylvanians. Looking forward, then, from British America's early seventeenth-century origins, there was nothing particularly "southern" about the colonies south of the Potomac.

But scholars do not simply stand at Jamestown Fort and explore the development of Virginia, followed by Maryland, Carolina, and Georgia in the abstract. Particularly those historians interested in the institution of slavery and the construction of racial power tend to interrogate colonial America while looking back: from the great houses of the mid eighteenth-century Chesapeake and Lowcountry; from the colonial rice and tobacco fields and antebellum cotton plantations that sealed the fates of generations of African Americans; from the early national era when the division between a free North and a slave South first took form. Historians who focus too much attention on these later developments run the risk of depicting the period as simply a prelude to the United States – a construct which colonialists rightly contest. Scholars studying slavery in colonial America therefore find themselves pulled between two competing impulses: appreciating the contingency and complexity of race and slavery in the colonies and revealing the connections between that world and the young United States to come.

Among historians engaged in explaining the colonial origins of racial slavery, no British colony has attracted more attention than Virginia. It was, after all, a cohort of slaveholding Virginia planters who served as the architects of the American republic: a nation that Thomas Jefferson, James Madison, and their contemporaries dedicated to liberty and equality but built on a foundation of racial slavery. Drawn by a desire to understand this seeming paradox, colonialists have searched seventeenth-century Virginia to find the roots of the racial values and regional distinctions that would emerge in the new nation. Other factors fuel interest in colonial Virginia. On the eve of independence, Virginia was home to the largest number of slaves in British North America. At the turn of the nineteenth century, half of all African Americans in the young nation, some 500,000, lived in the Chesapeake. (South Carolina, with a black majority, held the largest percentage of slaves among its population.) And Virginians shifted only gradually into this labor system, choosing in the late seventeenth century to change from white servitude to African slavery. South Carolinians, conversely, began their colony using slave labor, bringing slaves from the Caribbean with the first white settlers. Many scholars thus see in colonial Virginia the best opportunity for a full, nuanced, and compelling explanation of the development of racial slavery and its meaning for America.

Better than thirty years after publication, the finest work revealing the colonial origins of the American republic and the Old South remains Edmund S. Morgan's *American Slavery, American Freedom: The Ordeal of Colonial Virginia*. The opening half of Morgan's sweeping account of Virginia details the earliest conceptions of an American colony in Elizabethan London and the harrowing, deadly first years at Jamestown. He recounts the violent collisions with Powhatan Native Americans (when the settlers lowered the level of acceptable brutality to a shocking depth) and the cutthroat boom–bust tobacco market that emerged in the mid seventeenth century – which, in many ways, sealed the fate of Virginia. Tobacco, Morgan reminds his reader, made Virginia profitable, and so made the colony permanent. It also exacerbated among Virginia settlers a culture of avarice, exploitation, and violence. The second half of Morgan's book, passages of which are extracted in this chapter, turns to an explanation of why and how Virginia planters gradually shifted from cultivating tobacco with white servants to using African slaves. Both systems, Morgan shows, were brutal, and both commodified human beings. Each involved a deplorable cost-benefit analysis of a laborer's life expectancy. By the closing decades of the seventeenth century, as mortality rates in the colony rose, tobacco planters calculated that they could profit more from participating in the already thriving Atlantic slave trade than from continuing to depend on the increasingly unreliable immigration of English servants.

By turning to a permanently debased and racially defined labor force, Virginia planters also – if unintentionally – built a more stable society for themselves. Slaves could not easily run away, for they were immediately recognizable by their race, which had not been the case with white servants. They had little chance for freedom and, Morgan writes, "were without hope." So slaves posed no threat akin to that perpetuated by frustrated former servants during Bacon's Rebellion (a violent uprising of farmers and freedmen against the tidewater planter elite in 1676). Finally, slaves were systematically segregated from whites – in labor and in the law.

By the middle of the eighteenth century, Morgan argues, the Virginia colony was defined by a social order predicated not, as was the case in the mother country, on class but on race. The central division in society was between slave and free, black and white. The white solidarity that derived from this divide meant that even Virginia's poorest whites identified not with slaves but with planters; gentlemen slaveholders could believe that "all men are created equal" because all *white* men were equal in that they would never be black and so could never be enslaved. Racism, then, was not only a central factor in the transition from servitude to slavery, it became a foundational element in the creation of the American republic.

Since the publication of *American Slavery, American Freedom*, scholars have challenged and complicated many of Morgan's ideas, including his interpretation of the factors that led to the transition from servitude to slavery, his depiction of the relationship between racism and slavery, his characterization of slaves as living "without hope," as well as his central thesis about the intimate connection between slavery and freedom in the United States. It is a testament to the power of Morgan's work that so many scholars have contended with *American Slavery, American Freedom* and yet it remains widely recognized as a compelling interpretation of colonial Virginia.

One of those challenges came from Allan Kulikoff's *Tobacco and Slaves: The Development of Southern Cultures in the Chesapeake, 1680–1800*, which appeared a decade after Morgan's work and received widespread praise as a model of demographic and quantitative analysis. The excerpt from *Tobacco and Slaves* in this chapter reflects only a small part of Kulikoff's sweeping exploration of eighteenth-century Virginia and Maryland, which includes analysis of the region's developing tobacco economy, the rise of a planter elite, and the formation of African American communities and culture. Kulikoff explores not just the Virginia colony but the Chesapeake region. And he does not foreground his story around the American Revolution. Instead, Kulikoff's interest centers on a particular economic culture which eighteenth-century Maryland and Virginia shared. Kulikoff is principally interested not in ideologies associated with slavery but in the economic realities that led to its emergence in the Chesapeake, and the material consequences it produced.

In the brief selection below, Kulikoff offers an economically centered counter to Morgan's depiction of the transition from servitude to slavery. Economics, not ideology or notions of race, is what matters most in Kulikoff's assessment. The shift toward African slavery, he tells us, "resulted from a series of related economic and demographic events." Changes within Britain, the expansion of British North America, and problems internal to the Chesapeake combined to decrease the number of servants migrating into the colony in the late seventeenth century. Reflecting his economic focus and demographic methodology,

Kulikoff points out the influence of quantifiable factors: birth rates in England, tobacco markets in the colonies, migratory patterns of servants. It is these material realities that pushed planters to turn to African slaves. Planters, Kulikoff concludes, moved toward a racially based slave labor system only reluctantly, and only after the supply of British servants declined. (Morgan also makes this point but it is not nearly so central to his analysis.) Kulikoff's discussion of planters' interest in buying into African slavery, again reflective of his methodology, stresses quantifiable data: this time, the comparable prices of servants and slaves. Like Morgan, Kulikoff notes that, after the transition to slavery, political conflict eased among Chesapeake whites. But his work does not emphasize racial solidarity fostered by a race-based social order. Instead, Kulikoff points out that, after the large planters shifted to slave labor, poor whites could not easily compete with them. From Kulikoff's perspective the reality of economic life in Virginia and Maryland was what mattered most. And his evidence clearly demonstrates that the transition from white servitude to African slavery made the Chesapeake a far more economically divided and hierarchical society.

During the 1980s and 1990s, many historians shifted away from the demographic school exemplified by Kulikoff's work and focused instead on social and cultural history – including, not least, gender studies. Kathleen Brown's *Good Wives, Nasty Wenches, and Anxious Patriarchs: Gender, Race, and Power in Colonial Virginia* demonstrates the interpretive power of gender history. Like Morgan in *American Slavery, American Freedom*, Brown traces the story of Virginia from Elizabethan England through the American Revolution. And, like Morgan (and unlike Kulikoff), she is concerned more with ideas and perceptions than with demographic and economic realities. But for Brown, the transition to slavery and the relationship between racism and slavery cannot be understood apart from gender. She reads her sources seeking to understand how gender and racial power were constructed in Virginia.

An example of Brown's approach is provided in the third excerpt in this chapter, which looks at laws passed during the decades when Virginia planters were shifting from white servants to African slaves. Her reading of the legal statutes focuses on how white male lawmakers went about setting up a social hierarchy that not only subordinated black men and women but also white women. In the opening paragraphs, Brown refers to a number of legal innovations made after the 1670s that, for her, demonstrate the growing interest of white men in creating a more strictly defined social hierarchy: blacks' economic opportunities were circumscribed; legal proceedings became more formalized, and so increasingly excluded the influence of white women; slaves were precluded from entering into legally recognized marriages.

Focusing principally here on the legal regulation of sexual relationships across the color line, Brown concludes that policing interracial sex "became an increasingly important means of consolidating white patriarchal authority and defining racial difference." One example is the growing concern of

Virginia lawmakers about bastardy, particularly where white mothers bore children of African descent – resulting in "racially indeterminate people," who, Brown explains, threatened Virginia's social order. For Brown, the most important legal change came in 1691, when the Virginia legislature outlawed all interracial sexual relationships and characterized such unions as "abominable mixture" which produced "spurious issue." In Brown's reading, that law signified the exclusive power of white men over white women and African Americans. Only white men could have sexual access to white women; white women and black men who challenged that authority were subject to criminal prosecution. What white men accomplished with such laws and ultimately what they shared in common in the eighteenth century was, according to Brown, power defined by race and gender. That power bound Virginia men together and placed them at the head of a social order divided not simply by race, as Morgan argued, but by gender as well. This excerpt represents only a modest part of a wide-ranging work that has exerted tremendous influence over historians' understanding of the relationship between race, gender, and slavery in colonial Virginia. Brown's challenge to Morgan's work highlights both the continued significance of his interpretation of Virginia, as well as how much we can learn from scholars who interpret the same evidence and events from a new perspective.

The most sweeping analysis of slavery in colonial America undertaken in recent years is Ira Berlin's *Many Thousands Gone: The First Two Centuries of Slavery in North America*. Like Kulikoff, Berlin does not limit himself to colonial Virginia; his scope is even broader, including most of North America. *Many Thousands Gone* compares the evolution of slavery and of African American cultures in four regions that would become the United States: the Chesapeake, the North, the Lowcountry, and the Lower Mississippi Valley. Like Morgan, Berlin builds his story toward the coming of the American republic. He begins not at any particular point in colonial history, but rather with what he terms the "charter generations" – the moments when slavery was first introduced in these various regions. Berlin then investigates the "plantation generations," when some colonies shifted from societies with slaves, where slaves were used as simply one form of labor, into full-fledged slave societies, in which law, labor, and culture were all shaped by racial slavery. The book concludes with the "revolutionary generations," when northerners gradually rejected slavery and southerners grew increasingly protective of it.

Many Thousands Gone is largely a work of synthesis, drawing on Berlin's decades-long research into slavery and African American culture as well as the work of scores of other scholars, to present a wide-ranging overview of early America. The excerpts that conclude this chapter present Berlin's interpretation of how the Chesapeake shifted from being a society with slaves into a slave society. Like Brown, Berlin explains how laws denigrated African bondspeople and promoted racialized violence and power. Citing Kulikoff's work, Berlin also explains the demographic factors behind the transition from white servitude to African slavery. But in this selection, Berlin focuses most of his attention on the impact of those changes on the lives of African Americans.

The most important innovation in the historiography of slavery since the publication of *American Slavery, American Freedom* has been a concentration on the experiences of slaves themselves. Kulikoff, who investigated both the institution of slavery *and* the experience of bondage, was among the first to devote in-depth attention to the creation of black families and cultures in the colonial Chesapeake. Berlin's discussion of the contests of power between owners and slaves – and his explanation of both the fragility and resilience of the African American family – showcases how important that line of inquiry has become. Like Morgan, Berlin is greatly interested in the relationship between slavery and freedom. But his understanding of that connection extends beyond the intellectual leadership of the Founders, and includes enslaved men and women determined "to reclaim what their owners usurped," and defend the dearly bought, if modest, concessions they won from their masters. Berlin is less interested in charting how white power was enacted than in uncovering the creative ways in which slaves contested their bondage and the authority of slaveholders.

Directly or indirectly, the scholars whose path-breaking works provide these selections are in dialogue with one another. Sometimes they agree, often they do not. All of their books are important because of both the innovativeness of their approaches and their ability to recast the debate about slavery in the colonial South. What important connections do you see among these pieces by Morgan, Kulikoff, Brown, and Berlin? In what significant ways do their interpretations differ? Who do you think asks the best questions, and who provides the most compelling answers?

NOTES

1. In 2007 the *Journal of Southern History* devoted an issue to exploring "the South before there was a South." *Journal of Southern History*, 73 (August 2007), pp. 523–670.
2. Philadelphia and New York statistics provided in Berlin, *Many Thousands Gone*, pp. 54, 51.

* * *

FURTHER READING

Frey, Sylvia R. and Betty Wood, *Come Shouting to Zion: African American Protestantism in the American South and British Caribbean to 1830* (Chapel Hill: University of North Carolina Press, 1998).

Gordon-Reed, Annette, *The Hemingses of Monticello: An American Family* (New York: W. W. Norton, 2008).

Hall, Gwendolyn Midlo, *Africans in Colonial Louisiana: The Development of Afro-Creole Culture in the Eighteenth Century* (Baton Rouge: Louisiana State University Press, 1992).

Jordan, Winthrop D., *White Over Black: American Attitudes Toward the Negro, 1550–1812* (Chapel Hill: University of North Carolina Press, 1968).

Littlefield, Daniel C., *Rice and Slaves: Ethnicity and the Slave Trade in Colonial South Carolina* (Baton Rouge: Louisiana State University Press, 1981).

Merrell, James H., *The Indians' New World: Catawbas and Their Neighbors from European Contact through the Era of Removal* (Chapel Hill: University of North Carolina Press, 1989).

Morgan, Jennifer L., *Laboring Women: Reproduction and Gender in New World Slavery* (Philadelphia: University of Pennsylvania Press, 2004).

Morgan, Philip D., *Slave Counterpoint: Black Culture in the Eighteenth-Century Chesapeake and Lowcountry* (Chapel Hill: University of North Carolina Press, 1998).

Olwell, Robert, *Masters, Slaves, and Subjects: The Culture of Power in the South Carolina Low Country, 1740–1790* (Ithaca: Cornell University Press, 1998).

Perdue, Theda, *Cherokee Women: Gender and Culture Change, 1700–1835* (Lincoln: University of Nebraska Press, 1998).

Thornton, John, *Africa and Africans in the Formation of the Atlantic World, 1400–1800* (2nd ed., Cambridge: Cambridge University Press, 1998).

Wood, Peter H., *Black Majority: Negroes in Colonial South Carolina from 1670 through the Stone Rebellion* (New York: Knopf, 1974).

* * *

Edmund S. Morgan

American Slavery, American Freedom[†]

Slavery is a mode of compulsion that has often prevailed where land is abundant, and Virginians had been drifting toward it from the time when they first found something profitable to work at. Servitude in Virginia's tobacco fields approached closer to slavery than anything known at the time in England. Men served longer, were subjected to more rigorous punishments, were traded about as commodities already in the 1620s.

That Virginia's labor barons of the 1620s or her land and labor barons of the 1660s and 1670s did not transform their servants into slaves was probably not

---

[†]Edmund S. Morgan, *American Slavery, American Freedom: The Ordeal of Colonial Virginia* (New York: W. W. Norton, 1975), pp. 296–8, 308–9, 313–15, 369–70, 385–7.

owing to any moral squeamishness or to any failure to perceive the advantages of doing so. Although slavery did not exist in England, Englishmen were not so unfamiliar with it that they had to be told what it was. They knew that the Spaniards' gold and silver were dug by slave labor, and they themselves had even toyed with temporary "slavery" as a punishment for crime in the sixteenth century. But for Virginians to have pressed their servants or their indigent neighbors into slavery might have been, initially at least, more perilous than exploiting them in the ways that eventuated in the plundering parties of Bacon's Rebellion. Slavery, once established, offered incomparable advantages in keeping labor docile, but the transformation of free men into slaves would have been a tricky business. It would have had to proceed by stages, each carefully calculated to stop short of provoking rebellion. And if successful it would have reduced, if it did not end, the flow of potential slaves from England and Europe. Moreover, it would have required a conscious, deliberate, public decision. It would have had to be done, even if in stages, by action of the assembly, and the English government would have had to approve it. If it had been possible for the men at the top in Virginia to arrive at such a decision or series of decisions, the home government would almost certainly have vetoed the move, for fear of a rebellion or of an exodus from the colony that would prove costly to the crown's tobacco revenues.

But to establish slavery in Virginia it was not necessary to enslave anyone. Virginians had only to buy men who were already enslaved, after the initial risks of the transformation had been sustained by others elsewhere. They converted to slavery simply by buying slaves instead of servants. The process seems so simple, the advantages of slave labor so obvious, and their system of production and attitude toward workers so receptive that it seems surprising they did not convert sooner. African slaves were present in Virginia, as we have seen, almost from the beginning (probably the first known Negroes to arrive, in 1619, were slaves). The courts clearly recognized property in men and women and their unborn progeny at least as early as the 1640s, and there was no law to prevent any planter from bringing in as many as he wished. Why, then, did Virginians not furnish themselves with slaves as soon as they began to grow tobacco? Why did they wait so long?

The answer lies in the fact that slave labor, in spite of its seeming superiority, was actually not as advantageous as indentured labor during the first half of the century. Because of the high mortality among immigrants to Virginia, there could be no great advantage in owning a man for a lifetime rather than a period of years, especially since a slave cost roughly twice as much as an indentured servant. If the chances of a man's dying during his first five years in Virginia were better than fifty–fifty – and it seems apparent that they were – and if English servants could be made to work as hard as slaves, English servants for a five-year term were the better buy.

[. . .]

The plantation system operated by servants worked. It made many Virginians rich and England's merchants and kings richer. But it had one insuperable disadvantage.

Every year it poured a host of new freemen into a society where the opportunities for advancement were limited. The freedmen were Virginia's dangerous men. They erupted in 1676 in the largest rebellion known in any American colony before the Revolution, and in 1682 they carried even the plant-cutting rebellion further than any servant rebellion had ever gone. The substitution of slaves for servants gradually eased and eventually ended the threat that the freedmen posed: as the annual number of imported servants dropped, so did the number of men turning free.

The planters who bought slaves instead of servants did not do so with any apparent consciousness of the social stability to be gained thereby. Indeed, insofar as Virginians expressed themselves on the subject of slavery, they feared that it would magnify the danger of insurrection in the colony. They often blamed and pitied themselves for taking into their families men and women who had every reason to hate them. William Byrd told the Earl of Egmont in July, 1736, that "in case there shoud arise a Man of desperate courage amongst us, exasperated by a desperate fortune, he might with more advantage than Cataline kindle a Servile War," and make Virginia's broad rivers run with blood. But the danger never materialized. From time to time the planters were alarmed by the discovery of a conspiracy among the slaves; but, as had happened earlier when servants plotted rebellion, some conspirator always leaked the plan in time to spoil it. No white person was killed in a slave rebellion in colonial Virginia. Slaves proved, in fact, less dangerous than free or semi-free laborers. They had none of the rising expectations that have so often prompted rebellion in human history. They were not armed and did not have to be armed. They were without hope and did not have to be given hope.

[. . .]

It has been possible thus far to describe Virginia's conversion to slavery without mentioning race. It has required a little restraint to do so, but only a little, because the actions that produced slavery in Virginia, the individual purchase of slaves instead of servants, and the public protection of masters in their coercion of unwilling labor, had no necessary connection with race. Virginians did not enslave the persons brought there by the Royal African Company or by the private traders. The only decision that Virginians had to make was to keep them as slaves. Keeping them as slaves did require some decisions about what masters could legally do to make them work. But such decisions did not necessarily relate to race.

Or did they? As one reads the record of the Lancaster court authorizing Robert Carter to chop off the toes of his slaves, one begins to wonder. Would the court, could the court, could the general assembly have authorized such a punishment for an incorrigible English servant? It seems unlikely that the English government would have allowed it. But Virginians could be confident that England would condone their slave laws, even though those laws were contrary to the laws of England.

The English government had considered the problem in 1679, when presented with the laws of Barbados, in which masters were similarly authorized to inflict punishment that would not have been allowed by English law. A legal adviser, upon reviewing the laws for the Lords of Trade, found that he could approve them, because, he said "although Negros in that Island are punishable in a different and more severe manner than other Subjects are for Offences of the like nature; yet I humbly conceive that the Laws there concerning Negros are reasonable Laws, for by reason of their numbers they become dangerous, and being a brutish sort of People and reckoned as goods and chattels in that Island, it is of necessity or at least convenient to have Laws for the Government of them different from the Laws of England, to prevent the great mischief that otherwise may happen to the Planters and Inhabitants in that Island."

It was not necessary to extend the rights of Englishmen to Africans, because Africans were "a brutish sort of people." And because they were "brutish" it was necessary "or at least convenient" to kill or maim them in order to make them work.

The killing and maiming of slaves was not common in Virginia. Incidents like Robert Carter's application to dismember his two slaves are rare in the records. But it is hard to read in diaries and letters of the everyday beating of slaves without feeling that the casual, matter-of-fact acceptance of it is related to a feeling on the part of masters that they were dealing with "a brutish sort of people." Thomas Jones, of Williamsburg, was almost affectionate about it in writing his wife, away on a visit, about her household slaves. Daphne and Nancy were doing well, "But Juliet is the same still, tho I do assure you she has not wanted correction very often. I chear'd her with thirty lashes a Saturday last and as many more a Tuesday again and today I hear she's sick."

Possibly a master could have written thus about a white maidservant. Certainly there are many instances of servants being severely beaten, even to death. But whether or not race was a necessary ingredient of slavery, it *was* an ingredient. If slavery might have come to Virginia without racism, it did not. The only slaves in Virginia belonged to alien races from the English. And the new social order that Virginians created after they changed to slave labor was determined as much by race as by slavery.

[. . .]

[B]y the second quarter of the eighteenth century Virginians had established the conditions for the mixture of slavery and freedom that was to prevail for at least another century: a slave labor force isolated from the rest of society by race and racism; a body of large planters, firmly committed to the country, who had become practiced in politics and political maneuvering; and a larger body of small planters who had been persuaded that their interests were well served by the leadership of their big neighbors. The way was now prepared for the final ingredient that locked these elements together in a vital combination and enabled Virginians large and small to join with other Americans in devotion to freedom and equality, in abhorrence of slavery – and in the preservation of slave-holding.

That ingredient was a conglomeration of republican ideas that had gained popularity in England at the time of the Commonwealth. In England the ideas had not in the end prevailed, but they continued to be studied and refined and proclaimed by men who have come to be known as the eighteenth-century commonwealthmen. The commonwealthmen were not conspirators, hoping to overthrow the monarchy and restore the republic of the 1650s. But they were admirers of the Roman republic if not the English one, and caustic critics of the English monarchy. Along with other Englishmen they paid tribute to John Locke and the Revolution of 1688; but their favorite political philosophers were James Harrington and Algernon Sydney, who had championed the cause of republican government and suffered (the one imprisoned, the other executed) at the hands of Charles II.

The commonwealthmen believed that a monarch, if not curbed, would inevitably turn tyrant and reduce his subjects to slavery. In eighteenth-century England they saw in every exercise of executive power the signs of a drift toward tyranny and slavery, which they called on their countrymen to arrest. They suspected the army. They despised the churchmen who unflaggingly supported every infringement of liberty. They wanted to extend the suffrage and make representatives more responsive to the people. Above all, they wanted a wide distribution of property to create an enlarged enfranchised yeomanry who would see to it that government stuck to its proper business of protecting liberty and property. Their countrymen paid them little heed, and their names have not survived in fame: John Trenchard, Thomas Gordon, Robert Molesworth, Francis Hutcheson, James Burgh – these are scarcely household names today. But in the American colonies they were known and admired.

[. . .]

The English had come to view their poor almost as an alien race, with inbred traits of character that justified plans for their enslavement or incarceration in workhouses. Almost, but not quite. It required continual denunciations from a battery of philosophers and reformers; it even required special badges, to proclaim the differentness of the poor to the undiscerning, who might otherwise mistake them for ordinary men.

In Virginia neither badges nor philosophers were needed. It was not necessary to pretend or to prove that the enslaved were a different race, because they were. Anyone could tell black from white, even if black was actually brown or red. And as the number of poor white Virginians diminished, the vicious traits of character attributed by Englishmen to their poor could in Virginia increasingly appear to be the exclusive heritage of blacks. They were ungrateful, irresponsible, lazy, and dishonest. "A Negroe can't be honest," said Landon Carter and filled his diary with complaints of the congenital laziness and ingratitude of black men.

Racism thus absorbed in Virginia the fear and contempt that men in England, whether Whig or Tory, monarchist or republican, felt for the inarticulate lower classes. Racism made it possible for white Virginians to develop a devotion to the equality that English republicans had declared to be the soul of liberty. There were too few free poor on hand to matter. And by lumping Indians, mulattoes, and Negroes in a single pariah class, Virginians had paved the way for a similar lumping of small and large planters in a single master class.

Virginians knew that the members of this class were not in fact equal, either in property or in virtue, just as they knew that Negroes, mulattoes, and Indians were not one and the same. But the forces which dictated that Virginians see Negroes, mulattoes, and Indians as one also dictated that they see large and small planters as one. Racism became an essential, if unacknowledged, ingredient of the republican ideology that enabled Virginians to lead the nation.

How Virginian, then, was America? How heavily did American economic opportunity and political freedom rest on Virginia's slaves? If Virginia had continued to rely on the importation of white servants, would they have headed north when they turned free and brought insoluble problems of poverty with them? Would they have threatened the peace and prosperity of Philadelphia and New York and Boston, where the poor were steadily growing in numbers anyhow? Would Northerners have embraced republican ideas of equality so readily if they had been surrounded by men in "a certain degree of misery"? And could the new United States have made a go of it in the world of nations without Virginia and without the products of slave labor? Northern republicans apparently thought not. Some could not condone slavery and talked of breaking loose from the South in their own independent confederation. But the fact is that they did not. They allowed Virginians to compose the documents that founded their republic, and they chose Virginians to chart its course for a generation.

Eventually, to be sure, the course the Virginians charted for the United States proved the undoing of slavery. And a Virginia general gave up at Appomattox the attempt to support freedom with slavery. But were the two more closely linked than his conquerors could admit? Was the vision of a nation of equals flawed at the source by contempt for both the poor and the black? Is America still colonial Virginia writ large? More than a century after Appomattox the questions linger.

❧ ❧ ❧

Allan Kulikoff

Tobacco and Slaves[†]

The dominance of small planters in Chesapeake society began to disintegrate in the 1680s because the economic base that had supported their ascendancy crumbled. Ordinary planters had relied upon the labor of servants and freedmen to increase their income, but fewer servants came to the region in the 1680s and 1690s, and

---

[†] Allan Kulikoff, *Tobacco and Slaves: The Development of Southern Cultures in the Chesapeake, 1680–1800* (Chapel Hill: University of North Carolina Press, 1986), pp. 37–9, 40–1.

the servant trade nearly disappeared after 1700. Ex-servants had accumulated capital to set up their own farms when tobacco prices were high, but planters often made no profit in the decades between 1680 and 1720, and the rate of social mobility therefore greatly diminished.

The decline of the servant trade transformed the labor system of the region in two ways. It forced planters to substitute African slaves for white servants, and it permitted the whole white population to reproduce itself. Planters sought to retain a white labor force, but they eventually replaced indentured servants with black slaves, and by 1700 slaves produced much of the region's tobacco. As the number of servants and other white immigrants declined and the children of earlier immigrants reached maturity, the proportion of native-born whites in the population rose. Native whites married at young ages and had enough children to ensure a naturally increasing population.

The transformation of the Chesapeake labor force from one dominated by immigrant planters and white servants to one operated by planters and their black slaves revolutionized the social relations of production. Political conflict between groups of whites diminished because there were fewer servants and ex-servants in the population, and even poor whites sought to become slaveholders and thereby exploit the labor of people they considered inferior. At the same time, however, the probability that poorer whites would advance economically decreased because they did not have sufficient capital to purchase a slave. By the early eighteenth century, an indigenous group of slaveholders who inherited wealth and place had replaced the relatively egalitarian social order of mid-seventeenth-century society with a hierarchical society.

The adoption of slave labor resulted from a series of related economic and demographic events that stretched from the 1660s through the early decades of the eighteenth century. A decline in English birthrates during the second third of the seventeenth century, combined with rising real wages, had by the 1680s substantially reduced the number of men at risk to come to the New World. The new colonies of Pennsylvania and South Carolina, moreover, offered enticing opportunities. To attract their share of this diminished group of migrants, the Chesapeake colonies needed to offer opportunities for advancement that could compete with these new settlements.

But severe depression in the tobacco economy at the end of the seventeenth century decreased relative opportunities in the Chesapeake colonies.

[. . .]

These conditions did not bode well for immigrants, who frequently decided they had better chances elsewhere. The proportion of British immigrants who came to the Chesapeake colonies, in fact, declined from a high of over two-fifths in the 1670s to just over a third by the 1690s.

Chesapeake planters, however, still wanted servants, and some of them still had capital to purchase labor. The long depression hit some planters more severely than others. Farmers who grew tobacco on marginal land found they could no longer compete and substituted grains and livestock farming for tobacco. But planters who lived on more fertile lands, especially those who moved to new frontiers, often succeeded in improving their condition despite the general depression. These relatively prosperous families, unlike less fortunate farmers, could afford to buy servants.

These Chesapeake planters failed to entice a sufficient number of Englishmen to meet their needs by coming to their depressed region. From 1680 to 1699 only about thirty thousand whites migrated to Maryland and Virginia, about four-fifths the rate of the previous three decades. Since the number of households had greatly increased, the number of white laborers that planters could command drastically declined.

[. . .]

The decline of the servant trade transformed the labor force of the Chesapeake region. Planters preferred to employ English-speaking white servants rather than foreign whites or black slaves, but as the Chesapeake population rose and the number of men desiring white labor increased, they employed more and more alien workers. When the relative supply of servants began to decline in the 1670s and 1680s and they could no longer procure white English men, they turned first to English women, and when the supply of English women ran low, they purchased Irish men.

Once planters had exhausted the supply of white laborers, they turned reluctantly to African slaves. The slave trade to the Chesapeake colonies began slowly in the third quarter of the seventeenth century. In 1660 no more than seventeen hundred blacks lived in Maryland and Virginia, and by 1680 their numbers had increased to about four thousand. During the 1660s and 1670s most forced black migrants arrived in small groups from the West Indies, but about three thousand black people, including many Africans, were forced into slavery in the region between 1674 and 1695. Since the supply of servants had declined, these few blacks made up an ever-increasing proportion of unfree workers in the region in the late 1670s and 1680s. Only during the second half of the 1690 – two decades after the servant trade began to diminish – did planters buy substantial numbers of black slaves. They enslaved about three thousand Africans, as many as had arrived in the previous twenty years, between 1695 and 1700.

The racial composition of the Chesapeake labor force changed gradually during the last third of the seventeenth century, but by 1700 most unfree laborers were black.

[. . .]

Although planters clung to their preference for white servants over slaves for much of the late seventeenth century, they became reconciled, and even enthusiastic, about black labor by the early eighteenth century. When the supply of servants began to diminish during the 1670s and 1680s, the price of white men increased, both absolutely and relative to the price of full field hands. Planters in southern Maryland could buy three white men for the price of a single prime-age black male field hand in the early 1670s, but the same slave was worth only two servants by the end of the decade. This pattern strongly suggests that planters wanted servants more than slaves, for if they had believed that slaves were more profitable, the relative price of servants would have diminished. The ratio of servant to slave prices rose, however, over the 1690s and early 1700s and again reached nearly three servants per slave by the 1710s, despite the near-total disappearance of servants. By that time, planters had learned that slaves could be as productive as whites and sought them avidly every time a slave ship arrived.

∾ ∾ ∾

Kathleen M. Brown

Good Wives, Nasty Wenches, and Anxious Patriarchs[†]

After Bacon's Rebellion, white planters seeking new ways to reduce the rebellious potential of servants and slaves turned increasingly to African labor. Although enslaved men suffered disproportionately from many of the post-rebellion restrictions upon economic activity and geographic mobility, lawmakers also made new use of existing restrictions on white women's sexuality to refine the legal meanings and practical consequences of racial difference. Fornication between white women and black men threatened not only to compromise the utility of female servants – a perennial problem no matter what the race of the male offender – but to blur racial distinctions and increase the free black population. Previous legislation making slavery heritable through the mother had made it possible for white women to disconnect slavery from race by bearing children of African descent. By putting the traditional sexual regulations of white servant women to the service of patrolling racial boundaries, lawmakers created new legal meanings for race.

The sexualization of race occurred within the context of changing legal practices and new relationships between courtrooms and daily life during the last quarter of the seventeenth century. Three legal developments paved the way for the growing interdependence of definitions of racial difference and illicit sexuality. First, county courts narrowed the range of their prosecutions of sexual misdemeanors to focus on bastardy, punishing it with fines and whippings and abandoning ecclesiastical-style

---

[†]Kathleen M. Brown, *Good Wives, Nasty Wenches, and Anxious Patriarchs: Gender, Race, and Power in Colonial Virginia* (Chapel Hill: University of North Carolina Press, 1996), pp. 187–8, 196–8, 207.

punishments such as penance. Second, reflecting the growing sophistication of justices and the decline of women's influence over public spaces like courtrooms, the county courts also began to enforce more rigorous standards for proof of wrongdoing, giving less credence to hearsay evidence and the "common fame." The formality and uniformity of these legal standards eroded the influence of female speech and local customs over the judicial process, widening the distance between the legal identities produced by lawmakers and courtrooms and those that evolved through community negotiations and interactions. Third, in the context of these changes in legal practice, the colonial legislature refined its definition of whiteness to exclude individuals of African and Indian descent from Anglo-Virginian constructions of marriage and legitimacy.

Control over labor, white and black, provided a powerful motive for these legal shifts, as did the traditional concern to protect the masters of servant women from loss. But with the colonial legislature's exclusion of slaves from white definitions of marriage and legitimacy came new imperatives to maintain racial distinctions beyond the immediate needs of the labor system. What began with legal initiatives to defend the boundaries of slavery expanded to incorporate protections for legal concepts of race. Some of these legal constructs of racial identity filtered into popular attitudes toward racial difference and illicit sexual behavior. In most communities, however, some individuals continued, at the pleasure of their neighbors, to exercise privileges denied to them by law.

Having avoided some of the worst aspects of slavery through a combination of luck and perseverance, free Afro-Virginians were not completely excluded from white-centered definitions of marital sexuality before Bacon's Rebellion. But, at the end of the seventeenth century, they, too, were beginning to be distinguished from whites sexually. By the early eighteenth century, sexual and racial regulation had become interwoven components of social relations in the colony. The concern with the "foul crime" of white fornication had been replaced with attempts to punish bastardy, especially the "spurious issue" of interracial unions.

[. . .]

In the years after Bacon's Rebellion, sexual regulations became an increasingly important means of consolidating white patriarchal authority and defining racial difference. With the importation of large numbers of African slaves during the 1680s and 1690s, planter attention shifted from a concern with the laboring population in general to a specific interest in controlling black laborers. Between 1680 and 1699 . . . lawmakers passed new legislation aimed at subordinating potentially rebellious slaves. This legislation did not always apply to enslaved men and women equally, however, nor did it set uniform rules governing slave interactions with white men and women. Rather, several of the new laws targeted enslaved men and white female servants, distinguishing among slaves on the basis of sex and among white women on the basis of class and marital status. Codifying intervention in the lives of these potentially disruptive women and men, these laws fortified the rough alliance of white men along the lines of race and patriarchal privilege that had emerged after the rebellion.

[. . .]

In 1691, legislators explicitly addressed the problem presented by these relation-ships by refashioning older traditions for regulating servant sexuality to fit newer concerns with race. Expressing their anxieties about the sexual activities of white women in a preamble to the new statute, lawmakers noted the danger presented by the "abominable mixture and spurious issue which heareafter may encrease in this dominion, as well by negroes, mulattoes, and Indians intermarrying with English, or other white women." Provoked by the threat of a growing population of racially inde-terminate people, Virginia's planters took radical steps to enforce racial difference:

> Whatsoever English or other white man or woman being free shall intermarry with a negroe, mulatto, or Indian man or woman bond or free shall within three months after such marriage be banished and removed from this domin-ion forever.

The act further specified severe punishments for English women, free or servant, who bore illegitimate children by black or mulatto men. Even the children of these unions received the stigma of punishment. They were ordered to serve extended terms of indenture until age thirty, a measure that set them apart from other illegiti-mates who served only until age twenty-four.

The statute of 1691 made *all* interracial sexual acts illicit, criminalizing rela-tionships that might previously have been eligible for the protection of marriage. Sexual relationships between white people and Indians, moreover, became as subject to censure as those between white people and individuals of African descent. Despite the law's seeming concern to prevent all "spurious issue," however, its preamble revealed the special place that unions between white women and black men occupied in the thinking of Virginia lawmakers.

[. . .]

In their efforts to enforce the racial exclusivity of white women's sexual relation-ships, lawmakers also revealed the growing overlap between patriarchal privilege and racial domination. The 1691 law distinguished between the rights of black and white men, solidifying the patriarchal stake of all white men in a slave system that offered the greatest benefits to large planters.

[. . .]

With their access to white women sanctioned by law and protected from the dual threat of white female sexual autonomy and black male encroachments, moreover, white men could rest easy knowing that their authority over male slaves had been confirmed legally. By 1691, patriarchal authority had officially become a privilege of race as well as of sex.

[. . .]

Postrebellion laws knit together traditional measures for regulating the sexuality of poor people and servants with newer efforts to establish legal meanings for racial difference. Prohibitions on interracial marriages safeguarded white male access to white women, providing assurance that white female domesticity and sexuality would remain the preserve of white men. Harsh punishments greeted white servant women who threatened this arrangement by enjoying illicit pleasures with black men. Together, these legal measures racialized legal constructs of patriarchal privilege and female honor, creating a codependence between the two that excluded black men and women.

ᡐ ᡐ ᡐ

Ira Berlin

Many Thousands Gone[†]

During the seventeenth and into the eighteenth century, master, servant, and slave worked shoulder-to-shoulder, with the mistress and her children frequently joining them in the field as well. Although most planters appeared to presume people of African descent were slaves – since they were purchased from slave traders – no law yet enshrined African slavery in either Maryland or Virginia, and the laws that referred to black people were scattered and miscellaneous.

Since both white and black workers grew tobacco – subject to various degrees of coercion – black plantation hands labored according to customary English practices . . . Indeed, as the Chesapeake settlement grew during the seventeenth century, servants expanded the customary rights of English laborers, so that by midcentury they rarely worked more than five and a half days a week during the summer. Winter marked a general reduction of labor, as there was seldom enough work to fill the shorter days. Throughout the year, tobacco hands had not only Sunday to themselves but also half of Saturday and all holidays, which were numerous. The workday itself was punctuated with a long mid-day break.

Custom also required masters and mistresses to provide their servants sufficient

---

[†]Ira Berlin, *Many Thousands Gone: The First Two Centuries of Slavery in North America* (Cambridge, MA: Harvard University Press, 1998), pp. 31–3, 38, 109, 113–16, 126–7, 130–4.

food, clothing, and shelter, and it limited the owners' right to discipline subordinates. When planters wished to discipline workers, whether black or white, they often used the courts; not until the next century did slaveowners presume that they were absolute sovereigns within the confines of their estate. Although no slave took his owner to court for ill-treatment, as servants did upon occasion, the law and "Customs of the Countrey" that safeguarded servants provided a modicum of protection for slaves as well. In short, into the middle years of the seventeenth century and perhaps later, slaves enjoyed the benefits extended to white servants in the mixed labor force.

To be sure, the law was often ignored and customary practice forsaken; by all accounts, there was far more abuse of servants in the Chesapeake than in England, and slaves doubtless fared all the worse.

[. . .]

Thus, if the treatment of black laborers at the hands of planters differed little from that of white ones, it was in large measure because human beings could hardly be treated with greater disregard. While the advantages of this peculiar brand of equality may have been lost on its beneficiaries, it was precisely the shared labor regimen that allowed some black men . . . to obtain their freedom and join the scramble for land, servants, and status that characterized life in the seventeenth-century Chesapeake.

[. . .]

Small communities of free blacks sprouted up all around the perimeter of the Chesapeake Bay, with the largest concentration on the eastern shore of Virginia and Maryland. The number remained tiny – in 1665 the free black population of Virginia's Northampton and Accomack counties amounted to less than twenty adults and perhaps an equal number of children – but as the black population of the entire region was itself small, totaling no more than 300 on the eastern shore and perhaps 1,700 in all of Maryland and Virginia, the proportion of black people enjoying freedom was substantial. And, perhaps more importantly, it was growing. In Northampton County, free people of African descent made up about one-fifth of the black population at midcentury, rising to nearly 30 percent in 1668.

Although a minority, these free men and women defined the boundaries of black life and the character of race relations in the Chesapeake during the first fifty years of English and African settlement. The enslavement of most black people in the region – and, more importantly, the universal knowledge that people of African descent were enslaved throughout the Atlantic world – debased black people in the eyes of most whites, before Chesapeake lawmakers ruled that the children of enslaved black women were slaves for life and even prior to the enactment of other discriminatory legislation. But the free blacks' presence and growing numbers subverted the logic of racial slavery in the eyes of white and black alike. As long as the boundary between slavery and freedom remained permeable, and as long as white and black labored in the fields together, racial slavery remained only one labor system among many.

[. . .]

The plantation revolution came to the Chesapeake with the thunder of cannons and the rattle of sabres. Victory over the small holders, servants, and slaves who composed Nathaniel Bacon's motley army in 1676 enabled planters to consolidate their control over Chesapeake society. In quick order, they elaborated a slave code that singled out people of African descent as slaves and made their status hereditary. In the years that followed, as the number of European servants declined and white farmers migrated west, the great planters turned to Africa for their workforce. During the last decades of the seventeenth century, the new order began to take shape. The Chesapeake's economy stumbled into the eighteenth century, but the grandees prospered, as the profits of slave labor filled their pockets. A society with slaves gave way to a slave society around the great estuary.

Although black people grew tobacco as before, the lives of plantation slaves in no way resembled those of the charter generations. White indentured servants might graduate to tenantry or gain small holdings of their own, but black slaves could not. Planters restricted the slaves' access to freedom and stripped slaves of their prerogatives and free blacks of their rights. Rather than participate in a variety of enterprises, slaves labored single-mindedly under the direction of white overseers whose close supervision left little room for initiative or ambition. The slaves' economy withered and with it the robust network of exchanges that had rested upon the slaves' independent production. But even as the great planters installed the new harsh regime, African slaves and their descendants, sometimes in league with remnants of the charter generations, began to reshape black life. In the process, they created a new African-American society.

[. . .]

Whereas members of the charter generations had slept and eaten under the same roof and had worked in the same fields as their owners, the new arrivals [from Africa] lived in a world apart. Even the ties between black slaves and white servants atrophied, as blacks sank deeper into slavery while whites rose in aspiration if not in fact. The strivings of white servants necessitated their distinguishing themselves from African slaves, who were the recipients of harsh treatment that whites laborers would no longer accept. No matter how low the status of white servants, their pale skin distinguished them from society's designated mudsill, and this small difference became the foundation upon which the entire social order rested. Nothing could be further from the "drinkinge and carrousinge" that had brought black slaves and white servants together for long bouts of interracial conviviality than the physical and verbal isolation that confronted newly arrived Africans. Whiteness and blackness took on new meanings.

[. . .]

Such a social order required raw power to sustain it; and during the early years of the eighteenth century, planters mobilized the apparatus of coercion in the service of their new regime. In the previous century, maimings, brandings, and beatings had occurred commonly, but the level of violence increased dramatically as planters transformed the society with slaves into a slave society. Chesapeake slaves faced the pillory, whipping post, and gallows far more frequently and in far larger numbers than ever before. Even as planters employed the rod, the lash, the branding iron, and the fist with increased regularity, they invented new punishments that would humiliate and demoralize as well as correct. What else can one make of William Byrd's forcing a slave bedwetter to drink "a pint of piss" or Joseph Ball's placement of a metal bit in the mouth of persistent runaways.

[. . .]

Enslavement, Africanization, the imposition of the new plantation regimen, and the destruction of the charter generations – the various elements of the plantation revolution – altered black life in the Chesapeake region, almost always for the worse. But during the fourth decade of the eighteenth century, black society was again transformed as a new generation of African Americans eclipsed the African majority, ending the era of African domination. Native-born black people were healthier and lived longer than the African newcomers. Like members of the charter generations, they too were familiar with the landscapes and economies of the region. Perhaps most importantly, the new creoles had control of the word, as English was their native tongue. They could converse easily with one another, as well as with their owners and other whites. Indeed, many native-born slaves had developed particular variants of English and spoke in a "Scotch-Irish Dialect" or "Virginia accent."

Language allowed them to adjust their inherited cosmology, sacred and secular, to the requirements of tobacco cultivation and the demands of their status. Traveling through the countryside as messengers, watermen, and jobbing tradesmen, native-born slaves exuded confidence as they mastered the terrain, perfected their English, and incorporated the icons and institutions of their owners' culture into their African inheritance. The culture that emerged enabled African Americans to challenge their owners from a position of knowledge.

The passage from an African to an African-American majority began slowly. The transition had its demographic origins in the slaves' development of immunities to New World diseases and the steady growth in the size of slaveholding units. At midcentury, Chesapeake slaves not only lived longer but they also resided in units whose large size made it possible to find partners and form resident families. During the 1720s the slave population began to edge upward through natural increase. Planters, encouraged by the proven ability of Africans to survive and reproduce, strove to correct the sexual imbalance within the black population, importing a larger share of women and perhaps reducing the burdens on slave women during pregnancy. Although planters continued to purchase Africans at a brisk pace and the sex ratio remained imbalanced, by 1730 almost 40 percent of the black people in the Chesapeake colonies were native to the region. At midcentury, African Americans formed four-fifths of the slave population. On the eve of the American Revolution, the vast majority of Chesapeake slaves were native Americans, most several times over.

[. . .]

To create families to their liking, African-American slaves pressed their owners with demands for a modicum of domestic security. Husbands and wives petitioned for permission to reside together on the same quarter or to allow husbands to visit "broad wives" and other kin . . . Such off-plantation relationships disrupted the smooth operation of plantation life, making slaveowners reluctant to acquiesce. However, if the appeals to planter benevolence failed, slaves – particularly slave men – raised the cost of disapproval by withdrawing their labor.

[. . .]

The separation of family members was probably the single largest source of flight and the root cause of other dissension within the plantation.

In the end, few owners denied their slaves' requests to visit kinfolk on their own time. Where possible, slaveowners accommodated their slaves, allowing them to live together, and occasionally they purchased slaves to unite slave couples. By the middle of the eighteenth century, Chesapeake slaves had transformed their desire for domestic stability into a right, which, if not always honored by their owners, was recognized as a legitimate aspiration.

Slaves established other conventions to provide them with a modicum of domestic stability. While slave women demanded time to feed their children at the breast, slave men saw to it that their families were fed beyond their masters' rations. Slaves also began to wrench control of the naming process from their owners, and parents increasingly named their children after a respected ancestor or other notable . . . Before long, a system of inheritance emerged within the slave community. By the middle years of the eighteenth century, it became common for slave artisans and domestics to pass their skills and special positions within the plantation hierarchy to their children.

Slaves also won a measure of privacy for their domestic lives. Unlike the barracks that housed newly arrived Africans, native-born slave families generally resided in individual cabins, often of their own construction. Most were small, rude buildings, little different from the outbuildings where slaveholders housed their animals and stored their tools, although they generally took a neater, more permanent form in the great plantation towns. But even when ramshackle and dilapidated, the separate slave quarter marked the acceptance of the slaves' demands for an independent family life and a grudging concession to the slaves' right to privacy – a notion that was antithetical to the very idea of chattel bondage. With the maturation of the plantation generations, the family once again became the center of black life in the Chesapeake and the locus of opposition to the planter's rule.

[. . .]

Nevertheless, the slave family remained a fragile institution, as slaves had few resources to sustain ties and fewer still to protect – let alone advance – their interests. Slaveholders continually intervened in the slaves' family affairs, undercutting parents and other figures of authority, affirming their power as they rationed visitation rights and forced slaves to solicit their approval for the most routine engagements. Even under the best of circumstances, the long-distance relationships between husbands and wives were difficult to maintain and the authority of parents difficult to sustain, when they had no power to protect, few resources to reward, and little authority to punish. The frailty of family ties grew with the distance, as from afar kin relations did not even have the force of propinquity. Nonetheless, slaves recognized the centrality of their own domestic institution, and put it in the center of their own world.

[. . .]

The African-American family did not end at the household's edge. Sometimes extended families occupied a single plantation or quarter; sometimes slave families spilled across plantation boundaries. In Folly's Quarter of Charles Carroll's great Doorhoregan estate on the western shore of Maryland, [a slave woman named] Fanny lived surrounded by her children, grandchildren, and nephews and nieces, forty in number. Likewise, all but thirty of the 128 slaves residing on [another Carroll plantation] belonged to two extended families. Sometimes the quarter took the name of the family matriarch or patriarch. But the small size of most Chesapeake estates forced slave men and women to look beyond plantation borders for a spouse. As slaves intermarried across plantation lines, the extended network of kin spread through the countryside, joined together by consanguinity and shared obligations . . . The quarter, whether the home of a single extended family or a group of unrelated individuals who had been transmuted into kin, became the institutional embodiment of the slave community in the Chesapeake.

[. . .]

Within its bounds, slaves plotted their own ascent, socializing among themselves, educating their children to the harsh realities of enslavement, and honing the weapons which they would employ to reclaim what their owners usurped.

The slaves' weapons were many, and after a century in the tobacco fields they extended beyond revolt, maroonage, and truancy, for slaves understood the processes of tobacco cultivation as well as any owner. That many quarters took their names from the slave patriarchs or matriarchs who were their central figures and who often served as their foreman and occasionally as their forewoman suggests the degree to which black people had gained control over their work and their lives. As knowledgeable agriculturalists, these men and women appreciated how their strategic interventions could destroy a season's crop and ruin their owners. In their understanding of the complex process in which tobacco was cultivated and cured, Chesapeake slaves found strength.

Initially, slaves secured some substantial gains. Slaves stabilized the workday, which planters had stretched substantially beyond what had been customary during the early years of the eighteenth century, and began the process of rolling back the number of hours they were expected to labor. The planters' effort to counter this trend by lengthening the number of hours spent in the fields or speeding the pace of labor elicited immediate protests – sometimes in the form of shoddy work, broken tools, or increased truancy . . . Such small victories gave slaves a bit more control over their lives, and chastened those who desired to increase plantation productivity.

During the middle years of the eighteenth century, slaves recovered some of the prerogatives that members of the charter generations had taken for granted. The free Sunday had become an entitlement rather than a privilege, so almost all Chesapeake slaves had Sundays to themselves . . . Occasionally, slaves enjoyed part of Saturday as well. When owners impinged upon the slaves' free days, they generally compensated them in time or money.

Still, planters resisted, refusing to surrender the very essence of slavery's value. To prevent slaves from elevating customary practices into entitlements and from manufacturing yet additional rights, slaveholders sought to confine the slaves' economy. They were especially adamant about the independent trading, as they understood how the slaves' entry into the marketplace enlarged their understanding of the value of their own labor and sharpened their appreciation of the planter's usurpation. Moreover, planters were not above countering with new demands of their own – for example, requiring slaves to process as well as grow tobacco and to manufacture candles and other necessities for the Great House. The maturation of tobacco culture did not end the contest between master and slave; it only moved the struggle to new ground.

3

Adam Rothman

THE SOUTH IN THE AGES OF THE REVOLUTION AND THE NEW REPUBLIC

This chapter takes the South from the era of the American Revolution through the founding and early decades of the United States. Historical research on the late eighteenth- and early nineteenth-century South has revolved around a variety of questions. What role did the South (and the various actors within it) play in the origins, course, and aftermath of the American Revolution; and how, in turn, did the Revolution transform southern society? What was the legacy of the Revolution, and the founding of the United States, for the southern social order? Why did the slave labor system come to thrive and expand in the South, even as it receded up North? In what ways did the conflicting spirits of nationalism and sectionalism flavor southern political identity during the early national period? How were the tensions between these impulses framed by such vital developments as the market revolution, westward expansion, the spread of plantation slavery, the growth of federal power, and the hardening of partisan divisions?

These are the kinds of issues addressed in Adam Rothman's opening piece. But the central concern of his essay, and of the selections to follow, is the paradox famously noted on the eve of the Revolution by Dr. Samuel Johnson, when he asked how it was "that we hear the loudest yelps for liberty from the drivers of negroes." The clash between "the ideals of universal liberty and equality pronounced by the Declaration of Independence" and "the reality of American slavery," Rothman suggests, remains the "great paradox of the Revolutionary era." How did the South's dual heritage of slavery and liberty affect the character of the American Revolution? And how did southerners – black and white – engage and contest over this contradiction? Here is the focus of the probing analyses that follow.

Adam Rothman, Associate Professor of History at Georgetown University, specializes in the history of slavery and abolition in the Atlantic world. His first book, *Slave Country: American Expansion and the Origins of the Deep South* (2005), has been recognized as a pathbreaking narrative of how plantation slavery took root in what came to be known as the Deep South during the early decades of the new republic. More recently, he has co-edited two volumes: *Major Problems in Atlantic History* (with Alison Games, 2008), and *The Princeton Encyclopedia of American Political History* (with Michael Kazin and Rebecca Edwards, 2010). He is currently researching a book on the history of New Orleans "as a cosmopolitan city with dense and changing economic, political, and cultural connections to the rest of the world."

In March 1791, President George Washington left Philadelphia for a three-month tour of the "Southern States." His picaresque journey carried him through Annapolis and Georgetown, where he examined Andrew Ellicott's surveys of the new federal district. He stopped at Mount Vernon for a week to tend his plantations, and then proceeded southward to Richmond and Petersburgh in Virginia, then Halifax, Newbern, and Wilmington in North Carolina, and Charleston, South Carolina, whose inhabitants Washington found to be "wealthy – Gay – hospitable; appear happy, & satisfied with the Genl. Government." After being feted by the gentlemen and ladies of Savannah, Washington returned northward by an inland route that passed through Augusta, where he and Georgia's governor, Edward Telfair, discussed the ongoing problem of enslaved people fleeing to Spanish Florida. On his way to Charlotte, North Carolina, Washington met with "some of the Chiefs of the Cutawba Nation," who were concerned about encroachment on their lands. He drank tea with the women of Salisbury, and Moravians serenaded him in Salem. Although North Carolina had been an antifederalist bastion, Washington learned from the governor that "the discontents of the people were subsiding fast." The bad roads of Virginia's backcountry carried Washington back to Mount Vernon in mid June, where he rested for two weeks before returning to the nation's capital just after the "Anniversary of American Independence."[1]

Just as his previous tours through New England and the mid-Atlantic states had done for those regions, Washington's southern tour confirmed the existence of a "South" within the new United States, even as he tried to submerge any southern regional consciousness or solidarity under a broader American federal nationalism. Washington rode through the region for three months, tracing out its roads and rivers, judging the landscape, greeting the citizens and their leaders, and taking the pulse of their politics. Every town and locality staged rituals of civic pride, national patriotism, and veneration for Washington – military salutes, public dinners, elegant balls, ladies' teas, illumination of houses, and fireworks. Washington honored the memory of the Revolution in the southern theater by inspecting historic battlefields and military fortifications in Charleston, Savannah, Augusta, Camden, and Guilford Court House, always praising the soldiers' valor and patriotism. Rooted in republican ideology, a rhetoric of liberty suffused the public pronouncements of the various citizens' committees that welcomed Washington throughout his southern tour, as well as in his formal replies to them. Yet, beneath these paeans to liberty, peace, and an eternal Union lurked some difficult challenges, including land speculation, foreign intrigue, and, not least, the problem of slavery.

Southerners' memories of the Revolution were still vivid in 1791, and they claimed their share of laurels. What was the southern experience in the war for independence? Whether fueled by resentment against overseas creditors, suspicion of corrupt royal officials, or principled objection to the infringement of their political rights, many white southerners joined in the newly dubbed "American" cause against British tyranny. The southern colonial assemblies vigorously protested against Britain's imperial reforms following the Seven Years War, and the Sons of Liberty organized in the southern colonies as well as up north. Mobs harassed Stamp Distributors and other loyal subjects in Williamsburg, Wilmington, Charles Town, and Savannah. Consumer boycotts of imported goods closed down southern shops and markets. If Massachusetts was the cradle of revolution, Virginia (the most populous colony) was its crucible. It was Virginia's committee of correspondence that initiated the First Continental Congress in 1774; a Virginian, Thomas Jefferson, who drafted the Declaration of Independence; and another Virginian, George Washington, who took the reins of the Continental Army. But the Virginians were not alone. Almost 60,000 of the army's 232,000 enlisted men came from the southern states, and another 80,000 southerners fought in local and state "patriot" militias. Did all these men perceive a British conspiracy to "enslave" them, or did some simply seek to vindicate a new Creole identity? How many of them fought for more basic reasons, like money, revenge, or glory? Explaining individual motivation is a complex problem, especially since many colonials did not join the Revolution at all, preferring to risk neutrality, or to overtly support the Crown.

Anti-imperial resistance descended into civil war with international dimensions, as Tories and Patriots fought vicious partisan battles and foreign nations were drawn into the spiderweb of war. Even before the Declaration of Independence, loyalist and rebel militias skirmished throughout the southern colonies. Virginia's Lord Dunmore enraged many colonials by inviting slaves and indentured servants to earn their freedom fighting for the Crown, while a crushing defeat of the Cherokee Indians in the Carolina borderlands in June 1776 discouraged further Native American involvement in the war. Hence the charge in the Declaration: "He has excited domestic insurrections amongst us, and has endeavoured to bring on the inhabitants of our frontiers, the merciless Indian Savages whose known rule of warfare, is an undistinguished destruction of all ages, sexes and conditions." New England and the mid-Atlantic region took the brunt of the war until General John Burgoyne's victory at Saratoga in October 1777 compelled the British to reconsider their strategy. Hoping to tap much-vaunted reservoirs of southern loyalism, British commanders began to pursue a "southern strategy," taking Savannah late in December 1778 and fending off a combined French and Patriot siege in the fall of 1779. The British seized Charles Town in May 1780 and then, having secured the southern colonies' largest town, Cornwallis crushed General Horatio Gates's army at Camden in South Carolina in August. Another southern front opened when Spain declared war on Britain in 1779. Louisiana governor Bernardo de Galvez picked off British garrisons at Manchac, Baton Rouge, and Natchez and seized Mobile and Pensacola, laying the foundation for the Spanish takeover of Florida at war's end.

The tide slowly turned against the British after Washington replaced Gates with Nathaniel Greene, a raw but talented officer from Rhode Island, who bled Cornwallis's redcoats throughout the Carolina backcountry. Guerrilla warfare led by Francis Marion (the "Swamp Fox") and other savvy fighters also damaged the British effort to pacify the Carolinas and build loyalist strength there. Whipsawed by the brutality of British officers like Banastre Tarleton and the rebels' retaliatory violence, the southern states became the scene of what Greene called "savage fury." The ill-fated turn to Virginia sprang from the British commanders' inability to secure the Carolinas. Violence in the southern colonies did not end when Cornwallis surrendered to Washington and de Grasse at Yorktown in October 1781. John Laurens, the young and reckless South Carolina revolutionary who had proposed that his state recruit a regiment of slaves, was killed a year later at Chehaw Point on the Combahee River in one of the last skirmishes of the war. Another casualty was Andrew Jackson's mother, Elizabeth Hutchinson Jackson, who contracted cholera while tending to the sick and dying on board British prison ships in Charles Town harbor. Aside from Jackson's unquenchable rage, other legacies of the conflict included the exodus of thousands of southern loyalists, many of whom ended up in Florida, the West Indies, and (in the case of some enslaved people) Canada and Sierra Leone. This loyalist diaspora is beginning to receive closer scrutiny as southern historiography becomes more transnational.

What did this hard-won independence really achieve in the South? Drawing from postcolonial perspectives and the scholarly literature on early modern state formation, historian Jack Greene has recently identified fundamental continuities between the British North American colonies and the early United States, calling into question the idea that the new country made a sharp historical break with the colonial past or that the Revolution inaugurated a truly new society and politics.[2] The fundamental building blocks of the republic, the states, were inherited from the colonial political order. Even after the adoption of a new federal constitution strengthened the national government, the United States remained more a league of states than a bona fide nation-state. Moreover, territorial expansion merely repeated the processes of conquest, dispossession of the indigenous people, and settlement that had shaped the Atlantic seaboard in the seventeenth and eighteenth centuries. A stubborn dependence on slave labor and plantation agriculture, especially in the South, meant that "colonial" hierarchies of class and race persisted well after the southern colonies had become states. As some critics have charged, there was little that was *post*-colonial about the new United States – and the South in particular. The geography of Washington's southern tour also illustrates that a large part of what would become the US South was not yet enclosed within the nation. It might better be described in 1791 as the Spanish American Northeast or "native ground" belonging to the unvanquished Native Americans of the southeastern interior, Gulf coast, and lower Mississippi valley. Some of the most innovative recent scholarship in southern history focuses on these fractured and heterogeneous borderlands.

Yet an emphasis on continuity from the colonial to the national eras should not obscure the dynamism of the American South between the 1770s and the 1820s, an age of revolution in the broader Atlantic world. Under popular pressures, the oligarchs of the seaboard states enacted political reforms that began to expand voting rights for white men and equalize representation between eastern and western districts. An alliance of liberals and dissenting evangelicals sapped the old Anglican religious establishment, while thousands of white and black southerners were reborn as Methodists and Baptists. This religious awakening was arguably the most important development of the era for those who experienced it. Successful diplomacy and rapid western migration, including the forced relocation of enslaved people, led to the formation of six new slave states (Kentucky, Tennessee, Louisiana, Mississippi, Alabama, and Missouri) – although whether Kentucky and Missouri were truly "southern" remains in dispute. Thanks to the absorption of territory, natural reproduction, slave importation, and immigration, the southern population more than doubled to over four million, though it did not grow as quickly as that of the northern states. Overseas demand for short-staple cotton, the preferred fiber of Europe's textile manufacturers, spurred the invention of the cotton gin and reoriented the southern plantation economy. The cotton boom generated a clamor for slave labor from the Carolina piedmont to Louisiana's southwestern prairies, and buoyed the value of slaves in the seaboard states. As black and white people swarmed over the land, the southern Native Americans found themselves increasingly hemmed in, harried, and at the mercy of the United States. The defeat of the Red Sticks in the War of 1812 dealt a crushing, if not final, blow to southern Native American resistance against these intruders.

Amid these changes, a central question for white southerners remained how best to preserve republican liberty. As southern state legislatures raged through the 1780s with battles over issues of money and religion, key leaders, such as James Madison, perceived a need to restrain democratic exuberance, remedy the weaknesses of the Articles of Confederation, and strengthen the national union. Although supporters of the proposed federal Constitution eventually won ratification in the southern states, a powerful antifederalist tendency, especially in western districts, attested to small farmers' enduring suspicion of distant and overbearing government. Deference to George Washington sustained southern Federalism through the mid-1790s but the prospect of a powerful Hamiltonian state tilting toward northeastern financial and industrial interests appalled many southerners. The British model of economic development had no place in the South. As Drew McCoy has argued, the Jeffersonian alternative called for plentiful land and free trade to sustain the agrarian basis of a virtuous citizenry. It was this vision that appeared to triumph in the election of 1800, which catapulted Jefferson into the presidency. Yet, once in power, the Jeffersonians would discover that plentiful land and free trade invited their own perils. An overextended country could result in centrifugal fragmentation, while too many farmers producing for limited markets could result in rotting crops, collapsing prices, and a reversion to idleness. Standing up for free trade, moreover, drew the United States into a world at war. Navigating through the great power conflicts of the Napoleonic age was a tall order for a young country.[3]

And then there was the problem of slavery – the theme of the three selections that follow in this chapter. As Samuel Johnson put it in his much-quoted slap at the rebellious colonists, "How is it that we hear the loudest yelps for liberty from the drivers of negroes?" The great paradox of the Revolutionary era was that the ideals of universal liberty and equality pronounced by the Declaration of Independence clashed with the reality of American slavery, and nowhere was the clash more stark than in the states extending from Maryland to Georgia, where most of North America's enslaved people lived. Haunted by Johnson's query, modern scholars have tried to understand how slaveholders in the British North American colonies could have subscribed to a concept of freedom that endangered the moral basis of their society. One influential line of argument suggests that slavery clarified the meaning of liberty for white southerners and strengthened their passion for it. In his seminal book, *American Slavery, American Freedom*, Edmund Morgan argued that the existence of slavery relieved the Virginia gentry of the burden of a free, landless class of men. Republicans like Jefferson could therefore celebrate liberty without risking democratic assaults on property. In our first selection, Jack Greene draws from Edmund Burke, a more sympathetic observer than Samuel Johnson, to offer a rival explanation for American slaveowners' love of liberty. Focusing on South Carolina rather than Virginia, Greene suggests that the planters' own experience as slaveowners made them acutely aware of the horror of slavery. They cherished their own liberty all the more, and pursued political independence to preserve it.[4]

Since the 1970s, when Morgan and Greene called attention to the way slavery shaped the republican ideology of southern white elites, historians have focused more on patterns of division and conflict in the Revolutionary-era South. Backcountry "regulators" and evangelical dissenters bucked the hegemony of coastal elites in the 1760s and early 1770s. Loyalists offered counter-resistance to the rebels during the war, especially when bolstered by local British troops. And, as the selections by Sylvia Frey and Michael McDonnell demonstrate in different ways, slavery generated its own fissures during the war. Frey's *Water From the Rock* (1991) builds on earlier work by pioneering historians Herbert Aptheker and Benjamin Quarles in documenting African-American resistance and the contribution of black people to the American Revolution. Her work is a reminder that "the problem of slavery" was altogether different – more immediate and existential – for enslaved people than for their owners. Part of a generation of "bottom-up" social history, Frey places African Americans' own desire for freedom at the center of the story. Hundreds of enslaved people fought as soldiers; more still – voluntarily or not – assisted either the American or the British war effort as servants and laborers. As many as ten thousand enslaved people in the South found their way to freedom through the fog of war. In her selection, Frey shows that the British occupation of Georgia from 1778 to 1782 released "a flood tide of runaways," forcing British military and civilian officials to walk a fine line between disrupting and maintaining the slave plantation economy in the territory they controlled.

Michael McDonnell's 2006 essay returns the focus to Virginia, and the terrain of political history. Challenging Morgan's argument that slavery undergirded racial solidarity among white Virginians in the revolutionary era, McDonnell suggests that slavery created potentially dangerous class antagonisms among white citizens. Long latent, these antagonisms emerged in wartime. Poorer white men, resenting inequities in military service that favored wealthy slaveowners, did not exactly flock into militia service at the beginning of the Revolution. Their stubbornness forced the General Assembly to reform the system of military recruitment to make it fairer to men from the humbler classes. McDonnell shows that, as the British took the war to Virginia in 1780 and 1781, local fears of slave revolt kept white men at home to protect their own farms and families, rather than fend off the invaders. Virginia's difficulties in wartime mobilization led some patriot leaders to contemplate desperate policies, ranging from arming slaves to offering slaves as a bounty for military recruits. "Racial solidarity was no protection against class divisions in Virginia's Revolutionary War," concludes McDonnell. His essay offers a provocative new contribution to one of the enduring themes in southern historiography: the complex historical relationship between class and race.

The selections for this chapter concentrate on slavery and the Revolution, but the many dilemmas of slavery did not disappear once the war ended. They cropped up again at the local and state levels, as a national issue, and in the international arena. After the Revolution, a surprising number of white southerners recognized that slavery might be their country's fatal flaw. Jefferson famously warned in *Notes on the State of Virginia*: "I tremble for my country when I reflect that God is just." Slavery, he argued, threatened republican liberty by violating natural rights, stigmatizing labor, and nurturing discontent.[5] The prospect of revolt may have been a persuasive argument against slavery but its more immediate effect was to instill caution among slaveowners. They had reason to worry, since slave resistance did not cease once the British left. The discovery of Gabriel's conspiracy sounded the alarm in 1800, but still more unnerving (or perhaps inspiring, from the perspective of enslaved African Americans) was the slave rebellion and imperial war in the Caribbean that gave birth to Haiti. What was to be done?

It may appear that American slaveowners simply drew a color line around freedom, with whites on one side and blacks on the other. Yet, in the upper South, some slaveowners manumitted their human property, leading to a surge in the numbers of free people of color – a trend that was eventually curtailed by new restrictions on manumission and on the rights of free people of color. Many Jeffersonians hoped for what historian William Freehling has called the "conditional termination" of slavery. By prohibiting slave importation, diffusing the slave population throughout the southwest, and deporting freedpeople to Africa, slavery would dwindle and eventually disappear from the United States. Instead, the slave population continued to grow and spread, became ever more creolized and Christian, and perpetually warded off despair caused by violence and terror. The mirage of conditional termination never entirely dissipated, but southern whites drifted toward a rival pro-slavery vision, strongest in the lower South, that defended slavery's morality and set strict limits on the constitutional power of the national government to regulate slavery, let alone abolish it. Notwithstanding their partisan and ideological differences, southern politicians united against an emergent northern antislavery threat during the Missouri crisis in 1819–21, which capped three decades of political struggle over the fate of slavery in the young republic. As Michael Zuckerman has suggested, the fading of southern antislavery was part of a broader conservative reaction, a southern Thermidor, against the democratic-egalitarian promise of the revolutionary age. "We regard our negroes as the 'Jacobins' of the country," wrote Charleston's Edwin Holland after the suppression of Denmark Vesey's alleged slave revolt conspiracy in 1822.[6]

From the Revolution onward, inhabitants and outside observers recognized the southern states as a distinct but diverse region of the United States, with its own climate, unique history, and special interests. In a famous letter to Chastellux, Jefferson observed that northerners were cool, sober, and laborious, while southerners were fiery, voluptuous, and indolent. These distinctions grew sharper the further north or south one went, he asserted, "insomuch that an observing traveller, without the aid of the quadrant may always know his latitude by the character of the people among whom he finds himself." If Jefferson's *Notes on the State of Virginia* gave the transatlantic reading public a comprehensive portrait of the Old Dominion, William Bartram's 1791 *Travels* delighted readers with lavish depictions of unusual and occasionally dangerous flora and fauna in the semitropical lower South. David Ramsay, one of the country's first historians, wrote a history of the Revolution in South Carolina (1785) and another of the entire American Revolution (1789), but histories of "the South" were not yet in vogue. Closest to the mark was Henry Lee's 1812 *Memoirs of the War in the Southern Department of the United States*, which reminded readers of southern patriotism, heroism, and sacrifice at the altar of the nation – just in time for another war. Some historians suggest that an identifiable South in this era was mostly the invention of northern and foreign critics, but southern politicians themselves invoked an idea of the South and its interests in the national political arena. Delegates to the Continental Congress, the conventions that drafted and ratified the Constitution, and subsequently the US Congress, envisioned a southern regional identity – often, though not exclusively, in contests over slavery. Despite Washington's stern warnings, southern sectionalism did not dissolve in the waters of nationalism but remained in suspension, always ready to react under heat and pressure.[7]

NOTES

1. For Washington's diary of his southern tour, see Donald Jackson and Dorothy Twohig, eds., *The Diaries of George Washington* (Charlottesville: University of Virginia Press, 1979), 6: pp. 96–169, quotations on pp. 99, 132, 149, 155, 169.

2. Jack P. Greene, "Colonial History and National History: Reflections on a Continuing Problem," *William and Mary Quarterly*, 3d ser. 64 (April 2007), pp. 235–50.

3. Drew McCoy, *The Elusive Republic: Political Economy in Jeffersonian America* (Chapel Hill: University of North Carolina Press, 1980).

4. Quotation from Samuel Johnson, *Taxation no Tyranny: An Answer to the Resolutions and Address of the American Congress* (London: Printed for T. Cadell, in the Strand, 1775), p. 89; Edmund S. Morgan, *American Slavery, American Freedom: The Ordeal of Colonial Virginia* (New York: W. W. Norton, 1975).

5. Quotation from Merrill D. Peterson, ed., *Thomas Jefferson: Writings* (New York: Library of America, 1984), p. 289.

6. Quotation from Edwin C. Holland, *A Refutation of the Calumnies Circulated against the Southern & Western States, Respecting the Institution and Existence of Slavery among Them* . . . (Charleston: A. K. Miller, 1822), p. 61. For "conditional termination" see William W. Freehling, *The Road To Disunion*, Vol. 1. *Secessionists At Bay, 1776–1854* (New York: Oxford University Press, 1990), part III; for "Thermidor" see Michael Zuckerman, "Thermidor in America: The Aftermath of Independence in the South," *Prospects* 8 (October 1983), pp. 349–68.

7. Quotation from Peterson, ed., *Thomas Jefferson: Writings*, p. 827. William Bartram, *Travels through North and South Carolina, Georgia, East and West Florida, the Cherokee Country, etc.* (Philadelphia: James & Johson, 1791); David Ramsey, *History of the Revolution of South Carolina* (Trenton: Printed by Isaac Collins, 1785); Henry Lee, *Memoirs of the War in the Southern Department of the United States* (Philadelphia and New York: Bradford and Inskeep, 1812).

* * *

FURTHER READING

Abernethy, Thomas Perkins, *The South in the New Nation, 1789–1819* (Baton Rouge: Louisiana State University Press, 1961).

Alden, John Richard, *The South in the Revolution, 1763–1789* (Baton Rouge: Louisiana State University Press, 1957).

Boles, John B., *The Great Revival, 1787–1805: The Origins of the Southern Evangelical Mind* (Lexington: University Press of Kentucky, 1972).

Chaplin, Joyce, *An Anxious Pursuit: Agricultural Innovation and Modernity in the Lower South, 1730–1815* (Chapel Hill: University of North Carolina Press, 1993).

Crow, Jeffrey J., and Larry E. Tise, *The Southern Experience in the American Revolution* (Chapel Hill: University of North Carolina Press, 1978).

Davis, David Brion, *The Problem of Slavery in the Age of Revolution, 1770–1823* (Ithaca: Cornell University Press, 1975).

Frey, Sylvia and Betty Wood, *Come Shouting to Zion: African American Protestantism in the American South and British Caribbean to 1830* (Chapel Hill: University of North Carolina Press, 1998).

Holton, Woody, *Forced Founders: Indians, Debtors, Slaves, and the Making of the American Revolution in Virginia* (Chapel Hill: University of North Carolina Press, 1999).

Isaac, Rhys, *The Transformation of Virginia, 1740–1790* (Chapel Hill: University of North Carolina Press, 1982).

Klein, Rachel N., *Unification of a Slave State: The Rise of the Planter Class in the South Carolina Backcountry, 1760–1808* (Chapel Hill: University of North Carolina Press, 1990).

Rothman, Adam, *Slave Country: American Expansion and the Origins of the Deep South* (Cambridge, MA: Harvard University Press, 2005).

Sidbury, James, *Ploughshares into Swords: Race, Rebellion, and Identity in Gabriel's Virginia, 1730–1810* (New York: Cambridge University Press, 1997).

* * *

Jack P. Greene

Slavery or Independence[†]

"A love of freedom," Edmund Burke declared to the House of Commons in his speech on conciliation on March 22, 1775, "is the predominating feature" in the "character of the Americans." "Stronger in the English colonies, probably, than in any other people of the earth," a "fierce spirit of liberty," he said, "marks and distinguishes the whole." But in the southern colonies, he asserted in an opinion widely shared by contemporaries on both sides of the Atlantic, this spirit was "still more high and haughty than in those to the northward." Just a little over twelve years later, a delegate from one of these same southern colonies, long since become states, delivered the single most elaborate and passionate speech in celebration of American equality at the Federal Convention in Philadelphia. Equality, contended the South Carolina lawyer Charles Pinckney on June 25, 1787, with approval, was "the leading feature of the United States" and had to be the guiding principle in its future governance.

Yet, these southern societies, especially South Carolina, were the very ones in which chattel slavery was most deeply entrenched and social inquality [sic] among the free population most pronounced. For men to be such violent advocates for their own liberties while they were simultaneously, as one northern cleric put it, "trampling on the sacred natural rights and privileges of Africans" seemed to outsiders to be shamefully hypocritical. "How is it that we hear the loudest yelps for liberty among the drivers of negroes?," trenchantly asked Dr. Samuel Johnson, the English critic and lexicographer who deplored Burke's lenient attitude toward the Americans, in an oft quoted question. How could members of a society like that of lowcountry South Carolina, one that appeared to visitors such as the Boston lawyer Josiah Quincy, Jr., in 1773, to be sharply "divided into opulent and lordly planters, poor and spiritless peasants and vile slaves," possibly subscribe with any degree of sincerity to the pronouncement "all men are created equal" in the Declaration of Independence? Never systematically and thoroughly explored by modern scholars, these questions – the precise relationship among the commitment to liberty, chattel slavery, and the belief in equality – as they apply to Revolutionary South Carolina are the subject of this essay.

[. . .]

When in 1776 in his charge to the grand jury *On the Rise of the American Empire* William Henry Drayton said that the choice facing Americans was "Slavery or Independence," he was reiterating what, as Bernard Bailyn pointed out almost fifteen years ago, had been a consistent theme in American protests against

---

[†]Jack P. Greene, "'Slavery or Independence:' Some Reflections on the Relationship Among Liberty, Black Bondage, and Equality in Revolutionary South Carolina," in *South Carolina Historical Magazine*, 80 (July 1979), pp. 193–4, 197–205.

metropolitan efforts to tighten control over the colonies beginning with the revenue measures of George Grenville in 1764–65. To be required to pay taxes levied by the British Parliament without their consent, Americans claimed, put them in precisely the same position with regard to the metropolis as their slaves had in relation to them: they would be the "mere property" of Britain, which would thenceforth enjoy the absolute "disposal of their persons" and of course of their entire "substance and labour" as well. Once they had been driven "into servile submission," they would be in such an "abject and wretched" condition as to be, like all slaves, without "power of resistance," condemned "to groan and sweat under a slavish life," and an easy "Prey to the Ambition and Avarice, the Pride and Luxury of Masters, who will set no Bounds to their Lust; and in Order to keep Us in abject Slavery, will *rule Us with a Rod of Iron*."

[. . .]

As Bailyn has persuasively shown, such references to slavery were not simple hyperbole: "'Slavery' was a central concept in eighteenth-century political discourse," one that referred "to a specific political condition" in which the vast majority of citizens held their rights and property entirely at the will of the government. Far from being an abstraction, this condition of *political slavery* was in fact, early modern Anglo-Americans believed on both sides of the Atlantic and both before and after the American Revolution, characteristic of virtually all of the Earth's inhabitants. Almost everywhere, the South Carolina judge Aedanus Burke wrote in 1783, tyranny had been able to establish "her favourite principle, that mankind were destined by nature for slavery, and to be hewers of wood and drawers of water for *one* or a *few*."

[. . .]

Britain and Anglo-America alone, it was widely believed prior to the Revolution, still provided a refuge for liberty. As its restriction to the British world so dramatically revealed, however, liberty was a tender plant that, even in Britain, was in constant danger of being rooted up and killed by the malign forces of power and luxury. For over a century prior to the Revolution, opposition writers in Britain had fretted that evil ministers and corrupt courtiers would eat away at British liberty until, as an anonymous writer in the London *Public Ledger* put it in a piece reprinted in the *South Carolina Gazette*, they had turned Britain "from . . . a nation possessed of legal Freedom, which has been the envy and Admiration of the world," into a country of "the veriest Slaves that *ever* groaned beneath the rod of Tyranny" . . . "As the absolute political evil," slavery was thus by common political convention the polar opposite of liberty. Whereas liberty meant "to live upon one's own terms" and "to work for" one's "own profit and pleasure, and not for others," slavery meant "to live at the mere mercy and caprice of another" and to drudge for those who "live[d] in idleness, and would riot in luxury, rapine and oppression." Liberty, declared Hugh Alison in 1769, held out "the most attractive charms, adorned with the pleasant fruits of peace, plenty, science, virtue and happiness," while slavery, in all "its native horror and deformity, black with ignorance, wickedness and misery," offered only "a continual state of uncertainty and wretchedness; often an apprehension of violence; often the lingering dread of a premature death." Such powerlessness, as Aedanus Burke subsequently emphasized, quickly degraded "men in their own opinion" of themselves, and once impressed with their own "conscious inferiority" they soon manifested those "timid, cringing habits" that announced that they were "fit tools for the ambitious designs, and arbitrary dispositions of haughty aspiring superiors." So "habituated to Slavery" did some men become, wrote Thomas Tudor Tucker, in seconding Burke, that they "no longer" had even "the presumption to imagine themselves created for any other purpose, than to be subservient" to the will of their masters. They learned to be "patient of the Yoke, and" could not "be roused to throw it off." "Blind to their own Claims and Interest," they could scarcely be persuaded that they were "of the same Class of Beings" or were "made of the same Materials" as freemen.

[. . .]

When Americans expressed the fear that British measures would reduce them to slavery, they were undoubtedly, as Bailyn has argued, echoing the anxieties of several generations of metropolitan opposition writers who feared for the durability of liberty in Britain. But the "language of slavery" as expressed by South Carolinians strongly suggests that at least in South Carolina, a place where "the general topics of conversation," according to one visitor, were very largely "of negroes," and probably in all colonies with huge numbers of black slaves, that language was powerfully informed by local perceptions of the nature of chattel slavery. So many of the phrases quoted above – "mere property," condemned "to groan and sweat," ruled *"with a Rod of Iron,"* "emasculated eunuchs," forced to "bow the Neck," "hewers of wood and drawers of water for *one* or a *few*," "bowed down under the galling yoke," "treated like beasts of burden," "transferred without ceremony from one master to another," the "fruits of their bodily labours seized on" to "satisfy the repacious luxury of their rulers," living "at the mere mercy and caprice of another," "black with ignorance, wickedness and misery," impressed with their own "conscious inferiority," characterized by "timid, cringing habits," "patient of the yoke," not "of the same Class of Beings" as freemen – every one of these and other phrases employed to depict the terrors of political slavery were virtually interchangeable with those actually used by South Carolinians or visitors to describe actual conditions of chattel slavery in South Carolina.

[. . .]

If whites were so inured to slavery that, as one contemporary observer wrote, "they neither see, hear, nor feel the woes of their poor slaves, from whose painful labours all their wealth proceeds," these lingustic similarities might have represented nothing more than a subliminal awareness of an identification between political slavery and chattel slavery. But it is not necessary to rely on linguistic parallels to show that for South Carolinians such an identification was conscious and explicit. "Whatever we may think of ourselves," wrote Christopher Gadsden in the *South-Carolina Gazaette* in June 1769, "we are as real SLAVES as those we are permitted to command, and differ only in degree: for what is a slave," he asked, "but one that is at the will of his master, and has no property of his own, but on the most precarious tenure." Those too timorous to resist enslavement by Britain, advised an anonymous writer in the same newspaper seventeen months later, "should go and entreat some negro to change states with you. Don't fear that you will change for the worse. His situation is greatly superior to yours.

[. . .]

A comprehension of the very great extent to which South Carolinians made an explicit connection between political slavery and chattel slavery is an essential first step toward constructing an answer to the question of Dr. Johnson, quoted at the beginning of this essay, "How is it that we hear the loudest yelps for liberty among the drivers of negroes?" My argument is that it was precisely their intimate familiarity with chattel slavery that made South Carolinians, and other southern and West Indian colonists, so sensitive to any challenges to their own liberty as free men – and for at least two reasons.

First, the institution of chattel slavery, which David Ramsay once referred to as "our local weakness," rendered South Carolina, in Christopher Gadsden's words, "a very weak Province." "Their Number so much exceding [that of] the Whites," the slaves, as all white South Carolinians were aware, were "very dangerous Domestics" who posed an omnipresent threat of "domestic insurrections" and greatly limited the colony's capacity to resist the bonds its inhabitants thought the metropolis was forging for them. "We find in our case according to the general perceptible workings of Providence where the crime most commonly . . . draws a similar and suitable punishment," Gadsden wrote William Samuel Johnson in 1766, "that slavery begets slavery." The truth of this observation had already been demonstrated for Gadsden by the impotent responses of Jamaica and the other British West Indian colonies to the Grenville revenue measures, and, he and other South Carolina opponents of Britain's menacing measures believed, it behoved people who, like the South Carolinians, were similarly exposed by the presence of such a powerful domestic enemy to take a militant stand against any threat to their liberty before that threat had become so formidable that they had, like their slaves, lost all "power of resistance."

But their awareness of how vulnerable the large number of black slaves made South Carolina to metropolitan attacks upon the liberty of its inhabitants was not the only or even the primary reason why they yelped so loudly for liberty. Much more important, I would suggest, was their acute sensitivity, a sensitivity dramatically reinforced by daily experience, to the horrors and degradation of chattel slavery in South Carolina. Edmund Burke appreciated as much in 1775 when he attributed the peculiarly intense spirit of liberty in Virginia and the Carolinas to their "vast multitude of slaves." "Where this is the case in any part of the world," said Burke in persuasively underlining the most salient feature of the intimate connection between liberty and slavery in Revolutionary America, "those who are free are by far the most proud and jealous of their freedom. Freedom is to them," Burke continued,

> not only an enjoyment but a kind of rank and privilege . . . In such a people, the haughtiness of domination combines with the spirit of freedom, fortifies it, and renders it invincible.

So far from being inconsistent or incongruous with liberty, then, as Dr. Johnson's question implied, slavery, Burke appreciated, acted as its most powerful reinforcement – among free men.

Nor did Revolutionary South Carolinians fail to appreciate the vibrant dialectic between chattel slavery and liberty, as two political essayists of the mid-1790s, lawyers Timothy Ford and Henry William DeSaussure, made abundantly clear during the famous debate over whether the overrepresentation of the lowcountry was a threat to the liberty of the upcountry. Both argued that it was not . . . The constant example of slavery," Ford declaimed in language that could scarcely be more explicit, "stimulates a free man to avoid being confounded with the blacks; and seeing that in every instance of depression he is brought nearer to a par with them, his efforts must invariably force him towards an opposite point . . . DeSaussure made much the same point when he insisted that "where inequality of property pervails, the citizens are more jealous and watchful of their liberties from that very circumstance. In relation to the government of the United States, this remark is certainly true; for the southern states, where such an inequality exists, are the most jealous" . . . Dr. Johnson to the contrary notwithstanding, Ford and DeSaussure strongly argued, "domestic slavery, so far from being inconsistent, has, in fact, a tendency to stimulate and perpetuate the spirit of liberty."

℘ ℘ ℘

Sylvia R. Frey

Water from the Rock[†]

"This place," the King's Counsel, Chief Justice Anthony Stokes wrote of Georgia, "is the key to the southern provinces, and the Gibraltar of the Gulf passage; for

---

[†]Sylvia R. Frey, *Water from the Rock: Black Resistance in a Revolutionary Age* (Princeton: Princeton University Press, 1991), pp. 81–9, 94–5, 106–7.

to the south of this province there is not a port on the continent that will receive a sloop of war." The deep-draft navigation of Savannah harbor, which led to its development as Georgia's principal port or entrepôt, combined with heavy loyalist concentration in that city and throughout the state, were the principal factors in the decision made in 1778 by Lord George Germain, the American secretary, to renew offensive operations in the South. Exaggerated reports of the strength of loyalist support in the South had led Germain to conclude that renewed military operations there would lead to the restoration of royal government. Rich in supplies of ship timbers, staves, Indian corn, cattle, and hogs, Georgia was selected as the loyalist base for the reconquest of the southern colonies. Despite its rapid commercial development, at the outbreak of the American Revolution no one of the thirteen colonies was, in the words of a committee of the Georgia assembly, "so weak within and so exposed without." The presence of "vast numbers of Negroes . . . perhaps themselves sufficient to subdue us," made the prospect of an internal insurrection likely, while her defenceless borders made Georgia constantly vulnerable to external conquest.

Within Georgia's borders were approximately fifteen thousand slaves, most of whom were heavily concentrated in the low country and in the hands of a relatively small planter elite. To the west were the Creeks, Cherokees, Choctaws and other small Indian tribes. Regularly supplied with arms by the British through East and West Florida, they continually harassed the Georgia frontier. To the east stretched the flat coastal lands. Throughout the war British cruisers plied the waters around the sea islands plundering them of livestock and slaves. To the south lay the British province of East Florida, since the days of Spanish possession a haven for runaway slaves who escaped through the porous coastal passages or along the overland trails. Still a labor-scarce frontier region whose precarious circumstances probably produced relative freedom of movement for slaves, East Florida remained an attractive refuge for runaways after the British took possession in 1763. Beginning in 1776 with the collapse of the royal government and the passage of Georgia's confiscation acts, it became a haven for substantial numbers of white loyalists, many of whom migrated with their slaves. The influx of immigrants severely tested the struggling colony's resources and caused it very quickly to become a launching point for tory raiding parties and bands of "the Floridian banditti." The introduction of irregular warfare and raiding added a new dimension to the war in the South, the seizure of slaves as booty. Slave raids and kidnappings inevitably brought reprisals, thus giving to the war in the southern theater a more extreme and violent form than elsewhere.

[. . .]

Its borders ravaged by fratricidal war, Georgia was plunged into chaos by the British invasion of 1778. The expedition began in November when Lieutenant Colonel Archibald Campbell of the Seventy-first Scottish Regiment and thirty-five hundred troops were detached by military transports to Georgia, while General

Augustine Prevost was ordered to march two thousand troops from St. Augustine to the St. Mary's River to cooperate with Campbell in the conquest of Georgia. After experiencing unusually bad weather, the expedition finally landed on December 23, 1778. Intelligence reports had suggested a landing at John Giradeau's plantation two miles from Savannah as the most practical place in the area between the Savannah and Tybee rivers, a continuous tract of deep marsh interspersed by creeks of the St. Augustine and Tybee rivers and by other cuts of water. Although they encountered resistance from a rebel army led by Major General Robert Howe, "a Confidential Slave" guided the British down a path through a swamp, enabling them to surprise and rout the rebel force. On January 1 the British took possession of Savannah, a city of four hundred houses built along broad streets that intersected to divide the city into six equal parts. The following day a British force occupied Ebenezer. Within ten days the Georgia frontiers were under British control, except for Sunbury, which was taken shortly afterward by Prevost, making good Campbell's claim that "I have ripped one star and one stripe from the Rebel Flag of America."

[. . .]

The capture of Georgia confronted British army officers with a host of military, administrative, and political problems. Stretched thinly over large areas, the army depended heavily on the loyalty of powerful white families and on the neutrality of others. From the beginning, however, military relations with white southerners were bedeviled by a general fear and suspicion of the potentially revolutionary effects of the army's presence on southern society. Although whites were clearly uneasy about the dangers posed by the fighting, it was the internal threat of the resistance and rebellion of their slaves that was paramount. The scale of their response indicates the degree of their concern.

The extreme political instability created by the British invasion created panic among white Georgians. The first appearance of the British army precipitated a mass exodus of whites from Georgia and from South Carolina during the brief Prevost-led incursion against Charleston. Abandoning their plantations, white families, many of them with their slaves, took refuge in the swamps, or fled to the safety of St. Augustine, or to Virginia, or to more distant areas removed from danger, such as West Florida or the West Indies. Many of the refugees were women whose fathers, husbands, and sons had rushed away to join the ranks of the state militia or had simply fled in fear of their lives. As he traveled the hard, dry road to Purrysburg on the disordered Georgia–Carolina border, the whig Major General William Moultrie encountered "the poor women and children, and negroes of Georgia, many thousands of whom I saw . . . traveling to they knew not where." Accompanied by their owners or overseers, many of the slaves Moultrie saw were being moved to areas remote from the fighting to prevent them from falling into British hands, either by desertion or capture.

[. . .]

If the coming of the British excited fear and anxiety in white southerners, it raised hope and expectation among enslaved southerners. Between November, when the British expedition against Georgia was launched, and January, when the conquest was complete, an estimated five thousand slaves, roughly one-third of Georgia's prewar slave population, escaped their bondage. No previous occurrence in the history of North American slavery compared with the slave exodus that began in Georgia either in scale or consequences. Because of the scale and nature of the resistance, slave flight during the war in the South might be characterized as a type of slave revolt. Ironically, the high incidence of escapes and the actions of the British army, which was perceived by slave masters as the instigator of slave resistance, lessened the possibility of organized rebellion and prevented the revolt from becoming a revolution.

Despite the efforts of slaveowners to contain the exodus of their slaves, in their haste to escape, many white families left their slaves on abandoned plantations. Without supervision, restrictions, or control, thousands of slaves struck out on their own. Most fled on foot, following perhaps the same crisscross paths worn over the years by slave visits from one plantation to another. Others escaped in stolen canoes, steering a course through the small creeks and streams that in ordinary times were used to take produce to market. Advertisements in surviving issues of the *Royal Georgia Gazette* suggest that many of the fugitives fled to the woods and deep river swamps, which from the early days of slavery had been a sanctuary for maroon bands. Some fled to plantations or swamp farms away from the fighting and were concealed by family or friends. Although no offer of freedom had been extended, many slaves left the fields and farms to follow the British army.

Because of the special brutality of the war in the South, flight demanded genuine courage and a depth of commitment to freedom that white owners were loath to admit in their slaves. Once the initial shock of invasion had passed, whig forces began to try to recover as much of the state as possible. Georgia and South Carolina militia units, some of which had been actively engaged in defense of the frontier against Indian attack since 1775, were called up to contest British efforts to secure conquered areas with regular troops augmented by loyalist militia companies organized by Lieutenant Colonel Campbell. Ordered to crush political dissent and control social disruptions, the whig militia launched a campaign of terror, characterized by wholesale destruction of livestock, provisions, and carriages, which left the settlements from Ebenezer to Augusta "in a ruinous, neglected State; two-thirds of them deserted, some of their Owners following the King's troops others with the Rebels, and both revengefully destroying the property of each other."

Fugitive slaves were profoundly vulnerable to the arbitrary violence of the white belligerents. The experience of four runaways who tried to reach British lines during the invasion suggests the formidable obstacles they faced. Armed and mounted on stolen horses, the four ran into one of the whig patrols that roamed the swamps searching for runaways. With the patrol in close pursuit and firing blindly at every noise, the runaways plunged their horses into the Savannah River, swam to the opposite bank, and surrendered themselves to the startled British picquets who made up the advance guard for the army then preparing to launch an attack against Lytell's Point near Augusta.

[. . .]

The slave exodus was a result of the British conquest of Georgia, but it was not something the army had sought or encouraged. Although Parliament had briefly debated the possibility of arming slaves and Dunmore had conducted an abortive experiment with an armed black corps, the issue of using slaves as a matter of tactics remained officially unresolved, leaving commanders in the field and crown officials free to use their own discretion in deciding the question. The flood tide of runaways in Georgia transformed what had been a rather casual debate over political and diplomatic strategy into a historic decision about the future of slavery: whether to embrace the idea of an alliance with southern blacks, which implied the possibility of a political and social revolution, or to seek the thorough conciliation of white southerners, which of necessity implied the rejection of the strategy of racial manipulation.

[. . .]

As time and events were quickly to prove, civil and military authorities looked at slave labor from widely differing points of view. Civil authorities, whose own economic survival was closely tied to the restoration of the economic health of the state, tried to advance the pragmatic needs of the plantation economy. Because Georgia's economy was almost entirely dependent upon slave labor, they sought first and above all to check the exodus of slaves. Their efforts to assert control over the slave labor force precipitated a struggle with military authorities, who were motivated in some cases by military needs and in many cases by no larger purpose than private gain. Under the circumstances the freedom won by bondmen proved, in many cases, highly elastic.

When in July Sir James Wright, himself a casualty of the disasters wrought by war, returned to resume his duties as royal governor, he found the slave labor force severely depleted by desertion or military appropriation. A survey of plantations except those located south of the Ogeechee River, made by the commissioners of claims revealed that only nine hundred and twenty-five slaves remained on abandoned plantations in Georgia. As a result, agricultural production was drastically down and the plantation system was in ruins. Although some of the white families who had fled to St. Augustine or the West Indies at the collapse of royal government were beginning to return, there were still more deserted estates than there were "fit persons" to manage them. Unable to survive in the woods, or hoping perhaps to find refuge under the protective mantle of the British army, "a vast many" slaves had returned to Savannah on their own and "a great number" were returning to the city with Provost's army from South Carolina. They were, however, being appropriated by the army, which resorted increasingly to taking what it needed and then using or selling them as suited its purposes.

Besieged by protests from angry and disillusioned loyalists and by London merchants anxious to secure some £150,000s. in debts owed them by Georgia merchants, Governor Wright, with the approval of the American secretary, tried to stop the flight of the slave population and through their forced labor restore the health of the plantation economy. To reassert control over the freedom-minded slaves, civil authorities agreed to construct "a strong and convenient house or prison," to restrain slaves who were "unruly or abscond." In a series of moves designed to keep slaves on the plantations and to sustain the authority of the master class, they agreed to restore all slaves to their loyalist owners . . . In an effort to balance the need for military labor with the need to maintain plantation labor, the governor and his council unanimously agreed "that they should not interfere or attempt to meddle with any of the Negroes captured by the army, but leave that matter to be conducted by General Prevost in such manner as he may think it prudent and proper for him to do." At the same time, however, they reconstituted the office of commissioner of claims and authorized it to take charge of all rebel-owned estates as well as those belonging to absentee loyalists and to take control of "all fugitive slaves found in the province," together with all those "who may have been decoyed from their owners."

[. . .]

Under the pressure of practical politics, the provincial government had tried unsuccessfully to fashion a strategy for pacifying white southerners through the political manipulation of the slave population. The army's violent quest for pacification undermined those efforts. The wholesale destruction of property, the pillaging of homes, and the forcible impressment of slaves hardened the determination of many of the South's leading white families to resist British tyranny to the end. Paradoxically, by impressing slaves to work as military laborers, by forcing them back into the fields as agricultural laborers for the army or for loyalists, the army kept slavery functioning in many places and substantially reduced the enormous latent power of Georgia's black population; but the practice of receiving slaves, if it did not mean emancipation, at least raised the prospect of emancipation and suggested the clear possibility that some general somewhere might someday end slavery by proclamation, a fear that Clinton's pronouncement merely ratified. To the extent that it deprived slaveowners of their human property, even the highly exploitative practice of treating slaves as war contraband corroded the institution. Without meaning to do so, the British army had thus made the revolutionary war in Georgia a war about slavery. The result was to undermine British credibility and contribute significantly to Britain's ignominious retreat from Savannah, which presaged the failure of British efforts in the South and the ultimate collapse of the British cause in America.

For slaves the results were equally equivocal. Although they were not offered liberty, either as a general principle or as a reward for service, slaves generally tried to capitalize on the disruption that accompanied the war. Most made only elastic gains. Many of those who escaped in the early days of the British invasion were captured by one or the other of the contending forces and were, in many cases, reinslaved under different auspices. The constant fighting, which was a serious impediment to agricultural production, caused an increasing shortage of provisions. With no hope of permanent subsistence, and in many cases not even the hope of survival, large numbers were forced to return. Cynically mistreated by the provincial government and by state assemblies alike, they experienced massive disruptions in their lives. For those who fled to the British army, military service was, at best, a complex mixture of servitude and freedom, which for all its shortcomings, extended the tradition of slave resistance in a new direction. Although the slow growth of revolutionary consciousness did not bring Georgia's slave population all the way to revolution, the unprecedented size of the slave exodus demonstrated unequivocally that slaves constituted a potentially revolutionary force.

– – –

Michael McDonnell

Class War?†

After an extraordinary debate, even for an extraordinary time, legislators in the Virginia General Assembly in the fall of 1780 came up with a startling offer to needy whites in the state. For joining the Continental army, new recruits were promised not only a parcel of land large enough to enfranchise them but also an enslaved Virginian as an extra bounty. Yet this controversial offer was merely a compromise solution to conceal a more profound debate in the legislature that fall. Desperate for soldiers amid a series of British invasions, the Virginia legislature initially debated even more radical plans to redistribute property from the most wealthy in the state to the poorest in return for military service. Many legislators argued that the wealthiest slaveholders in particular, who generally had not fought in the war, ought to give up a larger share of their slaves to those who had.

[. . .]

What are historians to make of this revealing debate and recurring expressions of what seem to have been class divisions in a white society generally depicted as united in its opposition to Britain and in its shared social interests and coherent culture? Several interrelated issues seem to stand in the way of understanding this puzzle. Scholars have, perhaps understandably, focused a great deal of attention on race and slavery in Virginia. Most historians have, in a metaphorical sense,

---

†Michael McDonnell, "Class War? Class Struggles during the American Revolution in Virginia," in *William and Mary Quarterly*, 62 (April 2006), pp. 305, 307, 330–1, 333–9.

followed James Madison's cue and wondered about the contradictions inherent in a slaveholding society amid a war for supposed liberty. And in thinking about this paradox, historians are still under the influence of Edmund Morgan's powerful argument that the need for racial unity smoothed over class divisions in Virginia and created a shared commitment to racial slavery, which was the basis of a cohesive white culture in the eighteenth century. Moreover, whereas the imperatives of maintaining that system meant that elite literate Virginians were always reluctant to "air their dirty linen," as one scholar has put it, Morgan's persuasive argument has also meant that historians have seldom looked for divisions among whites and have not been sure what to do with, or how much weight to give to, comments such as those of Theodorick Bland when they have found them. Scholars have been too quick to accept elites' self-reassuring rhetoric about the apparent unity and harmony of the state, especially during times of stress.

[. . .]

Beginning in October 1780, the British mounted a series of devastating raids in the state, which would eventually culminate in the rendezvous of Benedict Arnold and Charles Cornwallis, the near capture of Governor Thomas Jefferson, and the almost complete breakdown of mobilization in Virginia. Throughout the yearlong ordeal, slavery cast a long shadow on events, and the paralysis Virginia experienced helps reveal the extent to which slavery affected mobilization in Virginia and intersected with class and gender.

[. . .]

Though many historians have assumed that slavery helped unify white communities in times of trouble or stress, the ownership of enslaved Virginians caused deep divisions among whites in wartime. From the start of the war, for example, militia throughout Virginia were quick to point out that slaveholding exacerbated the inequities of military service in different respects. In addition to complaints about wealthy slaveholders making themselves overseers to avoid military service, militia from Chesterfield County also pointed out as early as 1776 that even when elites did their part, military service for nonslaveholders was a much greater burden than for those who owned enslaved Virginians. Absent slave owners still had workers in their fields. In contrast, Chesterfield petitioners claimed, militia service was particularly "burthensome" for the "poorer sort who have not a slave to labour for them." Such complaints grew more common as the demands of war put a greater strain on farmers' abilities to maintain their independence in the face of numerous and intrusive callouts. Even as the British were chasing legislators out of Charlottesville, militia members from counties farther west especially claimed that the planter-dominated legislature did not understand how difficult it was for farmers without slaves to leave their farms for any length of time. More than one hundred militia members from Pittsylvania County made their gendered worries explicit when they pledged their money, their service, and their supplies to the war effort, but only "in such a manner as would not totally ruin themselves, their Wives and Children." The present recruiting law, they claimed, would do just that, as many of the petition-ers were "poor men without a single Slave, with a Wife and many small Children to maintain." Taking such men away from their families, the petitioners asserted, "would reduce them to the most indigent circumstances and hard grinding Want."

Slaveholding, then, particularly toward the end of the war, increasingly became the touchstone for class divisions among white Virginians. Time and again, on different issues surrounding mobilization, militia from across the state, not just slave-poor regions, made claims based on slaveholding inequality. Sometimes their claims implicitly contrasted slaveholders with nonslaveholders. Militia from Botetourt County, for example, explained that yet another militia callout in the spring of 1781 would bring ruin to nonslaveholders especially: "The Season of the year is Such, that to Call on men, with Families, and who have no Other possible means to support themselves and Families but by their own Labour, no other alter-native but inevitable Ruin, must be the Consequence, for before their Return the season for Sowing and planting will be over."

At other times, however, militia were explicit about the inequalities in Virginia. In the spring of 1780, for example, Charlotte County militia members, in a petition to the legislature, rendered an explicit analysis of the problem of wartime mobilization by laying bare what they saw as the class-based injustice of military service. They told the assembly that "in the personal services expected from the Citizens of this Commonwealth, the poor among us who scarce obtain a precarious subsistence by the sweat of their brow, are call'd upon as often and bound to perform equal Military duty in defence of their little as the great & oppulent in defence of their abundance." Yet the petitioners were angry that many wealthy Virginians were able to avoid even an equal amount of service. The "great & oppulent," the petitioners asserted, "who contribute very little personal labour in support of their families, often find means to screen themselves altogether from those military services which the poor and indigent are on all occasions taken from their homes to perform in person." What was worse, they claimed, was that slaveholders benefited twice over; whereas nonslaveholding whites – the "poor and laborious," they claimed – risked their lives, their families, and their estates through their personal service in the militia, slaveholding planters exempted themselves from service and grew person-ally rich on the backs of their slaves' labor. They particularly resented that "the poor who bear the heat and burthen of Military duty" were taxed the same amount as owners of enslaved Virginians were for their laborers who worked, the petitioners claimed, "only to support the extravagance of a Voluptuous master."

[. . .]

In the fall of 1780, Joseph Jones revealed the outlines of the radical new plan to raise a more permanent army with which this article began. The plan showed not only how far the representatives were prepared to go to avoid a draft but also to what extent legislators had listened to class-based complaints that the wealthy in Virginia had not borne their fair share in paying for the war. And, in the end, even the compromise solution reflected a significant concession to poorer Virginians. New recruits who enlisted for the duration of the war – in effect to create the more permanent army George Washington had wanted from the start and that more middling Virginians had begun to demand as the war wore on – were promised a "healthy sound negro" from age ten to thirty or £60 in gold or silver (at the option of the soldier), plus three hundred acres of land to be received at the end of the war. Thus lower-class Virginians were finally able to extract a huge wind-fall in return for their services to the state. They would get enough land to vote and also receive money enough to establish themselves or an enslaved Virginian to make that land more productive. For their part anxious legislators may have hoped that in addition to raising a more permanent army they were also making a judicious move to create some kind of alliance between poor whites and wealthy slave owners.

In the face of their desperate struggle with the British and their own population, however, some white patriots began exploring yet another, even more radical, alternative. James Madison, sitting as an observer in Congress, believed the idea of giving enslaved Virginians away as bounties was "inhuman and cruel." He thought it would be much better if patriot leaders in Virginia took the more obvious step and allowed the enslaved to serve in the army themselves. "Would it not be as well to liberate and make soldiers at once of the blacks themselves as to make them instruments for enlisting white Soldiers?" he asked Jones. Madison thought that such a move would "certainly be more consonant to the principles of liberty which ought never to be lost sight of in a contest for liberty."

A few months later, a Major Alexander Dick agreed with Madison. Trying desperately to recruit men for one of the three regiments for the new state forces in the spring of 1781, Dick suggested that Virginia formalize an already informal practice of allowing enslaved Virginians to enlist in the army. Dick was having trouble recruiting a new state regiment and believed that there was "no probability of recruiting the Regiment" with white Virginians. In the circumstances Dick, echoing Madison's suggestion, argued that they should consider accepting "likely young negro fellows" from planters who would then be given compensation. In turn the enslaved recruit would "be declared free upon inlisting for the War at the end of which, they shall be intitled to all the benefits of Conl. Soldiers." Dick believed that the plan would succeed because enslaved soldiers would make for good recruits and, apparently without a trace of irony, felt that the "the men will be equal to any."

Perhaps because Dick had inadvertently pointed out the perils of such a plan, the legislature did not take up his suggestion. Yet Madison and Dick may not have been the only proponents of such a move, for Jones countered Madison's proposal with some seemingly well-rehearsed objections to arming enslaved Virginians. Significantly, Jones thought there were practical reasons for keeping slaves at home. He admitted that enslaved workers were vital to the independence of those who owned them, thus at least implicitly acknowledging the arguments of nonslaveholding militia. Though the freedom of enslaved Americans was an important object, Jones protested that it should be done gradually so the planters could find laborers to replace them, "or we shall suffer exceedingly under the sudden revolution which perhaps arming them wod. produce."

But there were other objections, too. Perhaps white Virginians did not support the move in larger numbers because too many enslaved Virginians had, so far in the crisis, shown little inclination to support their patriot masters. Indeed Jones worried that arming enslaved Virginians might encourage the British to do likewise, as they had done before. No doubt with the nearly anarchic conditions of the fall of 1775 in mind, Jones thought that the British would be tempted once again to "fight us in our own way." They could probably count on full support from enslaved Virginians, unlike white patriots themselves. The consequences, Jones thought, would be disastrous. If the British armed the enslaved, "this wod. bring on the Southern States probably inevitable ruin."

With such a scenario in mind, patriot leaders tried their luck with lower-class whites instead. Giving slaves as a bounty for soldiers was an ingenious response on the part of some elites to avert the kind of ruin Jones talked about and save the state. Yet the idea of taking those slaves from the wealthiest of planters in the state revealed the extent to which class conflicts, defined as conflicts that grew out of economic inequalities, had permeated the political culture of the new state. Taking enslaved Virginians from the wealthiest class was a response to middle-class complaints about having to shoulder too much of the burden of the war. Offering slaves to lower-class whites was a response, in turn, to rising demands from that class of people to be paid adequately for their service. That new recruits would be given not only an enslaved Virginian but also land and thus the vote meant that many elite whites were willing to make at least some sacrifices and concessions to their middling and lower-class neighbors. The heaviest price for this deal would be paid by enslaved Virginians as well as Native Americans, in whose hands the land promised to new recruits almost certainly lay. Class conflict in Virginia during the Revolutionary War ultimately resulted not in radical solutions such as freeing enslaved Virginians to fight for freedom but rather in more ingenious yet conservative solutions that continued the expropriation of the labor of slaves and the land of Native Americans.

As it turned out, the debate over the new legislation was overshadowed when the British launched another series of devastating raids on Virginia beginning in January 1781. And though historians remember 1781 for George Washington's victory over Charles Cornwallis at Yorktown, it was also the year in which tensions among white Virginians reached the boiling point and the full implications of the previously simmering class divisions became clear. Perhaps the most intriguing aspect of Virginia's mobilization throughout the war, but especially in 1781, is that, despite the immediate threat posed by the British and enslaved Virginians, white Virginians failed to act in concert. Instead they divided and argued among themselves. They passively resisted and verbally protested against militia service, and some went even further. As the British roamed freely across the state in May and June, many militia throughout Virginia actually rioted in protest against military service. Several hundred militia members gathered in places including Augusta, Accomack, Hampshire, and Northampton counties to force local authorities to stop recruiting. In many other places, threats of such collective action were enough to stop worried officials from acting."

Though these riots and protests originated from diverse and sometimes particular causes, several began as a result of the smoldering resentment many poorer and economically vulnerable farmers felt toward wealthy slaveholding planters who had exempted themselves from military service or were quick to flee in the face of British raids. In one of the rare court martial records extant, such economically based grievances were laid bare. Amid a British raid up the Potomac in 1781, the militia of the Northern Neck were called out to defend the region. Instead several militia organized a barbecue in Richmond County to rally support among those who were fed up and unwilling to serve any longer. The barbecue ended in armed conflict against state authorities. The leaders made class-based appeals to their friends and neighbors. One man told authorities that the ringleaders of the conspiracy declared "the Rich wanted the Poor to fight for them, to defend there property, whilst they refused to fight for themselves."

Behind this revealing bravado were men living on the edge. One alleged leader of the barbecue, Edward Wright – described as a "hard-working" but "illiterate" man by authorities – had served often in the patriot militia. Yet in 1781 he found himself unwell and struggling to make ends meet in the face of constant callouts and increasing taxes. He had told another man that he would happily turn out in a few weeks' time after he could lessen his stock to free up basic food stores for his family, and after he returned to full health. In dire circumstances Wright, like others, may also have been tipped over the edge by the numbers of gentlemen in Richmond County who had used their genteel connections to get themselves declared exempt from any militia duty at all on account of their age or health. In a desperate effort to protect his patriarchy, Wright was prepared to incite civil war amid one of the more dense populations of enslaved workers in Virginia. Racial solidarity was no protection against class divisions in Virginia's Revolutionary War.

4

Stephanie J. Shaw

SLAVERY IN THE ANTEBELLUM SOUTH

American slavery was once a relatively quiet, marginal branch of historical scholarship. That would change dramatically in the 1960s and 1970s as the "peculiar institution" exploded into one of the busiest areas of southern, indeed American, historical study. And it was to the antebellum era – the period spanning from the maturation of the plantation economy in the 1820s to the coming of secession in 1860 – that most of this attention flowed. Inspired and informed by the contemporary upheavals of the Civil Rights era, a new generation of historians began to ask new questions about slavery – or brought fresh perspectives to old ones.

Some of these questions concerned the place of southern slavery in the political economy of the region, the country, and the wider world. In what measures did slavery promote, or stifle, the South's economic development? In what ways was the slave system an exception to, and in what ways essential to, the expansion of transatlantic capitalism? Other questions focused on the complex dynamics of the slave–master relationship. Which better describes antebellum slavery, "paternalistic" or "capitalistic"? Was it racial system or a class system? To what degrees were slaves able to weather the hardships and exploitations of slavery, to check the power of the slaveowners, and to establish their own realms of independence and autonomy? What were the features, and limits, of slave resistance? Historians devoted unprecedented attention to the experiences, sentiments, and initiatives of the slaves themselves; to the elements of culture and community in a "world the slaves made."

In her historiographical introduction, Stephanie Shaw traces the slaves' gradual transition from object of the narrative (whether as beneficiary or as victim) to active agent. The selections that follow illustrate the distance traveled over a century of scholarship on antebellum slavery – and the varied interpretations that continue to enliven the field.

Stephanie Shaw is Associate Professor of History at Ohio State University. Professor Shaw's research interests have centered around the family, work, and community lives of African Americans, from the days of slavery through the age of segregation. Her published works include *What a Woman Ought to Be and to Do: Black Professional Women Workers during the Jim Crow Era* (1996), "The Maturation of Slave Society and Culture" (in John B. Boles, ed., *A Companion to the American South* [2002]), and "Using the W. P. A. Ex-Slave Narratives to Study the Great Depression" (in *Journal of Southern History*, August 2003). She has a forthcoming volume about W. E. B. Du Bois's classic *The Souls of Black Folk*, and is currently working on a study of the antebellum slave experience, under the title, "Slave Generations, Migration, and the Antebellum Eras."

The centrality of slavery to America's history has made it an important topic of study from a wide variety of perspectives. For southern, political, and economic historians, for example, the big questions have focused on one set of issues. To what extent was slavery the catalyst for the Civil War? How did southern commitments to slavery either enhance or retard the region's development? Could the South have been the economic or political power it was without its slaves? Social historians and African Americanists have paid more attention to the ways people lived their lives. What were their families and communities like? How did they play, worship, work? How and on what terms did they interact with other people? While across time, new methods, new sources, and new questions have made it impossible to maintain the nice, neat boundaries that used to surround the social, political, and economic history of the South, the post-1960s expansion of interest in African-American history has also encouraged more attention to slaves.

Historical scholarship on slavery in the American South has evolved greatly over the past century. When U. B. Phillips published *American Negro Slavery* (extracted in this chapter) in 1918, it quickly became the most influential book published on slavery in the United States up to that time. Phillips's comprehensive study begins in Africa, covers the international slave trade, and explores diverse aspects (such as business, crime, law, etc.) of the domestic institution across time. But as illuminating as Phillips's book was (and remains), it reflected very little thought about slaves, their perspectives, or the way in which they actually lived their lives. The slaves in Phillips's study regularly fit stereotypes of the worst sort; they were lazy, backward, and/or childlike, and most of them could only have benefited from their enslavement. Indeed, in

Phillips's view, the plantation served as a "school" for slaves, and the master was a generous, benevolent teacher.[1]

Nearly a generation would pass before *American Negro Slavery* met its first major critiques. Chief among them were Herbert Aptheker's *American Negro Slave Revolts* (1943) and Kenneth Stampp's *The Peculiar Institution: Slavery in the Ante-Bellum South* (1956). Aptheker provided a dramatic alternative to Phillips's characterizations of American slaves as meek and mindless, while Stampp challenged Phillips's characterization of American slavery as mild and benevolent. Between the two books, and in subsequent studies, the image of the plantation system as "charming," which Phillips's study perpetuated, was turned on its head.[2]

It was not difficult to revise Phillips's work. He had, for example, included no sustained discussion of slave resistance. Despite his chapter on slave crime – with examples that some scholars would later interpret as resistance – Phillips's slaves were so content with their lot that there was no reason to resist. In Aptheker's study, however, not only were slaves not the pathetic, childlike vessels that Phillips described, they participated in major revolts and conspiracies, along with persistent, if subtle, efforts – Aptheker called them "individual acts" of resistance – which aimed to change the balance of power on plantations, even if only temporarily. Stampp's study continued the revisionist project by showing that what kept slaves from resisting even more than they apparently did was not their acceptance of, or satisfaction with, the system, but the brutality of slave owners. Stampp appropriately described the terror under which slaves lived in a chapter title – "To Make Them Stand in Fear" – which diametrically opposed Phillips's characterization of slaveowner reticence about punishing slaves.

Aptheker's and Stampp's books contributed much to the general shift in scholarly studies from the perspective of the slave owner to that of the slave. For John Blassingame, this new focus centered around *The Slave Community* (the 1972 work from which one of the following selections is drawn).[3] Looking inward – more, that is, at slaves than at slavery – Blassingame revealed a "slave culture" that had few participants resembling the imitative, backward, and/ or barbaric beings depicted by Phillips. Blassingame's slave culture had deep, vital, and diverse roots in Africa. From religion to music, family structure to social roles, Blassingame revealed cultural traditions that were absolutely positive and, in some respects, decidedly different from those of white folks.

Blassingame was responding to more than the old work of Phillips. He also took on some of the works that had incorporated new interdisciplinary methods. One of his primary targets was Stanley M. Elkins's 1959 study, *Slavery: A Problem in American Institutional and Intellectual Life*. Elkins employed the behavioral sciences, and personality theory in particular, to explain the Sambo-like (lying, lazy, and likable) character portrayed by Phillips. Elkins compared the plantation to a closed society, a "total institution" (much like a concentration camp) in which control from above was so overwhelming that subordinates regularly (often for the sake of survival) took on the culture, traditions, and values of the dominant group and sometimes even regressed to a dependent, childlike status. Elkins identified the primary environment of the slaves as one in which white control, expectations, and demands determined their behavior. He reasoned that slaves assumed social roles based on these expectations, and that they could easily have internalized those roles.[4] By contrast, Blassingame's study concluded that the slaves' primary environment was the slave community, one in which diverse slave personalities could and did develop that reflected the range of personality types likely to arise within any social group. In that context, Blassingame not only recognized the dependent, often childlike "Sambo," but his equally outstanding opposite, Nat (who evoked Nat Turner, the ultimate slave rebel). The most common personality type, however, the "average" man, was Jack.

In some ways, Blassingame's study reflected the influence of the modern civil rights movement, which, along with the highly nationalistic Black Power movement, made it nearly impossible to continue to look at the history of slavery in ways that ignored the agency that slaves surely possessed. In such an atmosphere, it is not surprising that Blassingame's study strove to make clear how far the lives slaves lived exceeded that which their owners defined for them.

Covering many of the same topics as Blassingame but in much more detail, Eugene Genovese's *Roll, Jordan, Roll: The World the Slaves Made*, paid special attention to the master–slave relationship in ways that reinforced some of Phillips's earlier conclusions. Yet, in his much more nuanced discussion of paternalism, Genovese also showed that slaves were neither the empty vessels portrayed by Phillips nor the powerless, infantilized victims suggested by Elkins. They were neither the thoughtless and reckless rebels that Aptheker's conclusions led some scholars (erroneously) to, nor people sheltered so well by their separate slave community as to lead quasi-independent lives, as some inferred from Blassingame's study. Genovese saw these slaves and slave owners as participants in a constant tug-of-war in which parties on both sides worked to maintain a standard within which each could live. Thus, many of the acts that Blassingame saw as resistance, Genovese saw as indications of accommodation.[5]

A general characteristic of the above studies is that they are large and sweeping in scope. They look, fairly consistently, at "the antebellum era," "the plantation South," "the slave community," and the like, with little discussion of the full range of diversity within any of these broad constructs. To be sure, there was much value in such studies as John Blassingame's *The Slave Community*, which made clear that looking literally at where slaves lived could provide a different perspective from that provided by Phillips. And George Rawick's *From Sundown to Sunup: The Making of the Black Community* accomplished as much as Blassingame's study in redirecting our attention to how slaves constructed their lives when they were not being managed, watched over, or otherwise controlled by whites.[6] But by the 1990s, a new generation of historians began to narrow the focus significantly, and in ways that affirmed the importance of focusing on slaves (not just slavery) while anchoring that experience in a world that remained dominated by whites.

Sharla Fett's *Working Cures*, for example, put slave health "at the nexus of plantation social relations," while centering those relationships within their political and cultural contexts. Providing a much more intimate examination of slave well-being than was possible in previous, broader explorations of antebellum disease and medicine, Fett's study also added much to the discussion of the day-to-day lives of *female* slaves.[7]

Narrowing the approach in a different way, Thomas Buchanan's *Black Life on the Mississippi* takes a world popularized in the American literary tradition by Mark Twain and completely subverts it by focusing on the slaves who were direct contributors to Mississippi river commerce. Buchanan's work moves beyond the general acceptance of the centrality of slave labor to agricultural production, and connects these workers to the next economic step of trade and transportation, that is, *commerce*. And Buchanan's study implicitly revises thinking related to the place traditionally defined as "the slave community." In Buchanan's study, "the slave quarter," the physical representation of Blassingame's slave community, practically disappears. By virtue of the nature of river work, "the slave community" stretched (for some slaves) from free states such as Ohio and Illinois up north, down to the Gulf coast, and as far inland from both sides of the Mississippi river as its tributaries and rivulets allowed.[8]

While it is still the case that most studies of non-agricultural/non-plantation slavery focus on urban slavery, general interest in commercial and industrial slavery continues to grow. Charles Dew's *Bond of Iron: Masters and Slaves at Buffalo Forge* (extracted in this chapter) focuses on industrial slavery in western Virginia from about the turn of the nineteenth century to the time of the Civil War. While looking at a very small segment of the slave population owned and hired by William Weaver (and his associates) this study yields illuminating results for slavery historiography. Not only does *Bond of Iron* help move us beyond the study of slaves who worked exclusively on farms but, equally important, Dew's volume is one of only a few to treat slave and slaveholder families with equal interest. And, finally, Dew's book provides a kind of detail about the family lives of slaves that rarely appears in other studies, regardless of the setting.[9]

The major impetus to reexamining slave families was Daniel Patrick Moynihan's 1960s study, which made the case for government support of social welfare programs by arguing that dysfunction in contemporary black families had roots in the days of slavery when fathers were not recognized by slave owners, and family structures supposedly became matriarchal. As well intentioned as the Moynihan study was, its characterization of the black family as historically dysfunctional set a tone that has proven difficult to overcome. Still, the publication in 1976 of Herbert Gutman's *The Black Family in Slavery and Freedom, 1750–1925* provided a momentous step in that direction.[10]

Gutman's study reflects all the important concerns of the new social history. *The Black Family in Slavery and Freedom* takes the long view, examining the black family from 1750 to 1925; it uses elaborate quantitative methods; it pays great attention to day-to-day life; and, obviously, it is a study from the bottom up. Gutman not only showed that the slave family was not matriarchal but, that from the earliest period for which records are available to well into the twentieth century, two-parent families were the norm. His discussion of naming patterns within the families reveals very important cultural traditions and social relationships within the slave community that not only suggest stability but also reinforce scholarly conclusions related to slave-identity formation apart from that of their owners.

Subsequent studies that focus on slave families have become a part of what might now be easily recognized as the Moynihan/Gutman debate. Brenda Stevenson, for example, not as convinced as Gutman of the stability of these slave families, showed that, even when slave families appeared to be intact in slaveowner records, the family members were often scattered across different (sometimes very distant) plantations. Ann Paton Malone posed the question differently by placing it in the context of the relocation of slaves to new settlements. Her important study of slave families and households revealed that, even after the fracturing of families and the relocation of some of its members as slavery expanded westward, new families and households formed rather easily, thus recreating stability among the slaves and within these communities. By taking advantage of the detailed records of slaveowners, Gutman, Malone, and Stevenson were all able to reveal detail about slave family life that was important to understanding the extensive efforts of nineteenth-century slaves to shape their lives within a system that gave them so little space to act as self-directed individuals.[11]

Charles Dew's study of slaves who worked in the western Virginia agricultural/iron belt (extracted in this chapter) adds to that tradition. The extraordinary and extensive records left by the William Weaver (slaveowner) family provided a new and up-close perspective on fairly intimate aspects of life inside the slave family, based especially on consumption patterns. While most studies reveal at least some detail about the material culture of slaves, suggesting much about the *possible* nature of their day-to-day lives, Dew connects family, work assignments, work routines, the accumulation of cash and property, and consumption patterns to give us a very fine-grained picture of what some slaves' home life looked like. For example, Sam Williams's purchases – coffee, sugar, clothes, furniture, fabric – reveal the ability of a slave to enhance the living conditions of his family. Among his various purchases, moreover, were things that suggest other important social-cultural conclusions. Williams's purchase of a fine blue coat for an astounding $20 not only speaks to his interest in looking a particular way but also his view of the importance of the Baptism ceremony for which he apparently bought it. In this purchase is the suggestion of an identity that was strong, positive, and self-determined. Williams's remarkable purchase of a mirror, whether for himself or for his wife and/or children, also signaled the possession of self-consciousness, and a personal identity that easily evokes a counterimage to Phillips's and Elkins's "Sambo" personality type.

Because many of the men in the families Dew described were highly skilled workers, they led a very different kind of life from that of most slaves, especially those who worked in agriculture. Their skills also made it possible for their families to live in a dramatically different fashion when compared to most slaves. (A slave husband and wife with bank accounts is but one example.) These differences not only relate to the historiography of slave family life but they complicate historiographical questions related to slave resistance, as well. As already noted, resistance has no place in Phillips's *American Negro Slavery*. Aptheker's *American Negro Slave Revolts* painted a radically different picture. And subsequent historians have shown that resistance was constant, though indirect and non-confrontational. Slaves designed forms of resistance to achieve a desired effect (that is, reduce the work load, gain more food) with the least amount of provocation and expenditure of effort and without risking loss of life. Not all historians regard these more subtle actions as "real" resistance because the slave(s) who engaged in them did not aim overtly to overthrow the system. But Dew's work shows that, even if we cannot call less dramatic actions "resistance," these iron workers manifested some real control over their lives and real thought about how to use it to their advantage.

There is no question but that William Weaver's forge and furnace men worked hard. Iron-making was a highly skilled, labor-intensive craft, and mistakes made during the process could be costly. (In extreme examples, a worker could lose his life or the foundry or forge could burn to the ground.) But, because Weaver realized that his business ultimately depended on slave willingness to work, when Sam Williams or Henry Towles refused to work, Weaver, who knew he could not easily replace them, simply allowed them the vacation. The two master refiners took similar care in their strikes, alternately taking a week off, thus allowing the foundry to continue to operate, albeit at a reduced level, and not causing Weaver to take on the added time and expense of having to restart (refire) the plant.

Dew's discussion makes it impossible to classify the slaves' actions as resistance or their owner's indulgence as paternalism. The two parties, as Genovese suggested in his work, in general, did a careful dance with and around each other in which each pushed, but not too far. Any effort to answer questions about resistance or paternalism becomes even more difficult when one considers that Weaver paid the men and women he owned for all their overwork at the same rate that he paid free (and white) workers. His slaves, skilled and unskilled, in turn, worked extra when they wanted to (usually coinciding with holidays and personal and family celebrations) to buy special clothes for themselves and/or gifts for family members or furnishings for their homes.

As the above discussion suggests, revisionist treatments of slavery and slaves seem always to carry some trace questions (or implications) about "agency," "resistance," and "identity." And historians have regularly related these phenomena to aspects of slave culture. But particularly fruitful discussions of slave culture have been based on the notion that American slaves were originally a transplanted population and that, over time, cultural transformations had to have taken place among them. Although the earliest discussions of these transformations concern slave religion, other discussions have been especially rich.

Both Blassingame and Charles Joyner showed the transmission, transformation, and meaning of slave folktales. The folktales were more than forms of entertainment: through these seemingly harmless and playful stories, slave children, and adults too, learned and conveyed many important lessons about social relations, power dynamics, and life in general. As Charles Joyner revealed in *Down by the Riverside: A South Carolina Slave Community* (extracted in this chapter), these tales provided exquisite examples of how one might (or ought to) live when the usual life chances are not available. They also suggested much about the ways in which slaves created alternative views of themselves in the form of these animal and human tricksters and teachers who met a variety of circumstances with caution, thoughtfulness, and/or recklessness, and had to deal with the consequences of their choice of action.

Charles Joyner's All Saints Parish was, in some ways, an ideal place for viewing the various processes of culture. In this somewhat isolated, self-contained community, African traditions would have been easier to maintain than in some other places. But Joyner adds to the usual discussion by showing not only the creolization of African culture – that is, its blending of diverse African and American elements – but also its subsequent decreolization – its becoming American. His most obvious examples are in the food ways and vernacular architecture of the lowcountry.

Although most studies since Phillips suggest the possibility of slaves' creating a life of their own beyond the eyes and ears of their owners, and even of slaves' directly influencing the culture of the whites around them, these studies should not create an impression of slaves, as a group, being fully in control of their lives. Despite all the scholarly efforts to balance the portrait of slavemasters' control with a counterimage of slave agency, it remains the case that the daily life of slaves was overwhelmingly defined by their owners, by where they lived, by the kind of work they performed, and by a myriad of other factors over which they had little control.

Perhaps no study has illustrated just how harsh the realities of slave life could be, and how completely beyond the control of the slaves it often was, as does William Dusinberre's *Them Dark Days: Slavery in the American Rice Swamps* (extracted in this chapter). Dusinberre found very little evidence in the South Carolina and Georgia lowcountry plantations he studied of the give-and-take between master and slave that, for instance, Genovese described, or that Dew found on William Weaver's holdings in western Virginia. Indeed, Dusinberre concluded in his study that capitalism, more than paternalism, defined the relationship between slaves and masters. And on the plantations he examined, Dusinberre found "unhappy families" for good reason: the rice swamps were virtually a "charnel house," as he titled a chapter, which easily destroyed families through disease and planter disregard.

The study of slavery in the American South has long been, and remains, a very dynamic field. Moving inward, from discussions of the institution itself to ones more narrowly focused on the people who created and functioned within it, historical scholarship reveals much about the ways slaves lived their lives at different times and in different locales. Increased attention to change over time has allowed not only a deeper understanding of the creolization of culture but also of diasporas, based on the notion that diverse "Africans" underwent changes beginning with their introduction to America. And so, not surprisingly, we now have a small but significant body of literature on these transplants becoming "African" and on their becoming "American."

While most such studies focus on the North and are weighted toward aspects of public culture, the limitations that southern slaves faced in their ability to move about at will in the public sphere, and our lack of deep access to their private lives, has, it seems, made it more difficult to talk about them in the same kind of extended discussions. Hence, in discussions of slave personality, very little has been added to Blassingame's triad of Nat, Jack, and Sambo. And perhaps because of the limitations within already sparse resources, virtually every action slaves took that did not especially reveal white control has come to be seen as an example of slave resistance. All this is to say that, despite the accomplishments of the above-cited studies, details of the "interior lives" of southern slaves continue to prove difficult to access, and much remains unknown or only superficially understood.

For example, though since the 1960s the slave family has been a favored topic among slavery scholars, we still know little beyond structural details. With more understanding of how, why, and with what effects its structure changed, we could gain greater insights into the shaping of family member roles, how they functioned, and under what circumstances. Similarly, we now understand that "slave communities" sometimes extended beyond the slave quarter. Generally, they functioned as "identity" communities, based largely on race and status. Dylan Penningroth's study of property and kinship among slaves, however, makes it clear that differing interests operated within these identity groups.[12] Thus, we could benefit greatly from more research into the ways that "the community" constituted something other than a place.

In every way, we could benefit by continuing to recall some of the old questions, and by carefully applying every useful method to their study. Dusinberre's stark portrait of life for slaves in the South Carolina/Georgia rice swamps is vivid and compelling precisely because of his use of quantitative methods which, one might assume, would make the story of slave life sterile and scientific beyond recognition. Sharla Fett's attention to what might otherwise be considered a mundane question (what happened when a slave became ill?) proved transformative for slavery historiography. And Daina Berry's recent reminder that Georgia slave women labored in three distinct regions, all with different demands and possibilities, really takes us back, fruitfully, to basics. Thus, to continue to move the historiography of slavery forward we have to assume that no question is too small. And we have to continue to look not only for change over time, but change over time and place.[13]

NOTES

1. U. B. Phillips, *American Negro Slavery: A Survey of the Supply, Employment and Control of Negro Labor as Determined by the Plantation Regime* (Baton Rouge: Louisiana State University Press, 1966 [orig. 1918]).
2. Herbert Aptheker, *American Negro Slave Revolts: Nat Turner, Denmark Vesey, Gabriel, and Others* (New York: International Publishers, 1978 [orig. 1943]); Kenneth M. Stampp, *The Peculiar Institution: Slavery in the Ante-Bellum South* (New York: Alfred A. Knopf, 1956).
3. John W. Blassingame, *The Slave Community: Plantation Life in the Antebellum South* (New York: Oxford University Press, 1972).
4. Stanley M. Elkins, *Slavery: A Problem in American Institutional and Intellectual Life* (Chicago: University of Chicago Press, 1980 [orig. 1959]).
5. Eugene D. Genovese, *Roll, Jordan, Roll: The World the Slaves Made* (New York: Pantheon Books, 1974).
6. George P. Rawick, *From Sundown to Sunup: The Making of the Black Community* (Westport: Greenwood Publishers, 1972).
7. Sharla M. Fett, *Working Cures: Healing, Health, and Power on Southern Slave Plantations* (Chapel Hill: University of North Carolina Press, 2002), p. ix.
8. Thomas C. Buchanan, *Black Life on the Mississippi: Slaves, Free Blacks, and the Western Steamboat World* (Chapel Hill: University of North Carolina Press, 2004).
9. Charles B. Dew, *Bond of Iron: Master and Slave at Buffalo Forge* (New York: W. W. Norton, 1994).
10. Daniel Patrick Moynihan, *The Negro Family: The Case for National Action* (Washington DC: United States Department of Labor, 1965); Herbert G. Gutman, *The Black Family in Slavery and Freedom, 1750–1925* (New York: Pantheon Books, 1977).
11. Brenda E. Stevenson, *Life in Black and White: Family and Community in the Slave South* (New York: Oxford University Press, 1996); Ann Patton Malone, *Sweet Chariot: Slave Family and Household Structure in Nineteenth Century Louisiana* (Chapel Hill: University of North Carolina Press, 1992).
12. Dylan C. Penningroth, *The Claims of Kinfolk: African American Property and Community in the Nineteenth-Century South* (Chapel Hill: University of North Carolina Press, 2003).
13. Daina Ramey Berry, *Swing the Sickle for the Harvest is Ripe: Gender and Slavery in Antebellum Georgia* (Urbana: University of Illinois Press, 2007).

* * *

Further Reading

Bolster, W. Jeffrey, *Black Jacks: African American Seamen in the Age of Sail* (Cambridge, MA: Harvard University Press, 1997).

Camp, Stephanie M. H., *Closer to Freedom: Enslaved Women and Everyday Resistance in the Plantation South* (Chapel Hill: University of North Carolina Press, 2004).

Creel, Margaret Washington, *"A Peculiar People": Slave Religion and Community-Culture Among the Gullahs* (New York: New York University Press, 1988).

Fett, Sharla M., *Working Cures: Healing, Health and Power on Southern Slave Plantations* (Chapel Hill: University of North Carolina Press, 2002).

Genovese, Eugene D., *Roll, Jordan, Roll: The World the Slaves Made* (New York: Vintage, 1974).

Gomez, Michael A., *Exchanging Our Country Marks: The Transformation of African Identities in the Colonial and Antebellum South* (Chapel Hill: University of North Carolina Press, 1998).

Gutman, Herbert G., *The Black Family in Slavery and Freedom, 1750–1925* (New York: Vintage, 1976).

Malone, Ann Patton, *Sweet Chariot: Slave Family and Household Structure in Nineteenth-Century Louisiana* (Chapel Hill: University of North Carolina Press, 1996).

Martin, Jonathan D., *Divided Mastery: Slave Hiring in the American South* (Cambridge, MA: Harvard University Press, 2004).

Rawick, George P., *From Sundown to Sunup: Slavery and the Making of the Black Community* (Westport: Greenwood Press, 1972).

Stuckey, Sterling, *Slave Culture: Nationalist Theory and the Foundations of Black America* (New York: Oxford University Press, 1987).

White, Deborah Gray, *Ar'n't I a Woman? Female Slaves in the Plantation South* (New York: W. W. Norton, 1985).

* * *

Ulrich B. Phillips

American Negro Slavery[†]

In general the most obvious way of preventing trouble was to avoid the occasion for it. If tasks were complained of as too heavy, the simplest recourse was to reduce the schedule. If jobs were slackly done, acquiescence was easier than correction. The easy-going and plausible disposition of the blacks conspired with the heat of the

---

[†] Ulrich B. Phillips, *American Negro Slavery: A Survey of the Supply, Employment and Control of Negro Labor as Determined by the Plantation Regime* (Baton Rouge: Louisiana State University Press, 1966 [orig. 1918]), pp. 306–9, 327–9, 339.

climate to soften the resolution of the whites and make them patient. Severe and unyielding requirements would keep everyone on edge; concession when accompanied with geniality and not indulged so far as to cause demoralization would make plantation life not only tolerable but charming . . .

There was clearly no general prevalence of severity and strain in the régime. There was, furthermore, little of that curse of impersonality and indifference which too commonly prevails in the factories of the present-day world where power-driven machinery sets the pace, where the employers have no relations with the employed outside of work hours, where the proprietors indeed are scattered to the four winds, where the directors confine their attention to finance, and where the one duty of the superintendent is to procure a maximum output at a minimum cost. No, the planters were commonly in residence, their slaves were their chief property to be conserved, and the slaves themselves would not permit indifference even if the masters were so disposed. The generality of the negroes insisted upon possessing and being possessed in a cordial but respectful intimacy. While by no means every plantation was an Arcadia there were many on which the industrial and racial relations deserved almost as glowing accounts as that which the Englishman William Faux wrote in 1819 of the "goodly plantation" of the venerable Mr. Mickle in the uplands of South Carolina. "This gentleman," said he, "appears to me to be a rare example of pure and undefiled religion, kind and gentle in manners . . . Seeing a swarm, or rather herd, of young negroes creeping and dancing about the door and yard of his mansion, all appearing healthy, happy and frolicsome and withal fat and decently clothed, both young and old, I felt induced to praise the economy under which they lived. 'Aye,' said he, 'I have many black people, but I have never bought nor sold any in my life. All that you see came to me with my estate by virtue of my father's will. They are all, old and young, true and faithful to my interests. They need no taskmaster, no overseer. They will do all and more than I expect them to do, and I can trust them with untold gold. All the adults are well instructed, and all are members of Christian churches in the neighbourhood; and their conduct is becoming their professions. I respect them as my children, and they look on me as their friend and father. Were they to be taken from me it would be the most unhappy event of their lives.' This conversation induced me to view more attentively the faces of the adult slaves; and I was astonished at the free, easy, sober, intelligent and thoughtful impression which such an economy as Mr. Mickle's had indelibly made on their countenances."

[. . .]

When Hakluyt wrote in 1584 his *Discourse of Western Planting*, his theme was the project of American colonization; and when a settlement was planted at Jamestown, at Boston or at Providence as the case might be, it was called, regardless of the type, a plantation.

[. . .]

The standard community comprised a white household in the midst of several or many negro families. The one was master, the many were slaves; the one was head, the many were members; the one was teacher, the many were pupils . . .

The separate integration of the slaves was no more than rudimentary. They were always within the social mind and conscience of the whites, as the whites in turn were within the mind and conscience of the blacks. The adjustments and readjustments were mutually made, for although the masters had by far the major power of control, the slaves themselves were by no means devoid of influence. A sagacious employer has well said, after long experience, "a negro understands a white man better than the white man understands the negro." This knowledge gave a power all its own. The general régime was in fact shaped by mutual requirements, concessions and understandings, producing reciprocal codes of conventional morality. Masters of the standard type promoted Christianity and the customs of marriage and parental care, and they instructed as much by example as by precept; they gave occasional holidays, rewards and indulgences, and permitted as large a degree of liberty as they thought the slaves could be trusted not to abuse; they refrained from selling slaves except under the stress of circumstances; they avoided cruel, vindictive and captious punishments, and endeavored to inspire effort through affection rather than through fear; and they were content with achieving quite moderate industrial results. In short their despotism, so far as it might properly be so called, was benevolent in intent and on the whole beneficial in effect.

[. . .]

In general the relations on both sides were felt to be based on pleasurable responsibility . . .

The negroes furnished inertly obeying minds and muscles; slavery provided a police; and the plantation system contributed the machinery of direction. The assignment of special functions to slaves of special aptitudes would enhance the general efficiency; the coördination of tasks would prevent waste of effort; and the conduct of a steady routine would lessen the mischiefs of irresponsibility. But in the work of a plantation squad no delicate implements could be employed, for they would be broken; and no discriminating care in the handling of crops could be had except at a cost of supervision which was generally prohibitive. The whole establishment would work with success only when the management fully recognized and allowed for the crudity of the labor.

The planters faced this fact with mingled resolution and resignation. The sluggishness of the bulk of their slaves they took as a racial trait to be conquered by discipline, even though their ineptitude was not to be eradicated; the talents and vigor of their exceptional negroes and mulattoes, on the other hand, they sought to foster by special training and rewards. But the prevalence of slavery which aided them in the one policy hampered them in the other, for it made the rewards arbitrary instead of automatic and it restricted the scope of the laborers' employments and of their ambitions as well. The device of hiring slaves to themselves, which had an invigorating effect here and there in the towns, could find little application in the country; and the paternalism of the planters could provide no fully effective substitute. Hence the achievements of the exceptional workmen were limited by the status of slavery as surely as the progress of the generality was restricted by the fact of their being negroes.

๛   ๛   ๛

John W. Blassingame

The Slave Community[†]

Personal relations on the plantation were, as in most institutions, determined by spatial arrangements, the frequency of interaction between high- and low-powered individuals, and how the high-powered individual defined the behavioral norms. In practice, of course, many of the institutionally defined roles were imperfectly played. Before one can examine the *actual* behavior on the plantation, however, the societal images and the planter's expectations of the slave must be compared. In the final analysis, the planter's expectations were more closely related to the slave's actual behavior than publicly held stereotypes. Even so, neither the planter's expectations nor the stereotypes were proscriptive. In other words, the slave did not necessarily act the way white people expected him to behave or the way they perceived him as behaving.

[. . .]

The portrait of the slave which emerges from antebellum Southern literature is complex and contradictory. The major slave characters were Sambo, Jack, and Nat. The one rarely seen in literature, Jack, worked faithfully as long as he was well treated. Sometimes sullen and uncooperative, he generally refused to be driven beyond the pace he had set for himself. Conscious of his identity with other slaves, he cooperated with them to resist the white man's oppression. Rationally analyzing the white man's overwhelming physical power, Jack either avoided contact with him or was deferential in his presence. Since he did not identify with his master and could not always keep up the façade of deference, he was occasionally flogged for insubordination. Although often proud, stubborn, and conscious of the wrongs he suffered, Jack tried to repress his anger. His patience was, however, not unlimited. He raided his master's larder when he was hungry, ran away when he was tired of working or had been punished, and was sometimes ungovernable. Shrewd and calculating, he used his wits to escape from work or to manipulate his overseer and master.

[†]John W. Blassingame, *The Slave Community: Plantation Life in the Antebellum South* (New York: Oxford University Press, 1979), pp. 223–6, 228, 230, 233, 238, 248.

Nat was the rebel who rivaled Sambo in the universality and continuity of his literary image. Revengeful, bloodthirsty, cunning, treacherous, and savage, Nat was the incorrigible runaway, the poisoner of white men, the ravager of white women who defied all the rules of plantation society. Subdued and punished only when overcome by superior numbers or firepower, Nat retaliated when attacked by whites, led guerrilla activities of maroons against isolated plantations, killed overseers and planters, or burned plantation buildings when he was abused. Like Jack, Nat's customary obedience often hid his true feelings, self-concept, unquenchable thirst for freedom, hatred of whites, discontent, and manhood, until he violently demonstrated these traits.

Sambo, combining in his person Uncle Remus, Jim Crow, and Uncle Tom, was the most pervasive and long lasting of the three literary stereotypes. Indolent, faithful, humorous, loyal, dishonest, superstitious, improvident, and musical, Sambo was inevitably a clown and congenitally docile. Characteristically a house servant, Sambo had so much love and affection for his master that he was almost filio-pietistic; his loyalty was all-consuming and self-immolating. The epitome of devotion, Sambo often fought and died heroically while trying to save his master's life. Yet, Sambo had no thought of freedom; that was an empty boon compared with serving his master.

The Sambo stereotype was so pervasive in antebellum Southern literature that many historians, without further research, argue that it was an accurate description of the dominant slave personality. According to historians of this stripe, the near unanimity of so many white observers of the slave cannot be discounted. While this is obviously true, it does not follow that the Sambo stereotype must be treated uncritically. Instead, it must be viewed in the context of the other slave stereotypes, and from the perspective of psychology and comparative studies of literature.

Any attempt to generalize about individual and group personality traits based on stereotypes must assess the degree to which "outsiders" are able to perceive someone else's behavior correctly. Since so much of one's personality is socially non-perceivable, hidden, or invisible, the way other people describe an individual is not totally reliable as an index of his attitudes and behavior.

[. . .]

Sambo became a universal figure in antebellum Southern literature partly because he belonged to a subordinate caste. Traditionally, writers in caste and slave societies, representing and identifying with the ruling class and supporting the status quo, have drawn unflattering stereotypes of the lowest caste . . . According to [David B.] Davis, "The white slaves of antiquity and the middle ages were often described in terms that fit the later stereotype of the Negro." Similarly, nineteenth-century Russian writers portrayed the white serfs as callous, shiftless, dishonest, lazy, hypocritical, and stupid.

[. . .]

Southern writers were also compelled to portray the slave as Sambo because of their need to disprove the allegations of antislavery novelists . . . Without Sambo, it was impossible to prove the essential goodness of Southern society.

Another of the important reasons for the pervasiveness of the Sambo stereotype was the desire of whites to relieve themselves of the anxiety of thinking about slaves as men. In this regard, Nat, the actual and potential rebel, stands at the core of white perceptions of the slave. With Nat perennially in the wings, the creation of Sambo was almost mandatory for the Southerner's emotional security. Like a man whistling in the dark to bolster his courage, the white man *had* to portray the slave as Sambo.

[. . .]

It is almost impossible to square the white's fear of Nat with the predominance of the Sambo stereotype in plantation literature. Apparently both slave characters were real. The more fear whites had of Nat, the more firmly they tried to believe in Sambo in order to escape paranoia. This psychological repression was augmented by public acts to relieve anxiety. Every effort was made to keep the slaves in awe of the power of whiteness, and ignorant of their own potential power.

[. . .]

Obviously, if Sambo represented the sum of the master's expectations, the slaveholder could not have survived. Lazy, inefficient, irresponsible, dishonest, childish, stupid Sambo was a guarantee of economic ruin.

[. . .]

If there is any validity at all in the essays on plantation management and publicly held stereotypes, there was a great variety of personality types in the quarters. The first premise of the planter was that there were so many different kinds of slaves that he had to combine several techniques in order to manage them. When the slaveholder considered the best way to get the maximum labor from his slaves he did not assume that a majority of them were Sambos; there was little room for romanticizing when there was cotton to be picked. Even in the publicly held stereotypes, slave behavior ran the whole gamut from abject docility to open rebellion. The predominance of the Sambo and Nat stereotypes explain[s] a great deal more about the white man's character than about the behavior of most slaves.

ॐ ॐ ॐ

Charles Dew

Bond of Iron[†]

Sometime in 1840, at age twenty, Sam Williams married a slave named Nancy Jefferson, twenty-three, who was also owned by William Weaver. The wedding may have occurred in the fall. In September, Sam bought two dress handkerchiefs for $1 and spent $10.50 on a store order that was not spelled out in detail; this store purchase was by far the largest single expenditure he had ever made. On October 10, he used his overwork credit to buy five yards of calico and three and a half yards of bleached muslin. These acquisitions suggest that Sam and Nancy were married in September 1840, and that Sam bought the calico and muslin the next month as a present for his new wife, probably for her to sew into a dress and petticoat.

Sam and Nancy's marriage was not a legal one, of course. Slave unions had no standing in Virginia law, or that of any other state. But time would clearly show that Sam Williams and Nancy Jefferson viewed themselves as man and wife. The date of their marriage was not recorded in the journals and papers kept at Buffalo Forge, but they knew the year was 1840 and they never forgot it.

The birth of their first child did appear in the Buffalo Forge records, however, and for good reason. The birth of a new baby in the slave quarters meant an addition to the master's wealth and potential work force. So, when Elizabeth Williams came into the world late that year, note was taken of the event. Elizabeth, or Betty as she was more frequently called, was undoubtedly named after Sam's younger sister, Elizabeth, who would have been fifteen years old in 1840.

Sam Williams's marriage and the birth of his daughter gave him added incentive to exploit the possibilities opened up by the overwork system. Early in 1840, he began devoting much of his spare time to "tar burning."

[. . .]

Sam would collect and sell this "tair," as it was spelled in the Bath Forge books. The managers at Bath were willing to pay 25 cents a gallon for it . . . and Sam's long hours in the woods produced fifty-nine gallons of tar before the year was out.

He also did something else in the year he was married that he had not done during the three previous years – he worked through the Christmas holidays. Forges almost always closed down for the holidays, but there were plenty of other things to do . . . His total overwork earnings for 1840 came to $26.73, well over seven times what he had made for himself in any previous year at Buffalo Forge or Bath Iron Works.

There is no way to be certain why Sam worked so hard in 1840, but it seems safe to assume that his efforts were spurred by a desire to be able to do more for

---

[†]Charles Dew, *Bond of Iron: Master and Slave at Buffalo Forge* (New York: W. W. Norton, 1994), pp. 176–8, 180–3, 185.

his wife and his baby daughter. During the summer, he bought a set of crocks, for household storage, and his other purchases during the year included molasses, sugar, and coffee, as well as the large store order and the cloth he obtained for Nancy in the fall. On January 15, 1841, he spent 40 cents for two yards of calico. Perhaps Nancy used this cloth to make a garment for herself or for their little girl.

Sam completed his apprenticeship and entered the ranks of Weaver's master refiners during 1841 . . . His purchases during the year again suggest that he was buying things his wife and daughter could use – sugar, bed ticking, striped drill, and calico cloth – and on December 17, 1841, he paid $1.25 for a silk handkerchief. Almost certainly this was a Christmas present for Nancy.

Their family grew steadily over the next several years. In 1842, a second daughter, Caroline, was born, and she was followed by two more girls, Ann, born in 1843, and Lydia, born the next year. Thus in the first four years of their marriage, Sam and Nancy Williams had four daughters. The births of these four girls would complete their family. Their marriage lasted a great many years, but no children were born to them after Lydia came into the world in 1844.

Sam's growing prowess as a refiner and his continued support of his loved ones are apparent in his overwork accounts during the next few years . . . On December 21, he bought four pounds of sugar for his mother, Sally, undoubtedly as a Christmas present (the cost was 77 cents). Three days later, on Christmas Eve, he took $1 in cash from his account, spent $2 for eight yards of calico, and drew against his overwork credit for $20 for a "Blue Coat Fine." Sam could have used the dollar in cash to buy treats for the girls; he almost certainly gave the calico to Nancy; but the "Blue Coat Fine" was his, and it was purchased for a very special reason.

Earlier that December, Sam Williams had stood before the members of the Lexington Baptist Church . . . "At a church meeting held on the 1st Lords Day in Dec 1844, Samuel, a colored man of Mr. Wm Weaver presented himself and after examination by the church was received and will be considered as a member of this church when baptized," noted Sam Jordan, the church clerk, in recording the minutes of this meeting. The blue coat was undoubtedly the coat in which he intended to be baptized.

[. . .]

The most fascinating items that he acquired during these years were the articles of furniture he bought for the cabin that he, Nancy, and the girls shared. His major Christmas gift to the family in 1845 consisted of a table ($3) and a bedstead ($9) . . . In April 1851, he made two acquisitions "at Blackford's Sale": a set of chairs, for which he paid $7.25, and probably his most revealing purchase of the entire antebellum era, "1 looking glass," priced at $1.75.

There are many reasons why any family would want to own a mirror – perfectly natural reasons, such as curiosity about one's appearance or a touch of vanity, perhaps. Sam and Nancy Williams had growing daughters, too . . . But the purchase of a mirror by a *slave* suggests something more. It indicates a strong sense of pride in one's self and one's family that transcended their status as slaves. Why else would Sam spend that kind of money on such a purchase? One dollar seventy-five cents represented the sweat and sore muscles that went into several hundred pounds of overwork iron. One almost suspects that the looking glass, packed carefully in a wagon and hauled home from "Blackford's Sale," stood as a symbol of Sam and Nancy's feelings about themselves and their children.

[. . .]

It was time for Sam to get his own name back.

On the page in the Buffalo Forge "Negro Book" covering his work for the year 1853, his name appears two ways: as "Samuel Etna" and as "Sam Williams."

[. . .]

From this point on, as far as the records were concerned, he was almost always identified as "Sam Williams." His father was "Sam Williams Senior."

[. . .]

Nancy Williams had a savings account, too, and in her own name. Since she was in charge of the dairy operations at Buffalo Forge and did a good deal of house-work at Weaver's residence, she clearly had opportunities to earn overwork pay in her own right . . . During the 1850s, she received money for raising calves, for a stone pitcher she sold Weaver, and for indigo she grew in her garden. She was given money on one occasion to buy starch, which indicates that she was ironing at Weaver's residence. And she also kept her own hogs at Buffalo Forge which were weighed, slaughtered, and put up in the smokehouse in her name when hog-killing time arrived. Some of this meat could have been sold to Weaver. By these means and other forms of overwork we unfortunately cannot identify, she had managed to accumulate savings that were fully two-thirds the size of her husband's. Between them, Sam and Nancy Williams had $153.27 in cash in 1856, the 1992 equivalent of approximately $2,500.

[. . .]

Through their overwork, both Sam and Nancy could help to shield and provide for each other and for their children. The psychological importance of this to them – the added access it afforded Sam to the traditional responsibilities of a husband and father, and Nancy to the role of wife and mother – cannot be overemphasized.

❧ ❧ ❧

Charles Joyner

Down by the Riverside[†]

Behind the Big House, beyond the kitchens, barns, stables, carriage houses, and other plantation outbuildings, were the cabins of the slaves. These slave quarters were known on the rice plantations of the Waccamaw as the street. They were built in settlements, often on named streets, and reminded an English visitor of a country village. There were three such settlements on Robert F. W. Allston's plantation, with houses about fifty yards apart on both sides of the street. Each village contained about twelve houses along each side of the street. In these villages the slaves lived more or less to themselves, although on some plantations the white overseer's house was at the end of the street, "so that watchful eyes and ears could know how the slaves behaved when not at work."

People are influenced by the space around them. They may be crowded, or awestruck, or comfortable. Their work may be made easier or harder; their personalities may be stimulated or relaxed by the space they inhabit. A proper orientation in space is essential to sanity and survival. Architecture, by giving form to space, brings space under human control. Vernacular architecture – that is, folk building, done without benefit of formal plans – is the immediate product of its users, forming a sensitive indicator of their inner feelings, their ideas of what is and is not appropriate.

[. . .]

The houses were built by the slaves, although the rice planters organized the process and usually provided the specifications. It is for that reason that most of the slave houses exemplify British house-types . . . At Hagley, for example, each slave house was said to have an upstairs and separate bedrooms for male and female children. This may have been an example of the southern I house, a very common two-story dwelling two rooms wide and one room deep.

Most of the slave houses in the old photographs appear to be of the British hall-and-parlor type. This rectangular, one-story, gable-roofed house is patterned closely after originals in England and northern Ireland. James R. Sparkman maintained that the slave cabins on his plantation contained "a hall and 2 sleeping compartments" – an apt description of the hall-and-parlor house. Appearances may be deceptive, however. The surviving slave houses at Friendfield Village exemplify the facade, but not the floor plan, of the hall-and-parlor house. The floor plan, on the other hand, is identical to that of the Yoruba two-room houses of Nigeria.

Another common folk house-type in the South was the double pen, in which a one-room cabin (or single pen) had another room added. Several double-pen cabins

[†]Charles Joyner, *Down by the Riverside: A South Carolina Slave Community* (Urbana: University of Illinois Press, 1985), pp. 117–20, 126, 172–9, 181–3.

are visible in the old photographs of Waccamaw slave streets, all of them examples of the saddlebag-type, with the additional room added to the chimney end, resulting in a double-pen cabin with a central chimney. Double-pen cabins may have sheltered two slave families, in which case their single-room spatial units were the same as the single-pen houses in spatial orientations. Some visitors, however, clearly described the double-pen house as a single-family dwelling. Whether or not the double-pens housed single families, however, the British single-pen house-type is conceptually equivalent to *half* of a common two-room Yoruba house. Thus, the floor plan of the double-pen house is similar to an African proxemic environment. Here, too, one finds a convergence of African floor plan and British facade. Nearly all the surviving slave cabins at Friendfield reflect the convergence of elements of African and of European culture. Outwardly the cabins were marked by European notions of symmetry and control, but inwardly they concealed interiors marked by African spatial orientations. The two-room house was crucial to the Yoruba architectural tradition, and its continuity in Waccamaw slave cabins was not accidental. That continuity is eloquent testimony that West African architecture was not forgotten in the crucible of slavery.

James R. Sparkman's claim that the slaves on his plantations lived in houses measuring eighteen by twenty-two feet hardly seems credible to contemporary scholars of slavery. But the lively debate over the adequacy of slave housing – based on unspoken Euro-American assumptions regarding optimum spatial dimensions – has obscured as much as it has revealed. By Euro-American standards the amount of living space available to the slaves would seem to compare favorably with that of the Pilgrims. The average dimensions of extant seventeenth-century houses in Plymouth, Massachusetts, measured sixteen by twenty-one feet. On the other hand, by Afro-American standards, the slave cabins may have been too large, not too small. Optimal dimensions in African architecture are small – nine by nine in Benin, eight by eight in Angola, ten by ten generally. Buildings throughout West Africa feature rooms small enough to facilitate intimacy in social relations. Slaves who came to All Saints Parish from Senegal and Gambia in the north all the way to Angola and the Congo in the south shared a cultural preference for such arrangements. Thus, the relatively small dimensions of slave housing may be taken less as evidence of the physical deprivation of the slaves than as evidence of cultural continuity with Africa. Despite the imposition by the planters of European symmetrical facades and construction techniques, slaves on the rice plantations of the Waccamaw built their houses in compliance with an undisrupted African sensitivity toward optimal dimension.

[. . .]

The broad front porches of the slave cabins helped to modify the steamy Waccamaw summers by providing both shade for the house and a shady place where one might catch the faintest stirrings of a late afternoon breeze. The absence of such porches in Europe suggests that the African slaves and their descendants may have taught their masters more about tropical architecture than has been generally credited.

[. . .]

Perhaps even more significant was that when the slave family was together in its home, gathered around the fireplace, the master and his power were shut out for the moment. Around that fireplace the young slave learned a language, heard stories of how Buh Rabbit outsmarted Buh Bear and of how the slave John outsmarted Ole Maussa, watched the grownups cook and quilt and dance to the music of fiddle and banjo, observed the spirited weekly prayer meetings, and prayed quietly in the family bosom. In short, it was largely around that fireside that the young slave acquired a rich creolized culture. The cabin may have been dark and stuffy, prone to drafts in the winter and insects in the summer, but its importance is nevertheless underscored by Hagar Brown's invocation: "God bless the house and keep the soul."

[. . .]

From Africa, with its long tradition of narrative and its great bestiary of tricksters, came a rich legacy of folktales that delighted both blacks and whites on the rice plantations of the Waccamaw. One of the persistent delusions of the slaveholders, of visitors to the plantations, and of several generations of others was that the trickster tales told by plantation slaves were mere entertainment. What the novel is to twentieth-century readers, the trickster tale was to the slaves of All Saints Parish. Its performance style was their synthesis of inherited and acquired artistry. Its theme was a satirical depiction of their own world and its social relations. Its function was to inspire and educate. Its telling and hearing helped to create the solidarity of the slave community . . . With no disposition to insist that the narratives – even those told as personal experiences – necessarily took place as told, one might at least observe that narrating such experiences had cultural meaning for the slaves who told them and the slaves who heard them. The cultural meaning may be probed by an examination of the slaves' stories and their storytelling, their continuity with Africa and their creativity in America, their themes and their functions. The animal and human trickster tales of the slaves exemplify language used as symbolic action. By manipulating the words that defined it, the slaves could verbally rearrange their world and turn it symbolically inside out.

[. . .]

The best-known and most widely collected folktales among both Africans and Afro-Americans are the animal tales, and the best-known and most widely collected animal tales are trickster tales. In All Saints Parish, too, animal trickster tales constitute the most common type of folk narrative. The most obvious feature of the All Saints animal tales is their emphasis on small but sly creatures, weak but wily animals who continually get the better of their bigger and more powerful adversaries through superior cunning. Despite physical puniness, the tiny trickster's personality is marked by audacity, egotism, and rebellion. Through the symbolic identification of nature with society the animal trickster tales defined the trickster and his actions as both necessary and good. Such symbolic identification served as a means of transforming the unavoidable into the desirable and of giving a certain freedom of individual action despite group restraints.

[. . .]

The animal trickster appears in many guises in black folktales in Africa and in the New World . . . This shifting of roles in the tales is important, for it underlines the educative function of folktale narration in the slave community. From such role switching, slaves learned not merely how to emulate the trickster but also how to avoid being tricked.

[. . .]

The central theme of the animal trickster tales is the struggle for mastery between the trickster and his adversary, as expressed in possession of the two most basic signs of status – food and sex.

[. . .]

While the possession of food is a common symbol of status and power, significantly the trickster found his greatest satisfaction not in the mere possession of food, but in *taking* it from the more powerful animals. In "De Buttah Tree," Buh Woof and Buh Rabbit are joint owners of a butter tree. While Wolf and Rabbit are hoeing rice one day, Rabbit keeps slipping off and eating some of the butter until he has eaten it all. Not only does he deny having eaten the butter, but also he rubs butter on Wolf's mouth while he is sleeping and accuses him of eating the butter. Were mere survival perceived by the narrators to be the theme of the stories, it is unlikely that the final episode would have remained part of the emotional core of the story. Clearly this story is not about food as a symbol of survival, but food as a symbol of power.

[. . .]

In yet another tale of the competition for food the tables are turned on the trickster. Buh Rabbit rarely meets his match; when he does, it is at the hands of even smaller, weaker creatures. "Buh Rabbit and Buh Guinea" involves the theft of a cow by Rabbit and Guinea. Rabbit sends Guinea to look for the sun in order to get fire with which to cook the cow. While he is gone, Rabbit gives away beef to all his friends. When Guinea returns, Rabbit tells him the cow has sunk into the ground. Only his tail is showing. They pull the tail up and Guinea eats it, then pretends to be poisoned. Rabbit desperately scurries off to get the meat back from his friends before they are poisoned, too.

The other basic status symbol in the animal trickster tales of the Waccamaw is sexual prowess. In tale after tale the trickster (Buh Rabbit usually) is engaged in deadly competition with the more powerful animals for the favors of "de gals." In "Buddah Rabbit and Buddah Gatah," for instance, Rabbit is jealous because "all de gals stuck on Buddah Gatah." Rabbit goes to a dance where Gator is fiddling and calling. As he calls instructions to the dancers, Gator repeats the refrain, "Eb'ry day good! Eb'ry day good!" Rabbit persuades Gator to let him call and fiddle while Gator rests. As Rabbit calls instructions, he repeats as a refrain, "Some day good! Some day bad! Some day good! Some day bad!" Gator does not like that refrain, because he says he has never seen any trouble. One day Rabbit finds Gator resting on some dried-up old swamp grass and encircles him with fire while Rabbit hollers at him, "Some day good! Some day bad!" Gator is forced to acknowledge that there is indeed trouble in the world. Here again the essential amorality of the trickster is depicted. Such duplicity and violence, in some cases (such as this) depicted for their own sake, are portrayed as everyday actions for the trickster.

In "Buh Partridge Pay Buh Rabbit Back," Rabbit is the victim, and a frailer creature, Buh Partridge, is the deadly trickster. Rabbit and Partridge are competing for the favors of a particular woman ("Dey lakin de same gal"). Rabbit finds Partridge sitting on a stump with his head tucked under his wing. Partridge pretends that his head has been cut off and grandly extolls the virtues of headlessness. He is even going to the dance without his head. Rabbit wants his head cut off, too, but neither his wife, his mother, nor his daughter will oblige him. Eventually Partridge agrees to behead him. He chops off Rabbit's head, then takes his own head out from under his wing and goes to the dance, where he will have the woman all to himself. Rabbit's cunning is offset by his stupidity, his vanity, and his inability to see when he himself is the butt of a trick. Rabbit's role-switching from trickster to tricked in different stories made it possible for slaves to empathize not merely with the trickster but with the tricked as well.

[. . .]

A notable theme of the trickster tales is the punishment of those who refuse to live up to the obligations of friendship or to come to the aid of their fellow creatures in time of need. The All Saints versions of the classic "Tar Baby" folktale exemplify the rhetorical device that shows things getting worse as the result of the neglect of sacred duties. The other animals seek revenge on Buh Rabbit for his not sharing water from his secret well during a drought. He tells them he gets up early in the morning to drink the dew. One night Billy Goat watches Buh Rabbit and discovers the secret well. Billy Goat hastens back to tell the other animals. They decide to teach Buh Rabbit a lesson and set a trap – the tar baby – for him near his well.

When Buh Rabbit comes for a drink, he says, "Hey, oh deah, Putty Gal!" but the tar baby does not answer. Buh Rabbit becomes angry. "You bettah talk wid me! Oh, ef I slaps you one time wid my right han', I broke you jaw!" The tar baby does not answer, and Buh Rabbit hits her. His hand sticks. "Ef I slaps you wid my lef' han' one time, I slaps you face one-sided!" The same result. "Ef I kicks you wid dis foot, I bus you belly open!" The same result again. "Oh, I wouldn' wantuh kick you wid muh lef' foot – Oh, Gal, ah ain' know whut 'e done fo you!" Both hands and both feet are soon stuck. "Well, I knows one ting! Uh got uh belly hyuh. I butt you wid my belly, buss you open!" Eventually even his head and teeth are stuck to the tar baby. Then the goat and other animals come and scold him for lying about the dew before releasing him. Buh Rabbit's selfishness is the reason *why* the other animals revenge themselves upon him; his vanity, boastfulness, and stupidity are the keys to *how* they are able to accomplish that revenge – a valuable lesson to slaves.

[. . .]

These folktales represent, perhaps preeminently, the artistic expression of the slaves – the means through which their creative artists present to posterity not merely the social, but also the artistic impulse of their community. In the animal tales they found the perfect vehicle to express those impulses, those often painful cultural truths, in an indirect, and thus less painful, way. Such indirection goes to the heart of African concepts of eloquence.

ഐ ഐ ഐ

William Dusinberre

Them Dark Days[†]

[Fanny] Kemble was appalled by her experiences on the Butler estate. Child mortality was frightful. The health of female slaves was shattered by the field labor required of them until soon before, and again soon after, their frequent pregnancies. Not even the most estimable slave woman could defend herself against the sexual demands of white overseers. Slaves were subject to revolting physical punishment and to degrading callousness. Both children and the aged were shockingly neglected.

[. . .]

The frequency with which children died, dismaying though it was to Kemble, should surprise no one acquainted with the rice kingdom. One evening a series

---

[†]William Dusinberre, *Them Dark Days: Slavery in the American Rice Swamps* (New York: Oxford University Press, 1996), pp. 234–9, 247.

of nine slave women came to Kemble after their work was done, petitioning her for bits of cloth and morsels of food, or simply paying her a visit. She asked each one her childbearing experiences. All nine women can be identified, a century and a half later, in the Butler records in Philadelphia; and with the possible exception of one (Sukey), the stories they told Kemble about the number of children they had borne appear to be consistent with the records of births and deaths kept by Roswell King Jr. from 1819 to 1834. The thirty-three-year-old Molly, for example, was the most fortunate of these women, because only three of her nine children had died. (Her nine children, the Butler records show, were born in 1824, 1826, 1828, 1830, 1831, 1833, 1834, 1836, and 1837: of these, the ones who had died by the time of Kemble's trip were those born in 1830, 1833, and 1834. A fourth child – the one born in 1831 – died subsequent to Kemble's visit but before reaching adulthood.) Sophy was not quite so lucky, for five of her ten children were already dead. Thirty-two-year-old Sukey said she had needed fifteen pregnancies to produce six living children: she had had four miscarriages, and five live children had later expired.

These were the only ones of the nine women who still had large families when Kemble spoke to them. Leah, twenty-six years old, had lost three of her six children, while Nanny at twenty-eight had seen two of her three die. (Nanny, Kemble noted, "came to implore that the rule of sending them into the field three weeks after their confinement might be altered.") Forty-eight-year-old Charlotte had had only two pregnancies, both ending in miscarriages. Sally at forty-four had also had two miscarriages, and one of her three live children had died. Fanny, thirty-eight years old, told Kemble that five of her six children had died. Her sole living child, the Butler records show, was her two-year-old Wallace.

The thirty-nine-year-old Sarah had had perhaps the hardest life of all those to whom Kemble spoke that evening. Her first husband, carpenter Ben, had died in 1825. Their only child had perished in infancy, and Sarah probably had also had several miscarriages before her husband's death. By a second husband Sarah bore children in 1827, 1828, 1830, 1832, 1833, and probably about 1836, of whom only two were still alive in 1839. Thus by the time she spoke to Kemble she had been pregnant eleven times, had had four miscarriages, and had seen five of her seven children die. Pregnant once again, Sarah

> complained of dreadful pains in the back, and an internal tumor which swells with the exertion of working in the fields; probably, I think, she is ruptured. She told me she had once been mad and had run into the woods, where she contrived to elude discovery for some time, but was at last tracked and brought back, when she was tied up by the arms, and heavy logs fastened to her feet, and was severely flogged. After this she contrived to escape again, and lived for some time skulking in the woods, and she supposes mad, for when she was taken again she was entirely naked . . . I suppose her constant childbearing and hard labor in the fields at the same time may have produced the temporary insanity.

This record of human misery undermines the claim of the eminent British geologist Sir Charles Lyell that the rapid growth of the slave population proved the happy condition of low-country slaves. The lives of these nine women – who among them had experienced twelve miscarriages and five stillbirths, and seen twenty-four more children die – were scarcely models of felicity; yet the nine women had produced twenty-six living children, far more than required to sustain the estate's labor force. As at [the] Gowrie [plantation], the majority of these families became small through dreadful child mortality; and the high incidence of miscarriage – suffered by four of these nine women – suggests an added dimension to the maternal woes of women at Gowrie, where miscarriages seldom found their way into the plantation records.

[. . .]

It has never been sufficiently realized how devastating infant mortality was on nineteenth-century rice plantations. Even Richard Steckel – whose valuable studies have done most to call attention to the phenomenon – originally suggested an infant mortality rate on rice plantations (to age one) of 31 percent; yet this figure, high though it seems, was surely an underestimate.

[. . .]

No doubt an even larger proportion of infants would have died at the Butler estate had the managers not granted pregnant mothers a certain respite from field labor. So clear was it that arduous labor in muddy or flooded rice fields would impair the health of pregnant women and their babies that – according to the younger Roswell King – "the labour of pregnant women is reduced one half, and they are put to work in dry situations." This sounded sensible, so far as it went; but how was King to determine whether a woman was pregnant? Evidently he had at first relied upon the women to notify him when a baby was on its way, and apparently as many as one-third of them had then pretended to be pregnant before they actually were. Dido's infant, King reported with exasperation in 1822, had been "15 mo[nths] breeding," Tina's 11 months, Elce's 17 months, and Mary's 16 months. Malingering seems to have been practiced even by the wives of the most trusted artisans. The admirable Betty (wife of that carpenter Frank whom King later promoted to be the head driver at Butler Island) was 12 months in breeding her infant; while the wife of carpenter Ned – later appointed chief engineer of the rice mill – took 15 months between the time she said her pregnancy had begun and the moment the child appeared. However much one may smile appreciatively at these women's successful deception of their master, this form of day-to-day resistance could be counterproductive; for it might impel the suspicious white man never to reduce a woman's task until he could see with his own eyes that she was indeed pregnant.

[. . .]

After her abortive attempt to flee to the North, Kemble listened more seriously than ever to the women's stories of hardship, often uttered with patient resignation. Thus Peggy – an "exceedingly decent woman" married to the literate carpenter John, who was one of Butler's most valuable slaves – suffered ill health in 1839 and said "she had been broken down ever since the birth of her last child." Asked how long after the confinement she returned to field work, "she answered very quietly, but with a deep sigh: 'Three weeks, missis; de usual time.'" Shocked by the sufferings of Mile and especially of Die (the woman whose miscarriage had been induced by a whipping), and shaken still by the explosion when Butler had refused her permission to intercede for the slaves, Kemble tried to "walk off some of the weight of horror and depression [she felt] surrounded by all this misery and degradation that I can neither help nor hinder." In the woods, the frightfulness of how people treat their own kind mingled with the horror nature sometimes displays. "Treacherous white moss" – like white slaveholders living off their slaves – parasitically depended from the "noble live oaks" of St. Simons Island and finally conquered them, "stripping [their] huge limbs bare." The seventh circle of Dante's hell came to Kemble's mind, where suicides, converted into trees, cried for compassion: "*Non hai tu spirto di pietate alcuno?*" – Have you no pity?

5

Victoria Bynum

CLASS AND CULTURE IN THE WHITE SOUTH

The white South of the antebellum era is classically portrayed as a world of stately planters and humble common folk. While there is some truth to this depiction, it obscures a more complex reality, one that has attracted continual research over the past century. Fueling such inquiry has been a series of compelling questions. What were the gradations of the white South's social hierarchy? How do we define such categories as "planter," "yeoman," "plain folk," "poor white trash"? In what regard can the social and political order of the white South be described as "aristocratic", in what regard, "democratic"? To what extent were class gulfs bridged by ties of kinship and locality or by common notions of race and gender, honor and religion, ethnicity and region? How fluid was social and economic mobility within the white South? What did the institution of slavery, and the presence of African Americans, mean to those whites (the majority, that is) who owned no slaves themselves? How well does the classic portrayal of nineteenth-century women as powerless inhabitants of a separate, domestic sphere describe the social realities of the white South? The essay by Victoria Bynum and the selections, old and new, that follow indicate how questions such as these have sustained interest in the white antebellum South.

Victoria Bynum, Distinguished Professor Emeritus of History at Texas State University–San Marcos, works on gender, race, and class relations in the nineteenth-century South. Among her published works are *Unruly Women: The Politics of Social and Sexual Control in the Old South* (1992), *The Free State of Jones: Mississippi's Longest Civil War* (2001), and *The Long Shadow of the Civil War: Southern Dissent and its Legacies* (2010). She currently moderates the blog 'Renegade South'.

In 1930, as the United States plunged into the Great Depression, twelve prominent southerners "took their stand" against the imperatives of modern industrial society. Calling for a return to agrarian traditions, the essays featured in
I'll Take My Stand were reactive rather than reformist. Contributor Frank L.
Owsley, professor of history at Vanderbilt University, disdained both industrial capitalism and its left-wing critics by invoking a lost past – one in which
independent yeomen farmed their own lands rather than toiling in the factories
of corporate bosses. Before the Civil War, he argued, plain white southerners
were contented agriculturalists and herders who asked only to be left alone by
the larger society. Slavery was incidental to their existence. Greedy northern
industrialists and zealous abolitionists, however, refused to leave the South
alone, and their meddling in southern affairs eventually precipitated the
"irrepressible conflict" of civil war.[1]

Owsley's version of southern history was perfectly consonant with
Confederate "Lost Cause" literature, and contributed much to its staying
power. His recognition of the Old South's vast middle class of rural farmers
and herders was embedded in familiar images of grasping, fanatical white
northerners and ignorant, rapacious black slaves, unleashed by emancipation and empowered by Radical Reconstruction. The leadership of southern
Reconstruction, he wrote, consisted of "half-savage blacks" armed by "half-
savage" white abolitionists. Owsley's impassioned words played to the racism
and sectional identification of many white southerners, while giving voice to
their frustration over stereotypical images of "poor white trash."

Just as racism blinded many white historians to the realities of slavery, so
have deeply ingrained images of poor white degradation long obscured the
history of class relations in the American South. Just five years before *I'll Take
My Stand* appeared, the 1925 Scopes "Monkey Trial" sensationalized the
image of plain white southerners as ignorant, degraded buffoons. Attorney
Clarence Darrow, in his defense of John Scopes against the charge of teaching evolution in a Tennessee public school, brilliantly lampooned prosecuting
attorney William Jennings Bryan for rejecting science in favor of a literal interpretation of the Bible – as did the news media, led by journalist H. L. Mencken.
The "forlorn mob of imbeciles" who cheered Bryan on, Mencken trumpeted,
was comprised of the lowest of white southerners; a "minority of civilized
Tennesseans" had capitulated to the masses and their "bigotry, ignorance,
hatred, [and] superstition."[2]

Novelists, film-makers, and even historians routinely drew on similar stereotypes to describe the majority of white southerners, past and present. The Old
South was routinely depicted as a land comprised only of slaveholders, slaves,
and poor whites (despite the fact that most antebellum white southerners were
propertied non-slaveholders). By the early twentieth century, popular depictions of the South featured scrawny, indolent, tobacco-chewing men, pipe-
smoking women, and hookworm-infested children – the quintessential "poor
white trash." In 1929, journalist Wilbur J. Cash fittingly published his essay,

"The Mind of the South" (forerunner to his 1941 book of the same name), in Mencken's *American Mercury*. Cash's message was clear: if a white man of the Old South did not own slaves and grow cotton, he likely scratched in the dirt to produce a few ears of corn.[3]

Owsley was not the first historian to recognize the South's middling yeoman farmer. In 1906, Ulrich B. Phillips acknowledged their presence in his landmark study of the Old South's Black Belt region.[4] Throughout the Progressive era and well into the 1920s, Phillips dominated the field of antebellum southern history. As a southern Progressive, he encouraged New South industrial growth by portraying an Old South in which the progress of rural capitalist planters had been hampered by inefficient slave labor. Economically, he argued, the ending of slavery had freed the South to move forward. Yet slavery, Phillips noted with approval, had protected the supremacy of the white race. Deeply racist, he did not question the morality of slavery, and approved of segregation as the New South's method of racial control. White antebellum southerners and northerners, he maintained, had always shared similar economic values; with slavery gone, they could now share common paths of progress.

Although Phillips and Owsley shared similar racial views, their takes on common whites differed profoundly. The Old South described by Phillips included small and large slaveholders, prosperous and not-so-prosperous yeoman farmers, and landless poor whites, all locked in a dynamic process of growth that tended to favor commercial staple-producing plantations. According to Phillips, the concentration of wealth by great planters resembled that of the large industrial organizations of his own time. Antebellum plantations, too, he argued, were specialized commercial units dependent on cheap labor – labor supplied by slaves rather than immigrants. Dependent also on fresh lands, plantation commerce expanded westward where, on each successive frontier, large planters drove small farmers off the Black Belt lands and thus out of business. Although Phillips recognized the middling yeoman farmer, he placed him in the midst of a process that marginalized and often impoverished him. As planters encroached on western lands settled first by frontier farmers, the latter either bought slaves and joined their neighbors in producing staple crops, moved on to new frontiers, or "drifted to the barren tracts" to become "anemic poor whites."[5]

As Progressive historians such as Phillips passed from the scene, a new generation, influenced by the Great Depression, the Second World War, and an incipient civil rights movement, brought major changes to the historiography of the Old South. New Deal-era emphasis on the "common man," horror over Hitler's genocidal policies toward Jews, and growing awareness of America's own systematized oppression of minorities – epitomized in racial segregation – drove scholars to rethink their understanding of the Old South.

Heightened scholarly interest in the southern common folk was marked by the 1939 publication of Roger Shugg's *Origins of Class Struggle in Louisiana*. Decrying the frequent equation of southern "po' white trash" with white people who were poor (by virtue of not owning slaves), Shugg more kindly designated non-slaveholders as the region's "common people."[6] His groundbreaking work was soon challenged, however, by a flurry of studies, emanating from Vanderbilt University, aimed at recovering the South's agrarian past.

Led by Frank Owsley, the "Vanderbilt group" mined the federal manuscript censuses to reveal an Old South populated primarily by middle-class farmers. Refuting Phillips's and Shugg's portraits of planter-class domination, they argued instead for widespread economic democracy. Propertied yeoman farmers, they insisted, lived lives of comfort and prosperity in the Black Belt, piedmont, and piney woods regions of the South. For those hardy pioneers who sought upward mobility, the western territories promised, and delivered, fresh lands.[7]

To the extent that Owsley avoided the inflammatory racism expressed in his 1930 essay, he joined mainstream white historians of the 1940s in publishing more racially sensitive works on the South. Owsley, however, continued to treat African Americans and slavery as irrelevant to understanding the Old South. Meanwhile, he rejected the class-based approach of Shugg, criticizing him for transforming Louisiana's yeoman farmers and urban artisans into "proletarians." In a foretaste of the Cold War politics of the 1950s, Owsley suggested that Shugg's fondness for the "Marxian bed" of class theory had rendered him less "alert" to relevant data.[8]

The Vanderbilt studies generated a good deal of excitement within the profession. Mainstream historians praised the new attention to the southern yeomanry, although some raised questions about the accuracy of their across-the-board claims of yeoman prosperity. The most critical assessment appeared in 1946, when Fabian Linden, at that time a Harvard graduate student, published a lengthy review of several of the Vanderbilt studies in the *Journal of Negro History*. While praising the group for its fresh approach and innovative use of sources, Linden characterized the image of a South populated only by planters, slaves, and poor whites as a "tedious cliché." Most devastating was Linden's critique of the methodology and conclusions of the Vanderbilt historians. Only by failing to recognize how planters controlled the greatest share of wealth and owned the most productive lands, Linden argued, could they maintain that economic democracy prevailed in the Old South.[9]

In 1947, Owsley vigorously defended the Vanderbilt approach against Linden's criticisms and, two years later, synthesized its arguments in his classic *Plain Folk of the Old South* (extracted in this chapter). Southern white farmers, he affirmed, were indeed self-sufficient and satisfied. Agricultural traditions were nurtured by plain folk and planters alike, leaving the former neither downtrodden nor deprived. Just as he had done almost twenty years earlier, Owsley presented the American past as a contest between urban industrial forces and rural agricultural traditions. His point was clear: not only was the Civil War *not* about slavery, but slavery had not played a significant role in creating distinct classes of white southerners.

The chief contribution of the Vanderbilt historians was their painstaking study of unpublished federal manuscript censuses and local state and county records as tools for recreating the lives of the South's non-slaveholding majority. That contribution, unfortunately, was largely forgotten amid withering criticisms of their conclusions. Perhaps even more important to the demise of the Owsley school's popularity, however, was its neglect of African Americans. The Vanderbilt thesis of economic democracy among southern whites seemed less relevant to historians in the wake of the Supreme Court's momentous *Brown* v. *Board of Education of Topeka* decision of 1954. Southern historiography was soon to be transformed again, this time by a burgeoning Civil Rights movement that convinced even mainstream historians that the study of blacks and race relations was fundamental to understanding the Old South. Owsley's "Lost Cause" approach, which pitted a villainous industrial North against a virtuous agrarian South, while ignoring slavery, appeared particularly dated in an era of dawning racial consciousness.[10]

As the field of African American history continued to grow during the 1960s, historical attention to plain white southerners declined. Whatever clues the Owsley school had offered about the world of southern plain folk – and there were many – were further submerged by the 1965 publication of Eugene Genovese's provocative collection of essays, *The Political Economy of Slavery*. Dismissing Owsley's contention that the non-slaveholding yeomanry was "strong and prosperous," Genovese revived U. B. Phillips's planter-domination thesis, urging readers to look past Phillips's racism and appreciate the sophistication of his economic arguments.[11]

Yet, in 1975, Genovese himself counseled historians, "in retrospect," to consider studying the white yeomanry as sympathetically as Owsley and his protégés had done. In his essay, "Yeoman Farmers in a Slaveholder's Democracy," Genovese chided historians for allowing their new fascination with race relations to eclipse those of class. Too often, he cautioned, historians reduced yeomen support for slavery and the Confederate cause to mere racism and ignorance of their own economic interests. But the South's apparent lack of class conflict, Genovese argued, was far more complicated than assumptions about yeoman ignorance, docility, and racism suggested. Raising the question of just how loyal the yeomanry actually was to the South's slaveholding regime, Genovese called for a "new wave of research," using the tools pioneered by Owsley to reconstruct the daily lives of ordinary white farmers. Special attention, he pointed out, should be given to cultural and economic differences between upcountry and plantation-belt farmers.[12]

Research on the southern yeomanry flourished during the 1970s and 1980s, as a "new" school of social history emerged. Historians rediscovered the value of local records and aggregate statistics, producing a host of regional studies that analyzed the place of small farmers in the southern political economy. Several studies presented yeomen who lived outside the Black Belt as more economically self-reliant than their Black Belt counterparts. Historians noted, however, that when railroads entered into backcountry regions during the 1850s, cotton production increased and yeoman self-sufficiency declined. Anxiety over fluctuations in national markets produced varying responses among the yeomanry. Some historians argued that yeoman farmers stubbornly resisted producing for the market while others found them all too willingly enmeshed in it by 1860. Some farmers embraced secession in 1861 as the only means of escaping the encroachment of northern industry, and thus retaining their independence, while others blamed the "big bugs" (southern planters and merchants) for disrupting the Union. Local divisions of power and political resentments, as well as market relations, often determined whether or not a particular community supported secession.

But what about the poor whites? If they did not constitute the rank and file of the Old South's non-slaveholders, were they, then, incidental to southern society, merely déclassé, as suggested by Owsley? Utilizing many of the same sources first tapped by Owsley, but adding criminal and civil action court records to the mix, recent historians have explored the lives of poor whites in more depth than ever before. Extracted here, Charles C. Bolton's 1994 study of poor white migration from North Carolina to Mississippi reconciled the conflicting portrayals of planter domination and plantation democracy. Through careful study of federal, state, and local records, Bolton found evidence of yeoman mobility yet disputed Owsley's vision of southern economic democracy and of the southwestern frontier as a harbinger of progress and equality. Not energy, ambition, nor even kinship ties, Bolton argued, overcame the class barriers faced by poor men and women moving west.

With co-editor Scott Culclasure, Bolton later analyzed a single court document – the dictated confession of convicted murderer Edward Isham – to produce a rich collection of essays on the effects of slavery, kinship networks, and conventions of white masculinity and femininity on the lives of poor whites of the Old South. The overarching message of this volume's authors – who drew upon court records, manuscript censuses, and newspaper accounts, as well as Isham's confession – was that, over time, class mobility decreased among landless people and small farmers as the concentration of wealth among slaveholding planters increased.[13]

Renewed attention to southern plain folk did not simply restore the old planter-domination thesis, however. While arguing against the notion of widespread democracy and opportunity, Bolton et al. insisted that poor whites, yeomen, and African Americans (free as well as enslaved) were vital participants in the shaping of antebellum southern society. And, just as race had become a fundamental tool for historical analysis of class, so too, by the 1980s, had gender. Challenging the assumption that women occupied a separate, private sphere bereft of political and economic influence, historians soon demonstrated that gender concerns – and women – played a central role in the creation of class and race systems in the Old South.

Michele Gillespie's extracted article on women millworkers in antebellum

Georgia is an important contribution to the debate on economic mobility among the southern plain folk. Neatly dovetailing with Bolton's focus on migration into the Southwest, Gillespie showed how the same migration stimulated industrialization in Georgia. By the 1820s, Georgia's rapid settlement stimulated congressional support for internal improvements, including transportation networks and textile mills, to facilitate the marketing of cotton.

By focusing on textile mill workers, Gillespie expanded the story beyond farmers on the move. Offering a gendered analysis of how white women and children emerged as Georgia's primary industrial workforce, she illuminated the importance of conventional norms of masculine independence and feminine domesticity to mill owners' ability to maintain a cheap labor force. Owners, Gillespie argued, touted their mills as a means to upward mobility for all poor whites, while benefiting from a low-paid, largely powerless workforce comprised mostly of young single women and children.

While historians such as Gillespie focused on women's paid work, others analyzed the ways in which class, race, and gender affected women's behavior in social and domestic settings. Victoria Bynum, Martha Hodes, Laura Edwards, Diana Sommerville, and Jeff Forret, among others, combed through state and local court records to find ordinary people who regularly transgressed the boundaries of southern society. By collapsing the theoretical walls between the political "public" world and the domestic "private" sphere, they revealed the deep roots and sweeping breadth of societal systems of power. Whether accused of theft, gambling, violent assault, illegal trade, or illicit sex, a defendant's gender, race, and class always mattered, as did kinship ties, community networks, and personal reputation. For example, a lower-class white woman, especially one who dared to cross the sexual color line, could expect little sympathy from lawmakers (or the broader white community) if she filed charges of rape – even when the accused was a black man.[14]

Ordinary folks were not mere victims, however, of a legal system stacked against them. Most wanted what rich folks had: material goods and power over others. Poor white men engaged in various predatory crimes (convicted murderer Edward Isham was an extreme but illuminating example), while poor white women ignored many conventions of womanhood to meet their physical and emotional needs. Interracial contact among all classes of people was both cooperative (as in the bartering of goods) and antagonistic (reflected in exploitive sexual relations), and was frequently illegal. Thus, when court officials attempted to administer justice and mediate relations between husbands and wives, masters and slaves, friends and neighbors, blacks and whites, they encountered a contested, often violent, world in which "dependents" and "inferiors" frequently asserted the powers of the weak. As Laura Edwards observed, "[t]he law had to assert continually the power of white male household heads precisely because, in practice, that power was neither complete nor stable."[15]

Historical debate over the level of economic mobility and political democracy among antebellum southern whites will continue, but the consensus to date is that the slaveholding class, though proportionately small, increased its share of wealth and power as the Civil War approached. Consequently, class consciousness grew among non-slaveholders during the decade preceding war but remained diffused and disorganized, hampered by the gulf between landowning and landless plain folk. Socially, non-slaveholding whites no longer appear as silent victims of a slaveholding patriarchy, or happy prosperous farmers who simply chose not to own slaves. Rather, they appear remarkably modern in their efforts to carve out lives in a society that privileged white over black, male over female, and slaveholder over non-slaveholder. Enclaves of prosperous small farmers did indeed exist throughout the South, but wretchedly poor white people were a common sight in virtually every community.

A century of scholarship has taught us much about planters, farmers, and poor whites – and the complex relations among them. Still, questions remain. Historians continue to debate the degree to which the southwestern frontier fostered class mobility, even while it extended the South's slaveholding empire. If class conflict existed, how and when did it become a politically conscious force? And we have only begun to understand the importance of women's labor to the celebrated "independence" of yeoman farmers. Other questions concern the legacy of the Old South for the New. How, for example, did early factories, such as the Georgia textile mills described by Gillespie, set the scene for industrial relations in the New South to come? To what extent, if any, did the frontier fulfill its promise as a poor man's paradise once slavery was abolished? Finally, how did Confederate defeat and the end of slavery stimulate political activism among blacks, white women, and poor farmers that set these groups on parallel, but conflicting, courses of change? The following selections provide a sampling of the lively historical debates that challenge Old South stereotypes of benevolent planters, passive farmers, and degraded poor whites.

NOTES

1. Frank Lawrence Owsley, "The Irrepressible Conflict," in Twelve Southerners, *I'll Take My Stand: The South and the Agrarian Tradition* (New York: Harper & Brothers, 1930), pp. 61–91.
2. Quoted from H. L. Mencken, "Tennessee in the Frying Pan," July 20, 1925 and "Aftermath," Sept. 14, 1925, both in *Baltimore Evening Sun*.
3. Wilbur J. Cash, "The Mind of the South," *American Mercury*, 17 (October 1929), pp. 310–18.
4. Ulrich B. Phillips, "The Origin and Growth of the Southern Black Belts," *American Historical Review*, 4 (July 1906), pp. 798–816.
5. Phillips, "Origin and Growth of the Southern Black Belts," p. 800.
6. Roger Shugg, *Origins of Class Struggle in Louisiana* (Baton Rouge: Louisiana State University Press, 1968 [orig. 1939]), pp. xi, 20–2.

7. Frank L. and Harriet C. Owsley, "The Economic Basis of Society in the Late Antebellum South," *Journal of Southern History*, 6 (February 1940), pp. 24–5; Blanche Henry Clark, *The Tennessee Yeoman, 1840–1860* (Nashville: Vanderbilt University Press, 1942); Harry L. Coles, Jr., "Some Notes on Slaveownership and Landownership in Louisiana, 1850–1860," *Journal of Southern History*, 9 (August 1943), pp. 381–94; Herbert Weaver, *Mississippi Farmers, 1850–1860* (Nashville: Vanderbilt University Press, 1945).

8. Frank L. Owsley, review of Shugg, *Origins of Class Struggle, Journal of Southern History*, 6 (February 1940), pp. 116–17.

9. Fabian Linden, "Economic Democracy in the Slave South: An Appraisal of Some Recent Views," *Journal of Negro History*, 32 (April 1946), pp. 140–89 (quoted passage, p. 187).

10. For example, in 1955, C. Vann Woodward, who had conducted research on behalf of the NAACP for the *Brown v. Board of Education of Topeka* case, published his landmark revisionist book on southern race relations, *The Strange Career of Jim Crow* (New York: Oxford University Press, 1955).

11. Eugene Genovese, *The Political Economy of Slavery: Studies in the Economy and Society of the Slave South* (New York: Pantheon, 1965), pp. 36–7.

12. Eugene Genovese, "Yeomen Farmers in a Slaveholders' Democracy," *Agricultural History*, 49 (April 1975), pp. 331–42.

13. Charles C. Bolton and Scott Culclasure, eds., *The Confessions of Edward Isham: A Poor White Life of the Old South* (Athens: University of Georgia Press, 1998).

14. Victoria Bynum, *Unruly Women: The Politics of Social and Sexual Control in the Old South* (Chapel Hill: University of North Carolina Press, 1992); Martha Hodes, *White Women, Black Men: Illicit Sex in the Nineteenth-Century South* (New Haven: Yale University Press, 1997); Laura F. Edwards, "Law, Domestic Violence, and the Limits of Patriarchal Authority in the Antebellum South," *Journal of Southern History*, 65 (November 1999): pp. 733–69; Diane Miller Sommerville, *Rape & Race in the Nineteenth-Century South* (Chapel Hill: University of North Carolina Press, 2004); Jeff Forret, *Race Relations at the Margins: Slaves and Poor Whites in the Antebellum Southern Countryside* (Baton Rouge: Louisiana State University Press, 2006).

15. Quoted from Edwards, "Law, Domestic Violence, and the Limits of Patriarchal Authority," p. 740; Victoria Bynum, "Mothers, Lovers and Wives: Images of Poor White Women in Edward Isham's Autobiography," in Bolton and Culclasure, eds., *Confessions of Edward Isham*, pp. 85–100.

* * *

FURTHER READING

Bynum, Victoria, *Unruly Women: The Politics of Social and Sexual Control in the Old South* (Chapel Hill: University of North Carolina Press, 1992).

Bolton, Charles C. and Scott Culclasure, eds., *The Confessions of Edward Isham: A Poor White Life of the Old South* (Athens: University of Georgia Press, 1998).

Brown, David, *Southern Outcast: Hinton Rowan Helper and the Impending Crisis of the South* (Baton Rouge: Louisiana State University Press, 2006).

Ford, Lacy K., *Origins of Southern Radicalism: The South Carolina Upcountry, 1800–1860* (New York: Oxford University Press, 1991).

Forret, Jeff, *Race Relations at the Margins: Slaves and Poor Whites in the Antebellum Southern Countryside* (Baton Rouge: Louisiana State University Press, 2006).

Genovese, Eugene, "Yeoman Farmers in a Slaveholders' Democracy," *Agricultural History*, 49 (April 1975), pp. 331–42.

Harris, J. William, *Plain Folk and Gentry in a Slave Society: White Liberty and Black Slavery in Augusta's Hinterlands* (Middletown: Wesleyan University Press, 1985).

Hyde, Samuel Jr., ed., *Plain Folk of the South Revisited* (Baton Rouge: Louisiana State University Press, 1997).

McCurry, Stephanie, *Masters of Small Worlds: Yeoman Households, Gender Relations, and the Political Culture of the Antebellum South Carolina Low Country* (New York: Oxford University Press, 1995).

Rockman, Seth, *Scraping By: Wage Labor, Slavery, and Survival in Early Baltimore* (Baltimore: Johns Hopkins University Press, 2008).

Shugg, Roger, *Origins of Class Struggle in Louisiana: A Social History of White Farmers and Laborers During Slavery and After, 1840–1875* (Baton Rouge: Louisiana State University Press, 1939).

Wright, Gavin, *The Political Economy of the Cotton South: Households, Markets, and Wealth in the Nineteenth Century* (New York: Oxford University Press, 1978).

* * *

Frank Lawrence Owsley

Plain Folk of the Old South[†]

The role of the Southern folk was scarcely that of a supernumerary in any phase of Southern life. To deal with them – as has been the tendency in studying the plantation economy – either as a formless mass or filler that settles into the cracks and crevices left by the planters is to take a narrow and incomplete view of Southern society. On the other hand to deal with the plain folk as a class-conscious group, bitter and resentful toward the aristocracy because of exploitation and neglect of the latter, is even farther from reality.

The Southern folk were, as has been repeatedly said, a closely knit people; but

[†] Frank Lawrence Owsley, *Plain Folk of the Old South* (Chicago: Quadrangle Books, 1965 [orig. Baton Rouge: Louisiana State University Press, 1949]), pp. 133–5, 138–49.

they were not class conscious in the Marxian sense, for with rare exceptions they did not regard the planters and men of wealth as their oppressors. On the contrary, they admired them as a rule and looked with approval on their success; and they assumed, on the basis of much tangible evidence, that the door of economic opportunity swung open easily to the thrust of their own ambitious and energetic sons and daughters. Indeed, it was considered a common occurrence outside the older states of Virginia and the Carolinas, for the rank and file to move upward in the economic scale, and for individuals in every community to become well-to-do planters, political leaders, and members of a learned profession. Relatively few of the plain folk, however, seem to have had a desire to become wealthy. Their ambition was to acquire land and other property sufficient to give them and their children a sense of security and well-being, to be "good livers" and "have something saved for a rainy day" as they would have put it. Nevertheless, the knowledge that the economic door was not bolted against themselves and their children tended to stifle the development of a jealous and bitter class consciousness.

The abundance of cheap land, the generally high prices received for farm products and livestock, and the rapidly developing political democracy were the principal means of keeping the economic door unlocked, and preventing the development of a sense of frustration and resentment against the more wealthy. There were, also, other important forces that diminished the feeling of class stratification and helped in the creation of a sense of unity between the plain folk and the aristocracy. Such were the association of rich and poor in all religious activities and in the schools, the frequent ties of blood kinship between them, and the generally folkish and democratic bearing of the aristocracy. This sense of unity between all social and economic groups can not be stressed too much, in view of the strongly and widely held opinion to the contrary.

[. . .]

A grazing and farm economy rather than a plantation economy was practiced by nearly all the nonslaveholders and by 60 to 80 per cent of the slaveholders. Farm economy meant a diversified, self-sufficient type of agriculture, where the money crops were subordinated to food crops, and where the labor was performed by the family or the family aided by a few slaves.

[. . .]

As a result of the self-sufficiency of farm economy, the farmers were seldom involved in indebtedness, once they had paid for their lands.

Farm economy, together with livestock grazing, not only furnished support for the farmers and herdsmen who composed the bulk of the Southern population but supplied a large portion of the hogs, cattle, and breadstuffs purchased for the plantations. Indeed, the farmers and graziers could have easily supplied the entire needs of the South for beef and pork, had not the greater portion of the cattle and hogs been driven to the seaports such as Philadelphia, Baltimore, Charleston, Savannah, Mobile, and New Orleans, where they were usually slaughtered and shipped to the Eastern markets or to the West Indies.

[. . .]

At this point I wish to say something about the role of the plain folk in political affairs, but space will permit of only a few general observations. Did the planter class as such dominate politics and determine the policy of government to the extent that has been usually claimed? If so, how did they control the mass of voters? Was it done by intimidation through threat of physical violence to the voter or his family? – a method quite common in Europe, today, and in many organizations in the United States. Such intimidation as a means of vote getting can of course be dismissed. It would have been physical and political suicide in a country where family ties and kinships were so numerous and close, and where such a threat would have been enthusiastically met – more than halfway – by men and boys handy with firearms. Did the aristocracy control the people by means of economic coercion? This also is a method too well known in the United States even to be discussed. This type of coercion was not possible in the antebellum South, however, since the Southern farmer usually owned his farm and was dependent on no one. All forms of coercion were in fact out of keeping with the character of either the common folk or the planters. What of the use of money to purchase votes necessary to win the election? Although there must have been in every community individuals whose vote could be purchased, there is no evidence of a widespread use of bribery to sway the vote of the people.

[. . .]

"These standards were high enough and clean enough to force aspirants for leadership to at least outward conformity with the popular ideal, and the very existence of such an ideal kept the political atmosphere in a measure pure." The truth of the matter is that whatever influence the planters exercised over the political action of the common people was of a personal and local nature. It was based upon the respect the plain folk of a community had for the character and judgment of individual planters in that community and such qualities of character and judgment in the planter were revealed only by his genuine participation in community affairs.

It must be remembered, however, that there were few genuine planters outside the black belt, and that such personal influence and leadership was [sic] relatively narrow. If the farmers who lived outside the black belt were to be brought to support the interest of the planters, a less personal means of gaining their votes would have to be used; and this method had to be that of persuasion.

[. . .]

The persuasive efforts made by both Whig and Democratic political leaders to win the political support of the rank and file was extraordinary.

[. . .]

Joint debates were a very popular mode of conducting a campaign. In these debates apt rejoinder, witty repartee and side comments were often more effective than oratory.

[. . .]

William H. Milburn tells of a political speaker, who, as he puts it, "was quite over-thrown at the summit of a gorgeous flight of eloquence, and left to slink dumfounded from the stage" when an unscrupulous adversary bawled out at his back "guess he wouldn't talk quite so hifalutenin if he knowed his breeches was torn out behind." These joint debates and political speeches . . . were usually successful in bringing together a great concourse of people. To make sure of a large attendance, scores of hogs, beeves, and young goats were barbecued, and barrels of lemonade were served.

[. . .]

"In consequence of this [observed Reuben Davis, the Mississippi politician] . . . there was never a people better educated on political questions than the Southerners of that day."

The significance of the role of the plain folk in politics may be partly evaluated from some of the provisions of the new state constitutions adapted under popular pressure between 1830 and 1860. Universal white manhood suffrage, the popular election of virtually all county and state officers, and the abolition of property qualifications for office holding in most cases were good examples.

[. . .]

Reference has been frequently made to the fact that outside the older states, indi-viduals were constantly rising from the farmer to the planter class. There are indi-cations, in fact, that in some areas a majority had thus risen from relative poverty as had the older planter class in the seaboard states. Much depended on when the immigrant settled . . . Settlers on rich soils usually rose more rapidly and further than those on poorer soils. Indeed, it appears that in many parts of the black belt most of the settlers were either nonslaveholders or small slaveholders, and that frequently both nonslaveholders and small slaveholders became large slaveholders.

But the plain folk made a much larger contribution to the leadership in other classes than they did to that of the planter class. It appears to be true in the lower South and in Tennessee and Kentucky that the bulk of lawyers, physicians, preach-ers, editors, teachers, businessmen, and political leaders below the national level were members of families who were poor or only comfortably well off. A young man of ability, energy, and determination – barring unusually bad luck – could scarcely fail of considerable success in any of the professions. He might never set the world on fire – in fact, he probably would have no such desire as a rule – but he could nearly always rise to local leadership.

[. . .]

If he were to be a lawyer, ofttimes he read law under the direction of an attorney while teaching school, though occasionally he would attend a law school. When he had been admitted to the bar he would usually enter a law office in a minor capacity – frequently as a sort of secretary and copyist for the firm. If he were shrewd and energetic – and young men of this type usually were – he would soon rise into a prominent position in the firm or as an independent attorney.

[. . .]

If the young man planned to become a physician, his preparation could be as little or as much as he desired and was able to pay for. The commonest procedure even for the most ambitious was to obtain employment with a practicing physician – such as keeping his books, driving his buggy, and running errands. In his spare time, if any, the apprentice read the medical books in the doctor's office and perhaps dissected a cadaver – at least for a while, until it spoiled completely.

[. . .]

An examination of the life histories of large numbers of the clergy seems to indicate that an overwhelming majority were recruits from the ranks of the people, and that they acquired their education in a fashion similar to that of the young men preparing for the other professions. Many began their careers as schoolmasters and, indeed, many continued throughout life to teach school.

[. . .]

Since education was for the poor but ambitious youth the gateway to success in business and the professions, what were the opportunities for acquiring the necessary education?

[. . .]

The first thing is to observe that the common folk of the South obviously received relatively more schooling than has generally been supposed. By comparing the illiteracy of the Southern people with that of the people of New England, where for well-known reasons a common school system had long existed, the South has been made to appear as a land where mass ignorance prevailed.

[. . .]

[I]n comparison with the situation in most countries of the world at that time the Southern folk were one of the most literate major groups of the entire world.

[. . .]

Only in the Scandinavian countries, Belgium, and Holland, Prussia, and Saxony was the literacy of the people comparable with or greater than that of the South.

[. . .]

Literacy is not education; however, if college attendance is any test of an educated people, the South had more educated men and women in proportion to population than the North, or any other part of the world. According to the 1860 census, out of a white population of 7,400,000 there were 25,882 students enrolled in Southern colleges, whereas in the North, with a white population of over 19,000,000, there were only 27,408 students in college; and quite a large number of these were from the South. That is, there was one college student for each 247 white persons in the South and one in 703 in the North.

[. . .]

It thus appears that the opportunity of acquiring an education – the gateway to the professions and to success was quite favorable for the ambitious youth, however poor he might be. Indeed, it can be rather positively asserted that most young men, at least, who *desired* an education, could obtain one. The catchword, let it be observed, is *desired*. Aye! There was the rub! – and it still is!

৯৮ ৯৮ ৯৮

Charles C. Bolton

Poor Whites of the Antebellum South[†]

During the early years of the Republic, the western lands of the United States held out great possibilities for widely shared prosperity among the country's white citizenry. Thomas Jefferson believed that the poor of the United States could be spared a Europeanlike dependent existence by becoming landed farmers on the

---

[†]Charles C. Bolton, *Poor Whites of the Antebellum South: Tenants and Laborers in Central North Carolina and Northeast Mississippi* (Durham: Duke University Press, 1994) pp. 66–78, 80–3.

vast acreage of the nation's western frontier. Almost a century later, looking back on the recently completed white settlement of that western frontier, the historian Frederick Jackson Turner echoed Jefferson's optimism by offering a generally positive assessment of the role westward expansion had played in the development of the United States. Although scholars have since modified or abandoned much of Turner's very influential frontier thesis, the era of westward settlement continues to linger in the American mind as a powerful cultural symbol of the equality and opportunity presumed to be inherent in the American experience. Indeed, popular memories of the westward settlement of the United States resonate with positive images: free land, hardworking settlers, the building of a nation out of wilderness.

In reality, the promising hopes many had for the western frontier collided with major roadblocks during the antebellum years. For one thing, it is important to recognize that the lands of the West were not free before the Civil War. During this period, when the best farming lands of the Old Southwest and the Midwest were settled, the Homestead Act to grant free western land to settlers languished in congressional debate for eighteen years.

[. . .]

Most southern politicians . . . opposed homestead legislation and played a key role in blocking federal action on a homestead measure in the years before the Civil War. Some feared that a policy of free land would encourage foreign immigrants with antislavery views to settle in the region.

[. . .]

Southern officials from many areas feared that a homestead measure might even hasten the immigration of landless white southerners to the free states.

[. . .]

Before the Homestead Act was finally passed by Congress in 1862 – following the exodus of the southern congressional delegations in 1861 – western settlers had to buy land from the government. Poor whites moving to the West generally did not have the money to make such a purchase.

Even without the promise of free land, however, millions of Americans from the original thirteen colonies left their homes for the new states to the south and west during the first half of the nineteenth century.

[. . .]

Poor whites, yeoman farmers, and rich planters from the South Atlantic seaboard states all joined the westward trek to the Old Southwest. The attraction for poor whites, as for other classes of southerners, was a seemingly inexhaustible supply of land that seemed suitable for growing cotton and making men wealthy. Besides the lure of western land, the crushing debt obligations created by credit-based systems of exchange also fueled the massive movement of poor whites to the south and west. When Jonathan Worth of Randolph County pressed one of his debtors, William Sluder, for payment in 1850, Sluder reacted in the same way as did many people in like circumstances – he left the area with his family. During the depression of the late 1830s and early 1840s, debts motivated the poor throughout the South to keep pressing westward.

[. . .]

In south Mississippi, large numbers of men were leaving for Texas during the late 1830s, some "running from wives[,] some from debts and some from the roap."

[. . .]

Poor whites who moved to the Old Southwest entered an area of expanding cotton production and rising individual incomes. Between 1833 and 1848, cotton production in the older South Atlantic States remained stable, while cotton production in the new lower South states tripled. Recognizing the growing affluence of the Old Southwest as a region, most scholars have accepted Frank Owsley's assessment that upward social mobility for poor white immigrants to the Old Southwest remained widespread because "vast quantities of cheap public lands [were] always available to the settlers during the antebellum period." In other words, scholars have often equated the prosperity of the new states of the cotton South with economic success for all classes of white immigrants.

The southern frontier clearly provided opportunities for poor whites. Many landless white southerners acquired land by emigration, and every success story went a long way in convincing others of the virtues of the West. For example, the story of Thomas Allred of Randolph County undoubtedly made a strong impression in the central Piedmont. In 1850, the twenty-seven-year-old Allred lived in Randolph County as a landless carpenter. Heavily in debt, he struck out for Missouri during the 1850s. By 1866, Allred owned 700 acres of land, a store, $2,000 in notes and interest, and a one-half interest in a mill. To top it off, he had served in the state legislature.

For the most part, however, poor white emigrants failed to become landowners. The story of Benjamin Scarborough is instructive.

[. . .]

Whatever plans Benjamin Scarborough had for improving his economic situation by selling his yeoman-sized inheritance in North Carolina and moving to the lower South, his dreams never materialized. After spending several years in Georgia, Scarborough moved in the late 1830s to Russell County, Alabama, in the east-central part of the state. In 1840 and 1841, he labored in Russell County as a sharecropper on a cotton plantation. Scarborough made enough to support himself and his family, but he did not generate any surplus income. He complained that "tho I have worked hard I shall git but little." Scarborough cautioned any potential North Carolina emigrants that if they had land that they "can make a liveing on[,] it is not worth his while to sell it for little or nothing and come hear with the expectation of gitting land on the same term." The high prices for cotton lands in the Old Southwest made purchasing quality land a difficult proposition, not only for destitute emigrants but also for men, such as Scarborough, who came to the Old Southwest with modest means.

[. . .]

A comparison of the status of individuals before and after migration suggests that opportunity did exist for landless emigrants to acquire land in the Old Southwest, although continued failure was more typical. In other words, the emigration experience of Benjamin Scarborough was apparently more common than that of Thomas Allred. An examination of the yeomen and poor whites living in Pontotoc County, Mississippi, in 1860 who had moved to the county during the 1850s reveals that the two groups had dramatically different histories. The yeomen hailed from a wide range of economic backgrounds. About two-fifths had been landless at their 1850 locations, with the remainder either yeoman or wealthy farmers. Clearly, a significant number of the yeomen living in Pontotoc County in 1860 could claim that moving had been a wise choice – one that had allowed them to acquire land and advance economically. A look at the landless population of Pontotoc County in 1860, however, provides a contrastingly bleak commentary on the economic benefits of the migration experience for poor whites. Around 80 percent of the landless population in Pontotoc County in 1860 – which represented about 39 percent of all households in the county – had not been landowners at their 1850 locations. Altogether, perhaps two-thirds of the landless immigrants to Pontotoc County during the 1850s had not improved their economic status by moving west.

During the antebellum years, the South – and indeed the entire country – had a significant population of poor people conducting frequent yet unsuccessful searches for places where they could own land.

[. . .]

Why did the search for a better life through migration prove to be an exercise in futility for large numbers of poor white southerners? The emigration pattern of landless whites does not appear to have been much different from that of yeoman farmers. Both landless and yeoman emigrants tended to travel to locations where they already knew family or friends, and like their yeoman counterparts, landless emigrants tended to migrate in groups.

[. . .]

Evidently, the migration strategies utilized by landless families mirrored those of yeoman emigrants, so it seems unlikely that the difficulties landless emigrants had in acquiring land were strongly connected with the way they migrated.

The major obstacle to landownership faced by landless emigrants in the antebellum period stemmed from the nature of land acquisition and distribution in the Old Southwest.

[. . .]

Northeast Mississippi, along with the rest of north Mississippi and parts of north Alabama, became available to white settlers in the early 1830s after the federal government took the land from the Chickasaws

[. . .]

The Chickasaws refused for several years to surrender their central holdings in north Mississippi, but in 1830, both the federal government and the state government of Mississippi took actions that made it extremely difficult for the Chickasaws to remain in their ancient homeland. The passage of the Indian Removal Act codified the federal government's resolve to move all southeastern Native Americans west of the Mississippi River, and Mississippi effectively destroyed tribal government by extending state law to cover the Chickasaw Nation. Consequently, Chickasaw leaders negotiated two treaties in 1830 and 1832 to relinquish the remaining Chickasaw lands in return for land farther west and individual allotments of land in Mississippi.

Thousands of landless white settlers poured into north Mississippi after 1830, but largely because of the way the federal government disposed of the Chickasaw cession, few of the immigrants had a chance to actually own any of the Chickasaw domain. On paper, the government's plan for disposing of the public lands appeared to be an orderly, fair process. After surveying the land, the government offered it at public sale to the highest bidder but at a price no lower than $1.25 an acre. In many areas, preemption rights allowed occupiers of the land at the time of a public sale the right of first option to purchase.

When the Chickasaw lands were made available for public sale in January 1836, preemptors had no rights and most of the best land had already been snatched up by private parties before the public sale even began. Before 1841 preemption rights had been granted only for limited areas and periods, but no such privileges were allowed in the lands of the Chickasaw cession.

[. . .]

In contrast to its active role in taking the lands of Native Americans, the U.S. government took no action to protect white squatters and settlers from land speculators once the removal of Native Americans was complete.

[. . .]

While it is generally understood that land speculators, not actual settlers, acquired a major share of the public domain sold in the first half of the nineteenth century, the implications of this development for the masses of poor people who moved west in search of land generally remain unexplored.

The early and almost complete control land speculators gained over the lands of the Old Southwest is the key to understanding why landless immigrants to the area had difficulty in obtaining land. Compared to poor settlers in the Midwest, landless whites in the Old Southwest faced a more daunting challenge from land speculators.

[. . .]

Anticipating that public lands of the Old Southwest could be transformed into sizable cotton plantations worked with slave labor, many planters from the older southern states came or sent agents to invest in the new lands. In addition, speculator companies from throughout the United States, believing that the public lands of the Old Southwest could be easily resold to planters at high prices, established powerful organizations to purchase as much land in the region as possible. In short, the presence of slavery and slaveholders made the public lands of the Old Southwest potentially more valuable than government land on other frontiers.

[. . .]

The nature of speculators' control over the public lands of the Old Southwest is clearly revealed by their maneuvers in north Mississippi to acquire the Chickasaw lands. They obtained much of the valuable land in the Chickasaw cession in the year *preceding* the public sale.

[. . .]

Northern capital stimulated much of the presale speculation.

[. . .]

Even small speculators sought the help of northern capitalists.

[. . .]

Speculators controlled the prime lands of the Chickasaw cession by the summer of 1835 and had already begun to resell the lands to wealthy planters or their agents six months before the government's public sale of the Chickasaw lands.

[. . .]

Speculators received considerable support in their land-grabbing efforts from local government officials. Each government land office had two officials, the register and the receiver. Throughout the country, these officials had a reputation for using their positions to assist their own efforts at land speculation.

[. . .]

These land officers/speculators had little inclination or incentive to protect the interests of poor white settlers.

For poor white emigrants, the decisive power wielded by land speculators meant continued poverty. Landless men seeking a western home obviously could not compete with the concentrated wealth controlled by big land companies or with the fortunes of wealthy planters.

[. . .]

In addition to gaining initial ownership of the lion's share of land in northeast Mississippi, land speculators continued to control the distribution of much of the area's land throughout the antebellum decades. The panic of 1837 struck on the heels of the government's disposal of the public lands in north Mississippi, a financial disaster that prevented land speculators from realizing the immediate, large profits they had anticipated. While the economic crisis crippled some smaller combinations of land hoarders, . . . the large organizations survived the crisis intact.

[. . .]

Many speculators kept the land they had acquired until after prosperity returned in the late 1840s and the 1850s. They then were able to obtain the high prices they desired.

[. . .]

In their efforts to secure profits, the land companies adopted credit policies that generally excluded landless customers.

[. . .]

Thus, as is typically true in an economy driven by credit, the people who needed credit most had to have ready cash to purchase, while those who had cash found credit easy to obtain. Although yeoman farmers may have had enough assets to be considered creditworthy, landless people undoubtedly appeared as poor credit risks.

[. . .]

Rather than take up the rejected lands of north Mississippi, many poor emigrants struck out farther west to Texas or Arkansas. Richard Bolton recognized that "emigration to Texas prevails to some extent with the poorer classes." This exodus from northeast Mississippi, however, did not trouble him because he realized that "not more than five or ten in the hundred are able to buy land in this country." By the 1850s, many poor emigrants completely bypassed northeast Mississippi for Arkansas or Texas, "where lands are cheaper."

Texas loomed as a potential promised land for all classes of emigrants, including landless ones. Under the terms of annexation, Texas owned its own public lands, and the state practically gave them away. A settler's only expenses were incurred when applying to the local commissioners and when arranging for a surveyor to locate an unoccupied plot. Each family could get up to 640 acres. Texas also passed the first homestead exemption law in the United States in 1838, protecting fifty acres of land and $500 worth of improvements from seizure for debt.

[. . .]

Even in Texas, however, landownership proved elusive for many settlers. In 1860, approximately 26 percent of the farmers in Texas remained landless. As in northeast Mississippi, many landless settlers arrived in Texas too late to claim any decent land.

[. . .]

The struggle of southern poor white emigrants to acquire land in the Old Southwest was frequently a losing battle. In a country that had wrested control of vast tracts of land from Native Americans, in part to provide homes for its white citizens, large numbers of poor whites could not lay claim to any of the land, despite persistent efforts. Even settlement of the vast lands of the West could not significantly alter the country's stratified social structure.

[. . .]

Ultimately, the migration of landless whites merely moved poverty west, a movement seemingly obscured by the fantastic fortunes generated in the new areas of the American South and by our own deeply held myths about the leveling nature of the nation's westward expansion.

൙ ൙ ൙

Michele Gillespie

To Harden a Lady's Hand[†]

"There is nothing in tending a loom to harden a lady's hand," stated Chief Justice Henry Collier, a strong advocate for textile manufactures in the antebellum South. Like many promoters of southern industrialization in the decades before the Civil War, Collier recognized that the employment of white females in textile mills secured an inexpensive, quiescent labor force that not only did not compete with but indeed complemented the dominant agricultural economy and its key labor source – slaves. To compel southern society to embrace white women's employment in the mills, he manipulated the conventions of gender and race in the antebellum South by invoking the southern lady ideal with his statement. Thus Collier was contending that a white female employee could remain a "southern lady," despite the unprecedented experience of toiling for fourteen-hour days in massive buildings filled with noisy machines and choking fibers, because her hands would not be callused by her labors. Her mythical gentility, in other words, along with her virtue, would remain intact, making millwork an ideal pursuit for white women, an implicit contrast to slave women, who were perceived by whites to lack such critical character attributes and whose work was generally agricultural, often extremely arduous, and rarely gender-specific.

When British traveler J. S. Buckingham passed through the region in 1842, he painted a very different picture of factory life in the Old South, one that did not include any reference to southern ladyhood. "The white families engaged in these factories live in log huts clustered about the establishment on the river's bank," he commented after meeting millworkers dwelling along the Oconee River in Athens, Georgia. "The whites look miserably pale and unhealthy; and they are said to be very short-lived, the first symptoms of fevers and dysentaries in the autumn appearing chiefly among them in the factories, and sweeping numbers of them off to death."

[. . .]

The majority of factory workers in Georgia in the antebellum era were white women. The truth about their origins and experiences remains largely unexplored, despite the fact that their entry into wage work represented a significant new development in the antebellum era. This essay explores the development of women as a mill labor force in Georgia, a key industrializing southern state in the antebellum period. It takes its cue from those scholars of nineteenth-century southern women's history, most especially Victoria Bynum and LeeAnn Whites, who have insisted

---

[†]Michele Gillespie, "To Harden a Lady's Hand: Gender Politics, Racial Realities, and Female Millworkers in Antebellum Georgia," in Susanna Delfino and Michele Gillespie, eds., *Neither Lady Nor Slave: Working Women of the Old South* (Chapel Hill: University of North Carolina Press, 2002), pp. 261–77, 279–80.

on exploring the critical connections between the presumably private world of the home and family and the public world of politics and commerce. In doing so, the essay highlights the interplay between seemingly straightforward economic concerns, perceptions about racial realities, uses of gender ideals, and new constructions of working-class identity that worked together to make paid female labor socially and politically palatable in the Old South.

Women from all walks of life had always toiled in the South prior to the advent of female factory work. Indeed, the vast majority of southern women, white and black, slave and free, worked the livelong day, just not in a factory in front of mechanized looms for wages. Wives, daughters, widows, and spinsters managed the household, hen house, and vegetable and herb gardens, ran the kitchen and the dairy, did the spinning, knitting, and making of cloth and clothes, the cleaning and laundering, and the bearing and caring for children. These same women were invariably expected to work in the fields, pick cotton, serve as midwives to the livestock and each other, break horses and drive cattle, handle the plow, build fences, protect the homestead, and in some cases, work with slaves.

[. . .]

The rural world of women's work described here, that of white and black, slave and free, in the southern household during the antebellum period, has become an increasingly well-documented subject. The introduction and maturation of industrialization in the antebellum South, along with the impact of the Civil War, slowly but surely brought an end to women's work as it once existed in this agricultural, slaveholding economy, yet this topic has not been a popular avenue for exploration.

[. . .]

At first, industrialization in the South began as little more than a modest trickle of change in the early nineteenth century. At that time, new industrialists in the South were faced with a dilemma in a region ripe for industrialization. Who would work in the mills? Slaves were needed in the fields, and most white men considered wage work beneath them. The only remaining workforce was that of white women and children, who were perceived to be a readily available, cheap, and malleable source of labor.

[. . .]

While industrialization's beginnings in the North grew out of a regional agrarian economy in the throes of a commercial revolution, its beginnings in the South were firmly rooted in a more traditional agrarian economy dependent on slave labor and a trans-Atlantic market.

[. . .]

As the market revolution's industrial manifestations began to take more permanent shape, men of means in the South grew increasingly disenchanted with the results. The advent of the cotton gin and the successful cultivation of short-staple cotton across the extensive southern piedmont – which stretched south from Virginia to Georgia and soon swung west across the upcountry of the newer Gulf states – promised quick and impressive profits as long as planters could be assured competitive prices from both European and American buyers.

[. . .]

In Georgia, migration westward created strong demand for internal improvements in communication and transportation as early as the 1820s. Piedmont planters could not get their valuable cotton crop to market without adequate roads, river transport, and, eventually, railroads. Private banks mushroomed across the upcountry to finance these ventures; regulated by the state and buoyed by the booming cotton economy, these banks proved surprisingly stable throughout the antebellum era. Entrepreneurs eager to establish textile mills believed the energetic state of Georgia's economy and the increasing regional divisiveness between North and South in the political arena meant the time seemed ideal for introducing manufacturing.

[. . .]

By 1851, the state boasted forty mills and by some reports more than 2,000 operatives.

Although scholars have long argued that industrialization lagged in the South, whether due to overinvestment of planter capital in land and slaves or the tenacity of the agrarian ideal, much evidence indicates that industrial development, despite its slow start, was very much on the ascendancy by the 1850s, only to be profoundly disrupted in the post-Civil War era.

[. . .]

The rapid drop in cotton prices in the 1820s followed by the constant stream of families westward convinced many politicians that industrialization offered an attractive alternative to the plantation economy and might help retain those Georgians who might otherwise look for better opportunities in the new Gulf states.

[. . .]

Although the textile industry was brand-new in the 1830s and 1840s, and local mill owners unsure who in fact constituted the ideal laborer, white women and children quickly became the majority workforce.

[. . .]

The population schedules show that factory work was a family affair. Eighty-six percent of all female factory workers were joined in the mills by at least one other family member. In some of these households, male heads listed their occupations as farmers, while one or more family members worked in the factory. Yet farming was no longer a productive pursuit in a mature plantation economy like that surrounding Athens, where the high cost of land and slaves, along with taxes, and the ups and downs of the cotton market had hurt all but the wealthiest of planters. Yeomen families, in rough straits, needed additional income to make ends meet. As industrialist Henry Merrell observed, rural families in the Georgia piedmont sent their daughters to the new mills to help their families eke out a rather meager subsistence.

The occupational identity of "farmer" undoubtedly allowed male household heads to save face, for many such "farm" families living in the factory district at the edge of town along the river listed no property in the census returns and hence could not have been truly farmers any longer.

[. . .]

Male household heads who claimed to be farmers despite their lack of land probably had moved their families to the mill district only recently, having been unable to turn a profit on their crops and steer clear of debt in the turbulent agricultural economy of the late 1850s. This family migration pattern from farm to mill town is significant, for it precedes the more well known migration of rural farm families to mill towns in the 1890s and 1900s. In this sense, late antebellum migration seems to have set an important social precedent for postbellum developments.

[. . .]

Herein lay the crux of the matter for many families. Men were reluctant to give up the independence that life on the farm or life as an artisan represented. As one critic stated about the impact of the textile industry, the arrival of the mills and the new economic order it represented undermined men's power and autonomy. "Labor-saving machines . . . employ more women and children . . . and with them must go a spirited and manly brother, husband, or father to cringe beneath the power of capital." To perform wage work for capitalists was emasculating in a southern culture where men's social and political status was rooted in their independence – a legacy of Jeffersonian republicanism.

If antebellum men believed their identity was at stake if they succumbed to millwork, it helps explain why over half of the households (58 percent) containing female factory workers were headed by women. What is equally interesting in these female-headed households is how infrequently the female heads worked in the mills. Sarah and Eliza Giles, adult daughters of Mrs. Giles, worked in the factory, while their mother claimed the occupation of "house business." Anne and Martha Brazzleton, eighteen and sixteen, respectively, worked in the mills while their younger sister and their mother, the latter listing her occupation as "housework," apparently stayed home. It is certainly likely that a number of female household heads could not work in the factory because they had young children; factories generally would not hire anyone under the age of ten. But in many instances, this was not the case; instead, adult women appeared to be choosing "house business" while their children labored in the mills.

[. . .]

The census records make it exceedingly apparent that the vast majority of female factory workers were young and single. Virtually all lived with family members and most in female-headed households. Without further evidence from other kinds of sources, it is dangerous to speculate further about the nature of these women's lives, except to conclude that for certain families in the piedmont, it was not unknown for young single women to work in the factory, mostly with sisters, sometimes with brothers.

[. . .]

Few of these households listed real estate holdings, and very few claimed personal property of any value, indicating that for most theirs was a marginal existence. Millwork attracted poor whites.

The fact that in many of these families men continued to seek independent work outside the mills and mothers stayed in the home suggests the broader power of southern culture to determine proper social roles for men and women regardless of class. These cultural dictates allowed poor men to retain their masculinity and independence and poor married women to retain their femininity and "ladyhood" despite their reduced circumstances. It would seem that these gendered expectations were such critical markers of social respect and status in the Old South that men and women were willing to forego earning wages, since they intimated weakness, vulnerability, and perhaps even unseemliness, and to have their empty purses filled by their children rather than themselves. Poor single women's identities, however, seem to have been more malleable and hence single women's lives viewed as more expendable.

[. . .]

While the evidence indicates that adult men and adult women skirted wage work in mills despite their straitened circumstances, sending their daughters to work in the mills in their stead – highlighting a significant degree of agency among parents in poor households, as well as their authority over their children – another interpretation remains equally plausible and even complementary. There is little question that mill owners preferred hiring white women and children over white males and slaves because they represented the cheapest labor source available. Cultural expectations about gender, age, and wage work, which compelled many white adults to avoid the factory, despite bad times, may in fact have aided industrialists in their search for bargain-basement laborers. Thus, familial roles and expectations worked in tandem with new economic developments to relegate white women, especially single white women, to subordinate status.

[. . .]

By the 1840s, promoters of industry in Georgia and across the South argued rather vociferously that factory work saved poor whites from destitution. Preferring to overlook the economic exigencies that compelled industrialists to seek out white labor, factory owners insisted upon the benefits of factory employment for Georgia's growing class of landless white families. The industrialists also stressed their own unique role as benefactors in this situation. In the wake of the panic of 1837, the depressions in the 1840s, and the spread of the plantation economy, with its skyrocketing land and slave prices in the 1850s, leaders throughout the South expressed concern about the dangers of a burgeoning population of poor whites.

[. . .]

Throughout Georgia, industrialists contended that employing poor whites prevented their impoverishment and ruin. In a sense, some state and regional leaders were coming to recognize that Jeffersonian republicanism was no longer applicable when growing numbers of whites were destitute. The power of a racialized *herrenvolk* sensibility that had bound whites together across significant class differences for so long in the South no longer proved operable when poorer whites lacked even the vestiges of independence – a decent crop and arable land.

[. . .]

Yet the actual use of textile mills as the solution to these growing numbers of impoverished whites had not been a foregone conclusion. Since the inception of the textile industry, politicians and promoters alike had debated whether to rely on white or black labor. In 1827, the Georgia legislature entertained a memorial to investigate the merits of supporting textile manufactures and in particular, to evaluate "the practicability" of using slave labor in the mills.

[. . .]

Not surprisingly, as more and more mills established largely white labor forces, mill owners publicly intimated that all-white labor forces prevented poor white peoples' collusion with slaves. Although racism was certainly endemic in this society and the color line represented significant social hierarchies that some whites were loath to cross, blacks and whites had always worked together in a number of settings, whether on small farms, in artisans' shops, or on the waterfront, and the possibilities for challenging the power and authority of the planter class had always concerned many elites. Blacks and whites could also work together in factories. Buckingham had found black and white factory hands working harmoniously in the Athens Manufacturing Company, the only Athens factory to own its slave hands.

[. . .]

The Athens mills notwithstanding, the Georgia textile industry as a whole relied far more on white than slave labor. Certainly a number of industry boosters penned editorials on the suitability of slave labor in Georgia manufactories, but these arguments did not sway general practice. More frequently, newspapers of the period were filled with invective detailing how black competition with free labor undermined white men's independence, arguments that industrialists used to explain their preference for white labor. Of course, the reality was far simpler. In the Georgia piedmont, where these mills predominated, white women and children were cheaper to employ, more readily available, and more tractable than white men, who were reluctant to engage in factory work and were presumed more likely to protest and perhaps even strike like their northern brethren. Moreover, white women and children were cheaper than slaves, who were more expensive overall, tied to the agricultural calendar, and ultimately controlled by their owners if industrialists elected to hire rather than own slaves outright.

[. . .]

The structural realities of the textile mill industry in Georgia forced owners and investors to cut corners wherever they could. Hiring the cheapest labor possible made good economic sense. Not surprisingly, although mill promoters argued to the contrary, factory wages in the Southeast in 1860 were lower than anywhere else in the nation, with the exception of Florida. Textile mills in antebellum Georgia relied on a workforce of predominately white women and children because they were the cheapest available labor source.

[. . .]

Because poor white women and children had few options for alternative employment, and could not easily migrate elsewhere, they were forced to accept employers' terms.

The mill industry justified this system by stressing the value of an all-white labor force both for poor whites and, by implication, for the citizens of the state as a whole who would not be required to support them if employed. These editorials skated around the fact that women and children were the bulk of their employees, however, rather than poor white men, whose growing presence was the stated cause for concern in the first place. They also ignored the hypocrisy of their rhetoric, labeling millworkers as worthy citizens and voters when in fact women and children, the bulk of these employees, were not entitled to the same privileges of citizenship as men.

[. . .]

[S]ome mill owners attempted to build a sense of community and create general goodwill by encouraging their workers to pursue their own advancement.

[. . .]

The Princeton Manufacturing Company offered religious services to factory workers twice a month. It also created a library for use by its employees. In nearby Graniteville, South Carolina, William Gregg . . . built a school with night classes, as well as a church to encourage moral virtue among his employees. The Howard Manufactory in Columbus furnished churches and schools, too. The *Augusta Chronicle* boasted that all Augusta mills offered "Sunday schools and evening schools, libraries, public lectures and public journals [as] no mean advantages for developing . . . intellectual and moral faculties."

However successful these sporadic efforts to create camaraderie, promote education, and encourage piety were, and however committed employers' writings appeared on these issues, few owners showed much respect for the actual workers themselves and largely ignored the gendered realities of their workforce. Henry Merrell, who supervised several textile operations, including the successful Roswell Mills, reflected about his management days. "I have worried through. I had to 'make out' . . . with hands who looked upon their employer as their natural enemy." He described these employees as "banditti."

[. . .]

Millwork was a last resort for many poor white women in the piedmont, and not an opportunity for advancement. Chief Justice Henry Collier, in his bid to make textile labor respectable, stressed that factory labor did not "harden a lady's hand."

[. . .]

Industrialists stressed their own critical role as providers for poor white Georgians and advocates for their advancement. But the story is more complicated than that. The industry used economic concerns about labor and race, social expectations about gender, and political fears about class not only to create a new workforce that was cheap and relatively tractable but to justify it as well. Poor white families supported these developments and in many cases relied on these new working women to sustain them. Although the end of the Civil War would halt the industrialization movement in the South, it would pick up steam again. By the late nineteenth century, southern industrialists would rely once more on a predominantly white female labor force, dredging up the same sets of arguments and assumptions about gender and class employed a half century earlier to construct this working class, and in doing so, confirming the power of paternalism to prevail across time and place in the South.

6

Frank Towers

THE COMING OF SECTIONAL CRISIS

Few developments in American history have proven more captivating for scholars – or for that matter anybody interested in the American past – than the origins of the Civil War. Feeding this fascination is a set of questions that are easy to raise, yet not so readily resolved. What explains the mounting of sectional tensions during the 1830s, 1840s, and 1850s – tensions culminating in a bloody, traumatic, and deeply transformative Civil War? In what ways did these tensions reflect such momentous trends as westward expansion, the market revolution, Jacksonian democracy, and the impulse for moral reform? How did these trends relate, in turn, to the growing debates over the "slavery question"? How inevitable, or inexorable, was the coming of civil war between North and South?

This chapter reviews the ways historians have understood the South's gradual drift towards secession. Brought into view are some of the leading points of inquiry and debate. What were the particular threats from the North that southern whites perceived; in what degrees were they "threats" to the material benefits flowing from slavery, or to white supremacy, or to the rights and liberties of white southerners? How did these perceptions vary between large planters and yeoman farmers, slaveholders and nonslaveholders, women and men, urban dwellers and rural dwellers, people of the Deep South and those of the Upper South?

In his opening essay, Frank Towers shows how each of the authors extracted for this chapter seeks in his or her own way to illuminate the passage of the South toward secession: from the cultural ambivalence of a paternalistic planter class over the expanding capitalist economy in which it was enmeshed; to the emergence of gender, and social relations in the "private," domestic realm, as a key terrain of southern politics and white male "mastery"; to the widening political gulf between the Lower South, where slavery was robust, and the Upper South, where it was increasingly marginal; to the urgency planters felt about preserving the right to hold their highly valuable slaves as property. One comes away from Towers's opening essay, and from the selections that follow, with an appreciation for how complex the sources of secession were – and how much the effort to sort through them can teach us about mid nineteenth-century southern society.

Frank Towers is Associate Professor of History at the University of Calgary. His various research projects have explored issues of race, politics, labor, and violence in the nineteenth-century South. Of particular note has been his work on the origins of southern secession. His first book, *The Urban South and the Coming of the Civil War* (2004), showed how the region's main urban centers served as little-remembered settings for the coming of secession. He is the co-editor of *The Old South's Modern Worlds: Slavery, Region, and Nation in the Age of Progress* (2011) and is at work on a history of proslavery politics and the causes of the Civil War.

The sectional crisis refers to the prolonged conflict between North and South that culminated with eleven slave states seceding from the Union in 1860–1. Not only did the sectional crisis end in secession, it also drew upon most major developments of United States history up that point. To understand American history between the revolution and the Civil War, one must have some appreciation for what this struggle was about.

At the center of the sectional crisis was slavery. During the early national period, slavery came increasingly to define the border between the South, where it expanded and thrived, and the North, where it was gradually abolished after the American Revolution. Conflict over slavery engaged many issues. Religious leaders differed over whether slavery had divine sanction. Economists debated its profitability. Reformers disagreed as to whether slavery hindered progress. While these debates produced intense discord, the political dimensions of this conflict posed the greatest threat to the survival of the federal union.

Since the founding of the republic, Congress had wrangled over questions that, in one way or another, involved conflict over slavery. Should slaves be counted when apportioning seats in the House of Representatives? Did Congress have the power to regulate the slave trade? Should slavery be allowed to expand onto new territory? To what extent should the federal government aid in the capture of runaway slaves? These were only some of the problems that pushed voters and legislators to identify with the interests of their respective sections – and, which ultimately drove the South to secede.

The leading proponents of southern secession owned slaves, came from the planter class (the group that held the most slaves and dominated southern governments), and frequently proclaimed the need to quit the federal government should it fall into the hands of northerners opposed to slavery's expansion – which is what happened when Republican Abraham Lincoln won the presidency in 1860.

Typical of such claims, the South Carolina legislature declared that it seceded because Lincoln's Republican party "has announced that . . . a war must be waged against slavery . . ." Jefferson Davis, president of the breakaway Confederacy, had predicted that slavery was "the rock upon which the old Union would split." His vice president, Alexander Stephens, called slavery "the cornerstone" of southern society. Secessionists had other grievances, of course, but, as New York Republican William Seward put it, "Every question, political, civil, or ecclesiastical, however foreign to the subject of slavery, brings up slavery as an incident, and the incident supplants the principal question. We hear of nothing but slavery, and we can talk of nothing but slavery."

In highlighting slavery's centrality to the sectional crisis, Seward hinted at a problem for later historians. Slavery appears to have been the "incident" behind the many disputes tied up in the conflict, but it is no simple task to determine *how* it figured in any number of issues, ranging from the organization of federal territory, to railroad building, to family ethics.

Because sectional conflict for decades dominated American politics and culminated in the Civil War, historians have devoted considerable effort to understanding how it came to pass. As the following selections show, their explanations can differ greatly, often dramatically. The essays by Eugene D. Genovese, James L. Huston, Stephanie McCurry, and William W. Freehling engage in a tradition of enquiry into the sectional crisis that stretches back more than a century. The relationship among these varying interpretations can be best understood when we explore their place in this larger scholarly dialogue.

As it does now, slavery figured prominently in the older debate over Civil War inevitability (was it destined to happen, or could it have been avoided?). Disillusioned with militarism in the wake of the First World War, so-called "revisionists" such as James Randall and Avery Craven thought that a "blundering generation" of inept politicians had created a needless war by encouraging the extremes of abolition and pro-slavery.[1] To Randall and Craven, the furor over slavery masked similarities in northern and southern opinion. While Republicans opposed slavery's expansion, they promised to preserve it where it already existed. Although some abolitionists talked about racial equality, most northerners – including Lincoln – backed white supremacy. For sections so close on race and slavery, the revisionists argued, a solution short of war could surely have been found.

At the time the revisionists wrote, Jim Crow racial segregation ruled the South, and a less formal racist order characterized much of the rest of the country. In this climate, critics of the revisionists tended to share in their derision of abolitionists; rather, they made the case for the inevitability of Civil War on economic grounds. For example, Charles and Mary Beard traced the rupture to the conflict between the rising industrial system of the North and the powerful agricultural interests of the South.[2]

But over time, the climate would change. The war against Nazi racism and the civil rights movement of the 1950s and 1960s prodded scholars to look anew at the racial ideology of the northern antislavery movement. A growing chorus of historians – led by Kenneth Stampp and David Potter, and later James McPherson and Eric Foner – found that, despite their racism, northern whites truly feared slaveholder aggressiveness and wanted to put the institution on the road to extinction.[3] The role of abolitionists, black and white, loomed larger in these studies, as did the significance of pro-slavery thought in the case for secession. By the 1960s, historians were coming to agree that war had been inevitable given the deeply felt convictions on each side. In advancing this viewpoint, scholars reaffirmed Lincoln's assessment that the sectional crisis represented a "house divided against itself," one that could not stand forever half slave and half free.

Writing at this time, Eugene Genovese sought to explain why the South was so committed to slavery that it would risk – indeed, precipitate – civil war. He argued that the master–slave relationship was the taproot from which the sectional identity of the South grew. Unlike capitalist bosses, who hired workers for set portions of time and then sent them away, slaveholders had an enduring personal relationship with their laborers. Slavery, then, was more than simply a means of making money. Masters exercised total control over slaves. That control gave slaveholders a unique sense of power and independence. But independence had its flip side. Because slaves provided masters with all their material possessions, masters were dependent on slaves.

Like slaveholders, employers of free (wage) labor depended on their workers to produce a profit. Paying cash for units of work, however, contributed to many capitalists' belief that labor was equivalent to other goods exchanged in the market rather than the essential element in the production of all other commodities. According to Genovese, slaveholders' awareness of their reliance on labor was one way that the master–slave relationship engendered a "special psychology" in the planter class that committed it to slavery – the source of its independence – and sensitized it to threats that might expose its dependence on slaves. Planters reacted hostilely as northern criticisms of slavery increased during the 1840s and 1850s.

Genovese's rethinking of the master–slave relationship moved the study of the sectional crisis onto new territory. Historians had long been debating whether the antebellum South was a region characterized by quasi-self-sufficient small farmers and egalitarianism (among whites), or rather, a hierarchical society dominated by capitalist-minded planters. Genovese advanced this discussion by arguing that the slave South was part of the capitalist world, even as its embrace of slavery violated bourgeois values.

This conception of the South as a region with an ambivalent relationship to nineteenth-century capitalism enabled Genovese to relate other sectional differences to the divide over slavery. Southern investors preferred land and slaves to other forms of wealth, such as factories. The former, they felt, brought independence whereas the latter did not. Similarly, Genovese argues, the comparative absence of cities and railroads in the South stemmed from planters' refusal to develop sources of profit and power that rivaled slave ownership.

Genovese's look at the underlying economic structure of society cast contemporary debates over states' rights and slavery's future in a new light. For example, where many had regarded southern demands to take slaves into Kansas and California as legalistic gestures that had little practical benefit, Genovese found that slaveholders' indifference to capitalist efficiencies of soil conservation or investment outside of plantation agriculture compelled them to seek out the fresh land of the West.

This reinterpretation of the antebellum South went along with fresh ways of understanding the prewar North. Although not spelled out in the extracted essay, Genovese implies that a middle-class or "bourgeois" capitalist spirit motivated the policies of northern businessmen and politicians, and that "quasi-aristocratic" planters were standing in their way. Genovese's planters represented the "closest thing to feudal lords imaginable in a nineteenth-century bourgeois republic." Although unique in his interpretation of the antebellum South, Genovese echoed earlier historians, such as the Beards, who viewed economics as the cause of the sectional crisis. For Genovese, however, the struggle went beyond mere sources of income to encompass clashing worldviews. As he puts it, "[t]he ideology and psychology of the proud slaveholding class" drove them to secede. The essay remains influential because it challenges readers to think about connections between society and politics, and provides a compelling explanation not just for the coming of the sectional conflict but for the meaning of southern history at large.

Among those historians influenced by Genovese is Stephanie McCurry. True, she breaks new ground by bringing gender into the story of the sectional crisis, a subject about which Genovese says little. McCurry's debt to Genovese becomes apparent, however, when we explore her case for gender as a source of sectional identity. Building on the work of feminist scholars who argue for breaking down barriers between public and private, McCurry examines the role of the household in the politics of secession's heartland, the South Carolina lowcountry.

Household politics, McCurry argues, made for a double-sided, or two-faced, brand of "republicanism," a term for the representative democracy practiced in the United States and other parts of the Americas and Europe. The face presented in the "high politics" of governing and electoral campaigns treated all white men as equals. This equality disappears when one turns to the other face of republicanism, the one that subordinated white women and African American slaves of both genders to the authority of white male household heads. Here is where the link to Genovese comes in. Similar to the way in which he conceived of slave mastery as buttressing slaveholder independence, McCurry explains how the mastery that white men, slaveholders or not, exercised over dependents in their families defined them as independents, equal in this regard to all other household heads.

In thus expanding the scope of southern independence to include all white male heads of household, McCurry offers a solution to one of the enduring puzzles of Civil War historiography: that is, what induced non-slaveholding southern whites to ally with much wealthier slaveholders to defend an institution that provided them with no obvious material rewards? Her answer of household paternalism, a form of authority based on the ideal of fatherly dominion, echoes Genovese's claim that "the paternalism of the planters toward their slaves was reinforced by the semipaternal relationship between the planters and their neighbors." Like Genovese, McCurry rejects the notion that the South was egalitarian, even when it came to the relationship among white men. Because all political claims made by yeomen rested on their status as household masters, they had difficulty challenging demands from planters that used the same logic. When wealthy slaveholders told yeomen to "'set aside womanly fears of disunion' in favor of 'manly and resolute action'" (that is, secession), yeomen followed the logic of household paternalism and, in large numbers, joined the cause.

"The Two Faces of Republicanism," the 1992 article from which her selection in this chapter is extracted, drew upon a decade of pioneering research on gender in southern history. McCurry's essay shows how students of the past can connect the seemingly separate phenomena of legislative politics and family organization. In tandem with McCurry's work, historians Drew Faust and Elizabeth Varon, among others, have explored how gender shaped southerners' approach to the sectional crisis.[4]

If we shift our attention from the master–slave relationship to other aspects of slavery, different explanations of the sectional crisis emerge. Such is the case in William Freehling's *The South vs. The South* (extracted in this chapter), which examines how slaveholders maintained power in the face of rebellious slaves and a white non-slaveholding majority. While agreeing that slavery represented a powerful interest, Freehling argues that the uneven geographic distribution of that interest created tensions within the South over slavery's survival.

In so-called Black Belts of the Lower South, where slaves and slaveholders were numerous, rich and poor whites banded together in shared concern over the prospects of rebellion, abolition, and imperiled profits. Here, Freehling reconfirms the picture painted by Genovese and McCurry.

But the South consisted of more than just Black Belts. Closer to the sectional border, the presence of slaves and slaveholders thinned, while that of non-slaveholding whites thickened. What Freehling terms the "attenuation" of slavery in the Middle and Border Souths posed difficulties for slaveholders needing help from non-slaveholding whites, both near and far, to keep slaves in check. Pro-slavery politicians understood that, if slavery continued to decline in the Border South, then voters in those states might join the North in pushing for its restriction. Maintaining slaveholders' physical hold on their human property, therefore, required maintaining their political hold on the white belts, making the sectional conflict as much a contest of the "South vs. the South" as it was of free versus slave states.

Freehling's emphasis on the geography of political conflict allows him to reinterpret some famous sectional confrontations. For example, in Freehling's hands, the Fugitive Slave Act, which historians have often characterized as an unnecessary overreach for power on the part of the South, makes more sense as an effort to shore up slavery in the Border South.

Readers should consider how Freehling's geographic focus raises questions about the applicability of Genovese's and McCurry's accounts to slave-scarce states in the Border and Middle South. He also has a different take on the strength of democracy in southern politics. For Genovese and McCurry, paternalism helped planters to quiet calls for equality; for Freehling, the problem is more complicated. He finds Middle and Border whites to have been committed democrats who resisted being pushed by fire-eating planters to the South or, for that matter, by abolitionists to the North. Freehling stands between those who regard the South as having been significantly less democratic than the North and those who highlight the section's egalitarian heritage (associated with southerners like Thomas Jefferson and Andrew Jackson).

Finally, Freehling places greater importance on the timing of secession. Had the entire South been required to act in unison, secession may never have been adopted, because the Middle and Border South saw less reason to fear free-soil Republicans than did Lower South whites. South Carolina's decision to act alone and act first pressed other southerners into choosing not between secession and Union but rather between defending a sister slave state or opposing it. By highlighting the stages of secession, Freehling illustrates the significance of slavery's geography, and of the sequence of decisions made by political leaders during the critical weeks between Lincoln's inauguration on March 4, 1861 and the firing on Fort Sumter on April 12.

The possibility that the war might have been postponed, if not entirely avoided, is explored in detail in Freehling's two-volume history of secession, and in recent books by historians Edward Ayers and Nelson Lankford.[5] These studies focus on moderate Unionists in border slave states like Maryland and Virginia who had blunted earlier drives for secession, and almost stopped the effort early in 1861. While it echoes some aspects of the revisionists' case against the Civil War's inevitability, this renewed consideration of the war's contingency comes out of a more recent effort by scholars to assess the matter of timing – that is, why secession occurred in 1860–1, and not earlier or later.

Beginning in the 1970s, political historians, such as Daniel Crofts and Michael Holt, began investigating the role of antebellum party politics in promoting nationalism and suppressing sectionalism.[6] During the 1830s and 1840s, they argue, the Whig and Democratic parties contained the sectional crisis by interesting voters in national institutions and issues. The collapse of the Whigs in 1852, the rise of the Republicans in 1856, and the breakup of the Democrats in 1860 explain why secession occurred when it did.

In his article, "Property Rights in Slavery and the Coming of the Civil War" (extracted in this chapter), James Huston arrives at a very different outlook on the war's timing. Treating the collapse of political parties as more a symptom than a cause of the crisis, Huston seeks to explain why and when sectional concerns became strong enough to realign the parties. While he identifies technological advances in transportation as the immediate catalyst for change in sectional attitudes, his deeper focus is on slavery. For Huston, the material value of slaves, and the perceived need to preserve the right to hold them as property, were the underlying causes of the sectional crisis.

Most economic treatments of slavery consider how the labor of slaves contributed to the wealth of their masters. Huston takes one step back to ask what slaves themselves were worth, as property, to their owners. He finds that the value of slaves on the eve of the war comprised a staggering $3 billion, or more than the combined assets of railroads, banks, and factories, a point illustrated in Huston's table on wealth in 1860. If one looks only at economic measurements favorable to the North, such as the number of factories or acres of improved farmland, the South appears to have been on the defensive. The South's economic power becomes clearer with Huston's accounting for the value of slaves, which shows that slaveholders were far richer than northern capitalists.

Behind this analysis stands an illuminating explanation of how property rights functioned, and how slavery figured, in the political economy of antebellum America. Government, Huston argues, is essential to defining and defending property. If Congress outlawed slavery, a vast investment would have been wiped out; hence, the tenacious defense of slavery by white southerners. Huston notes that, although slavery rewarded the wealthiest slaveholders disproportionately, it generated enough income for poorer southern whites to win their support for the peculiar institution.

In a sharp disagreement with Genovese, who sees slavery as maladapted to the modernizing economy of the 1800s, Huston contends that slavery could compete in the same enterprises as free labor, and that its products sold for less when wages rose above the amount masters spent to feed and clothe their slaves. When the threat of head-to-head competition between slave and free labor became real, Huston argues, northerners organized to defend their social order (a way of life encapsulated in the "free labor ideology") from what they perceived as an aggressive Slave Power. Northern unrest over slavery grew in the 1850s largely, perhaps pivotally, because improved rail and water transportation made goods produced in one region so much more accessible

THE COMING OF SECTIONAL CRISIS

to consumers in another. As Huston states, "individuals from a locality at a great distance from another locality could *compete* in the *distant* locality's *market*."

Huston's attention to the value of slaves, moreover, helps him to recast the balance of power between the sections. Instead of a defensive South fending off a more dynamic North – as suggested in some of the other selections – Huston's slaveholders were the aggressors against a beleaguered, poorer North. With this change in the perceived balance of power, the question of why northerners elected a free-soil president in 1860 (and not earlier, or later) becomes more complicated than does the issue of southern secession, which makes sense from the perspective of power and profit.

Huston's findings fit within a larger body of recent work that emphasizes slaveholders' power in national politics.[7] These historians hark back to the case against the Slave Power made by the Republicans of the 1850s. But, unlike those contemporaries and many subsequent historians, these scholars find troubling indications that slavery could have flourished into the future as long as its supporters remained politically powerful. Even if the war was inevitable, according to this viewpoint, freedom's triumph was not.

Presented with these competing explanations of sectional conflict and secession, readers might naturally ask: Which one is right? As the foregoing suggests, readers would do better to ask what assumptions guide each explanation and what evidence each historian uses to prove his or her point. Where their interpretations differ, look for the absent pieces of the larger story, and ask how those missing elements might affect the explanation. For example, would more attention to the master–slave relationship change the way Huston explains the importance of slavery to the South? Or, how might Freehling's account of Middle and Border southerners' commitment to slavery look if gender figured more prominently in his analysis?

Finally, readers should use these essays as a jumping-off point for further study. In addition to reading other histories mentioned in this introduction, they might devise their own research questions. One place to start is to consider some of the common issues raised in these essays, such as the role of slavery in federal politics, the nature of the master–slave relationship, the part played by economics in the fracturing of the Union, or the extent to which non-slaveholding whites supported slavery and the political power of slave-holders. What new questions and new evidence can be used to study these problems? Just as McCurry's pathbreaking study of gender changed the way scholars understood sectionalism, is there a neglected category of analysis, the environment for example, that could open up an alternative reading of the sectional crisis? Another way to reconsider these interpretations would be to bring in evidence from beyond the confines of mid-1800s American South, perhaps by comparing the US sectional crisis with separatist conflicts in other nations. Formulating new questions in dialogue with other scholarship is the way historians answer the question: Which interpretation is right?

NOTES

1. Avery O. Craven, *The Repressible Conflict, 1830–1861* (Baton Rouge: Louisiana State University Press, 1939); James G. Randall, *The Civil War and Reconstruction* (Boston: D. C. Heath, 1937).

2. Charles A. Beard and Mary R. Beard, *The Rise of American Civilization* (New York: Macmillan, 1927).

3. David M. Potter, *Lincoln and His Party in the Secession Crisis* (New Haven: Yale University Press, 1942); Kenneth M. Stampp, *And the War Came: The North and the Secession Crisis, 1860–1861* (Baton Rouge: Louisiana State University Press, 1950); James M. McPherson, *The Struggle for Equality: Abolitionists and the Negro in the Civil War and Reconstruction* (Princeton: Princeton University Press, 1964); Eric Foner, *Free Soil, Free Labor, Free Men: The Ideology of the Republican Party before the Civil War* (New York: Oxford University Press, 1970).

4. Drew G. Faust, *Mothers of Invention: Women of the Slaveholding South in the American Civil War* (Chapel Hill: University of North Carolina Press, 1996); Elizabeth R. Varon, *We Mean to Be Counted: White Women and Politics in Antebellum Virginia* (Chapel Hill: University of North Carolina Press, 1998).

5. William W. Freehling, *The Road to Disunion* (New York: Oxford University Press, 1990–2007): Edward L. Ayers, *In the Presence of Mine Enemies: War in the Heart of America, 1859–1863* (New York: W. W. Norton, 2003); Nelson Lankford, *Cry Havoc: The Crooked Road to Civil War, 1861* (New York: Viking, 2007).

6. Daniel W. Crofts, *Reluctant Confederates: Upper South Unionists in the Secession Crisis* (Chapel Hill: University of North Carolina Press, 1989); Michael F. Holt, *The Political Crisis of the 1850s* (New York: Wiley, 1978).

7. Robin L. Einhorn, *American Taxation, American Slavery* (Chicago: University of Chicago Press, 2006); Don E. Fehrenbacher, *The Slaveholding Republic: An Account of the United States Government's Relations to Slavery* (New York: Oxford University Press, 2001); Leonard L. Richards, *The Slave Power: The Free North and Southern Domination, 1780–1860* (Baton Rouge: Louisiana State University Press, 2000).

* * *

FURTHER READING

Ayers, Edward L., *What Caused the Civil War? Reflections on the South and Southern History* (New York: W. W. Norton, 2005).

Barney, William L., *The Road to Secession: A New Perspective on the Old South* (New York: Praeger, 1972).

Bonner, Robert E., *Mastering America: Southern Slaveholders and the Crisis of American Nationhood* (New York: Cambridge University Press, 2009).

Crofts, Daniel W., *Reluctant Confederates: Upper South Unionists in the Secession Crisis* (Chapel Hill: University of North Carolina Press, 1989).

Dumond, Dwight L., *The Secession Movement, 1860–1861* (New York: Macmillan, 1931).

Holt, Michael F., *The Fate of their Country: Politicians, Slavery Extension, and the Coming of the Civil War* (New York: Hill and Wang, 2004).

Onuf, Nicholas and Peter Onuf, *Nations, Markets, and War: Modern History and the American Civil War* (Charlottesville: University of Virginia Press, 2006).

Potter, David, *The Impending Crisis, 1848–1861*, edited and completed by Don E. Fehrenbacher (New York: Harper and Row, 1976).

Schoen, Brian, *The Fragile Fabric of Union: Cotton, Federal Politics, and the Global Origins of the Civil War* (Baltimore: Johns Hopkins University Press, 2009).

Towers, Frank, *The Urban South and the Coming of the Civil War* (Charlottesville: University of Virginia Press, 2004).

Varon, Elizabeth R., *Disunion: The Coming of the American Civil War, 1789–1859* (Chapel Hill: University of North Carolina Press, 2008).

* * *

Eugene D. Genovese

The Political Economy of Slavery[†]

The uniqueness of the antebellum South continues to challenge the imagination of Americans, who, despite persistent attempts, cannot divert their attention from slavery. Nor should they, for slavery provided the foundation on which the South rose and grew. The master–slave relationship permeated Southern life and influenced relationships among free men.

[. . .]

The hegemony of the slaveholders, presupposing the social and economic preponderance of great slave plantations, determined the character of the South. These men rose to power in a region embedded in a capitalist country, and their social system emerged as part of a capitalist world. Yet . . . they imparted to Southern life a special social, economic, political, ideological, and psychological content.

[. . .]

[†]Eugene D. Genovese, *The Political Economy of Slavery: Studies in the Economy and Society of the Slave South* (New York: Random House, 1967 [orig. 1965]), pp. 13, 16–18, 20, 23, 28, 30–6.

Slave economies normally manifest irrational tendencies that inhibit economic development and endanger social stability. Max Weber . . . has noted four important irrational features. First, the master cannot adjust the size of his labor force in accordance with business fluctuations. In particular, efficiency cannot readily be attained through the manipulation of the labor force if sentiment, custom, or community pressure makes [sic] separation of families difficult. Second, the capital outlay is much greater and riskier for slave labor than for free. Third, the domination of society by a planter class increases the risk of political influence in the market. Fourth, the sources of cheap labor usually dry up rather quickly, and beyond a certain point costs become excessively burdensome.

[. . .]

There are other telling features of this irrationality . . . Capitalism largely directs its profits into an expansion of plant and equipment, not labor; that is, economic progress is qualitative. Slavery, for economic reasons as well as for those of social prestige, directs its reinvestments along the same lines as the original investment – in slaves and land; that is, economic progress is quantitative.

In the South this weakness proved fatal for the slaveholders. They found themselves engaged in a growing conflict with Northern farmers and businessmen over such issues as tariffs, homesteads, internal improvements, and the decisive question of the balance of political power in the Union. The slow pace of their economic progress, in contrast to the long strides of their rivals to the north, threatened to undermine their political parity and result in a Southern defeat on all major issues of the day. The qualitative leaps in the Northern economy manifested themselves in a rapidly increasing population, an expanding productive plant, and growing political, ideological, and social boldness. The slaveholders' voice grew shriller and harsher as they contemplated impending disaster and sought solace in complaints of Northern aggression and exploitation.

[. . .]

Most of the elements of irrationality were irrational only from a capitalist standpoint. The high propensity to consume luxuries, for example, has always been functional (socially if not economically rational) in aristocratic societies, for it has provided the ruling class with the façade necessary to control the middle and lower classes.

[. . .]

One wealthy planter with a great house and a reputation for living and entertaining on a grand scale could impress a whole community and keep before its humbler men the shining ideal of plantation magnificence.

[. . .]

[E]very dollar spent by the planters for elegant clothes, a college education for their children, or a lavish barbecue contributed to the political and social domination of their class.

[. . .]

We must concern ourselves primarily with capitalism as a social system, not merely with evidence of typically capitalistic economic practices. In the South extensive and complicated commercial relations with the world market permitted the growth of a small commercial bourgeoisie.

[. . .]

Independent merchants found their businesses dependent on the patronage of the slaveholders. The merchants either became planters themselves or assumed a servile attitude toward the planters. The commercial bourgeoisie . . . remained tied to the slaveholding interest, had little desire or opportunity to invest capital in industrial expansion, and adopted the prevailing aristocratic attitudes.

The Southern industrialists were in an analogous position.

[. . .]

The preponderance of planters and slaves on the countryside retarded the home market. The Southern yeomanry, unlike the Western, lacked the purchasing power to sustain rapid industrial development. The planters spent much of their money abroad for luxuries. The plantation market consisted primarily of the demand for cheap slave clothing and cheap agricultural implements for use or misuse by the slaves. Southern industrialism needed a sweeping agrarian revolution to provide it with cheap labor and a substantial rural market, but the Southern industrialists depended on the existing, limited, plantation market.

[. . .]

The planters were not mere capitalists; they were precapitalist, quasi-aristocratic landowners who had to adjust their economy and ways of thinking to a capitalist world market. Their society, in its spirit and fundamental direction, represented the antithesis of capitalism, however many compromises it had to make.

[. . .]

The planters commanded Southern politics and set the tone of social life. Theirs was an aristocratic, antibourgeois spirit with values and mores emphasizing family and status, a strong code of honor, and aspirations to luxury, ease, and accomplishment. In the planters' community, paternalism provided the standard of human relationships, and politics and statecraft were the duties and responsibilities of gentlemen.

[. . .]

At their best, Southern ideals constituted a rejection of the crass, vulgar, inhumane elements of capitalist society. The slaveholders simply could not accept the idea that the cash nexus offered a permissible basis for human relations.

[. . .]

The slaveholders generally, and the planters in particular, did identify their own ideals with the essence of civilization and, given their sense of honor, were prepared to defend them at any cost.

This civilization and its ideals were antinational in a double sense. The plantation offered virtually the only market for the small nonstaple-producing farmers and provided the center of necessary services for the small cotton growers. Thus, the paternalism of the planters toward their slaves was reinforced by the semipaternal relationship between the planters and their neighbors. The planters, in truth, grew into the closest thing to feudal lords imaginable in a nineteenth-century bourgeois republic. The planters' protestations of love for the Union were not so much a desire to use the Union to protect slavery as a strong commitment to localism as the highest form of liberty.

[. . .]

The Southerners' source of pride was not the Union, nor the nonexistent Southern nation; it was the plantation, which they raised to a political principle.

[. . .]

The slaveholder, as distinct from the farmer, had a private source of character-making and mythmaking – his slave. Most obviously, he had the habit of command, but there was more than despotic authority in this master–slave relationship.

[. . .]

The slaveholder commanded the products of another's labor, but by the same process was forced into dependence upon this other.

[. . .]

This simultaneous dependence and independence contributed to that peculiar combination of the admirable and the frightening in the slaveholder's nature: his strength, graciousness, and gentility; his impulsiveness, violence, and unsteadiness. The sense of independence and the habit of command developed his poise, grace, and dignity, but the less obvious sense of dependence on a despised other made him violently intolerant of anyone and anything threatening to expose the full nature of his relationship to his slave.

[. . .]

Any attempt, no matter how well meaning, indirect, or harmless, to question the slave system appeared not only as an attack on his material interests but as an attack on his self-esteem at its most vulnerable point. To question either the morality or the practicality of slavery meant to expose the root of the slaveholder's dependence in independence.

The South's slave civilization could not forever coexist with an increasingly hostile, powerful, and aggressive Northern capitalism. On the one hand, the special economic conditions arising from the dependence on slave labor bound the South, in a colonial manner, to the world market. The concentration of landholding and slaveholding prevented the rise of a prosperous yeomanry and of urban centers. The inability to build urban centers restricted the market for agricultural produce, weakened the rural producers, and dimmed hopes for agricultural diversification. On the other hand, the same concentration of wealth, the isolated, rural nature of the plantation system, the special psychology engendered by slave ownership, and the political opportunity presented by the separation from England, converged to give the South considerable political and social independence. This independence was primarily the contribution of the slaveholding class, and especially of the planters. Slavery, while it bound the South economically, granted it the privilege of developing an aristocratic tradition, a disciplined and cohesive ruling class, and a mythology of its own.

Aristocratic tradition and ideology intensified the South's attachment to economic backwardness. Paternalism and the habit of command made the slaveholders tough stock, determined to defend their Southern heritage. The more economically debilitating their way of life, the more they clung to it. It was this side of things – the political hegemony and aristocratic ideology of the ruling class – rather than economic factors that prevented the South from relinquishing slavery voluntarily.

As the free states stepped up their industrialization and as the westward movement assumed its remarkable momentum, the South's economic and political allies in the North were steadily isolated. Years of abolitionist and free-soil agitation bore fruit as the South's opposition to homesteads, tariffs, and internal improvements clashed more and more dangerously with the North's economic needs. To protect their institutions and to try to lessen their economic bondage, the slaveholders slid into violent collision with Northern interests and sentiments. The economic deficiencies of slavery threatened to undermine the planters' wealth and power.

[. . .]

The planters faced a steady deterioration of their political and social power. Even if the relative prosperity of the 1850s had continued indefinitely, the slave states would have been at the mercy of the free, which steadily forged ahead in population growth, capital accumulation, and economic development. Any economic slump threatened to bring with it an internal political disaster, for the slaveholders could not rely on their middle and lower classes to remain permanently loyal.

When we understand that the slave South developed . . . a special civilization built on the relationship of master to slave, we expose the root of its conflict with the North. The internal contradictions in the South and the external conflict with the North placed the slaveholders hopelessly on the defensive with little to look forward to except slow strangulation. Their only hope lay in a bold stroke to complete their political independence and to use it to provide an expansionist solution for their economic and social problems. The ideology and psychology of the proud slaveholding class made surrender or resignation to gradual defeat unthinkable, for its fate, in its own eyes at least, was the fate of everything worth while in Western civilization.

ৡ ৡ ৡ

Stephanie McCurry

The Two Faces of Republicanism[†]

Prompted by theories about the complexities of power in modern society, a number of historians, feminists most prominent among them, have joined the recent debate over the proper definition and boundaries of "the political."

[. . .]

The history of republican political ideology and culture in the antebellum South may seem a long way from the concerns of contemporary theorists, but it is not so far, perhaps, as it appears at first glance.

[. . .]

In the antebellum South, where the defense of domestic institutions and relations were matters of the utmost political significance, one finds . . . compelling reason to eschew conventional historiographical boundaries, and particularly those

[†]Stephanie McCurry, "The Two Faces of Republicanism: Gender and Proslavery Politics in Antebellum South Carolina," in *Journal of American History*, 78 (March 1992), pp. 1245–52, 1254–5, 1257–60, 1263–4.

that separate the public from the private sphere and the history of women and gender relations from that of "high" politics. In the Old South, "high" politics *was* the politics of the household, and all relations of power in what we would call the "private sphere," including those of men and women, were inevitably politicized. Indeed, the gender and class relations contained in southern households were the distinctive social conditions to which proslavery politicians pointed as permitting the South, and the South alone, to retain the proper political arrangements of republican government.

The slave South was commonly represented as the last republic loyal to the principle of government by an exclusive citizen body of independent and equal men. However inadvertently, that portrait revealed the two faces of republicanism in the antebellum South. The first gazed outward on the public sphere and countenanced a purportedly egalitarian community of enfranchised men. This is the familiar face of slavery republicanism privileged by antebellum politicans and, for the most part, by historians. But to view the political edifice solely from that perspective is to remain captive to the designs of its proslavery architects. For southern men, like other republicans, established their independence and status as citizens in the public sphere through the command of dependents in their households. The modern slave republic was defined above all else, as its defenders never tired of saying, by the boundary that separated the independent and enfranchised minority from the majority of dependent and excluded others. Republicanism had another, more conservative face that gazed inward on the private sphere and countenanced inequality and relations of power between masters and their dependents: slaves, women, and children.

Any assessment of antebellum southern political culture, and especially of the yeoman–planter relations on which it hinged, must confront the republican edifice whole. This broader perspective is most pressing with respect to the politics of the yeoman majority. As independent proprietors, yeoman farmers were (and knew themselves to be) empowered by the exclusionary boundaries of the public sphere. Their republicanism, no less than that of the planters, was centrally configured around the politics of the household and around the public meaning of domestic dependencies.

The South Carolina low country, from which much of the material in this essay is drawn, provides a dramatic case in point. Nowhere did proslavery republicanism find more momentous expression; and nowhere was its social basis more starkly displayed in ways that confound a conventional focus on the public sphere in the interpretation of the yeomanry's politics.

[. . .]

Republican and proslavery politics already had a long and intimate relationship in South Carolina by the beginning of the antebellum period.

[. . .]

But the crucial moment was the nullification crisis; then, in the midst of the state's greatest religious revival, South Carolina's antebellum political culture and ideology was [sic] forged.

As fire-eater politicians (not a few of whom were, like Robert Barnwell Rhett, newly born again) met the challenge of an unprecedented political mobilization, they embraced the language of evangelicalism, and with it the faith of its primarily yeoman congregants. Evangelicalism and popular politics were thereafter indissociable in South Carolina.

[. . .]

Evangelical ministers did the main work of the proslavery argument . . . Indeed, the Biblical defense of slavery was the centerpiece of an organic or familial ideology that encompassed far more than the relation of master and slave. Thornwell . . . insisted that the central tenet of that conservative social theory, that "the relation of master and slave stands on the same foot with the other relations of life," was grounded in scriptural proof. "We find masters exhorted in the same connection with husbands, parents, magistrates," and "slaves exhorted in the same connection with wives, children and subjects." Such stitching together of all social relations into the seamless fabric of southern society became the mainstay of the proslavery argument, and it drew proslavery advocates inexorably into a struggle with abolitionists in which the stakes were no less than the nature of society and the republic itself. Thornwell characteristically minced no words: "The parties in this conflict are not merely abolitionists and slaveholders . . . They are atheists, socialists, communists, red republicans, Jacobins on the one side, and the friends of order and regulated freedom on the other."

[. . .]

The real measure of the effectiveness of proslavery arguments . . . was their social breadth. For the ideological work of slavery assumed the greatest significance precisely where it confronted the greatest challenge: in binding nonslaveholders and small slaveholders to planters within a common system of meanings and values. In reaching beyond masters and slaves to all relations of southern households, proslavery ideologues bid for the loyalties of all white male adults. They repeatedly reminded white southerners of all classes that slavery could not be disentangled from other relations of power and privilege and that it represented simply the most extreme and absolute form of the legal and customary dependencies that characterized the Old South – and their own households.

The conjoining of all domestic relations of domination and subordination enabled proslavery spokesmen to tap beliefs about the legitimacy of inequality that went and, sadly, still go so deep in the individual psyche and social structure that for most historians they are still unrecognizable as the subject of history. In the dual task of painting both the abolitionist image of social disorder and their own benevolent and peaceful social order, proslavery spokesmen returned repeatedly to gender relations . . . On the common ground of gender they sought to ensure that every white man recognized his own investment in the struggle over slavery.

[. . .]

By equating the subordination of women and that of slaves, proslavery ideologues and politicians attempted to endow slavery with the legitimacy of the family and especially marriage and, not incidentally, to invest the defense of slavery with the survival of customary gender relations. In this sense, the subordination of women bore a great deal of the ideological weight of slavery, providing the most concrete example of how public and private distinctions were confounded in political discourse and culture.

[. . .]

In their efforts to impress on ordinary southerners the seamlessness of the social fabric, proslavery ideologues were afforded assistance from the most unlikely of quarters. In the 1830s, a handful of Garrisonian abolitionists also came to the conviction that the fate of dependents, slavery, and the subordination of women were inseparable, and that conventional gender relations were at stake in the national struggle over slavery.

[. . .]

Abby Kelley, a committed Garrisonian and a leading figure in the antebellum women's rights movement, articulated the radical meaning most concretely in acknowledging a debt of gratitude to slaves: "In striving to strike his irons off, we found most surely that we were manacled ourselves." Garrisonians' yoking of the subordination of women and slaves and their public commitment to a dual emancipation proved a perfect foil for proslavery politicians.

If all men should have "equal rights," more than one South Carolinian worried, "then why not women?" That some northern . . . abolitionists . . . asked the same question lent credibility to proslavery threats.

[. . .]

In the most literal sense, the subordination of women was at issue in the struggle over slavery; in another sense, however, the larger question was the social and political status of dependents, men and women alike, and thus the proper parameters of the republican polity. Although the debate was a national one, the conservative South . . . had more to gain than the North from the politicization of gender relations.

[. . .]

The recognition that the social relations of the private sphere profoundly shaped political ideas and actions in the public sphere has important . . . implications for the political ideology and culture of the South Carolina low country and, especially, for the position of the yeoman majority within it.

[. . .]

Low-country yeoman farmers . . . articulated their world view . . . in the colloquial language of familialism. They represented Christian society most commonly as an extended family replete with paternal head and fixed ranks of dependents, a formulation that bore striking resemblance to the organic ideology of published proslavery ministers and politicians.

[. . .]

Their commitment to the slave regime owed as much to its legitimation of dependence and inequality in the private sphere as to the much-lauded vitality of male independence and formal "democracy" in the public sphere. As good republicans, yeomen appreciated both of Columbia's faces.

[. . .]

Many historians, however, see only the public face of slavery republicanism, perhaps because they employ such a narrow definition of "the political," one more theirs than antebellum southerners'. As a result, they mistake ideology for description of social and political reality; the common interpretation of the South as a *Herrenvolk* or white man's democracy bears an unsettling resemblance to the portrait proslavery politicians themselves drew. But the slave republic was emphatically not a democracy, racial or otherwise, as its defenders readily acknowledged in boasting of the restriction of political rights to a privileged few as its distinctive and superior characteristic.

[. . .]

The banner of "free men" was an emblem of the conservatism of "American republicanism," waved to distinguish it from "French democracy," or mobocracy, as so many low-country planters referred to the bastardized politics of the North. Thus the "MEN of the South," yeomen and planters, were challenged repeatedly to "set aside womanly fears of disunion" in favor of "manly and resolute action," not . . . of an egalitarian and democratic regime, but of a hierarchical and republican one.

[. . .]

Yeoman farmers were committed to the defense of social hierarchy and political privilege, including slavery, in large measure because of the relations of personal domination on which their own independence rested. But . . . the very values in which yeomen and planters found agreement also drew yeomen into a political culture and ideology in which planter prerogatives were difficult to resist. They were left, as a result, with few resources to represent effectively their specific interests as small farmers in a region of great planters, and they were overmatched in every aspect of South Carolina politics. Empowered by a system that rewarded privilege, yeoman farmers found themselves overpowered by vastly more privileged planters.

[. . .]

[E]verywhere in the United States, from the early days of the republic to the Civil War, the commitment to government by the virtuous and independent lent a special and contradictory character to political culture and ideology. In some times and places, it generated universal manhood suffrage; in others, an abhorrent and brutal program of geographical expansion; in yet others, the defense of slavery through Civil War. And always the disfranchisement of women.

ᔓ ᔓ ᔓ

William W. Freehling

The South Vs. The South[†]

The Old South! Those words call to mind cotton and slaves, masters and mansions, heat and humidity, plantations and lashes. A myth? Not wholly. *The* reality? Only in the southernmost Old South, and only during the final quarter of slavery's U.S. history.

[. . .]

Farthest south lay the [slave] system's . . . titans, the seven Lower South states. This most tropical North American area stretched westward from South Carolina, Georgia, and Florida on the Atlantic Ocean through Alabama and Mississippi to Louisiana and Texas across the Mississippi River. The Lower South . . . possessed 58.5 percent [of US slaves] in 1860 . . . [and] grew 85 percent of the South's cotton, 96 percent of its sugar, and 100 percent of its rice.

Farthest north . . . bordering on free labor states, lay the . . . attenuated top of the slave system, the four Border South states. This coolest tier of mid-nineteenth-

[†]William W. Freehling, *The South Vs. The South: How Anti-Confederate Southerners Shaped the Course of the Civil War* (New York: Oxford University Press, 2001), pp. 17–20, 22, 28–32, 35, 37–43.

century U.S. enslaved areas stretched westward from Delaware and Maryland on the Atlantic Ocean through Kentucky to Missouri across the Mississippi River. The Border South . . . contained 11.3 percent [of US slaves] in 1860 . . . [and] grew almost none of the South's cotton, sugar, or rice.

Sandwiched between Lower and Border Souths, the four Middle South states stretched westward from Virginia and North Carolina on the Atlantic Ocean through Tennessee to Arkansas across the Mississippi River. The Middle South . . . contained . . . 30 percent [of US slaves] in 1860 . . . [and] grew almost none of the South's sugar and rice and only 15 percent of its cotton.

Not so much proportions of slaves as proportions of thickly enslaved neighbor-hoods distinguished these three tiers of slave states. Compared to the Middle and Border South, the Lower South contained many more black belt neighborhoods (locales with 20 percent or more of their population enslaved) and many fewer white belt neighborhoods (locales with 5 percent or fewer slaves).

[. . .]

Nothing was slack or attenuated about the brotherhood of whites in black belts. In thickly enslaved areas, fancied racial dangers united white classes and sexes. Whites in black belts shared horror images about freed blacks as rioters, rapists, arsonists, and cannibals. These whites characteristically thought that using slavery to control alleged barbarians meant saving civilization.

[. . .]

Whether poor whites lashed rich whites' supposedly unequal blacks as patrolmen or as overseers, slaveless plebians eased their own discomfort about inequality.

[. . .]

Northern abolitionists provoked slaveholders to fury . . . Uneasily unequal non-slaveholders shared slaveholders' outrage. They resented those who would raise lowly blacks to lowly whites' level . . .

In the vast southern white belt areas with few or no slaves, nonslaveholders felt less brotherhood with slaveholders. The geographic point cannot be overempha-sized. Before fault lines between nonslaveholders and slaveholders could open wide, physical separation of the classes usually had to compound class differences. Even when geographic spaces separated the classes, little prewar contention over slavery exploded. White belt folk usually remained neutral rather than hostile about far-off slaveholders, until the black belts' disunion obsessions threatened white belts' Unionist priorities.

[. . .]

The Slave South's survival hinged on effective deterrence *between* as well as inside masters' private realms. Controlling slaves depended not only on masters . . . but also on police power beyond the estate.

Slave runaways could easily sneak out their masters' gates.

[. . .]

For the Slave South to deter its most potentially destructive slave resistance, potential fugitives had to dread coercion outside as well as inside their masters' estate.

[. . .]

Slaveholder police regulations ended at the South's northern border . . . If border slaves' sprints to the North increased, border slaveholders' sales to the South might multiply . . . [and] hasten the dilution of the borderland's incrementally diminishing institution . . . Border slaveholders . . . demanded that the federal government close the open border . . . They prevailed in Congress. They thereby helped push their beloved Union down their most dreaded path: the road to disunion.

[. . .]

[The] Fugitive Slave Law, passed . . . [in] 1850 . . . could force Yankee citizens to serve as . . . slave-nabbers. After the alleged fugitive had been captured, the commissioner alone tried the case, with no other judge, no jury, no right of appeal, no writ of habeas corpus, no defendants' right to call witnesses in their own behalf.

The new national law brought southern limits on white men's democracy to the North. Nationally as in the South, liberty for whites had to be curtailed, wherever danger to black slavery began.

[. . .]

Four years later, the Kansas–Nebraska Act increased northern distress about white liberty lost. Missouri's U.S. senator, David Atchison . . . demand[ed] that Congress allow previously barred slaveholders to enter Kansas and Nebraska territories. Atchison sought slaveholder opportunity to cross over the Missouri border, secure a Kansas majority, and pass antifugitive edicts.

[. . .]

Congress turned Atchison's remedy for Missouri slaveholders' exposure into the Kansas–Nebraska Act. Then Davy Atchison led his constituents over the Kansas border to vote for the first territorial legislators. Missouri's one-day Kansans won the election . . . and passed the most draconian slave code in the Americas, making agitation for antislavery and aid to slave runaways illegal. In defense of these . . . edicts, secured by not-so-democratic one-day settlers, slaveholders called debate and majority decision on slavery, in the presence of slaves, not a democrat's right but an insurrectionist's madness . . . A rising northern Republican Party replied that to protect black slavery, slaveholders must not destroy white democrats' right to discuss and decide in open republican processes . . .

Two regions, two labor systems, two conceptions of whether white men's democracy should be shuttered, whenever an opening for abolition intruded. The Fugitive Slave and Kansas Controversies, by bringing clashing conceptions of white men's democracy to the fore, pitched the nation toward a shattering secession crisis.

[. . .]

The more Northerners raged that Southerners' expanding defenses of black slavery enslaved the white republic . . . the more Middle and Lower South black belts raged at Yankee critics. This fury above and below the Border South left border folk caught in the middle . . . perhaps in a position to determine the victor if a secession crisis yielded a civil war.

[. . .]

Northerners invented two words to describe slaveholders' offensive-minded defense: Slave Power.

[. . .]

In 1856, the new northern Republican Party almost won the presidency with an anti-Slave Power agenda. Republicans distinguished between antislavery radicalism and anti-Slave Power conservatism. They eschewed all proposals to impose abolition inside southern states. They embraced all efforts to stop the Slave Power from imposing minority law on northern majorities. They would allow the southern minority no more national proslavery laws. They would permit no further slaveholder expansion into national territories. They would subsequently hope that the nation's restriction of slavery to southern states would someday, somehow, lead to the institution's extinction.

[. . .]

On that anti-Slave Power program . . . [Republican Abraham] Lincoln swept to the presidency in November 1860. The question now became, would this anti-Slave Power hater of slavery become a menace to the institution inside southern states?

Southern disunionists preferred to dwell on more certain matters. They called Lincoln's antislavery insults bad enough. No honorable Southerner could tolerate the castigation. Some secessionists claimed that no institution could endure without expanding. Some ridiculed northern protestations about never interfering in the South.

[. . .]

They prophesized that within a decade, slavery would wither away in Maryland and throughout the Border South. They calculated that within twenty-five years, the North and the liberated Border South would possess a three-fourths free labor state majority. Then would come the knockout punch, the antislavery constitutional amendment.

[. . .]

[S]peculation that Lincoln would immediately begin to fasten a hangman's noose around slaveholders remained only a guess. The huge majority of Southerners deplored the prospect of smashing their Union over a guess. They preferred to wait and see whether Lincoln would attack slavery inside the South.

[. . .]

Secessionists possessed a trump card to rout a southern majority deaf to Lincoln's alleged menace. According to the southern version of American republicanism, a majority of the people *in any state* could withdraw their consent to be governed. One majority in one slave state could force a secession crisis that a Southwide majority deplored. South Carolina had long aspired to be that state. As A. P. Aldrich, one of the most important South Carolina secessionists, exclaimed, "whoever waited for the common people when a great move was to be made – We must make the move and force them to follow."

[. . .]

On December 20, 1860, South Carolina's Aldrich followers swept their state out of the Union, in defiance . . . of a large southern majority's unionism.

South Carolinians thereby canceled other Southerners' debate on whether a revolution should be started. Now antisecessionists had to decide whether an accomplished revolution should be joined.

[. . .]

After the disunion decision took this Carolina-altered form, disunionists secured 56 percent of the key vote in Georgia as well as 54 percent in Alabama and Louisiana. Elsewhere in the Lower South, South Carolina's precipitancy galvanized more comfortable disunion majorities. When 77 percent of Texas voters went for secession on February 23, 1861, the entire Lower South stood with South Carolina.

But the eight Border and Middle South states (together called the Upper South) stood against the new Confederacy when Abraham Lincoln assumed the presidency.

[. . .]

No shooting would begin unless Lincoln attempted to enforce federal laws or to protect federal property inside Confederate states.

[. . .]

In March and April of 1861, Union troops protected only two Lower South sites: Fort Sumter outside Charleston, South Carolina, and Fort Pickens outside Pensacola, Florida. Neither fort contained sufficient troops or food. If Lincoln sent reinforcements, he might be seen as provoking a civil war. Upper South states, wishing to avoid that combat, might punish the precipitator for initiating the horror.

[. . .]

But Lincoln felt compelled to enforce majoritarian laws at least symbolically at Sumter or Pickens, lest he symbolically accept rebels' destruction of majority rule.

[. . .]

Lincoln faced trouble no matter who fired the first shot, for many Southerners would call any federal shot wrong. They believed that minorities could legitimately depart a majoritarian republic. Like American Revolutionaries . . . they emphasized that the people of any state could withdraw their consent to be governed. So here was the (arguably unanswerable) question: When the minority exercises its right to withdraw consent and the majority exercises its right to rule, who is right?

Moderate Southerners saw virtue in both arguments. These men in the middle might blame the warrior who fired the first shot for turning a legitimate debate into an illegitimate war.

[. . .]

In early April 1861, Lincoln wrote the South Carolina governor that he was sending ships to Fort Sumter. The ships would unload "provisions only," and no "men, arms, or ammunition," assuming that the "attempt be not resisted."

[. . .]

Confederate rulers saw no choice. The bread would sustain troops that by their very presence denied any right to withdraw consent to be governed. The South Carolina governor sped news of the coming expedition to Jefferson Davis in Montgomery, who rushed back orders to conquer the fort before Lincoln's bread-bearing expedition arrived. As first Confederate and then Union shots lit the sky above Fort Sumter, both sides endeavored to save their half of democratic theory. Just as Davis sought to show symbolically that consent to be governed could be withdrawn, so Lincoln sought to show symbolically that election winners must be obeyed.

To the men in the middle, now forced to decide which side best sustained democracy, the answer looked as uncertain as Lincoln's immediate menace to slavery. Again, the answer . . . hinged . . . on how deeply slavery had penetrated a given region. To the blackest belts, Davis seemed the supreme democrat, for a majority must never coerce a minority that withdrew its consent. To the whitest belts, Davis seemed democracy's destroyer, because he ordered the first shot and because a majority must enforce its laws.

In the Middle South, where black belts outnumbered white belts, the crucial facts seemed to be that Lincoln had sent the provoking ships and that he subsequently called up 75,000 troops to coerce provoked Confederates.

[. . .]

The Border South offered richer hope. None came close to secession over Fort Sumter, just as none had come close to secession over Lincoln's alleged immediate menace.

ჾ ჾ ჾ

James L. Huston

Property Rights in Slavery and Civil War[†]

This article proposes an economic explanation for the origins of the Civil War – an explanation based on the existence of a dual system of property rights. The thesis is that southern secession grew out of the irreconcilability of two regimes of property rights: one in the South that recognized property in humans and one in the North that did not.

[. . .]

[†]James L. Huston, "Property Rights in Slavery and the Coming of the Civil War," in *Journal of Southern History*, 65 (May 1999), pp. 251, 253–5, 257, 259–60, 265–8, 279–2, 276, 278–9, 283–6.

Property rights became a crucial element in the sectional controversy because slavery was such an imposing demographic presence in southern society. The slaveholding states in 1859 had a total of 12,240,300 people; 65.7 percent of these were white, 2.0 percent were free blacks, and 32.3 percent – some 3,950,511 or about 4 million – were slaves.

[. . .]

More important was the wealth that slavery represented, for slavery was a labor system in which slave masters owned the slaves as property, and the property had an evaluation.

[. . .]

TABLE 1
WEALTH ESTIMATES OF THE U.S. IN 1860 BY ECONOMIC CATEGORY

Category	Estimated $ Value (1860 dollars)
Slaves	$3,000,000,000
Farms	6,638,414,221
Farm Implements	246,125,064
Investment in Manufacturing	1,050,000,000
Investment in Railroads	1,166,422,729
Bank Capital	227,469,077
Home Productions	27,484,144
Livestock	1,098,862,355
Total of above categories	$13,452,000,000
Total Assessed Real Estate and Personal Property by Census	$16,159,616,068
Unaccounted-for Wealth	$2,707,616,000 (rounded)

Relative to other endeavors in the economy, the investment in slaves was massive. (See table; unaccounted-for wealth probably reflects urban residences, investments in canals, river and oceanic transportation devices and supply facilities, and various sundry items of personal wealth.) The comparison of wealth in slaves to wealth (or investment) in other areas of the economy is shocking. The table shows that slaveholding comprised far more national wealth than railroads and manufacturing enterprises *combined*.

The vast amount of wealth in Africans . . . by itself yields an obvious economic motive for the defense of the peculiar institution, but the overall impact of slavery on southern life must be delineated because slavery stitched most of the South together. It did so because slavery was productive wealth: From it flowed a stream of income.

[. . .]

Income stitches a society together and generates social inertia, a conservatism in the population at large. With a reliable income stream, even if it is paltry in its flow to numerous individuals, life at least becomes predictable. This is how modern wealth, even though unevenly distributed, produces social stability. As long as the wealth yields an income stream that includes the general population, a society becomes less willing to attempt institutional upheaval for fear of disrupting that income stream.

[. . .]

Income from slavery aided in financing industry, transportation, government, and various urban and legal services. As long as cotton was king, it produced a per capita income comparable to the national average and a growth rate that augured a rosy future. Southerners understood that slavery caused the economic prosperity of their region, and that knowledge created an economic bond among all classes of whites.

[. . .]

Property rights in slaves was absolutely crucial to the existence of the peculiar institution . . . [and] property rights could exist only via authority or sanction of government – no sanction, no property rights, no slavery.

[. . .]

[In] the federal government of the United States . . . power was shared by people from societies representing different regimes of property rights, between slave states and free states. Property rights were defined and enforced by government, and the nature of the federal Union gave power in the national Congress to individuals who had absolutely no material interest in slavery. Here lay the danger to the longevity of slaveholding.

[. . .]

The federal government was under no obligation to recognize property rights in slaves at the federal level and had certain powers reserved to itself that could affect such rights: foreign diplomacy, control of interstate trade, rulings by the federal judiciary, and governance of newly acquired territories.

[. . .]

Federal authorities could damage slave owning by adopting a position hostile to the enforcement of those property rights.

[. . .]

The dilemma that property rights in slaves posed for southerners can be explicitly stated. Property rights dictate an investment path, and if the property involved will yield a good return to the owner, then continuous investment will result. Over the years, the time and effort to build up the store of property produces a strong attachment to the property and, perhaps, a sense of purpose and achievement.

[. . .]

By the time of the American Revolution, let alone by 1860, southerners knew that the investment process had inseparably fused their society with slaveholding.

[. . .]

The behavior and attitudes of northerners toward slavery and its expansion present more analytical difficulty than do those of southerners.

[. . .]

The essence of the dilemma with the northern position is, first, the timing of the decision to combat slavery's expansion. The second part of the dilemma is what led northerners to see aggression in southern behavior.

[. . .]

Expectations about property holding governed northerners' social vision [, known as] . . . the "free labor ideology." In the free labor scheme of the good society, the ultimate goal was . . . economic independency. . . . But before this "competency" could be obtained, many, if not most, men would have to go through a period of dependency, or wage earning, until enough knowledge and savings were accumulated to permit the jump to ownership.

[. . .]

A crucial assumption of the free labor ideology . . . was the wage. Economic independency . . . could be obtained only if wages were high . . . If wages were low, there could be no saving and no eventual move to self-employment and property ownership. Therefore, the free labor experiment in the North, the entire experiment in self-government and republicanism, required ample remuneration to all who labored.

The political battles of the Jeffersonian and Jacksonian periods made it plain how the laborer was to claim the full fruits of his (never her for the early part of the century) labor. There was to be no partiality, no advantage given to a few, and as much economic equality as legislation could generate, recognizing that "natural" conditions might favor some over others. This was the egalitarianism of the age, arising from the anti-aristocratic impulse of the American Revolution.

[. . .]

Contemporaries believed that slavery depressed wages because slaveholders held a monopoly, which grew out of property rights; his property rights in the laborer (the slave) permitted the slaveholder to usurp the fruits of labor.

[. . .]

For the republican/democratic society of the North to continue, wages simply had to be substantial.

[. . .]

No high wages, no accumulations, and no freeholders; no freeholders, no self-government.

Concern about the impact of slavery upon free white workers has a long history. Why did concern over it rise to a boiling point in the late 1840s and especially in the 1850s? Certainly one answer is that the territorial acquisition from the Mexican–American War sparked the debate over whether slavery would expand into that region or not. But also fueling northern fears was an understanding that the economic structure of American life had changed: the transportation revolution portended a much closer relationship between free labor North and slave labor South than had existed before 1850. Slavery had always been profitable in the production of the great southern staple crops . . . But outside of those staples, slavery affected only local labor markets . . . The transportation revolution augured the end of the local market and local prices. Steamboats, canals, and railroads created a rudimentary national market that connected the East Coast to the Mississippi River by 1854 . . . The transportation revolution remolded the economy of the United States by breaking down the price barriers that separated local economies. Because transportation was widely available and the cost of shipment so greatly reduced, individuals from a locality at a great distance from another locality could *compete* in the *distant* locality's *market*.

The application of this economic change to the sectional controversy over slavery seems obvious. The effects of slavery on the labor market could no longer be confined to small geographical areas in the South. Slavery could potentially affect the national labor market by permitting the employment of southern slaves in the same occupations as northern workers. Products made by slave labor then competed against products made by free labor – and the cost advantage would be to the southern producer on the basis of the wages paid to slaves.

[. . .]

Understanding how the transportation revolution affected the sectional controversy begins to clarify the reasoning behind the belief of northerners that they were
the victims of southern aggression.

[. . .]

Perhaps slavery would not have planted itself north of the Mason–Dixon line, but
over time the effect of slavery on product prices would go northward.

[. . .]

This contingency fed the northern notion of an aggressive South.

[. . .]

The two regimes of property rights were colliding. For northerners, the only way
to rectify the economic imbalance was to end property rights in people

[. . .]

The battle over property rights in slaves was joined when Representative David
Wilmot of Pennsylvania proposed in August 1846 to prohibit slavery in the territories acquired by the United States at the end of the Mexican War.

[. . .]

Southerners immediately reacted to northern advocacy of the Wilmot Proviso
with the conviction that their property rights were in jeopardy. They insisted that
the territories were common property to all the states and that the federal government could not discriminate between different types of property.

[. . .]

Two issues – first, the sanctity of property rights in slaves and, second, what
authority had control over those rights – made the territorial issue crucial.

[. . .]

[What] concerned southerners was their property rights in slaves and the federal
government's potential control over those rights. To defend such rights, southerners demanded that the national government recognize in all its dealings the sanctity
of property in slaves.

[. . .]

Abraham Lincoln's election to the presidency in November 1860 sparked the fire-eaters in the South to sever state ties with the Union.

[. . .]

Secessionists left little doubt that the sanctity of property rights in slaves was the reason for their drastic action. [According to] the South Carolina "Declaration of Causes" for secession . . . the Constitution had been a compact that recognized "[t]he right of property in slaves."

[. . .]

Given the smorgasbord of explanations for the Civil War, it might be asked why this explanation should be given more credence than any other. The answer is that the property rights dilemma by itself, cloaked behind the rhetoric of states' rights, was capable of producing secession . . . And as questions of authority . . . over property escalated in the 1840s, both northerners and southerners believed that their societies were endangered, and those perceptions reached paranoid proportions by the 1850s. The existence of two systems of property – both of which produced income from massive amounts of investment and one of which intruded with damaging effects upon the other – is sufficient to generate massive conflict. One additional aspect of human behavior, however, must be invoked in order to obtain the final result, civil war: In order to preserve accumulated property, or even to extend the bounds of property ownership, some people will kill other people.

7

Anne Sarah Rubin

THE RISE AND FALL OF THE CONFEDERACY

If the Civil War is generally cast as the dramatic high point of American history, then the Confederacy may, in turn, rank as the most fabled aspect of the Civil War. The sheer audacity of secession and rebellion; the sacrifice borne and tenacity exhibited over four years of war; the ordeal of defeat at the hands of a formidable adversary, and the radical transformations that followed – all combine to lend the Lost Cause an aura of poignancy, and an abiding mystique. And the moral issues brought to the fore by the Civil War – with each side laying claim to the cause of freedom and casting the other as the embodiment of tyranny – continue to render the southern rebellion a charged topic even a century-and-a-half later. Not for nothing does the Confederate flag retain its power to spark searing controversy in early twenty-first-century America.

The history profession has not been immune from this enduring fascination with the Confederate rebellion – or from the passion it has long inspired among so many Americans. Ever since Appomattox, the rise and fall of the Confederacy has been told and retold, as historians explore its many facets. Sustaining scholarly interest in the Confederacy is a cluster of ongoing questions. What did the Confederacy stand for? How did its leaders make the case for secession and mobilize southerners to support it? What motivated so many non-slaveholders to rally around a war to preserve slavery? What were the main sources and themes of popular dissent under the Confederacy? How did slaves respond to the opportunities and uncertainties opened up by the war, and what roles did they play in the outcome? How did the demands and disruptions of war transform the place of women in the white South – and how in turn did they affect the course of the war? To what extent was Confederate fervor dampened – and to what extent, deepened – by the mounting hardships and waning fortunes of the war? What accounts most for the defeat of the Confederacy: the superiority of northern might or the lack (or loss) of a popular will to win? Together, the readings in this chapter provide a taste of the kinds of focal points and interpretations – some long familiar, some more recent – that have made the rise and fall of the Confederacy a fixture in southern historical study.

Anne Sarah Rubin, Associate Professor of History at the University of Maryland–Baltimore County, specializes in the Civil War-era South. Her first book – *A Shattered Nation: The Rise and Fall of the Confederacy, 1861–1868* (2005) – offered a fresh look at how a Confederate identity was constructed following secession, and how it persisted and evolved over the course of the war, and beyond. Professor Rubin is also co-author, with Edward Ayers, of the electronic project, *Valley of the Shadow: Two Communities in the American Civil War: The Eve of War* (2000). Her current book project, a history of the way Americans have remembered Sherman's legendary March through Georgia, will be published in 2014. (An online component of this project can be seen at www.shermansmarch.org.)

Whenever I tell people that I wrote a book about what happened to Confederates' sense of national identity when the Confederacy ceased to exist, someone always jokes that it hardly seems to have happened, that the Confederacy seems to still exist today. Certainly conflicts over its symbols – battle flags, statues of generals, names of schools – flare up repeatedly. While the Civil War itself was over in the spring of 1865, it left legions of unanswered questions, and the failure of Americans – both northern and southern – to resolve festering issues of race and citizenship has kept the war alive to this day. While the Confederacy lasted for only four years, its brief existence allows us to see the process of nation-building in a compressed way. Ironically, while the majority of white southerners shifted their allegiance to the Confederacy with startling speed, their connection to this nation endured, at an emotional level, for generations.[1]

Confederate historiography has been remarkably complex and changeable. From the moment the war ended, participants and historians have struggled to make sense of its origins, its meanings, and its ultimate fate. Why did white southerners vote in favor of secession? What led non-slaveholders to enlist in droves? To what extent did the presence of slavery shape Confederate identity? And finally, what of the outcome – was it more that the Union *won* the war or that the Confederacy *lost* it? These basic questions raise a host of others, cutting across issues of race, class, and gender. Some historians have argued that the

Confederacy foundered on the shoals of class conflict, others that women did not feel the same degree of patriotism that men did. Writers have attributed Confederate defeat to such factors as the Union's overwhelming numbers, the oppositional efforts of southern Unionists and African Americans, and guilt over slavery. Recently, scholars have begun to pay closer attention to conflicting loyalties within families. This introduction to Confederate historiography will focus particularly on questions of national loyalty and allegiance. By understanding the ways in which Confederates saw themselves, we can better understand their commitment to their new nation. But before getting to these issues, and to the ways in which the selections for this chapter address them, some background is in order.

There were, of course, opponents to secession within the slaveholding states, particularly in the border states of the Upper South. Also, African American southerners, both free and slave, felt no loyalty to this newly created nation, and would work to sabotage it from within. Still, the Confederate nation came into being with remarkable ease, largely spared the struggles that have afflicted other emergent nations. This was because the delegates to the Montgomery convention, whatever differences they might have had, shared a conviction that they and their new nation were the true heirs of the Founding Fathers. Therefore, they drew heavily on the United States Constitution, and also on the iconography and language of the American Revolution. This served a double function: first, it allowed them to create a nation quickly, without having to build everything from scratch; second, and more importantly, it also gave the Confederate people a ready-made myth of national origin, and eased the shifting of their allegiances from the United States to the Confederate States. Secession also took on an air of emotionalism and celebration, particularly in the Lower South. For southerners who had felt under siege for over a year, withdrawal from the Union provided a sort of catharsis. Standard manifestations of nineteenth-century political culture – parades, fireworks, and celebrations – accompanied each secession convention.

Confederates wanted to believe that they were better than the Americans they left behind, and that their politics were more pure, less tainted by partisanship. In this spirit, the delegates at Montgomery emphasized consensus; there were no political parties in the Confederacy. While this rejection of factionalism was perhaps admirable, it would remain to be seen how effectively a nation based on a foundation of states' rights would be able to govern and wage war.

The vast majority of white southerners, even those who had been Unionists throughout the winter of 1860–1, transferred their allegiances to the Confederacy with a minimum of backward glances following the firing on Fort Sumter and Lincoln's call for troops. For many whites, secession provided a sense of relief – they were now masters of their political destiny, no longer subject to the whims of Yankees. If the Confederates invoked the heritage of the American Revolution, they also imbued their political identity with a healthy dose of Christian rhetoric. Confederates believed themselves to be

God's chosen people, and they saw confirmation of that in their early victories of 1861–2. As the tide of battle turned against them in 1863–4, Confederates shifted their rhetoric, and believed that God was testing or chastening them.

As much as Confederates argued that their nation was based on constitutional principles, revolutionary antecedents, and Christianity, it also included a potent mix of fear and rage. The fear was of an end to slavery, couched often in warnings of "black rule" or "race-mixing"; the rage was against those demonic Yankee invaders. White supremacy and the protection of slavery were integral to the Confederacy, and even non-slaveholders understood that benefits and status accrued to them. Thus, discussions of slavery per se appeared only rarely in public forums. For the most part Confederates took slavery as a given, albeit a sometimes problematic one, subject neither to challenge nor to conversation.

Confederates had a second reason to keep silent on the subject of slavery, and that was the matter of how their nation would be perceived by foreign countries. The ever-present search for diplomatic recognition, a sort of national status anxiety, underlay Confederate calls for indigenous schoolbooks and literature, and it influenced the language in which Confederates framed their national aspirations. They were sensitive to foreign, particularly British, opposition to slavery. By de-emphasizing bondage as a cause of secession, stressing instead state rights and political domination, Confederates sought to shift the terms of debate, and thus make their cause more palatable to conditional Unionists, non-slaveholders, and especially outside nations.

The first historians to write about the Confederacy got going as soon as the war ended, and most had themselves held positions in the government or the army. These "participant historians" included Richmond's Edward Pollard (who actually began writing his history while the war was still going on), dozens of members of the Army of Northern Virginia who contributed to the Southern Historical Society Papers, and later Confederate Vice President Alexander Stephens and President Jefferson Davis. Viewing the past through the gauzy haze of the Lost Cause, these writers tended to present the Confederacy as a doomed agrarian last stand against the crushing forces of industrial modernity.

What this story virtually ignored, however, was the issue of slavery and its role in the Confederate nation, a telling omission that persisted for close to a century (and continues, in some quarters, to this day). This uncritical assessment of the Confederacy eased the culture of reunion at the turn of the twentieth century. In this version, the Civil War was a quarrel between white brothers, over lofty principles, rather than one about the place of blacks in the American nation. Confederate soldiers came in for the same praise as Union men, honored for their service to a fabled (if unspecified) "cause."

For almost a hundred years after the war, historians of the Civil War and the Confederacy rarely addressed questions of nationalism and identity. To do so would be to challenge the notion of a brothers' war, to disrupt the idea that Confederates were still fundamentally American. But the 1960 publication of David M. Potter's seminal essay, "The Historian's Use of Nationalism and Vice Versa," changed all that, and inspired military, social, and political historians to produce a voluminous literature on Confederate nationalism. Beginning, too, with Potter's work, historians have tended to focus on the origins of Confederate nationalism, testing its "strength" against a range of theories. In the extracted section, however, Potter actually warns against this. First, he cautions against the position that taking the Confederacy seriously as a nation implies some sort of endorsement of what it represented. Drawing on the conviction that historians ought not to examine only those with whom they agree, he tries to divorce the study of the Confederacy from the moral question of whether it should have existed.

Potter also addresses another intriguing question – that of whether Confederates were nationalists or sectionalists. He challenges the view that, while northerners felt a loyalty to their nation, southerners put their regional interests above all else, perhaps a result of the burgeoning field of southern regional studies. Rather, Potter argues that northerners were just as motivated by regional interests as their southern counterparts – the difference was that northern interests tended to be aligned with Union policies while southern ones did not. Potter reminds us that northerners, like southerners, had alternative interests and multiple loyalties. Neither side had a monopoly either on patriotism or on internal conflict.

The Confederacy struggled mightily as the war went on, pressured not only by the Union army but by a host of internal divisions and instabilities, and historians in turn have struggled to gauge the impact of these pressures. Consider the range of tensions that plagued the wartime South. First, there was the place of national government in the polity of the new nation. Confederates quickly discovered that states' rights (particularly when guarded jealously by state governors) was not a strong foundation from which to launch a nation and fight a war. Thus, each time President Davis attempted to increase centralization – whether through taxation, impressment, or conscription – he encountered considerable opposition. But, because of the Confederacy's avowed antipartyism (perhaps compounded by the six-year presidential term), there was no real channel for that opposition. Rather than having it diffused by partisan competition, disenchantment became more and more focused on Davis personally. At the same time, while all Confederates struggled with shortages of foodstuffs and runaway inflation, the effects hit lower-class whites especially hard. Shortages of food and supplies, loss of labor, and the class resentments inspired by the twenty-slave exemption (a law that allowed one white man to stay home on plantations of over twenty slaves, ostensibly to help grow food and keep the peace), alienated even supportive yeomen. In 1863 there were bread riots in cities around the South, as working-class women stormed stores and government warehouses to get food for their families. Family interests might take precedence over the national interest, as letters from women begging their husbands and sons to desert suggest. The South also had the problem of slaves, who, when not running away, might simply refuse to work. A combination of labor unrest, slowdowns, and escape all rendered the southern economy much less efficient, and contributed to a general sense that the world was falling apart around the Confederates' ears. The myriad difficulties that the Confederacy faced have led some historians to attribute its eventual defeat to a failure of will. Essentially these historians claim that Confederate patriotism was not strong enough to sustain a viable nation, and that a withdrawal of public support at home ultimately led to defeat on the battlefield.[2]

Historians ranging from Paul Escott to Drew Faust to co-authors Richard Beringer, Herman Hattaway, Archer Jones, and William N. Still, Jr., have sought to explain, in the words of Beringer, et al., "why the South lost the Civil War." Did it, as one historian has suggested, die of democracy? Can the blame be placed at the feet of the leadership, particularly Jefferson Davis? Was it a casualty of class conflict or was it that women, no longer protected by the patriarchy, withdrew their crucial support? Historians who have asked these questions have tended to find that the Confederacy failed to secure its independence because it failed to secure and retain the loyalty of its people. This "loss of will thesis," best exemplified in Paul Escott's *After Secession* and in Beringer et al.'s *Why the South Lost the Civil War*, argues that Confederate nationalism was built on a shallow foundation of superficial difference from that of the United States. Therefore, it was by definition unable to inspire citizens and too weak to sustain the Confederate war effort. Escott, in particular, puts much of the blame for the Confederate defeat on divisions of class as captured by the cry that "it's a rich man's war and a poor man's fight." Yet, while southern yeomen and poor whites may appear to have had no direct class interest in a war to perpetuate slavery, they had other reasons for which to fight, most notably a perceived need to defend themselves against northern invasion. And, in the end, they were as subject to nationalist exhortations as anyone else.

A more subtle form of this argument came in Drew Gilpin Faust's 1996 *Mothers of Invention: Women of the Slaveholding South in the American Civil War*. Faust argues that the ebbing of support from elite white women over the course of the war led eventually to the collapse of the Confederacy. Faust's women are conditional nationalists – they support the Confederacy while it can protect them and their status as women, and withdraw support as the patriarchal and paternalistic society collapses around them. The section extracted here shows women begging male relatives – fathers, sons, and husbands – to desert the army and come home. This increasing self-interest on the part of white women, Faust argues, was essentially conservative in nature. These women wanted a return to the status quo antebellum with white women on a protected pedestal. For Faust, self-interest ultimately triumphed over patriotism.

Other historians, like Gary Gallagher, Anne Sarah Rubin, and Aaron Sheehan-Dean, have taken a different approach to the question of

Confederates' patriotism or will to fight, arguing that the rebellion was defeated much more by the North's superior resources, both material and personal, than by internal weaknesses. For these historians, the relevant question is not so much "why did the Confederacy lose?" as "why was the Confederacy able to exist as long as it did?" The breakaway nation, for all its shortcomings, did possess all the necessary apparatus of government – an executive, a legislature, a judiciary, a treasury, a postal service, a state department. Most importantly – for the Confederacy had no real existence apart from war – it raised and kept an army in the field. These may not have always functioned well – indeed, in many cases they barely functioned at all – but they did exist. Also, for each expression of war-weariness or resentment, one could find a countervailing desire to fight to the end, to continue on to independence. In fact, I would argue, too many historians have conflated frustration over the war with a desire to return to the Union. To the contrary, when Confederates longed for peace, they almost always meant peace with independence.[3]

The extract from Gary Gallagher's *The Confederate War* explores the many challenges that Confederates faced, both at home and in the field. Where Faust and other proponents of the loss-of-will thesis might find grounds for their position in shortages, desertion, and class tension, Gallagher suggests how these stresses can be overstated. The North faced similar internal challenges, from draft riots and labor unrest to a significant peace Democrat movement. Until the final months of the war, Gallagher finds, the Confederate desertion rate scarcely exceeded that of the Union. He reminds us, too, that many men counted as "deserters" could more accurately be considered as "away without leave"; that is, they went home temporarily, especially during the wintertime when campaigning was suspended. In a sense, the issue of desertion is similar to that of Faust's elite women. Both populations may have chosen to place personal or familial concerns above national interests, but that doesn't necessarily mean that they no longer supported the Confederacy or no longer cared about the outcome of the war.

This idea that loyalty could have multiple meanings and, indeed, that the Confederacy itself could stand for multiple ideologies was put to the test in the winter of 1864–5. At that point, Jefferson Davis, knowing how desperately his armies needed manpower, began to entertain proposals to arm slaves, with the understanding that those men might eventually need to be emancipated. Predictably, Davis's suggestion met with scornful, even angry, opposition. By suggesting that at some point the Confederacy should think about turning to slave soldiers, Davis had brought to the surface simmering questions about the meaning of the Confederacy. Could a nation born out of the desire to defend slavery at any cost survive emancipation, even emancipation on its own terms? Davis and other supporters of arming slaves argued that, in fact, they were seeking to protect the peculiar institution. Emancipate a few slaves in order to win the war, they claimed, and preserve the system of slavery intact; let the Confederacy be destroyed and slavery would be lost forever. As an added benefit, support for any level of emancipation would demonstrate to foreign nations – not to mention wavering yeomen – that this was not a war exclusively to preserve the property of a wealthy few.

The extract from Bruce Levine's *Confederate Emancipation: Southern Plans to Free and Arm Slaves during the Civil War*, describes in fascinating detail the rationales of Confederate emancipation supporters. Levine also explores the motivations of slaves who had long been struggling for their freedom. This effort would ultimately come to nothing. A company of black soldiers was hastily recruited in Richmond in March 1865, and their drilling was reported in the city's papers with somewhat patronizing praise for their military aptitude. But within days, Richmond itself was evacuated. Reports a few days later placed some of these African Americans at a rearguard action or at the building of earthworks. But they do not appear on the surrender rolls – the only blacks who do were the cooks, teamsters, and musicians who had served throughout the war.

What does this all mean? Was the movement to arm Confederate slaves nothing but desperation? Or did it signify a shift, at least for some, in the meaning of the Confederacy itself? If the Confederacy was supposed to have died from failures of will and nationalism, on which side of the argument does this incident fall? I would argue that the willingness of many Confederates to arm their slaves, thus bringing to life their greatest fear, shows the depth of their attachment to their nation. Born in slavery, the Confederacy had become about more than that for many people. It had become a viable alternative to life within the United States, one in which slavery was no longer the only marker of differentiation.

This more expansive vision of the Confederacy – as an identity that could outlive the nation-state – has powerful implications, not just for understanding post-Civil War America but for tracing nationalism throughout the world. The Confederate example shows us that national identity, loyalty, patriotism – these were ever-changing phenomena during the war and we need to stop seeing them as fixed categories. It also reminds us that it may be easier to adopt a new national or political identity than it is to shed one. The processes of nation-building and of national dissolution are going on all over the world, from the Balkans to the Caucasus to the Middle East, and we ignore the lessons of history at our peril.

NOTES

1. A word on terminology is in order. In this essay, I am using "Confederate" to refer to those white southerners who supported the Confederacy. Southerner refers to all people – black and white – living south of the Mason–Dixon line.
2. Richard E. Beringer, Jr., Herman Hattaway, Archer Jones, and William N. Still, *Why the South Lost the Civil War* (Athens: University of Georgia Press, 1986); Paul D. Escott, *After Secession: Jefferson Davis and the Failure of Confederate Nationalism* (Baton Rouge: Louisiana State University Press, 1978); Escott, "Southern Yeomen

and the Confederacy," *South Atlantic Quarterly*, 77 (Spring 1978), pp. 146–58; and Escott, "The Failure of Confederate Nationalism: The Old South's Class System in the Crucible of War," in Harry P. Owens and James J. Cooke, eds., *The Old South in the Crucible of War* (Jackson: University Press of Mississippi, 1983), pp. 15–28.

3. Gary W. Gallagher, *The Confederate War* (Cambridge, MA: Harvard University Press, 1997); Anne Sarah Rubin, *A Shattered Nation: The Rise and Fall of the Confederacy, 1861–1868* (Chapel Hill: University of North Carolina Press, 2005); Aaron Sheehan-Dean, *Why Confederates Fought: Family and Nation in Civil War Virginia* (Chapel Hill: University of North Carolina Press, 2007).

* * *

Further Reading

Ash, Stephen V., *When the Yankees Came: Conflict and Chaos in the Occupied South, 1861–1865* (Chapel Hill: University of North Carolina Press, 1995).

Beringer, Jr., Richard E., Herman Hattaway, Archer Jones, and William N. Still, *Why the South Lost the Civil War* (Athens: University of Georgia Press, 1986).

Bonner, Robert E., *Mastering America: Southern Slaveholders and the Crisis of American Nationhood* (New York: Cambridge University Press, 2009).

Dirck, Brian R., *Lincoln & Davis: Imagining America, 1809–1865* (Lawrence: University Press of Kansas, 2001).

Doyle, Don H., *Nations Divided: America, Italy, and the Southern Question* (Athens: University of Georgia Press, 2002).

Escott, Paul D., *After Secession: Jefferson Davis and the Failure of Confederate Nationalism* (Baton Rouge: Louisiana State University Press, 1978).

Faust, Drew Gilpin, *The Creation of Confederate Nationalism: Ideology and Identity in the Civil War South* (Baton Rouge: Louisiana State University Press, 1988).

Gordon, Lesley J. and John C. Inscoe, eds., *Inside the Confederate Nation: Essays in Honor of Emory M. Thomas* (Baton Rouge: Louisiana State University Press, 2005).

Grant, Susan-Mary, *North over South: Northern Nationalism and American Identity in the Antebellum Era* (Lawrence: University Press of Kansas, 2000).

Rable, George, *The Confederate Republic: A Revolution against Politics* (Chapel Hill: University of North Carolina Press, 1994).

Rubin, Anne Sarah, *A Shattered Nation: The Rise and Fall of the Confederacy, 1861–1868* (Chapel Hill: University of North Carolina Press, 2005).

Sheehan-Dean, Aaron, *Why Confederates Fought: Family and Nation in Civil War Virginia* (Chapel Hill: University of North Carolina Press, 2007).

Thomas, Emory M., *The Confederate Nation, 1861–1865* (New York: Harper & Row, 1979).

* * *

David M. Potter

The Historian's Use of Nationalism[†]

I have already suggested that the element of sanction in the institutional concept sometimes makes it difficult for the historian to attribute nationality to movements of which he morally disapproves, since the attribution itself would imply that the movement has a kind of validity. This factor has certainly influenced the treatment of the question whether the Southern Confederacy was a nation, for the issue between the Union and the Confederacy also became an issue between freedom and slavery. To ascribe nationality to the South is to validate the right of a proslavery movement to autonomy and self-determination. Since few historians in the twentieth century have been willing to do this, their moral position has sometimes run counter to their theory of nationality and has impelled them to shirk the consequences of their own belief that group identity is the basis for autonomy. In other words, once the ethical question of the character of Southern institutions becomes linked with the factual question of the nature of the group loyalties in the South, it becomes very difficult for the historian to deal with the factual question purely on its own merits. If the finding that a majority of Southern citizens wanted a nation of their own is inseparable from the conclusion that the institution of slavery enjoyed a democratic sanction, it is always possible to reverse the reasoning and to argue that since slavery could not have enjoyed a democratic sanction, therefore the Southern people must not have been a "people" in the sense that would entitle them to want a nation of their own.

The position of the strongly antislavery historian on the question of Southern nationality tends to be particularly ironic, for he usually emphasizes more than do most writers the depth of the division between the North and the South. No one stresses more than he the profound authoritarian implications of slavery for the entire intellectual and social life of the South, and the sharpness of the contrast between this society, with its system of legalized caste status, and the free, democratic society of the North. Yet, after making this case, the antislavery historian often takes the view that the Southern assertion of nationality was not justified. Of course, he might simply follow the logic of his moral position and argue that war is justified if waged by one nation to compel another nation to give up slavery. But since he also attaches moral value to the right of self-determination, the recognition of Southern nationality would place him in a moral dilemma. The only way he can have his crusade against slavery and his right of self-determination too is to deny that the principle of self-determination is involved in the case of the crusade against slavery, or in short to deny that the

[†]David M. Potter, "The Historian's Use of Nationalism and Vice Versa," in Don E. Fehrenbacher, ed., *History and American Society: Essays of David M. Potter* (New York: Oxford University Press, 1973), pp. 89–93.

slaveholding belligerent was endowed with such nationality as his own analysis has pretty well demonstrated.

This statement, it might be added, is not intended to deny or question the primacy of moral considerations. It may well be that the abolition of slavery is worth more to mankind than the right of self-determination of peoples, especially since slavery itself denies this right to the slaves. Even if coercion is an evil, it may not be the worst of evils, and a war of subjugation may well be justified by the emancipation of 3,950,000 slaves. It may also be, as Lincoln apparently believed, that the preservation, even by force, of the Union which had been formalized by the Constitution of 1787 has a higher value than the purely voluntary self-determination of peoples. All I mean to argue is that a historian should not assert that he regards the right of self-determination as an absolute and then argue that it is not involved in cases where he is unwilling to apply it, or where he thinks some other value has a higher priority.

The equation of Northernism with nationalism and Southernism with sectionalism not only denies by prejudgment, and without actual analysis of group feelings, that the Southern movement could have been national; it also leads to an easy assumption that all Northern support for federal authority must have been nationalistic rather than sectional. But this view tends to obscure the fact that in the North as well as in the South there were deep sectional impulses, and support or nonsupport of the Union was sometimes a matter of sectional tactics rather than of national loyalty. For instance, Northern support for a sectional tariff or for sectional internal improvements, adopted by sectional majorities in the national government, was no less sectional than Southern opposition to them. Northern efforts to put the terminus of a Pacific railroad at Chicago were no less sectional than Southern efforts to put it at New Orleans. Northern determination to keep Negroes (rather than just slaves) out of the territories was no less sectional than Southern determination to carry them there. Even Northern support for Lincoln, who did not so much as run in most of the slave states in 1860, was perhaps just as sectional as Southern support for Breckenridge or for Bell, who did not carry a single free state.

But in the North, sectional forces tended to support a strong Union because it was evident that this Union was becoming one in which the sectional forces of the North would be dominant. Thus the national Union could be made the instrument of these sectional interests. The South, on the other hand, finding itself in a minority position, could not hope to secure national support for sectional objectives, nor even to keep sectional and national interests in coordination with one another, and therefore it was forced to choose between section and nation. If the proslavery elements seemed less nationalistic than the antislavery elements, it was not because one more than the other put peace or national harmony above the question of slavery – for neither of them did – but because the antislavery elements could expect, with their majority status, to employ the national authority for their purposes, while the proslavery forces could not. A Northerner could, and many

Northerners did, support the Union for sectional reasons; no Southerner was likely to support it for any other than national reasons.

The historian certainly should make some distinction between the nationalistic motive to support the Union as the embodiment of the "people" as a whole, and the tactical motive to use the authority of the Union for the promotion of sectional interests; but very often both of these impulses are called by the same name, i.e. nationalism.

If the antithesis of Northern nationalism and Southern sectionalism conceals the sectional motivation of much that was done through national means in the North, it also obscures another important reality: namely that a mixture of regional and national loyalties prevailed on both sides. These mixed loyalties did not seem ambiguous or inconsistent in the North because they were not in conflict there, whereas in the South they did conflict and, because they did, were made to seem evidence of what amounted to duplicity – as if devotion to the section in itself demonstrated alienation from the nation and as if nationalism could flourish only as regional loyalties withered away. But in fact, this view is mistaken. To take one concrete example, there was no equivocation on the part of Josiah Quincy of Massachusetts when he declared in 1811 that "the first public love of my heart is the Commonwealth of Massachusetts . . . the love of this Union grows out of this attachment to my native soil." Nor was there ambiguity in Sam Houston of Texas when he asserted that he was a Southerner and a Unionist too, with "a Southern heart, large enough, I trust, to embrace the whole Union if not the whole world"; nor in J. D. B. De Bow when he appealed to his fellow citizens, "as Southerners, as *Americans*, as MEN"; nor in Alexander H. Stephens of Georgia when he said, "I have a patriotism that embraces, I trust, all parts of the Union . . . yet I must confess my feelings of attachment are most ardent toward that with which all my interests and associations are identified . . . The South is my home, my fatherland."

If the point here were only that the people of the South became trapped in a conflict of loyalties, it would hardly be worth stating; historians have known it as a truism for a long time. The point is rather that the Northerners and the Southerners were not distinguished from one another by a singularity of loyalty on one side and a multiplicity of loyalties on the other, as though one had been monogamous and the other polygamous. In fact, they both had multiple loyalties, and what distinguished them was that one, being in a majority, was able to keep all its loyalties coordinated, and therefore undivided, while the other, being in a minority, was not able to keep them coordinated, with the result that they did become divided. Multiple loyalties do not inherently produce conflict, and the question whether conflict will develop is entirely separate from the question whether loyalties are multiple.

৯ ৯ ৯

Drew Gilpin Faust

Mothers of Invention[†]

The patriotism women had so enthusiastically embraced in 1861 began to erode before seemingly endless – and increasingly purposeless – demands for sacrifice. After the defeats of the summer of 1863 Julia Davidson exclaimed to her husband, John, "Oh how I do pray this war was at an end. If the Yankees are going to whip us I wish they would hurry about it." Gertrude Thomas expressed a similar "impatience to have it over." As a New Orleans woman wrote her soldier son, "je ne vois que des sacrifices, des victimes, la ruine, la misère, rien de gagné." By 1864 the war's battles seemed no longer glorious but "massacres sans résultat." Women's willingness to be selfless, to embrace the needs of the nation as prior to their own, had begun to disappear. Their initial dedication to the Cause proved to be conditional, dependent on their own capacities to endure war's hardships and on a hope for the Confederacy's future that was rapidly evaporating. On a tour of the battlefield at Seven Pines in search of her wounded cousin, Constance Cary reported seeing men "in every stage of mutilation" and proclaimed herself "permanently convinced that nothing is worth war!" Margaret Junkin Preston greeted news of the death of her stepson and several of his friends by protesting, "Who thinks or cares for victory now!" Sarah Jane Sams proclaimed herself "sick and tired of trying to endure these privations to which we are all subjected," and as early as 1862 Julia Le Grand had come to believe that "nothing is worth such sacrifice."

[. . .]

As Confederate women discussed the war, they increasingly employed words such as *worth* and *gain*, scrutinizing their circumstances with a new attention to costs and benefits and with a new sense of self-interest born of what was for most elite southerners the novelty of privation and loss. Commitment to the Cause was not unbounded but had to be calculated in a balance sheet on which the burden of further hardship and the growing likelihood of ultimate defeat figured large. An elderly Virginia lady confessed her growing doubt about the whole Confederate experiment as she experienced the escalating trials of war. "I cannot help being unpatriotic – to feel a little selfish sometimes – and," she continued significantly, "regret our peace and comfort in the old Union." In October 1864 Sal Mabry of North Carolina asked her husband Robert, "what do you think of going back into the Union[?] dont you think it would be better than to have all our men killed[?] . . . I often think if I could make peace how soon I would have you and all my loved ones with me."

By the last years of the conflict, war with its hardships and shortages had begun

[†]Drew Gilpin Faust, *Mothers of Invention: Women of the Slaveholding South in the American Civil War* (Chapel Hill: University of North Carolina Press, 1996), pp. 238–47.

to nurture not nobility and sacrifice so much as a new selfishness, a novel awareness of individual needs and desires, of requirements for minimal personal survival, even if not happiness. In the Confederacy at large an emerging venality was evident in widespread speculation and extortion, problems that consumed considerable public attention, prompted state and national legislation, and won religious notice as the besetting sin of the South. Women were most often victims rather than perpetrators of these economic and moral crimes, however, for they participated in the market chiefly as consumers.

Women instead displayed their new self-absorption and self-interest in a growing reluctance to continue to yield their loved ones to the Confederate army. At the outset of the war, women had urged husbands and brothers into service, but by the later years of conflict quite a different attitude became evident. Even at the expiration of men's first terms of enlistment, as early as 1862 or 1863, many wives insisted that their husbands had already given enough to the Cause. As Mary Bell of North Carolina bluntly proclaimed to Alfred in July 1862, "I think you have done your share in this war." An initial romantic fascination with military heroism had quickly given way to a sobering recognition of war's dangers. Louisa Rice of Georgia wrote her husband, Zachariah, at the end of 1862 urging him to leave the army for a post that would shield him from conscription. "You have served long enough," she declared, "to rest awhile." Mary Williams Pugh, a refugee in Texas in the fall of 1862, warned her husband that both she and her slaves required his return. Not only had he "done enough now to satisfy yourself & everyone else," but she had borne his absence so "patiently and cheerfully," she calculated, "that surely now I deserve some reward." Pugh urged him either to hire a substitute or to take advantage of the October 1862 law exempting slave supervisors. "My good behavior now is all put on & will soon disappear unless I see something brighter ahead." The expectation of his imminent return, moreover, was the only cause of his slaves' "good behavior," she warned. "The truth is . . . you *must* come home." In Florida during the same year, Octavia Stephens urged her husband, Winston, to "give up now while you have life." In her view it was foolish to "talk of the defense of your home & country for you can not defend them, they are too far gone now so give up before it is too late." Losing the war and keeping her husband seemed to Tivie Stephens a far better bargain than losing both, but Winston would fight for another two years before fulfilling Octavia's worst fears.

Mounting draft calls prompted first reluctance then resistance from mothers, wives, and sisters. "We felt like clinging to Walter and holding him back," a Virginia woman explained. "I for one had lost my nerve. I was sick of war, sick of the butchery, the anguish . . . the fear." Emily Harris declared that she felt as much like fighting the men who kept her husband in uniform as she did the Yankees. In South Carolina, Margaret Easterling balanced the dictates of patriotism against her own desires and decided firmly in favor of the latter. With two sons in the army, she wrote Jefferson Davis, "I need not tell you of my devotion to my country, of the sacrifices I have made, and of the many more I am willing to make . . . But I want my oldest boy at home." Facing the conscription of her last son, Mary Scales wrote movingly and revealingly to the Confederate secretary of war. "I know my country needs all her children and I had thought I could submit to her requisitions. I have given her cause my prayers, my time, my means and my children but now the last lamb of the fold is to be taken, the mother and helpless woman triumph over the patriot."

[. . .]

In one sense the erosion of women's patriotism simply represented a reversion to conventional female concerns, an almost reactionary reassertion of the private and domestic and a rejection of the more public and political burdens women had been urged to assume. But at the same time, women's new perspectives involved an articulation of individual right and identity, of self-interest, that was strikingly modern in its implications. Their retreat from the public realm was fueled in considerable part by their recognition that in the Confederacy the public interest did not encompass their own, for it threatened to kill their loved ones, deprive them of life's basic necessities, and require them to manage recalcitrant, rebellious, and often frightening slaves. A nation that had acknowledged no legitimate female political voice had in crisis failed adequately to consider women's needs.

Before the war, women of the southern elite had regarded themselves as dependents within an organic social order in which female subordination was accepted in return for protection and support. Yet white men's wartime failure to provide women with either physical safety or basic subsistence cast this world and its social assumptions into question. Relationships of unchallenged status, of assumed superiority and inferiority, were transformed into what political theorists would call social relations of contract. Women came to regard their sacrifice and subordination as no longer inevitable but contingent on men's fulfillment of certain expectations. The notions of "virtual" political representation – which argued that women's interests would be protected by their men – had proved hollow indeed. Women began to acknowledge and defend their own interests apart from those of their families and their nation and to regard themselves as individuals possessing rights and legitimate desires, not just duties and obligations.

This warborn evolution in female self-perception parallels a much broader transformation in American political life, one that many scholars have designated as a shift during the early and middle years of the nineteenth century from republican to liberal political forms and values, as a replacement of virtue and community by faction and self-interest. The changing outlook of southern women in the course of the Civil War helps remind us of the psychological foundations of such a transformation, for women's shifting understanding of their larger social place arose from a newfound ability to perceive themselves as more than simply appendages to other, more important social actors.

In their recognition of individual needs and desires amidst all but unbearable emotional and even material deprivation, Confederate women discovered both new self-interest and new selves. It was not, however, as so many discussions of women and war would have it, that new achievements and new accomplishments – as nurses or teachers or plantation managers – yielded the basis for enhanced self-esteem; this new sense of self was based not in the experience of success but in desperation, in the fundamental need simply to survive. "Necessity," as Confederate women so often intoned, was in this sense truly "the mother of invention"; only "necessity," as Julia Davidson wrote her husband, John, could "make a different woman of me."

[. . .]

Put simply, upper-class southerners had a greater investment than their poorer countrywomen and -men in the system that had given them their superior status. For all their disillusionment with slavery, with Confederate leadership, and with their individual men, elite southern women clung to – even reasserted – lingering elements of privilege. Even when patriotism had been exhausted by war and even when the Confederacy had died, elite white women of the South held fast to the traditional hierarchical social and racial order that had defined their importance. Indeed, their disillusionment with the Confederacy arose chiefly from its failure to protect and preserve that privilege, to serve white female self-interest

In ladyhood southern women accepted gender subordination in exchange for continuing class and racial superiority. Yet their understanding of that bargain had changed profoundly in the course of the war. Their expectations for male protection had all but disappeared; their new sense of themselves, born in necessity rather than opportunity, made them sharply aware of both the dangers of dependence and the daunting demands of autonomy. Filled with doubts about both themselves and their men, elite southern women faced the postwar world with a new realism, a deep-seated bitterness, and a frightening sense of isolation. The social order they were determined to preserve offered them only the best of a bad bargain; the ideal of male strength and competence that had justified the paternalistic southern world had been proven mythical, and women had discovered little foundation in their own competence or effectiveness for trying to replace male power and authority with their own. In the face of the frightening reality of black emancipation, however, white women came to regard the rehabilitation of patriarchy as a bargain they were compelled to accept. The postwar commemoration of male courage and wartime achievement by the Daughters of the Confederacy, the Confederate Memorial Society, and other female celebrants of the Lost Cause represented women's effort to make what they regarded as necessary seem once again legitimate. If white men were once again to run the world, southern ladies would struggle to demonstrate the confidence in male superiority that would convince both themselves and others that such a social order was both natural and desirable.

ﭗ ﭗ ﭗ

Gary W. Gallagher

The Confederate War[†]

The Confederate populace waged a determined struggle for independence. No other segment of white American society has persisted in any endeavor so destructive of human and physical resources. Yet despite an unparalleled level of loss, Confederates often have been judged wanting in devotion to their cause. Scholars have described in abundant detail waning Confederate morale and have speculated at length about why white southerners did not resist longer. They have argued that political dissension, class strife pitting the yeomanry against planters, doubts about the morality of slavery, fears that God favored the North, the absence of a shared sense of purpose, and other factors explain why the Confederate experiment in rebellion failed. For more than half a century, the overriding scholarly question almost always has been "Why did the Confederacy collapse so soon?" Not only have scholars usually failed to place the Confederate resistance within a comparative context of broader American history, but they also too often have slighted or ignored entirely an equally important question, namely, "Why did so many Confederates fight for so long?" Until the second question receives the detailed attention long accorded the first, the history of the Confederacy will remain imperfectly understood.

Preoccupation with fissures within the wartime South arises from an understandable tendency to work backward from the war's outcome in search of explanations for Confederate failure. Historians begin with the fact that the North triumphed. Large and well-equipped Union forces remained in the field in April 1865. No apparent social upheavals rent northern communities as the armies played out the war's closing scenes at Appomattox, Durham Station, and elsewhere. After four years of conflict, the North seemed able to continue to fight the war and maintain social equilibrium, which has suggested to many historians a stronger northern will to win. What weaknesses in Confederate society, scholars have wondered, eroded southern will at a rate more rapid than that experienced in the North?

[. . .]

Desertion by Confederate soldiers has been a main beam supporting the lack-of-will edifice, but its strength may be more apparent than real. The presence of Union armies on southern soil generated a type of Confederate desertion unknown among Union soldiers – and one that did not necessarily indicate weak will or unhappiness with the Confederacy. In a letter representative of a large body of evidence, a Georgia soldier in the Army of Tennessee informed his wife in mid-July 1864 that "a great many Tennesseans and up [country] Georgians are leaving the army and say they are going back home . . . They know that their families are

[†]Gary W. Gallagher, *The Confederate War* (Cambridge, MA: Harvard University Press, 1997), pp. 17–18, 31–2, 55–8.

left behind at the mercy of the Yankees, and it is hard to bear." This man assured his wife that he and most of his comrades remained confident of final victory, but if the southern army retreated beyond his home county "and we were to pass on by you and the children, I could not say that I would not desert and try to get to you." Thousands of other Confederates left the ranks when they marched close to the areas where their families lived but later returned to their units. In her pioneering work on desertion, Ella Lonn estimated that 8,500 of 12,000 deserters from Virginia and nearly 9,000 of 24,000 from North Carolina rejoined the army. How should these men be categorized?

At the least, historians should avoid portraying Confederate desertion as a linear problem of constantly increasing gravity. A recent study of the Old Dominion described a bulge of desertions in 1862 that probably represented anger at implementation of the Conscription Act, the terms of which extended the service of thousands of men who originally had signed on for one year. After this initial wave, rates dropped off until the final months of the war. "Virginia's experience," concluded William A. Blair, "calls for modification of explanations of desertion as demonstrating a lack of will to fight or identity with the Confederate cause." Similarly, Kevin Conley Ruffner's examination of desertion in the 44th Virginia Infantry contradicted the image of a steadily mounting problem. Ruffner found that most deserters left the 44th during the early period of the war, "a product of the recruitment of men unsuited for military life." At the end of 1864, a time when many historians have argued that desertion swept unchecked through southern armies, the 44th "had a desertion rate of less than 3 percent of its effective strength." A recent comparative study of the 24th and 25th North Carolina Infantry regiments concluded that an "overwhelming majority" of each unit's initial volunteers performed steadfastly throughout the war. The 25th suffered a much higher overall rate of desertion among replacement troops, however, "because of the instability and poor quality of its company-grade command structure."

[. . .]

A fuller picture of how morale changed over time and across regions will yield a greater understanding of the Confederacy. There may have been generational differences between men and women reared during the bitter sectional debates of the late antebellum years and those who grew to maturity in less contentious times. It may be possible to sort out the hard-core deserters from those who returned to service after leaving the army, the bitter opponents of the Confederacy from those who expressed unhappiness with specific Confederate policies but still wanted southern independence.

Many historians have stressed material deprivation and class tensions fueled by a sense that wealthier people had access to more goods and sacrificed less than poorer Confederates. All too often, analysis has consisted of little more than applying a crude formula wherein increased privation equals growing disenchantment. This overlooks the fact that common suffering can produce greater resolve to oppose those causing the physical distress. By the end of 1863, prolonged resistance against an enemy with seemingly unlimited manpower and industrial capacity had created among many Confederates a sense of accomplishment against long odds and a determination to carry on the fight. As the pro-administration Richmond *Dispatch* proudly announced in April 1864, the Yankees, according to their own newspaper accounts, had sent more than two million men against the Confederacy, created a 600-ship navy, occupied much southern territory, and built an unparalleled industrial war machine – all "without producing the slightest disposition to succumb, or in the remotest degree shaking the firm and confident faith" of the Confederate people. Although the *Dispatch* attributed too little impact to the Union effort, its basic point merits close attention.

William Tecumseh Sherman, who scrutinized the Confederate nation as he prepared for a new military campaign in the spring of 1864, would not have disputed the *Dispatch*'s conclusions about the state of southern morale. The spectacle of white southerners still apparently devoted to winning independence after three years of hard conflict prompted a perceptive assessment by the North's master of psychological warfare. "The devils seem to have a determination that cannot but be admired," wrote Sherman to his wife on March 12, 1864. "No amount of poverty or adversity seems to shake their faith – niggers gone – wealth and luxury gone, money worthless, starvation in view within a period of two or three years, are causes enough to make the bravest tremble, yet I see no sign of let up – some few deserters – plenty tired of war, but the masses determined to fight it out." Sherman's subsequent actions and statements underscored his belief that severe measures would be necessary to break the dogged Confederate resistance.

Historians typically have emphasized only religion and guilt about slavery as nonmaterial factors that affected Confederate morale, portraying both as ultimately destructive. But what of the ideology and ideals, which bolstered Confederate will to varying degrees throughout the conflict, and the interplay between beliefs and material circumstances? James M. McPherson discussed these issues in his preliminary study of Confederate soldier motivation: "The concepts of southern nationalism, liberty, self-government, resistance to tyranny, and other ideological purposes . . . all have a rather abstract quality. But for many Confederate soldiers these abstractions took a concrete, visceral form: the defense of home and hearth against an invading enemy." Confederate definitions of freedom and liberty may not accord with modern ones, but they resonated at the time and helped keep men in the ranks and foster support behind the lines.

The relative importance of military and nonmilitary influences on fluctuations in morale has not been clearly defined. There has been a good deal of interest in how disaffection behind the lines promoted desertion and how the presence of deserters in turn exacerbated problems on the home front. Unfortunately, the ways in which campaigning armies hardened civilian will have garnered far less attention. Most scholars have assumed that northern incursions into the Confederacy dampened southern enthusiasm for the war. In fact, the Union army probably had the opposite effect on many Confederates, acting as a catalyst for muting grievances about issues such as the tax-in-kind, impressment, and the draft. When the question came down to accepting heavier economic burdens and greater governmental infringement on personal liberty or submitting to Yankee soldiers who had killed thousands of their men and wreaked havoc on their society, many Confederate civilians chose the former.

ဆ ဆ ဆ

Bruce Levine

Confederate Emancipation[†]

The Confederate military and political figures who took the lead in pushing for the arming and emancipating of slaves were . . . by no means hostile to slavery on principle. They certainly did not eagerly await its early demise. It is equally mistaken to believe that their purblind southern nationalism had led them to discard or devalue the interests of the planter class. Confederate nationalists they may have become, and haters of the Yankee-dominated Union they certainly were. But they had come to their iconoclastic proposals because they were able, sooner or later, to recognize unpleasant realities and to reformulate their plans in the light of those realities.

The combined efforts of Union armies and the slaves themselves, they saw, had driven the plantation system and the planters' government to the brink of destruction. If events continued to unfold in that way, the rest of the South's military-age male slaves would likely also be drawn into Union ranks. Thus reinforced, the enemy's forces would overwhelm their already outnumbered foes. Confederate military defeat would inevitably follow. The social and political consequences of such a defeat, Davis and his co-thinkers believed, would be disastrous for southern patriots generally but for slaveholders in particular. A militarily triumphant Republican government would surely make good its 1864 platform promise to complete the destruction of chattel slavery. "If we fail in the establishment of our independence," as one North Carolinian pointed out, "slavery is lost beyond the possibility of a doubt."

Bleak as the prospect of imposed emancipation seemed, moreover, it would only constitute the first step in the Union's postwar program. As experience along the Atlantic coast and in the lower Mississippi valley seemed to prove, Republicans would also confiscate southern farms and plantations and turn them over to their own supporters, black and white. Complete Yankee victory would mean our utter "robbery and spoliation and ruin," explained the Richmond *Sentinel*. If the Confederacy is conquered "all our property [will] be swept from us into the public coffers of the Yankees, or divided out in portions and rewards to a hireling soldiery."

The organization of political life and the distribution of civic liberties in the South would also change dramatically for the worse. The conquerors would wrench

---

[†]Bruce Levine, *Confederate Emancipation: Southern Plans to Free and Arm Slaves during the Civil War* (New York: Oxford University Press, 2005), pp. 93–5, 98, 143–6.

legislative, executive, and judicial power from the grasp of the region's traditional leaders (the planters) and place it instead into the hands of northern interlopers, southern white traitors, and – worst of all – the South's black former laborers and servants.

To those willing to arm and free slaves on the Confederacy's behalf, this apocalyptic vision of defeat's consequences justified even the most extreme sacrifices. "If Lincoln succeeds in arming our slaves against us," the Jackson *Mississippian* had warned in August of 1863, "he will succeed in making them our masters. He will reverse the social order of things at the South." Patrick Cleburne had begun his December 1863 memo by urging his fellow officers "to understand the meaning of subjugation before it is too late. We can give but a faint idea when we say it means the loss of all we now hold most sacred – slaves and all other personal property, lands, homesteads, liberty, justice, safety, pride, manhood" and acceptance of a world in which "our former slaves" will control us like a "secret police." Lose this war, Louisiana Governor Henry W. Allen warned his state's legislature in mid-January, and "your negroes will be made your equals, your lands will be declared confiscate, and you will become the slaves of the very hirelings who are now waging war upon you."

There was only one way to avoid this terrible fate, Cleburne, Davis, and company agreed. The Confederacy must deprive the Union of thousands of potential black soldiers and place them instead in the Confederate ranks. And – given the starkly displayed slave desire for freedom and the Union emancipation policy already in place – only a Confederate promise of manumission could conceivably induce slaves to risk death on the South's behalf.

But, claimed R. M. T. Hunter and many others, implementing such a policy was incompatible with the status quo antebellum. Of course it is, calmly replied Benjamin, Davis, and Lee; but antebellum life no longer provided the proper yardstick with which to measure current policy options. Prewar southern society was already irrevocably lost. Davis and his allies flatly denied that arming and freeing slaves was to abandon – indeed, was to betray – the cause of the plantation South. They did grant that the course they advocated involved large costs and real risks. They nonetheless insisted that their plan – and their plan alone – offered a way to salvage at least something of slavery from the Old South's wreckage.

[. . .]

Just how might Confederate emancipation differ from a Union-imposed version? Perhaps in its pacing, the Wilmington *North Carolinian* suggested. The Confederate government could choose to slow the emancipation process, perhaps drastically. "If, to secure our independence, the abolition of slavery be necessary," the editor volunteered, he for one was "prepared to adopt a conservative, safe and practical course in the matter." One such would be "the extinguishment of the institution after a series of years" so that "a century hence, it would be extinct in these Confederate States."

But ultimately, the key difference between Union and Confederate emancipation would be found in the nature of the legal status that would replace slavery. Judah

P. Benjamin's old college friend, Prof. Frederick A. Porcher, elaborated. Porcher was no less ardent a devotee of slavery than was Davis, Benjamin, or Lee. During the 1850s he had published a series of essays that movingly evoked the miseries and injustices borne by the Northern poor and the hypocritical justifications thereof favored by the Northern rich. They also enthused that the South had been spared such shameful abominations because paternalistic slavery had inculcated into masters an "unselfish consideration of the claims of others." Indeed, Porcher contended further, this "considerateness pervades our whole civilization" precisely because "our whole fabric of society is based upon slave institutions." So it had been, and so it would continue to be. "The fact of slavery is here," he asserted, "and a fact it must remain," not only in the short run, indeed, but "until the end of time." Porcher's secessionism grew directly out of his regard for southern distinctiveness. For the South to remain bound to the philosophically and culturally alien free states would be, he concluded, "under any circumstances" a mistake.

[. . .]

White Confederates' doubts that very many slaves would fight on their behalf were well-founded. Speculation about why slaves would refuse to cooperate accurately read both the mood and the calculations of the South's bondspeople. Word of Davis's initiative had spread among the black population through the slave grapevine and elicited an energetic discussion there, too. A freedman in Petersburg, Virginia, subsequently told a Northern writer how he had first reacted to the Confederate black-soldier plan. Like most prudent bondspeople, he had previously "never felt at liberty to speak my mind." But now, perhaps emboldened by the Confederacy's evident crisis, the man could contain himself no longer. "They asked me if I would fight for my country," he remembered. "I said, 'I have no country.'" Then "they said I should fight for my freedom." To which the man had retorted that "to gain my freedom" on their terms "I must fight to keep my wife and children slaves."

In early February 1865, Thomas Morris Chester, the African American correspondent for the Philadelphia *Press* who was traveling with Union troops in the Old Dominion, talked with Richmond-area blacks about the emerging Confederate policy. They had discussed the subject among themselves, Chester learned, and those deliberations had "rapidly spread throughout Virginia." In the process, tactical disagreements had emerged about how to respond to the expected offer. Only a loyalist handful would genuinely welcome the chance to serve their masters arms in hand. The "great majority" was thoroughly hostile to the Confederacy and was interested only in calculating how best to frustrate its plans. But therein lay the principal disagreement. Some thought it best to flee to Union lines rather than serve in gray uniforms. But "the more thoughtful" and "best informed bondmen and freemen," Chester reported, had settled upon a bolder and more ambitious strategy. They decided "that black men should promptly respond to the call of the Rebel chiefs, whenever it should be made, for them to take up arms." And then, when they found themselves in battle, black Confederate soldiers should "raise a shout for Abraham Lincoln and the Union" and, in alliance with Union troops on the field, "turn like uncaged tigers upon the rebel hordes."

Other expressions of slave opinion revealed strikingly similar sentiments and calculations at work. In early December 1864, William T. Sherman's troops were in eastern Georgia on their way to Savannah. The Union general and his entourage spoke with a group of older black men who had only recently obtained their freedom, and an officer recorded in his diary the conversation that ensued. Sherman told one of the freedmen that Jefferson Davis "was talking about arming the negroes." "Yes, Sir, we knows dat," the man replied. "Well," Sherman asked, "what'll you all do – will you fight against us?" "No, *Sir*," came the reply. "De day dey gives us arms, *dat day de war ends*!" The words according to the soldier diarist, were "eagerly spoken – and the rest [of them] as eagerly assented." About six weeks later, Union Gen. Alpheus S. Williams conversed with another group of freedmen outside Savannah. Williams asked one of these black men if they, too, had heard about plans to raise black Confederate army units. This man had also heard of them but, he assured the general, "Massa, they can't make us fight de Yankees, I habe heard de colored folks talk of it. They know'd all about it; dey'll turn the guns on the Rebs."

[. . .]

Other southern loyalists also acknowledged that slaves understood both what the North and South really stood for and which of them enjoyed the military advantage when – and acknowledged as well that slaves were making choices in the light of that knowledge. In early April 1865, Mississippi's governor heard that "our negroes are again stampeding" for fear of being pressed into the Confederate army because they "know *too well* on which side to *fight*." Some four year's earlier, South Carolina planter and Confederate official James Chesnut had queried some of his most trusted bondsmen about the matter and discovered (as his wife later recorded) that "they were keen to go in the army" if afterward they would receive their freedom and a bounty. But the readiness of 1861 had disappeared by November 1864, the Chesnuts discovered; "now they say coolly they don't want freedom if they have to fight for it." What accounted for this apparent change of heart? Simply the fact that they could now see a shorter and straighter route to freedom, could see that "they are pretty sure of having it anyway" when Union troops arrived. Why, then, take up arms precisely against those Union troops? A Confederate officer told of a slave named Jack who cautiously tried to explain that reasoning to a southern white physician. Jack told the doctor that he didn't want to fight. "But," the doctor prompted him, "you surely won't allow the Yankees to come here and rob your master and carry you and all the boys away for Yankee soldiers." "Tell you, massa, I knows nothing 'bout politics," Jack replied. "Why," urged the doctor, "if you become a [Confederate] soldier you'll be free. Surely you'd like to be a free man." "Dat's berry well, massa," Jack countered. "We niggers dat fight will be free, course; but you see, massa, if some ob us *don't* fight, we *all* be free, massa Lincum says."

8

Kate Masur

EMANCIPATION, RECONSTRUCTION, REDEMPTION

"Easily," the legendary black scholar W. E. B. Du Bois once wrote, "the most dramatic episode in American history was the sudden move to free four million black slaves." Appomattox had, after all, left unresolved, or opened up, questions that went to the heart of the American experience. How would a region steeped in the culture and economics of slavery make the transition to freedom? What, indeed, would "freedom" mean – and who would get to decide? How closely, in the end, would the realities of life in a reconstructed South align with the national ideals of democracy, liberty, and equality? The drama of emancipation and Reconstruction emerged in the impassioned, often fierce, battles waged among the various parties involved – from the freedpeople, to the former slaveholders (large and small), to common white folk who had never owned slaves, to a diverse range of actors up North – as all sought to leave their stamps on a malleable, post-slavery South.

If the course and outcome of Reconstruction were sharply contested, so, too, have been historical representations of the topic over the century-and-a-half since. In her opening essay, Kate Masur reviews what one historian long ago dubbed "the dark and bloody ground of Reconstruction historiography." Surveying a succession of interpretive schools – from the racially charged "Tragic Era" approach, to the more favorable "revisionist" depiction, to the more skeptical "post-revisionist" portrayal – Masur shows how closely the shifting currents of Reconstruction historiography have mingled with those of contemporary trends.

Reconstruction remains a lively field of historical research and debate. How did the freedpeople envision, and pursue, their freedom? How did Reconstruction-era contests over these aspirations play themselves out in the realms of work, politics, community life, and daily interaction? How close, at its peak, did Reconstruction come to fulfilling the promise of interracial democracy? What, ultimately, accounts for the defeat of Reconstruction? The selections for this chapter sample several recent treatments of one of the more explosive and pivotal developments in the story of Reconstruction: the engagement of African Americans on the field of southern politics.

Kate Masur, Assistant Professor of History at Northwestern University, works on issues of race and citizenship in nineteenth-century America. She is the author of *An Example for All the Land: Emancipation and the Struggle over Equality in Washington D.C.* (University of North Carolina Press, 2010). Before joining the faculty at Northwestern, she served as an assistant editor at the Freedmen and Southern Society Project at the University of Maryland where she co-edited *Freedom: A Documentary History of Emancipation, 1861–1867*, ser. 3, vol. 2: *Land and Labor, 1866–1867* (forthcoming from University of North Carolina Press).

If the Civil War had been shorter or less bitterly contested, the Confederacy's defeat might have been followed by an attempt to resume the status quo antebellum, complete with the enslavement of people of African descent and rule by a landed elite. But after four years of war – years during which some 620,000 soldiers died, thousands of people escaped slavery, the Union adopted emancipation as a war aim, and black men enlisted as soldiers – there would be no going back to the old order. The United States government faced questions shared by victors of other modern wars: Which policies would ensure the maintenance of peace? Was it necessary to punish the losers; and if so, which ones and how much? Such questions were complicated because the goal was not, as in other conflicts, to secure the sovereignty of a separate nation but, rather, to bring the defeated territory back into the national fold. How could such reintegration be accomplished in a country historically committed to a weak national government? Complex questions were rendered still more difficult by the paramount question of the era: What constituted freedom for former slaves, and how could such freedom be guaranteed?

The answers depended not only on federal government policies but also on the actions of southerners, who were divided among themselves along lines of class, region, and race. Faced with the material devastation of war and an immense loss in human property, the southern elite recognized the need for considerable "reconstruction" – from the reinvigoration of staple agriculture to the rebuilding of economic infrastructure. Yet few would concede that Confederate surrender should mean significant change in their region's social, economic, or racial order. Poorer whites, particularly in areas where Unionism had flourished during the war, saw in the Confederacy's defeat the chance to challenge traditional planter dominance. Freedpeople, for their part, sought to reunite with lost kin, establish lives outside the purview of former owners, and become full-fledged members of the polity. Northerners, black and white, migrated to the South in search of economic and political opportunities, and they too contributed to the messy and often violent struggle to define the post-bellum South.

Given the contentiousness of the period, and its significance in southern and national history, it is not surprising that historians have examined Reconstruction from many angles. They have explored federal policy, as well as changing southern labor relations, family forms, and gender roles. They have investigated racial segregation and changes in landholding and business patterns of the southern economic elite. Among the most exciting and fruitful avenues of recent inquiry concern how southern African American men, the vast majority of them former slaves, became voters, what their political power meant, and what kind of political culture emerged in the postwar South. The entry of black men into politics was arguably the defining aspect of that era's history and, as such, it also makes a useful lens for understanding historians' changing approaches to the period as a whole.

The enfranchisement of black men in the former Confederacy began with an epic political conflict in Washington DC. When the war ended in the spring of 1865, President Andrew Johnson took charge of federal Reconstruction policy. Johnson, a man of humble origins who became president after Lincoln's assassination in April 1865, was a former Democrat and wartime Unionist from Tennessee. Although hostile to the southern ruling class, he was also a vehement racist who opposed voting rights and other forms of legal equality for people of African descent. During presidential Reconstruction, Johnson restored full economic and political rights to virtually all former Confederates who sought them, emboldening white southerners to keep such men in high political office and to unleash repressive action against freedpeople.

Republican congressmen and their constituents saw such developments as evidence that southern whites remained defiant, and they laid considerable blame on Johnson's lenient policies. The confrontation between Congress and the president intensified during 1866, when Johnson opposed several Reconstruction bills that congressional Republicans considered quite moderate. Congressional Republicans won a resounding victory in the fall 1866 mid-term election, giving them sufficient power to chart their own course for Reconstruction policy, regardless of the president's wishes. Thus, in the spring of 1867, a tenuous coalition of radical and moderate Republicans in Congress passed the Reconstruction Act, a reflection of their vision of how to place the former Confederate states on a new political footing and readmit them to the Union.

The Reconstruction Act placed the states of the former Confederacy under military control while their residents created new constitutions. Black and white men, enfranchised on an equal footing, must elect delegates to the mandatory constitutional conventions. The new state constitutions must implement universal manhood suffrage, ratify the Fourteenth Amendment, and receive voters' approval. The Reconstruction Act represented the Republican coalition's attempt to balance a mandate for significant change in southern politics with attention to the American tradition of state sovereignty and, in particular, states' authority over voting rights. Though moderate from a constitutional perspective, the act's mandate for black men's enfranchisement promised to transform dramatically the southern political, economic, and racial order.

Historians have always recognized, as contemporaries did, that the enfranchisement of black men in the South was an epic change. But before the second half of the twentieth century, most professional historians interpreted that change as an unmitigated disaster. Probably the most important among them was renowned Columbia University professor William A. Dunning, who – along with a stable of graduate student advisees – interpreted congressional Reconstruction and black men's voting rights as a tragedy for the South. They believed, as Eric Foner put it in 1988, that "childlike blacks . . . were unprepared for freedom and incapable of properly exercising the political rights Northerners had thrust upon them." Such scholars depicted corrupt southern Republican governments formed by avaricious northern "carpetbaggers," scheming and traitorous southern white "scalawags," and ignorant "Negroes." Democratic "Redeemers" were, in their telling, heroes who rescued the South from the fiasco of corrupt government, driving out the Republicans and reestablishing order and prosperity. The "Dunning School" of Reconstruction history meshed with the popular culture of the Jim Crow era, including most prominently the epic Hollywood blockbuster, *Birth of a Nation* (1915), which portrayed the Ku Klux Klan heroically restoring white supremacy and national peace. Such interpretations of Reconstruction helped legitimate the racially repressive order of early twentieth-century America.

African American scholar W. E. B. Du Bois was the most prominent early critic of the Dunning School. Du Bois began writing about Reconstruction at the end of the nineteenth century and, in a 1910 article provocatively titled "Reconstruction and Its Benefits," argued that black men's voting rights had not brought about unusually corrupt governments, that southern African Americans were no more venal than anyone else, and that federal policies during the period had been reasonable rather than extreme. In the same era, black historian Alrutheus A. Taylor's studies of African Americans in post-emancipation South Carolina, Virginia, and Tennessee also disputed Dunningite caricatures of African American politicians and voters. At the end of his wide-ranging 1935 reinterpretation of the period, *Black Reconstruction in America,* Du Bois argued that the field of Reconstruction history was "devastated by passion and belief" and called for a more "scientific" approach to the period.[1] He demanded that historians look beyond sources generated by white southerners who had adamantly opposed black men's enfranchisement, to other documents, heretofore ignored or deemed untrustworthy, including slave narratives and government reports.

By the 1930s, some white historians were also challenging the Dunning School, primarily through interpretations that stressed economic interests and class conflict. Historian Howard Beale, for example, argued that Reconstruction was fundamentally about opening the South to capitalism and that the southern Democratic onslaught represented above all the consolidation of power by a new southern elite seeking to marginalize African Americans and poor whites alike.[2]

By the end of the 1930s, then, historians such as Du Bois, Taylor, and Beale had set the stage for the wholesale scholarly reinterpretation of Reconstruction that began after the Second World War. In the midst of growing attacks on the Jim Crow order, increasing numbers of historians took aim at the Dunningites. They showed that African Americans' political power had not been nearly so imposing as claimed by redeemers of the era and their latter-day apologists. They also began to complicate heretofore one-dimensional portraits of "carpetbaggers" and "scalawags." Northern migrants emerged as variegated figures, at turns pragmatic, idealistic, and corrupt, while white yeomen became a class of southern dissenters who unsuccessfully fought for economic policies favorable to small landholders. Congressional Republicans now appeared not as the cabal of radicals described by the Dunningites but rather as a tenuous coalition in considerable disarray over southern policy and ambivalent about how much to support its southern wing and how forcefully to insist on continued federal intervention in states' affairs.

Historians debated the significance of the Freedmen's Bureau, a short-lived federal agency designed to oversee the transition from slavery to free labor in the South. For Dunningites the bureau had exemplified misguided northern efforts to intervene in southern labor relations. Some historians now argued that the bureau was a useful but perpetually underfunded pioneer of federal poverty policy, while others insisted that its agents promulgated an oppressive vision of "free labor" that served planters better than it did freedpeople.

So dramatic was the unseating of the Dunning School consensus that, by the mid-1960s, historians were arguing not over whether northern Republicans had intervened too much in the South but whether they had done as much as possible to secure the era's most expansive promises of racial equality. "Post-revisionists" of the 1960s and 1970s, such as Louis Gerteis and Michael Les Benedict, emphasized the Republicans' tentative, conservative sides. Party leaders, they noted, opposed breaking up large plantations or redistributing southern land on more equal terms – reforms that might have empowered freedpeople and poor whites far more than could the right to vote on its own. They showed that leading Republicans often proved more committed to stability and capitalist development in the South than to the well-being of freedpeople, and that Reconstruction's three constitutional amendments were designed not so much to expand the power of the federal government as to maintain the traditional balance of power between the states and the US government.[3]

In keeping with a growing interest in the histories of everyday people – sometimes called the "new social history" – some historians now focused on how southern African Americans' lives changed in the wake of emancipation. In the mid-1960s, John Hope Franklin observed that historians still understood very little about how former slaves made the transition to freedom, from what backgrounds black leaders emerged, what political programs African Americans supported, and what difference the entrance of black people into politics made.[4] Historians now embarked on biographies of Reconstruction-era black leaders, as well as state studies of the impact of African Americans in politics. "Community studies" also explored the post-emancipation development of black institutions, including churches, schools, voluntary associations, labor unions, families, and neighborhoods. Over time, historians began to emphasize conflicts as well as cooperation in African-American communities, which they increasingly saw as divided along lines of wealth, status, gender, religious denomination, and place of origin. Although community studies were often little concerned with formal politics, they were a direct rejoinder to the Dunningite conception of freedpeople and black leaders as passive and unresourceful.

New questions about the lives of everyday people pointed historians to heretofore unused sources, including labor contracts and account books, from which they could discover how the war and emancipation shaped family and labor relations. Historians documented considerable fluidity in labor relations in the years following emancipation. Freedpeople sought to maximize their control over their own labor and their families' time, while planters strove to keep their labor force dependent and immobilized. One compromise was sharecropping, an arrangement in which landless farmers paid for rented land with a "share" of the crop while retaining a significant measure of control over how and when they and their family members labored. Historians also explored how the era's upheavals pushed people to question, and sometimes remake, traditional gender roles. With so many men killed or wounded in the war, elite white women of the South had opportunities to cultivate new kinds of independence, from plantation management, to migration to cities, to teaching and other professional work. Meanwhile, freedpeople sought to reconstitute family relationships severed by slavery, and to rebuild kinship networks in freedom. To the frustration of employers, freedwomen insisted on devoting more time to childcare and subsistence farming – tasks that benefited their own families – and less to augmenting the employer's harvest. Some historians saw that change as evidence that freed families aspired to conventional visions of "separate spheres" for men and women; others viewed it as evidence of a determination to keep women away from predatory male employers; and still others emphasized that women's household production generated income that might make it possible for families to purchase land.

Historians of Reconstruction since the 1950s thus reoriented the field in three major ways. First, using new sources, and putting known sources to new uses, they wrote more thorough and objective accounts of the period. Second, they opened to investigation new sides of the story, looking more closely at everyday people to learn how life changed in the South amid the end of slavery and the devastation of the Civil War. Third, they changed the moral valence of the historical literature, replacing the Dunning School's deep revulsion against black men's enfranchisement with more nuanced accounts, premised on egalitarian and anti-racist assumptions.

Eric Foner's monumental 1988 study, *Reconstruction: America's Unfinished Revolution*, synthesized many revisionist themes, placing particular emphasis on the role of African Americans in postwar politics. Foner also explored the relationship between Reconstruction and the expansion of industrial capitalism, both North and South. His book was more than simply a synthesis, however. Foner argued that the entry of black men into electoral politics was crucial to the story of American emancipation. In the following extract from this now classic overview, Foner explains how African Americans became increasingly assertive in politics after enfranchisement in 1867. Reflecting a continuing effort to refute the Dunningite vision of pernicious "Negro rule," the author emphasizes that even at the peak of black political power, African Americans rarely held state-wide office, and only South Carolina had a black majority in its state legislature. Yet Foner also shows that the election of black and white Republicans to crucial local offices, such as sheriff and tax collector, had a great impact on the lives of everyday southerners. Once in office, Republicans pursued policies and practices that favored poor southerners far more than past regimes ever had. Under Republican rule, state governments created many of the South's first public schools systems, taxed land more heavily than personal property, and strove for impartial administration of justice.

Some historians who noticed African Americans' remarkable commitment to formal politics in the wake of emancipation became interested in precisely how freedpeople mobilized for politics so quickly and effectively. In *The Work of Reconstruction: From Slave to Wage Laborer in South Carolina, 1860–1870*, Julie Saville examines how freedpeople's visions of labor, family, community, and politics coincided in post-emancipation South Carolina. In the selection printed here, she argues that freed men and women built political associations upon existing networks of kin and community. Viewing "political discipline" as "a community affair," she shows how people exerted pressure on one another to mobilize, to vote – and to vote Republican. Saville unearths a political world very different from our own. Ballots, or "tickets," revealed a voters' choice for all to see, and the act of voting was often accompanied by military drills and the threat of violence, by freedpeople, by their opponents, or by both.

Local studies such as Saville's, which emphasize freedpeople's everyday politics and the inseparability of politics and violence, opened the way for a sweeping look at rural southern black politics across most of the nineteenth century – Steven Hahn's *A Nation under Our Feet: Black Political Struggles in the Rural South from Slavery to the Great Migration*. Like Foner and Saville, Hahn portrays a world in which African Americans' political power was locally meaningful. Indeed, Hahn cautions that historians' determination to debunk the "Negro rule" stereotype must not blind them to the fact that "Radical Reconstruction occasioned a massive transfer of power at the state and local levels." Hahn also develops the argument, suggested by Saville, that politics and violence were inseparable in the postwar South. In his selection on the backlash against black enfranchisement and the southern Republican party, Hahn demonstrates that conflagrations often called "riots" by contemporaries and historians were, in fact, organized campaigns of violence by whites against African Americans. The "Camilla riot" of 1868, described here, is but one example of how both Republicans and Democrats entered electoral politics heavily armed. Whites, often with superior arms and the force of the Democratic party behind them, typically prevailed. The increasing strength of white "paramilitary politics" during the 1870s, coupled with the United States government's growing refusal to defend Republican state governments in the South, set the stage for the contested elections of 1876, and the federal government's official abandonment of Reconstruction.

After violent and closely fought contests that fall, state election results remained contested in South Carolina and Louisiana, and presidential election results unclear in those states and in Florida. It was up to Congress to resolve the confusion. After complex negotiations involving businessmen and members of both parties, Republican candidate Rutherford B. Hayes gained the presidency. Weeks after becoming president, Hayes ordered US soldiers away from their posts defending Republican state governments in Louisiana and South Carolina, effectively handing the contested gubernatorial elections to the Democrats. As Hahn suggests, the South was not the only place where violence saturated politics or where governments used force to ensure victories for the economic elite. The army's disengagement from the South allowed it greater opportunities for deployment in other regions – from the West, where it fought Native Americans to clear the way for railroads and white settlement, to the North, where it stymied laborers' strikes for higher pay, better working conditions, and the right to organize.

Although Hahn highlights the resolution of the 1876 election as an important moment of transition, historians emphasizing social history and local heterogeneity have questioned whether it is useful to "end" Reconstruction there. It is clear that many of the broad phenomena unleashed by the Civil War – the swift penetration of capitalism into the South, the development of southern agriculture on a free labor basis, the "reconstruction" of southern households in new economic conditions – continued almost regardless of whether federal troops remained posted in southern state capitals or whether Democrats or Republicans controlled the presidency. Even in politics, 1877 did not mark the end of black voting or of the southern Republican party. To the contrary, particularly in hill country regions where farms were of modest size and black populations relatively small, bi-racial political coalitions continued to challenge Democratic dominance into the 1890s. Perhaps Reconstruction ended in the mid-1890s, with the defeat of Populism and consolidation of the one-party Democratic South. Perhaps it continues to this day, as some historians have argued, since the promises of equality and democracy remained unfulfilled. Or maybe it is most useful to define the period more conventionally – ending around 1880 – so as to demarcate a special period of economic, political, and social transformation. When did Reconstruction end? The answer depends on where one looks. And we know now that there are many places to look: local politics, families, communities, labor, the states, and the federal government. In such a rich field of inquiry, many more questions remained to be explored.

NOTES

1. W. E. B. Du Bois, *Black Reconstruction in America* (New York: Atheneum, 1992 [orig. 1935]), p. 725. Alrutheus A. Taylor, *The Negro in South Carolina during the Reconstruction* (Washington DC: The Association for the Study of Negro Life and History, 1924); Alrutheus A. Taylor, *The Negro in the Reconstruction of Virginia* (Washington DC: The Association for the Study of Negro Life and History, 1926); Alrutheus A. Taylor, *The Negro in Tennessee, 1865–1880* (Washington DC: The Associated Publishers, 1941).
2. Howard K. Beale, *The Critical Year: A Study of Andrew Johnson and Reconstruction* (New York: Harcourt, Brace, & Co., 1930).
3. Louis S. Gerteis, *From Contraband to Freedman: Federal Policy toward Southern Blacks, 1861–1865* (Westport: Greenwood Press, 1973); Michael Les Benedict, *A Compromise of Principle: Congressional Republicans and Reconstruction, 1863–1869* (New York: W. W. Norton, 1974).
4. John Hope Franklin, "Reconstruction and the Negro," in Harold M. Hyman, ed., *New Frontiers of the American Reconstruction* (Urbana: University of Illinois Press, 1966), pp. 59–76.

* * *

FURTHER READING

Benedict, Michael Les, *A Compromise of Principle: Congressional Republicans and Reconstruction, 1863–1869* (New York: W. W. Norton, 1974).

Brown, Thomas J., ed., *Reconstructions: New Perspectives on Postbellum America* (New York: Oxford University Press, 2006).

Du Bois, W. E. B., *Black Reconstruction in America, 1860–1880* (New York: Atheneum, 1992 [orig. 1935]).

Edwards, Laura F., *Gendered Strife and Confusion: The Political Culture of Reconstruction* (Urbana: University of Illinois Press, 1997).

Fields, Barbara Jeanne, *Slavery and Freedom on the Middle Ground: Maryland during the Nineteenth Century* (New Haven: Yale University Press, 1985).

Frankel, Noralee, *Freedom's Women: Black Women and Families in Civil War Era Mississippi* (Bloomington: Indiana University Press, 1999).

Gillette, William, *Retreat from Reconstruction, 1869–1879* (Baton Rouge: Louisiana State University Press, 1979).

Hahn, Steven, Steven F. Miller, Susan E. O'Donovan, John C. Rodrigue, and Leslie S. Rowland, eds., *Freedom: A Documentary History of Emancipation, 1861–1867*, Series 3, Volume 1: *Land and Labor, 1865* (Chapel Hill: University of North Carolina Press, 2008).

Holt, Thomas C., *Black over White: Negro Political Leadership in South Carolina during Reconstruction* (Urbana: University of Illinois Press, 1977).

Litwack, Leon F., *Been in the Storm So Long: The Aftermath of Slavery* (New York: Knopf, 1979).

McKitrick, Eric L., *Andrew Johnson and Reconstruction* (Chicago: University of Chicago Press, 1960).

* * *

Eric Foner

Reconstruction[†]

Initially . . . blacks stood aside when the political "loaves and fishes" were divided up – not only because white Republicans so desperately coveted office, but because many black leaders did not wish to embarrass their party, heighten internal contention, or lend credence to Democratic charges of "black supremacy." Georgia blacks "went from door to door in the 'negro belt'" seeking white Republican candidates, and in North Carolina, James H. Harris, fearing his selection "would damage the party at the North," declined a Congressional nomination. Others deemed themselves unqualified for office ("I refused to run because I knew nothing about what was needed to be done," Georgia schoolteacher Houston H. Holloway later recalled of his decision to refuse a legislative nomination). Not all blacks, of course, proved so retiring . . . In South Carolina, the Northern-born in particular insisted that blacks must be "admitted to a full participation in the control of affairs." Over white opposition, they placed one of their own, Benjamin F. Randolph, at the head of the state Republican committee in 1868. Even here, however, most blacks feared doing "anything that would injure the party." Francis L. Cardozo

---

[†] Eric Foner, *Reconstruction: America's Unfinished Revolution, 1863–1877* (New York: Harper & Row, 1988), pp. 351–6, 362–3.

(boosted for the lieutenant governorship) and Martin R. Delany (promoted for a Congressional seat) declined to run in 1868, citing the need for "the greatest possible discretion and prudence," and the legislature's lower house, which contained a black majority, chose white scalawag Franklin J. Moses, Jr., as Speaker over black carpetbagger Robert B. Elliott.

From the top of the political order to the bottom, blacks initially received a lower share of offices than their proportion of the party's electorate warranted. Sixteen blacks sat in Congress during Reconstruction, but of these only three served in the Forty-First Congress (which met from 1869 to 1871). Hiram Revels of Mississippi, a North Carolina-born minister and educator, in February 1870 became the first black to serve in the United States Senate. In the House sat freeborn South Carolina barber Joseph H. Rainey and Jefferson Long, a Georgia freedman elected to the two-month short term of 1871 . . . In the Forty-Second Congress, the black component rose to five, two of whom, however, spent much of their time fending off charges of election irregularities and were eventually unseated.

Nor were blacks well-represented at the highest levels of state government. In five states – Texas, North Carolina, Alabama, Georgia, and Virginia – none held a major office during Reconstruction. Philadelphia-born missionary and educator Jonathan C. Gibbs was the only black to win a major post in Florida, serving as secretary of state from 1868 to 1872 and then as superintendent of education. Blacks came to exercise far greater power in Mississippi and South Carolina, but here, too, whites initially all but monopolized statewide positions. In Mississippi, Secretary of State James Lynch was, at first, the only black state official, and until 1870, Secretary of State Francis L. Cardozo was his lone South Carolina counterpart. Only in Louisiana did blacks hold more than one major position from the beginning of Republican rule. In 1868, Oscar J. Dunn became lieutenant governor and wealthy free sugar planter Antoine Dubuclet state treasurer, a post he retained until 1877.

It did not take long for black leaders to become dissatisfied with the role of junior partners in the Republican coalition. Especially in states with large black populations, they increasingly demanded "a fair proportion of the offices" and began to assume a larger role in party affairs. The results were most dramatic in South Carolina, where in 1870 black leaders, as the result of a concerted campaign for greater power, received half the eight executive offices, elected three Congressmen, and placed Jonathan J. Wright on the state supreme court, the only black in any state to hold this position during Reconstruction. In Mississippi, they mobilized effectively against Governor Alcorn. "The complexion of political affairs in our State perceptibly *darkens*," a white Mississippi Republican remarked in 1872; the following year, blacks engineered the replacement of Alcorn's handpicked successor, Ridgely Powers, by Adelbert Ames and won half the statewide offices for themselves. Arkansas in 1872 elected its first black state officials; Superintendent of Education Joseph C. Corbin, a college-educated editor from Ohio, and Commissioner of Public Works James T. White, a minister from Indiana.

By the end of Reconstruction, eighteen blacks had served as lieutenant governor, treasurer, superintendent of education, or secretary of state.

[. . .]

It is difficult to gauge precisely how much power these men enjoyed. During Reconstruction more blacks served in the essentially ceremonial office of secretary of state than any other post, and by and large, the most important political decisions in every state were made by whites. On the other hand, the four black superintendents of education exerted a real influence on the new school systems, and black lieutenant governors presided over state senates and exercised gubernatorial powers when their chief executives were ill or out of the state. In December 1872, P. B. S. Pinchback became the only black governor in American history when he succeeded Henry C. Warmoth, who had been suspended as a result of impeachment proceedings.

A similar pattern of initial underrepresentation, followed in some states by growing black influence, appeared in state legislatures.

[. . .]

Despite the overall pattern of white political control, the fact that well over 600 blacks served as legislators – the large majority, except in Louisiana and Virginia, former slaves – represented a stunning departure in American politics. Moreover, because of the black population's geographical concentration and the reluctance of many scalawags to vote for black candidates, nearly all these lawmakers hailed from plantation counties, home of the wealthiest and, before the war, most powerful Southerners. The spectacle of former slaves representing the lowcountry rice kingdom or the domain of Natchez cotton nabobs epitomized the political revolution wrought by Reconstruction.

An equally remarkable transformation occurred at the local level, where the decisions of public officials directly affected daily life and the distribution of power. Although the structure of government varied from state to state, justices of the peace generally ruled on minor criminal offenses as well as a majority of civil cases, while county commissioners established tax rates, controlled local appropriations, and administered poor relief, and sheriffs enforced the law, selected trial jurors, and carried out foreclosures and public sales of land. Such officials, in the words of an Alabama lawyer, dealt with "the practical rights of the people . . . our 'business and lives.'" In the antebellum South, these positions had been monopolized by local elites, and the prospect of Republicans, whether former slaves or whites of modest wealth, occupying them alarmed the old establishment even more than their loss of statewide control. Howell Cobb said he could tolerate freedmen sitting in the Georgia legislature, "but when it comes to the home municipal government – all the blacks who vote against my ticket shall walk the plank."

Although the largest number served in South Carolina, Louisiana, and Mississippi, and the fewest in Florida, Georgia, and Alabama, no state lacked its black local officials. A handful held the office of mayor . . . A far larger number served on city and town councils in communities from Richmond to Houston. The nation's capital itself elected two black aldermen in 1868. Some of the South's most important cities, and many towns of lesser note, became centers of black political power during Reconstruction. Republicans controlled the major rail and industrial center of Petersburg from 1870 to 1874, and blacks held posts ranging from councilman to deputy customs collector and overseer of the poor. Nashville's council was about one third black, and Little Rock's at times had a black majority. Black aldermen were even elected in predominantly white upcountry Republican communities like Rutherfordton, North Carolina, and Knoxville and Maryville in East Tennessee.

In virtually every county with a sizable black population, blacks served in at least some local office during Reconstruction. Atop the pyramid of local power stood the sheriff, described by one Mississippi politico as "the best paying office in the state," with annual salary and fees often amounting to thousands of dollars. In most Republican counties the post remained in white hands throughout Reconstruction, partly because black aspirants found it nearly impossible to post the bond required to assume office. But as time went on, black sheriffs appeared in many plantation counties. Eventually, nineteen held the office in Louisiana, and fifteen in Mississippi (where over one third of the black population lived in counties that elected black sheriffs). Blacks in increasing numbers also assumed such powerful offices as county supervisor and tax collector, especially in states where these posts were elective. By 1871, former slaves had taken control of the boards of supervisors throughout the Mississippi black belt. Most local black officials served in lesser posts like school board member, election commissioner, and justice of the peace. Yet even these positions, as former Alabama Governor Patton remarked, were "of considerable importance to the people."

[. . .]

The presence of sympathetic Republican officials, whether black or white, made a real difference in the freedmen's day-to-day lives. Many took an active interest in improving blacks' neighborhoods and securing them a fair share of jobs on municipal construction projects. "They look upon me as a protector," wrote the white mayor of Salisbury, North Carolina, "and not in vain . . . The colored men placed me here and how could I do otherwise than to befriend them." In Louisiana, the state employed blacks, whites, and Chinese to work repairing the levees, and, in a departure from traditional practice, all received the same wages. As the chief engineer reported, "our 'Cadian friends were a little disgusted at not being allowed double (colored) wages, and the Chinamen were astonished at being allowed as much and the American citizens of African descent were delighted at being 'par.'"

To those accustomed to experiencing the law as little more than an instrument of oppression, moreover, it seemed particularly important that the machinery of Southern law enforcement now fell into Republican hands. Tallahassee and Little

Rock chose black chiefs of police, and New Orleans and Vicksburg had black captains empowered to give orders to whites on the force. By 1870, hundreds of blacks were serving as city policemen and rural constables . . . In the courts, defendants now frequently confronted black magistrates and justices of the peace, and racially integrated juries. One white lawyer observed that being compelled to address blacks as "gentlemen of the jury" was "the severest blow I have felt."

Throughout Reconstruction, planters complained it was impossible to obtain convictions in cases of theft and that in contract disputes, "justice is generally administered solely in the interest of the laborer." Nor could vagrancy laws be used, as they had been during Presidential Reconstruction, to coerce freedmen into signing labor contracts. "There is a vagrant law on our statute books . . .," observed an Alabama newspaper in 1870, "but it is a dead letter because those who are charged with its enforcement are indebted to the vagrant vote for their offices." Black criminals, in fact, did not commonly walk away from Reconstruction courts scot-free. Indeed, as frequent victims of violence, blacks had a vested interest in effective law enforcement; they merely demanded that officials, in the words of one petition, "rise above existing prejudices and administer justice with . . . an even hand." Yet this basic notion of equal justice challenged deeply rooted traditions of Southern jurisprudence. Republican jurors and magistrates now treated black testimony with respect, the state attempted to punish offenses by whites against blacks, and minor transgressions did not receive the harsh penalties of Presidential Reconstruction.

ҩ ҩ ҩ

Julie Saville

The Work of Reconstruction[†]

With an assurance variously remarkable or distressing to their contemporaries, ex-slaves rallied to political life. Registration tallies compiled in the Second Military District's office of civil affairs in Charleston suggest the successes of the unprecedented canvassing. By mid-November 1867, nearly ninety percent of the state's eligible black electorate had registered to vote in the referendum on the constitutional convention.

[. . .]

Tantalizing puzzles surround ex-slaves' broad political participation. People largely bereft of animal transport showed up at meetings, and at registration and election sites. Men, most of whom could neither read nor write, and the few

[†]Julie Saville, *The Work of Reconstruction: From Slave to Wage Laborer in South Carolina, 1860–1870* (New York: Cambridge University Press, 1996), pp. 166–77.

who could decipher print but not script, cast written ballots in large numbers. Moreover, these rank-and-file Republicans met and registered and voted in explicit opposition to a more mobile, literate electorate composed in bulk of their employers. Disparities of power did not determine the disposition of ex-slaves' political behavior. The forging of their political courage began outside the arena of formal politics.

The social fabric of popular Republican clubs wove together threads of association that originated outside party organizations. Women and men, young and old poured into public meetings called in the wake of the Reconstruction Acts. Between fifteen hundred and two thousand men, women, and children attended a mid-April 1867 Republican rally in Beaufort called to "ratify" the platform adopted in Charleston the previous month. Most probably arrived aboard the steamers provided by the meeting's organizers. When word reached outlying plantations that people were being summoned to Beaufort "by the order of the Government to vote for Mr. Lincoln's son," rare was the man or woman willing to be left behind. Skiffs, carts, and "every mode of transportation which the wit of man could devise" were pressed into service. Even those for whom the process was still hazy found it worthwhile to seize the closest of human, animal, and waterborne resources within reach in order to vote. Keen popular interest expanded the transportation arrangements that carried people to the first public meeting whose size approached earlier gatherings in Charleston.

Curiosity knew no bounds of age or sex when speakers or convention candidates made an appearance . . . Rallies on behalf of candidates for the constitutional convention kindled anew freedpeople's expectations that rights withheld since the conclusion of the war would soon be gained. Work halted when the arrival of "any person known to be in sympathy with the Republican party and the North" suggested that hoped-for changes might be at hand. Planter Augustus Shoolbred complained during campaigning for the constitutional convention on the Santee in November 1867, that the region's rice workers "are easily led astray & imposed upon by any one (especially of their own color) encouraging this hope [of rights to be gained] & they eagerly run off to any call for a public meeting however unauthorized in total disregard of their contracts, keeping the labor uncontrolable [sic] at best; constantly disorganized."

Freedpeople's widely shared sense that emancipation was incomplete, compromised, or perhaps betrayed outright ensured spokesmen for a new order an eager and attentive audience.

[. . .]

Multiple social identities intertwined in the neighborhood clubs that flowered during "registration summer," where compounded social ties made for strong alliances. Members regarded their associations as perpetual, more like lineages than leagues. In July 1867, Wesley Staggers, an ex-slave soldier who had organized a military company on Fenwick's Island, "positively refused" a provost marshal's order to disband an organization that, a planter had charged, promoted "[c]onduct tending to disorganize labor." According to the officer, Staggers insisted that members "were sworn into service for life," and that he "would stick by them until compelled to break up, by force of arms." A fellow society captain, Monroe McDowell, reportedly reinforced Staggers's stand, insisting that the company "was formed for life" and that he "*would* stick by it." Neighborhood radical clubs linked captains, brothers, cousins, friends, church members, "fellow servants," and neighbors for lifetime projects.

Club members shared overlapping social attachments, woven from ties of marriage, kinship, common workplace, and close residence. A rich realm of informal political power therefore shaped the elaboration of formally political roles. Gossip, ridicule, nonlethal assault, and regulated vandalism were among the means by which a laboring community kept its voters faithful to Union League principles.

To enforce political loyalty, neighborhoods drove their hardest bargains with the currency of social support. Social isolation and humiliation had a value greater than money dues in sustaining large league memberships among people for whom cash was ever short. Church members refused to help bury a man who had voted the Democratic ticket; neighbors abducted and subjected to "all manner of indignities" short of lasting physical injury a fellow society member who quit attending Loyal League meetings.

Voting was too important a matter to be entrusted only to the enfranchised. Women guarded muskets brought to defend public meetings against attack. Wives and lovers wielded sanctions of bed and board on behalf of political action . . . Women and men alike rallied to Henry McNeal Turner's appeal to "save their Congressional districts from the wicked designs of men who are trying to prevent our people from registering." In the summer of 1867, employing a pattern of parallel gender organization widespread among freedpeople, freed women and men in central Georgia formed separate associations of "fifty subscribers" each and assessed each member ten cents weekly in order "to pay a lecturer to travel through their Congressional district." Male adolescents not yet of legal voting age often brought previous military experience to ardent league activities on behalf of legal voters.

Monday, foreman of a Santee River rice estate, vividly described popular mechanisms for enforcing political loyalty. His employer recalled how Monday explained why he would again vote the Republican ticket in the first state elections after the 1876 campaign that marked the political end of Reconstruction:

> I got tuh vote de 'Publican ticket, suh. We all has. Las' 'lection I voted de Democrack ticket an' dee killed my cow. Abum, he vote de Democrack ticket; dee killed his colt. Monday counted off the negroes who had voted the "Democrack" ticket, and every one had been punished. One had been bombarded in his cabin; another's rice crop had been taken – even the ground swept up and every grain carried off, leaving him utterly destitute.

Extending a working-class variant of patronage, Monday explained that he actually safeguarded the interests of his Democratic employer and his own effectiveness as a plantation foreman by voting the Republican ticket. "I tell you, suh," said Monday, "I got tuh do it on my 'count, an' on yo' 'count. You make me fo'man an' ef I didn' vote de 'Publican ticket, I couldn' make dese niggers wuk. I couldn' do nothin' 'tall wid 'em."

Political discipline was a community affair.

[. . .]

Although political discipline was embedded in networks of community life, the act of voting remained, for the most part, man's work. In the councils of their radical societies, union clubs, and Loyal Leagues, freedmen invented new forms of mass behavior to safeguard recent rights of suffrage. The political practices that they created made them effective partisans at the polls. E. W. Seibels, leader of an 1870 opposition party, bestowed grudging praise. Popular organization of Republican voting was "so perfect a system," Seibels informed a congressional committee, "that it is impossible to break through it." Seibels believed that his conservative coalition had managed to gain some black men's votes "by [the voters'] mistake" in 1870 state elections. "But," he reflected, "it was the hardest matter I ever undertook to do."

[. . .]

Of necessity, clubs kept a sharp watch over ballots. Illiterate Republican voters could scarcely comply with the expectations of the Second Military District's chief civil officer, Ammiel J. Willard, that voters themselves would supply ballots for or against a constitutional convention "in Conformity with the usual custom." Even so, voters who could not read letters well knew how to read men. Club members therefore pledged to accept a ticket at the polls or other prearranged sites from the hands of only one designated person, who would have received his tickets under the same strictures in a chain that linked small numbers of literate voters to the nonliterate majority of club "captains" . . . When Republican tickets could not be distributed . . . "of course [freed men] could not write them, and they had no vote the next day." Most men who handed out Republican tickets in 1867 and 1868, however, probably fulfilled their duties to standards achieved by ex-slave Willis Johnson, who judged that he had "done right smart" when he "took the tickets around among the black people."

Before voting proceeded against a grim backdrop of terror, it went forward as rough sport. Agents who distributed tickets were fair game, as when, during state elections in 1870, groups of freed men watching various polling places in the low country seized the opposing Union Reform Party's ballots and drove their distributors from the polls. To approach the ballot box was sometimes to begin a strenuous athletic match. A crowd surrounded the bearer of an unfavored ticket, who then had to run a gauntlet of blocks and shoves in order to deposit his ballot. The object often was to occupy the polls early and thereby impede the opposition's access to the ballot box. The four hundred freedmen – some wearing their old army uniforms – who "took possession" of the Grey's Hill polls in Beaufort, or the eight hundred men who similarly occupied the polling place on St. Helena Island during November 1867 elections, had clearly mastered the strategy. Voters deposited their tickets to raucous cheering. However, charges that former slave Robert Smalls, during elections for the constitutional convention in which he was a candidate, had urged freedmen at a polling place in Beaufort district "to shoot, knock the brains out, or kill any man who attempted to vote any other ticket than the so called red ticket" seem exaggerated. A former Union Reform candidate, bested (in part) by rough tactics at the hands of "a rabble of colored men, sometimes by white republicans," better conveyed the rules of the game. "A crowd can push a man off," Robert Aldrich explained, "without laying hands on him." Athletic confrontations helped male voters size up the competition at many polls on election days.

Printed ballots kept few secrets; on the contrary, local ballots were emblems whose distinctive designs and colors broadcast a voter's allegiance to all who watched. And many watched. Authorized men from both parties tallied ballots as they were cast. Staged dramas of intimidation followed the voter to the ballot box. Tench Blackwell, a white Republican manager of elections in Spartanburg County, recalled, "When a republican would go up to vote," Democratic watchers "would jerk their repeater strap, and look as if they were whipping somebody, looking at the man who was voting."

The public nature of voting provoked more secretive adherence to party tickets among white Republican voters, whereas ex-slave Republicans tended more toward strategies relying on amassing large numbers. Literacy enabled some Republican voters, usually yeoman partisans, to camouflage how they had voted. Pasting a newly written Republican slate inside a visibly Democratic covering was one favored stratagem. Black rank-and-file Republicans opted for monopolizing particular polls and voting en masse. C. H. Suber, a Democratic lawyer, irritatedly recounted how black Republicans voted at the courthouse in Newberry village in 1870: "[T]he colored people were invited to come from all parts of the county to the court-house and vote. They came from the remotest parts of the county to vote . . . They congregated around the boxes at 4 o'clock in the morning, before they were opened, and monopolized all the precincts until about 10 or 11 o'clock in the day."

Force more or less restrained and stylized hovered in the very act of voting. Rank-and-file Republicans accepted certain forms of physical assault as being within bounds when political enemies confronted each other at the polls. Election "riots" that erupted at polls in St. John's, Berkeley and outside Charleston during elections of local officeholders in June 1868 suggest the limits of popular political coercion . . . of one Sigwald, the Democratic candidate for sheriff . . . became occasion for direct action at the Club House poll in St. Andrew's Parish outside Charleston. On arriving at Club House, a squad of men from Buleau plantation, led by ex-slave minister and schoolteacher Ishmael Moultrie, discovered that some ex-slave voters had placed tickets for Sigwald in the election box . . . Moultrie charged the election managers "that by allowing the Freedmen to vote the Sigwald Ticket, which was a Rebel Ticket, they were trying to bring them into slavery." On hearing Moultrie's claim, the crowd rallied and "demanded that the Sigwald Tickets be taken out, and they be allowed to vote over." When the managers refused, large numbers of men, brandishing sticks, clubs, or firearms, seized the election box, removed 190 Sigwald tickets, and replaced them with an equal number of tickets for the Republican candidate.

For better and for worse, ex-slave voters wielded coercion rooted in the non-lethal force of neighborhood sanctions for strictly political ends. Roughing up a wayward voter of their own relative social position, or forcibly replacing ballots in order to "vote over," gained victory for Republican candidates. Party regulars of local influence tolerated what were at most overly zealous indiscretions when the most severe consequences stayed within class bounds. Arriving at the Club House polls later that same day, Charleston party stalwart Samuel Dickerson remarked that the men from Buleau plantation had "acted right." The Republican candidate for sheriff gained victory. Five of the "rioters" including Ishmael Moultrie (regarded as "manager of the spiritual, political, and business affairs of his people" at Buleau plantation) gained one month at hard labor in military custody. Moreover, conservatives loath to concede legitimacy of Reconstruction governments gained propaganda for the view that such clashes left "lives imperiled."

જ જ જ

Steven Hahn

A Nation under Our Feet[†]

There are no better markers of African-American political struggle and advance in the immediate postemancipation period than the vigilantism of the Ku Klux Klan. Like previous paramilitary outfits, Klans sought to enforce the general subordination of former slaves and to punish whites and blacks who challenged or threatened a variety of racially defined hierarchies. But Klans were particularly involved in combating the social and political repercussions of Radical Reconstruction, and their targets make up a roster of the individuals, institutions, and developments that made those repercussions tangible. Klansmen attacked and murdered local leaders and organizers. They intimidated and coerced Republican party supporters and voters. They tried to force out objectionable officeholders and election registrars. They harassed and abused black men and women who had gained measures of personal and economic independence. They disturbed white landowners who

---

[†]Steven Hahn, *A Nation under Our Feet: Black Political Struggles in the Rural South from Slavery to the Great Migration* (Cambridge, MA: Harvard University Press, 2003), pp. 272–3, 288–92, 310–13.

rented or sold land to black laborers, white merchants who bought crops from and sold goods to black customers, and white employers who enticed black workers with higher wages. They burned down black churches and schoolhouses and drove off repugnant teachers and ministers. Most of all, they set out to destroy the Union League.

[. . .]

Klan-style paramilitarism always existed alongside other forms of political violence and coercion and cannot be easily dissociated from them. They included personal intimidation, threats of dismissal from employment, harassment of Republican party voters and supporters, manipulation of ballots and returns, and what contemporaries (and later historians) called "riots." Together they came to compose the materials of various "plans" for ridding the former Confederate states of Republican rule and black power: the Georgia plan of 1870, the Alabama plan of 1874, the Mississippi plan of 1875, or the South Carolina plan of 1876. Each, with its own peculiar mix, meant the use of violence, fraud, and intimidation to achieve the political end of "redemption." But what appear to be mere variations on a theme were rather increasingly organized and tenacious battles. For if the Klan managed to weaken the institutional bases of rural black politics, it was generally too diffuse and uncoordinated to dislodge Republican regimes and reclaim political supremacy in more than limited areas. That work would be left to the rifle clubs, the White Leagues, and the Red Shirts – the true paramilitary wings of the Democratic party. They would not only have to overawe, outmuscle, and outgun the Republicans through most of the individual states and often across state lines; they would also have to destroy the African-American capacity for armed resistance.

The Klan's effectiveness depended on a wider political climate that gave latitude to local vigilantes and allowed for explosions of very public violence. Louisiana and Georgia, which alone among the reconstructed states supported Democrat Horatio Seymour for the presidency in 1868, had at least seven bloody riots together with Klan raiding that summer and fall. The term "riot," which came into wide use at this time, quite accurately captures the course and ferocity of these eruptions, claiming as they did numerous lives, often over several days, in an expanding perimeter of activity. But "riot" suggests, as well, a disturbance that falls outside the ordinary course of political conduct, and so by invoking or embracing it we may miss what such disturbances can reveal about the changing dynamics and choreography of what was indeed ordinary politics in the postemancipation South. Simultaneously harking back to forms of struggle prevalent under slavery while illuminating new sites of tension and conflict that came with freedom and the franchise, the "riots" demonstrated in convulsive ways something far more generally applicable: that the ballot box registered not so much the balances of public opinion as the results of paramilitary battles for position.

Consider the Camilla riot in southwest Georgia, which captured the greatest attention but shared many features of the others. In late August 1868, Republicans in the state's Second Congressional District, most of whom were black, met in the town of Albany and nominated William P. Pierce, a former Union army officer, failed planter, and Freedmen's Bureau agent, for Congress. It would not be an easy campaign . . . In early September, moderate white Republicans joined with Democrats to expel thirty-two duly elected African Americans from their seats in the state house and senate, and as Pierce began his canvass it appeared that the district's Democrats had become emboldened . . .

News of the rally – which would feature Pierce, several other white Republicans, and Philip Joiner, a former slave, local Loyal League president, and recently expelled state legislator – circulated through the neighboring counties. So, too, did rumors of a possible attack by armed whites who, it was said, proclaimed that "this is our country and we intend to protect it or die." Freedpeople did have ample cause for alarm. Camilla, the seat of relatively poor, white-majority Mitchell County in an otherwise black majority section of the state, crackled with tension. Gunfire had broken out there during the April 1868 elections, and many of the blacks had resolved that they would "not dare . . . go to town entirely unarmed as they did at that time." The white Republican leaders tried to quell these fears when the Dougherty County contingent gathered on their plantations on Friday night the 18th; and as the group moved out on Saturday morning for the twenty-odd mile trek to Camilla, most heeded the advice to leave their weapons behind and avoid a provocation.

The procession was led by a wagonload of musicians playing fifes and drums. Moving southward, it attracted the attention of growing numbers of freedmen, women, and children, who left the fields and joined the ranks . . . Perhaps half of the men toted firearms of some kind for protection and effect (most only had bird-shot for ammunition), while many of the others carried walking sticks. Collecting at China Grove, a short distance from Camilla, they numbered between two and three hundred. In several important respects – finding safe havens the night before, marching in quasi-military fashion, sounding fife and drum, welcoming the partici-pation of the entire community – they displayed practices associated with Union Leagues, Republican political clubs, and drilling companies, and expressed their intent to claim the full rights of citizenship.

But to the whites of Camilla, such a procession could only constitute a "mob," with no civil or political standing, and mean "war, revolution, insurrection, or riot of some sort." Once spotted on Saturday morning, it thereby sparked another round of rumors, these warning of an "armed body of negroes" heading toward the town. Although evidence suggests that local Democrats had been busy for at least two days accumulating weapons and preparing to respond with force, the rumors clearly sped the mobilization of the town's "citizens," who appointed a committee to ride out with the sheriff and "meet the approaching crowd." A tense exchange followed, with the Republican leaders explaining that they only wished "to go peaceably into Camilla and hold a political meeting," and the sheriff warning them not to enter the town with arms. It was not hard for the seasoned leaders to see the risks of accommodating the sheriff and stacking their weapons . . . [and] they determined to continue as planned, with their arms, and have speeches at the Camilla courthouse, as was their "right." For his part, the sheriff returned to town and effectively deputized the entire white male population.

Two of the white Republican leaders riding in a buggy entered Camilla's courthouse square first. Some fifty yards back of them, the procession followed in what the sheriff described as a martial demeanor: "side drums and fifes going on, some commanding them in military order, they marching four deep" with "about twenty mounted negroes" who "seemed to act as outriders." But with their walking sticks and birdshot, the marchers could be no match for the "squads" of heavily armed whites waiting on the south and west sides of the square . . . Suddenly, a local drunkard, waving a double-barreled shotgun, ran out to the wagon and . . . demanded that the drumming (associated both with a citizens' militia and slave communication) cease. A moment later he fired, and the "squads" of white townsmen immediately joined in. Freedmen who had guns briefly returned the volleys and then, with the others, commenced a desperate flight for safety. The sheriff and his "deputies" followed them into the woods and swamps with deadly purpose, some looking for "that d——d Phil Joiner." Joiner escaped, but eleven days later he reported that "the mobing crowd is still going through Baker County and every Colored man that is farming to his self or supporting the nominee of grant and Colfax he either have to leave his home or be killed."

Prospects for black retaliation briefly ran very high. As word of the shooting spread through Dougherty County that Saturday evening, agitated freedmen in Albany sought out the local Freedmen's Bureau agent. Some talked of going immediately to Camilla to rescue and protect those who remained at risk. A few hours later, African Methodist minister Robert Crumley . . . suggested traveling there en masse the next day to "burn the earth about the place." The Freedmen's Bureau agent managed to discourage such a course by promising a full investigation and urging his superiors in Atlanta to send federal troops. The investigation showed Camilla to be a massacre that had left at least nine African Americans dead and many more wounded. But all that came out of Atlanta was a proclamation by Republican governor Rufus Bullock urging civil authorities to keep the peace and safeguard the rights of the people. Election day proved to be remarkably quiet in southwest Georgia because the contest was over well before. Only two Republicans bothered to cast ballots in Camilla, and the turnout was so low elsewhere in the district that the Democrats, despite being greatly outnumbered among eligible voters, registered an official victory. There would be resurgences of local black power in the future, but this was the beginning of the end for Republican rule in Georgia.

[. . .]

As Republicans and Democrats struggled to reach an accord before Grant's term expired in early March . . . what appeared to be taking shape was less a "compromise" than a shared political sensibility in northern ruling circles that questioned the legitimacies of popular democracy. That sensibility had always been in evidence among conservatives and had spread during the 1850s, only to be pressed to the margins by the revolutionary mobilizations of the 1860s. It now expressed itself as weariness with the issues of Reconstruction, as skepticism about the capabilities of freedpeople, as concerns about the expansion of federal powers, as revulsion over political corruption, and, especially, as exasperation with the "annual autumnal outbreaks" in the Deep South and the consequent use of federal troops to maintain Republican regimes there.

It required elaborate fictions and willful ignorance for critics to argue, as some did, that the military had no business rejecting the popular will in the South. For if detachments of federal troops at the statehouses in Columbia, South Carolina, and New Orleans, Louisiana, alone enabled Republicans to hang onto the last threads of power, their Democratic rivals made no effort to conceal their own dependence on superior force of arms. In Louisiana, Democratic gubernatorial claimant and former Confederate brigadier general Francis T. Nicholls . . . designated local White League units as the legal state militia, commandeered the state arsenal, and took control of the New Orleans police. In South Carolina, Wade Hampton's allies succeeded in garrisoning the state capitol with as many as six thousand Red Shirts, while rifle clubs drove out Republican officeholders in upcountry counties. Although the Democrats, in both cases, avoided a direct resort to violence . . . the threat of violence hung palpably in the air . . . And as efforts to resolve the national crisis proceeded, these large-scale paramilitary deployments made Nicholls and Hampton the de facto governors of their states.

But it was not, in fact, the continued use of federal troops per se that repelled most northern critics of Reconstruction. It was rather the use of federal troops to empower certain groups over others. The problem of American political life, as the editors of *The Nation* saw it in the spring of 1877, was that the very notion of "majority government" had been transformed in such a way as to threaten the fate of the republic. At one time, it had meant "a majority of taxpayers, or a majority containing a fair representation of the intelligence, sagacity, and social and political experience of the population" . . . But now, in the "great cities" as well as in the Reconstruction South, "political power" was being severed from "intelligence and property," and the "rule of a mere numerical majority" was being "made visible."

[. . .]

[F]ar from "condemning the people of South Carolina and Louisiana" for their "determination to overthrow [Ring rule] by hook or by crook," *The Nation* felt "indebted to them" despite "their occasional resorts to violence."

The withdrawal of federal troops from the statehouses of South Carolina and Louisiana in April of 1877 did not therefore mark the end of their role in protecting the rights and property of American citizens; it only marked the end of their role, at least for nearly another century, in protecting the rights and property of African Americans and other working people. If anything, the collapse of Reconstruction and the defeat of Radicalism nationwide ushered in a new era of state-organized violence in defense of private property and respectable propertyholders at all levels of government: the deployment of federal troops in labor disputes and to secure the trans-Mississippi West for white settlement; the professionalization of state militias and the National Guard; the expansion and retraining of urban police forces. Unlike their Republican predecessors, Democratic governors in the redeemed South would not hesitate to use (now white) state militia companies – if local paramilitary outfits did not suffice – to maintain "order" in black-majority districts.

African Americans in the countryside were not vanquished politically with the ending of Reconstruction. There remained significant enclaves, owing to numbers and organizational strength, where blacks could still exercise their electoral muscle and place their representatives in the seats of local and state governments, if not in Congress.

[. . .]

But it also seemed dishearteningly familiar. From the birth of the American republic until the spring of 1861, blacks as slaves and free people had conducted their politics in a context of official hostility and repression, where the apparatus of the state was in the hands of those who denied or ignored their claims and aspirations. Then, for nearly two remarkable and revolutionary decades, they not only gained a dramatically new standing in civil and political life; they also had an access to state power that few other working people had ever or would ever enjoy. Now the state was again controlled by their avowed enemies or by those who were indifferent to them.

Yet if this appeared to be merely another example of a revolution gone backward, appearances could be deceiving. The revolution that African Americans . . . had played such a signal role in advancing had substantially weakened the old guard, and the Redeemers, well-armed and enthusiastic as they may have been, were in fact a motley and rather fractious crew . . . They did not have a unified vision of the redeemed South's future, and the restoration of "home rule" did not bring with it a return to the national power they had once shared. The consequences would be felt by all southerners in the last depression-ridden decades of the nineteenth century, and for African Americans the economic hardships would be accompanied by the old fists of exploitation and oppression. But there would be new possibilities as well.

9

Alex Lichtenstein

TRIALS OF THE NEW SOUTH

In 1886, *Atlanta Constitution* editor Henry Grady famously
heralded the arrival of a "New South," one that had made its
peace with Appomattox and abolition, embraced northern values
of industry and innovation, and become an oasis of material
opportunity, cultural uplift, and social harmony. The term caught
on, and has been used ever since to denote Dixie's passage into the
post-Civil War, post-Reconstruction decades of the late nineteenth
and early twentieth centuries. But how well did the gauzy images
offered by "New South" boosters convey the emerging realities
of southern life? Thrashed out by contemporaries, the origins and
character of the New South would later become a focus of debate,
lively and lasting, among historians.

Research on the New South has revolved around a series of
enduring questions. How substantial a break did the architects,
and agendas, of the New South represent from those of the
Old South? In what ways did the commercial and industrial
transformations of the region (in both city and countryside)
improve, or undermine, the lives of southerners? What
accounts for the region's continuing problems of poverty and
underdevelopment? In what ways did New South tenant farming
represent an extension of, and in what ways a departure from,
the coercions of slavery? In what measures were the "common
folk" – rural and urban, black and white – able or inclined to
mobilize against the class and racial orders of the New South?
What were the thrust and legacy of early twentieth-century
southern Progressivism; how did it either challenge or fortify the
prevailing values and hierarchies of the New South? Developments
and issues such as these are addressed in the introductory essay by
Alex Lichtenstein, and in the selections to follow.

Alex Lichtenstein, Associate Professor of History at Indiana

University, has researched extensively in the fields of labor, African American, southern, and comparative history. His first book – *Twice the Work of Free Labor* (1996) – showed how integral convict labor was to the political economy of the New South. Among his many published articles and book chapters are: "Was the Emancipated Slave a Proletarian?" *Reviews in American History* (March 1998); "Proletarians or Peasants? Sharecroppers and the Politics of Protest in the Rural South, 1880–1940," *Plantation Society in the Americas* (Fall 1998); "'The Hope for White and Black'? Race, Labour and the State in South Africa and the United States, 1924–1956," *Journal of Southern African Studies* (March 2004); and "Rethinking Agrarian Labor in the U.S. South," *Journal of Peasant Studies* (October 2008). He is currently working on a study of the civil rights and labor movements in 1940s Florida.

Following the violent overthrow of Reconstruction in the 1870s, an emerging cohort of southern business entrepreneurs and newspaper editors set about promoting a "New South" based on the growth of regional industry, the diversification of agriculture, and the attraction of northern investment. With the removal of Union Army troops and the restoration of "home rule," it became time to "put business before politics" – or so proclaimed Henry Grady, the young editor of the *Atlanta Constitution* and quintessential New South booster, in his landmark 1886 "New South" address. "The Old South rested everything on slavery and agriculture," Grady informed his northern audience. "The New South presents a perfect democracy . . . and a diversified industry that meets the complex needs of this complex age." In advocating a "New South," Grady asked his northern listeners for their cooperation in promoting sectional reconciliation and regional economic development.[1]

Historians have long debated whether the program advocated by Grady and his compatriots ushered in genuine change, or if the New South era might better be understood as an extension of patterns established during slavery. Prior to the Second World War, an influential generation of scholars emphasized continuity in southern history. Journalist Wilbur J. Cash popularized this notion in his 1941 masterpiece, *The Mind of the South*, when he argued that, even after the cataclysm of the Civil War, "the Old South was preserved virtually intact" and the "pride of the ruling class was not weakened" by defeat and slave emancipation, "but even distinctly enhanced." In his 1948 presidential address to the Southern Historical Association, historian Robert S. Cotterill gave this widely held view his professional imprimatur when he proclaimed that "in no essential way did the war [Between the States] alter or deflect the course of southern development."[2]

Only three years later, C. Vann Woodward set the standard for several generations of revisionist historians by roundly rejecting the notion of a traditional South impervious to change. The stakes of this challenge were great. As Woodward later noted, "the legitimacy of the New South regime – and . . . the legitimacy of the social order still in place in the 1950s – was dependent upon a certain reading of history," one that above all regarded white supremacy as the South's timeless foundation. "According to the orthodox historical credo" of the New South, Woodward complained, the world ushered in by Grady and company was "thought of as the fulfillment and continuation of ideals, convictions, folkways, and institutions" deeply rooted in the region's past. Even Grady himself, Woodward observed, claimed that the New South was "simply the Old South under new conditions."[3]

Woodward's 1951 work *Origins of the New South* (extracted below) overturned that reading of history, contending instead that the society that emerged from the ashes of civil war, federal occupation, and counterrevolution differed profoundly from that of the slave South. Far from being led by a reinvigorated planter aristocracy, as the traditionalists claimed, Woodward argued that an emergent middle class spearheaded the New South. This new class based its wealth and power on residence in growing towns, ownership of movable property, and hard-nosed business investment. Driven not by some bygone values of *noblesse oblige* and racial paternalism, the avatars of the New South embraced a ruthless capitalism that put profits ahead of the well-being of the majority of the region's people. And far from restoring the precepts of good government, supposedly tarnished by the corruption of Reconstruction, Woodward's "Redeemers" themselves wrested special privileges from the state, such as the use of inexpensive prison labor. The result was not a harmonious social order overseen by a beneficent regional ruling class but one riven by class conflict, and subjected to the economic control of outsiders.

In challenging the New South's dual claims to upholding tradition and promoting sectional progress, Woodward subjected to withering scrutiny the sunny picture painted by contemporaries like Grady and reaffirmed uncritically by subsequent historians. "Rising above logic," Woodward acidly remarked, advocates of the New South "professed to be equally loyal to the Old South of the Lost Cause and to the New South of Yankee ideals and business and nationalism." In trying to paper over that contradiction, the term New South "had the color of a slogan, a rallying cry." Paul Gaston, in his 1971 work *The New South Creed* (excerpted below), explored the nature of that slogan, examining closely the set of myths that disguised the harsh realities of southern life described by Woodward. Where *Origins of the New South* offered a critical account of the social and political history of the New South, Gaston's work explored the intellectual and cultural climate that created a world-view that was so at odds with the society it described. As the promise of economic growth, racial harmony, and stable class relations failed to materialize, Gaston showed, the "creed" of New South progress hardened into a "myth" that denied its limitations, and blocked challenges to the status quo.

Current scholarship on the New South continues to look behind the promotional rhetoric of the "New South Creed" to investigate the lives of ordinary southerners, and now seeks to move beyond the debate about "continuity and change" stimulated by Woodward's classic text. Perhaps the social order which was baptized the "New South" during the late nineteenth century is best understood as a series of compromises struck by various contending parties striving to place their stamp on the region's future while, at the same time, laying claim to its past. Driven by the desire for sectional reconciliation and economic growth, northerners agreed to abandon Reconstruction and leave the southern states alone politically. This entailed abandoning African Americans to their fate at the hands of southern whites, even while investing more capital in the region. In exchange, promoters of the New South promised to share the profits of industrial growth with their northern business partners and to insure regional political and social stability – and thus a congenial investment climate.

Such stability, however, required a series of settlements internal to the southern states, often touted by defenders of the New South as compromises but usually representing, as Woodward put it, "a capitulation" to the "new masters" of the region. These included the paternalistic promise by powerful whites to share some of the New South's vaunted prosperity with blacks, as long as the latter gave up their claim to political rights and conformed to segregation laws. Similarly, New South boosters claimed to ensure working-class whites access to jobs without competition from blacks or immigrants, bolstered by the supposed advantages conferred by white supremacy. In return, white workers – especially in the southern Piedmont's burgeoning textile industry – were expected to bring entire families off the land and into the mills, to steer clear of trade unions, and to accept without protest their subordinate position in company towns. Finally, in the absence of widespread redistribution of land to freed slaves after the War – and indeed as many small farmers found themselves hard pressed to hold on to land in the face of declining cotton prices – New South agriculture rested on a compromise between the landed and the landless that came to be called sharecropping. These compromises, the delicate political equilibrium they entailed, and their fundamentally negative consequences for the majority of the South's people – black especially, but poor white as well – exemplify the ability of the architects of the New South simultaneously to perpetuate older models of hierarchical social relations while fully embracing the rush to modernity.

Since all of these social settlements depended, at least in theory, on tapping the region's bountiful natural resources – from coal and iron to tobacco to timber – the first priority of the New South's leading businessmen and policymakers was, indeed, economic development. This proved an especially pressing need not only because Dixie remained an overwhelmingly agrarian region but also because of the destruction of the South's economy wrought by the Civil War. There is no denying that the New South experienced waves of economic growth fueled largely by outside capital, just as its boosters had hoped. Entrepreneurs and investors established coal mines in East Tennessee and Alabama, erected blast furnaces in Birmingham, opened phosphate pits in Florida, built tobacco factories in Winston-Salem and Durham, and turned Savannah and Jacksonville into the world's largest exporters of turpentine. Between 1869 and 1899 the region's manufacturing output and value of products multiplied six times, and capital investment increased tenfold.

Despite these apparent gains, the South continued to lag behind the rapidly expanding manufacturing base of the North; with nearly a third of the nation's population in 1900, the region claimed only 10 percent of America's nonagricultural income. Although the per capita income of the region went from only 51 percent of the national average in 1880 to 62 percent by 1920, this latter figure still marked a far cry from the South's prewar position. (In 1860, with slavery intact, the figure had stood at 72 percent.) And much of the South's economic development rested on industries based on the exploitation of the land's resources, such as timber, naval stores, and mining, or low-wage manufacturing based on agricultural products, like tobacco and cotton textiles.

For the most part, New South industry produced unfinished or low value-added goods for distant markets. Moreover, low wages and a manufacturing environment hostile to labor organization, along with a lack of state regulation, represented the region's primary competitive advantage over the North. Here was a formula that would attract outside capital and bedevil labor reformers and organizers for decades to come. Child labor, for example, expanded in southern industries even while northern states began campaigns to abolish it. Economic growth of this sort did little to lift ordinary southerners out of poverty. Thus, visions of industrial progress notwithstanding, by the end of the century the New South measured up poorly against most indicators of national progress. Per capita income, literacy, infant mortality, access to electricity, mechanization of agriculture . . . by any measure of modernity, the region continued to lag behind its northern and western competitors. "Even by 1920," concludes historian Howard Rabinowitz, "the rhetoric of New South spokesmen failed to square with the realities of southern economic life."[4] By that date, as the nation as a whole discovered that more than half its citizens resided in urban areas, some four-fifths of the South's population remained rural, much of it trapped in relentless poverty.

Yet, when it came to agriculture, despite incessant calls for diversification and modernization, the region's farm sector had stagnated. To be sure, between 1859 and 1900 the number of cotton bales harvested in the South nearly doubled, from 5.4 to 10 million, much of it destined for the region's growing textile industry. But the emphasis on cotton encouraged overcultivation which, in turn, led to land exhaustion and falling prices.

By 1910, historian Albert Bushnell Hart estimated that nearly half of the South's population was engaged in some fashion in raising cotton.[5] With the steady increase in bales of cotton and lack of diversification, the price of the region's main commodity crop failed to promote investment in the modernization of southern agriculture; mules and plows continued to characterize the southern countryside well into the twentieth century, long after farmers in other parts of the country had begun to employ tractors, combines, and mechanical reapers. Worse still, low prices and steep mortgages drove many once independent landholders into the ranks of tenants and sharecroppers; by 1900, two-thirds of all southern cotton producers worked land owned by someone else, a dramatic increase from only a generation before.

Designed at first to establish the untested relationship between freed slaves and their former masters, sharecropping emerged as a "compromise" between cash-poor landlords and land-poor tenants. Under this arrangement, landowners relied on the cheap and readily available – if woefully inefficient – labor of the South's poor, and to profit from the exorbitant rates of interest they charged to "furnish" their tenants in advance, with the unpicked cotton crop as collateral, or a "lien" on the tenants' share. For their part, tenants and sharecroppers, black and white, found themselves entirely dependent on the landlord or merchant for fertilizer, rent, food, and other services that the declining price of the crop could not meet. Without access to alternative forms of subsistence, tenants had to seek loans from landowners, and the "lien" on their labor gave landlords powerful leverage over their daily lives. Ultimately, this system, in conjunction with a redefinition of common rights on the land, allowed the landowning class, as Steven Hahn said in his 1983 book *The Roots of Southern Populism* (extracted below), "to withstand the demise of slavery and reassert their authority in the realm of [agricultural] production." Yet that authority came at the expense of efficiency, modernization, and the long-term health of the land.

Hahn, a former student of Woodward, placed the social experience of dispossessed white farmers at the center of the economic transformations of the rural New South. In *The Roots of Southern Populism*, Hahn detailed how once independent landholders in Georgia's "Upcountry" districts found themselves sucked into the "vortex" of the postbellum cotton economy. Their resistance to fence laws, stock laws, and other encroachments on their customary agrarian rights, Hahn argued, was a precursor to the political revolt of the 1890s against the merchants and landholders – those who seemed to benefit from the New South's economy at their expense.

The unrelenting reign of "King Cotton" had economic and political consequences that went well beyond the realm of agriculture, however. "The South is destined at no distant day to not only raise cotton," proclaimed a Georgia newspaper in 1882, "but to manufacture it, thus keeping at home all the profits."[6] Such was the hope but, in fact, the rapid growth of the South's textile industry demonstrated the close relationship between the decline of agricultural self-sufficiency described by Hahn, the expansion of industrial employment, and the mass impoverishment of Dixie's common folk. The South's most impressive industrial success, the rapid expansion across the

Piedmont of textile manufacturing, drew primarily on the cheap and unskilled labor of white tenant farm families who could no longer make a living on the land. Textile workers, commonly scorned by middle-class town dwellers as lazy, ignorant "lintheads," lived and labored in mill towns completely dominated by the textile company owners. (By one estimate, more than 90 percent of textile workers lived in villages owned by their employers.) Moreover, under the family labor system that prevailed in the Piedmont, nearly a quarter of southern textile workers in the 1880s and 1890s were children under the age of sixteen, and over 40 percent were women. The southern economist Broadus Mitchell, even while he later came to oppose child labor, continued to insist that in the early years of the "cotton mill campaign" it had proved a necessity. He went so far as to declare in 1921 that the employment of children during the 1880s and 1890s "was not avarice, but philanthropy; not exploitation, but generosity and cooperation and social mindedness."[7]

Despite their carefully cultivated self-image as the benefactors of poor whites, southern textile entrepreneurs did little to lift the mass of displaced rural whites out of poverty and dependence. "We work in *his* mill. We live in his houses. Our children go to *his* school. And on Sunday we go to hear his preacher," complained North Carolina millworkers in 1913. Long hours, low wages, a family-based labor system, and dependence on the millowners were the lot of the textile workers who left field for factory in the New South. And while it is true that local investors generated the cotton mill expansion in the early years of New South boosterism, by the turn of the century, northern firms had invested heavily in the southern mills, in part to hedge against the competition rooted in the region's cheap labor costs and lack of regulation. By 1904, southern mills consumed more cotton than their long-time competitors in New England. Tax exemptions, subsidies, low wages, anti-unionism, and the absence of social legislation were among the chief advantages the South offered as inducements to capital. "The social costs" of this program, C. Vann Woodward wryly remarked, "were charged up to 'progress'."

The persistent gap between rhetoric and reality in the New South thus proved especially conspicuous for the region's working class. For rural workers, African Americans in particular, the system of sharecropping meant dependence on landlords, little income, and scant possibility of upward mobility. Many fell into a state of peonage, and found themselves bound by debt to a landlord or turpentine camp operator in perpetuity, or sent to a chain gang or convict camp. Coal miners competed against the forced labor of convicts, leased to mine owners for a pittance. Certainly, black and white workers attempted to better their condition during this period, at times in concert with one another. The interracial United Mine Workers successfully organized the coalfields of Alabama and Tennessee, the Knights of Labor made comparable inroads in Richmond and other cities, and dockworkers in New Orleans built an effective biracial union, to name but three examples. The company-run textile towns, however, remained by and large impervious to organization.

Unionized or not, most southerners continued to labor long hours, under difficult conditions, for low wages or, in the case of sharecroppers, peons, and convicts, no wages at all. The prevailing current of African American leadership, personified by Booker T. Washington, urged black workers to accept their degraded place in the labor market and make their peace with the economy of the New South in lieu of pursuing political or civil rights.

By the 1890s the increasingly desperate plight of farmers, sharecroppers, and tenants drove many to join a new political movement that shook the New South order and the confidence of its leadership: the People's Party, or Populists. Building on rural protest movements that struggled to shore up the farmers' declining economic position, the Populists sought to boost crop prices, reduce interest rates and crippling mortgages, and end the farmers' growing dependence on monopolized finance, railroad transport, and means of communication. As Woodward points out, by the time of the Populists' creation of their national "Omaha Platform" in 1892, the southern wing of the movement had already begun to build alliances across regional, class, and racial lines. It was the last of these three that proved the boldest challenge to a New South order that rested upon white supremacy. "You are kept apart that you may be separately fleeced of your earnings," Populist firebrand Thomas Watson told the South's black and white tenants in 1892. "You are made to hate each other because upon that hatred is rested the keystone of the arch of financial despotism which enslaves you both."[8] With these words, while surely no advocate of integration or "social equality," Watson urged rural folks of both races to join forces on the basis of common economic interests and to vote the New South Democrats, the local enforcers of this despotism, out of office.

This effort to organize whites and blacks in a single party would seal the political fate of southern Populism by the end of the decade. Just as the previous generation had done during Reconstruction, the defenders of the Democratic party as the South's guarantor of white supremacy used a combination of rumor, fraud, violence, and the "defense of white womanhood" to drive all biracial political challenges from the ballot box during the 1890s. Wilmington, North Carolina, a city governed by a Republican white–black "fusion" alliance, essentially underwent a white *coup d'état* sponsored by Democrats in 1898. North Carolina newspapers declared that "when the white men had control of the government . . . peace and concord prevailed. Wherever the negro and his allies have obtained power the politicians have become offensive and the brutal have become lawbreakers." Even a one-time champion of biracial cooperation such as Watson concluded in the wake of the Populist defeats of the 1890s that "the white people dare not revolt so long as they can be intimidated by the fear of the negro vote," and eventually came to advocate disfranchisement of the black voters he had once courted.[9] Congressman George White, elected in eastern North Carolina's second congressional district in 1898, proved to be the last southern black congressman to win office until the 1970s.

Henry Grady himself insisted that "the relations of the southern people with the negro are close and cordial," thereby placing former slaves and their children outside the category of "southern people" even though he claimed to have their best interests at heart. "No section shows a more prosperous laboring population than the negroes of the South," Grady claimed, "none in fuller sympathy with the employing and land-owning class. He shares our school fund, has the fullest protection of our laws and the friendship of our people." Despite this sort of paternalism, however, blacks in the New South faced an upsurge in racial violence, suffering from frequent lynching (over 190 a year during the 1890s) and brutal race riots, like the one that shook Grady's home town of Atlanta in 1906. For blacks, the outcome of the era's political jostling was disfranchisement, segregation, and single-party rule by the Democrats.[10]

Ironically, many of these features of white supremacy were fashioned by Grady's successors in the South's Progressive movement. As historian Jack Temple Kirby puts it, "the official work of undoing Reconstruction was concluded in the midst of the twentieth century's first reform movement." Indeed, as Kirby suggests in the extract below, the political turmoil generated by the Populist revolt of the 1890s spurred planters and businessmen to advance a reform agenda – Progressivism – that would help them secure their power over poor whites as well as blacks. Such reforms included efforts to prohibit liquor; to limit, if not abolish, child labor; to "uplift" the degraded millhands of the cotton mill villages; and to replace the notorious convict lease system with state-controlled chain gangs, with the added benefit of improving rural roads with their forced labor. But above all, the reformers sought to purge once and for all blacks – and many poor whites as well – from the voter rolls, ending the conflicts they believed ensued from political competition for black votes. Thus the region's Progressive movement bequeathed to the twentieth century the so-called "Solid South," a virtual one-party state that reduced all politics to a narrow competition between different factions of the Democratic party, and relied on a severely constricted electoral base. The election in 1906 of the Progressive Hoke Smith as Georgia's governor (with the support of former Populist leader Thomas Watson) led directly in that state to prohibition, the abolition of convict leasing, and, not least, the disfranchisement of black voters.

As historian Howard Rabinowitz observed of the New South era, "white supremacy supplied a needed element of continuity [for whites] in the midst of rapid social, political, and economic change."[11] Acknowledging this, we might still recognize that the New South was perhaps even newer than Woodward himself imagined. The planter class reconstituted its power on the basis of sharecropping, debt, and legal strictures, not slavery. A ruthless, rising business class seized the reins of power in the name of progress and sectional reconciliation; as a result, the South experienced industrialization but suffered a colonial relationship with the North. Racial segregation was not merely the legal codification of the way race relations had "always been" but sprang from the economic and political conflicts of the 1890s. Populism was a rational, democratic and, at times, radically biracial challenge to the power of the region's new capitalist elite. Its defeat marked the triumph of the rapacious modernizers, who consolidated their power and white supremacy in the disfranchisement conventions and the subsequent Progressive movement, often at the expense of the poor of both races. Ultimately, as Paul Gaston notes, the New South advocates "created a gospel of union that became an integral part of the New South creed." But, if the leaders of the New South movement accepted the industrial regime and its attendant social costs as the price of reconciliation, their northern counterparts embraced much of the myth of a bygone aristocratic south swept away by the war. In both political and economic terms, this romanticized version of the past was combined with the acquisitiveness of the present to insure the continued subordination of workers to owners of former slaves and their children and their children's children to former masters and their children and their children's children; and, of South to North.

NOTES

1. "The New South," in Edwin DuBois Shurter, ed., *The Complete Orations of and Speeches of Henry W. Grady* (New York: Hinds, Noble & Eldredge, 1910), p. 19.
2. Wilbur J. Cash, *The Mind of the South* (New York: Knopf, 1941), pp. 110, 126; Robert S. Cotterill, "The Old South to the New," *Journal of Southern History*, 15 (February 1949): pp. 3–8.
3. C. Vann Woodward, *Thinking Back: The Perils of Writing History* (Baton Rouge: Louisiana State University Press, 1986), pp. 61–3.
4. Howard N. Rabinowitz, *The First New South, 1865–1920* (Wheeling: Harlan Davidson, 1992), p. 6.
5. Albert Bushnell Hart, *The Southern South* (New York: D. Appleton & Co., 1910), p. 252.
6. Quoted in Broadus Mitchell, *The Rise of the Cotton Mills in the South* (Baltimore: Johns Hopkins University Press, 1921), p. 84.
7. Mitchell, *Rise of the Cotton Mills*, p. 95.
8. Thomas E. Watson, "The Negro Question in the South," *Arena*, 6 (October 1892), pp. 540–50.
9. David Cecelski and Timothy B. Tyson, eds., *Democracy Betrayed: The Wilmington Race Riot of 1898 and Its Legacy* (Chapel Hill: University of North Carolina Press, 1998), p. 4; Watson quoted in C. Vann Woodward, *Tom Watson: Agrarian Rebel* (New York: Oxford University Press, 1963), p. 371.
10. "The New South," in Shurter, ed., *Complete Orations of and Speeches of Henry W. Grady*, pp. 16–17.
11. Rabinowitz, *First New South*, p. 174.

* * *

Further Reading

Ayers, Edward L., *The Promise of the New South: Life after Reconstruction* (New York: Oxford University Press, 1992).

Brundage, W. Fitzhugh, *Lynching in the New South: Georgia and Virginia, 1880–1930* (Urbana: University of Illinois Press, 1993).

Cohen, William, *At Freedom's Edge: Black Mobility and the Southern White Quest for Racial Control, 1861–1915* (Baton Rouge: Louisiana State University Press, 1991).

Gilmore, Glenda Elizabeth, *Gender and Jim Crow: Women and the Politics of White Supremacy in North Carolina, 1896–1920* (Chapel Hill: University of North Carolina Press, 1996).

Grantham, Dewey W., *Southern Progressivism: The Reconciliation of Progress and Tradition* (Knoxville: University of Tennessee Press, 1983).

Hahn, Steven, *A Nation under Our Feet: Black Political Struggles in the Rural South from Slavery to the Great Migration* (Cambridge, MA: Belknap Press of Harvard University Press, 2005).

Kousser, J. Morgan, *The Shaping of Southern Politics: Suffrage Restriction and the Establishment of the One-Party South, 1880–1910* (New Haven: Yale University Press, 1974).

Lichtenstein, Alex, *Twice the Work of Free Labor: The Political Economy of Convict Labor in the New South* (London and New York: Verso, 1996).

Link, William A., *The Paradox of Southern Progressivism, 1880–1930* (Chapel Hill: University of North Carolina Press, 1997).

Litwack, Leon F., *Trouble in Mind: Black Southerners in the Age of Jim Crow* (New York: Knopf, 1998).

Rabinowitz, Howard N., *The First New South, 1865–1920* (Arlington Heights: Harlan Davidson, 1992).

Wright, Gavin, *Old South, New South: Revolutions in the Southern Economy since the Civil War* (New York: Basic Books, 1986).

* * *

C. Vann Woodward

Origins of the New South[†]

It would have been difficult to find a climate more hostile to the cultivation of radical movements than the South in the 1890s. For a generation the South had practiced a political romanticism that dissociated politics from realities and masqueraded shabby expedients and doubtful concessions in the garments of the past. A cult of

---

[†]C. Vann Woodward, *Origins of the New South, 1877–1913* (Baton Rouge: Louisiana State University Press, 1951), pp. 249–54.

racism disguised or submerged cleavages of opinion or conflicts of interest in the name of white solidarity, and the one-party system reduced political intolerance to a machine of repression.

Southern Populists challenged the New-South romanticism head on. The farmers mingled politics frankly with questions of land, markets, wages, money, taxes, railroads. They spoke openly of conflicts, of both section and class, and ridiculed the clichés of Reconciliation and White Solidarity. The bolder among them challenged the cult of racism with the doctrine of common action among farmers and workers of both races. The very existence of the third party was, of course, a challenge to the one-party system as well as to white solidarity.

Populists would never have overcome their handicaps had they not been able to appeal to a great body of native Southern tradition and doctrine. A mine of such tradition they uncovered in eighteenth-century revolutionary writings and in the ideas upon which Southerners had drawn when they provided the national leadership for the struggle against Hamiltonian Federalism and later against Whiggery.

[. . .]

Important in the Populist credo, however, was the declaration found in their national platform of 1892: "We believe that the powers of government – in other words, of the people – should be expanded," and this was to be accomplished "as rapidly and as far as the good sense of an intelligent people and the teachings of experience shall justify." The Populists did not intend the expansion to play the Hamiltonian godfather to corporate interests. Rather the expansion was to be at the expense of those interests, especially in the three fields in which the majority of their demands lay – those of money, land, and transportation.

On the question of money the Populists believed that the government had abdicated its sovereign power in favor of private corporations which were manipulating coinage, credit, and public finance to their own gain. They called for abolition of the national banking system, the enlargement of currency in circulation, and a system of commodity credit such as that of the subtreasury plan. Secondly, they believed the government had failed as custodian of public land, "including all the natural sources of wealth," and had permitted rapacious interests to steal the people's heritage. They demanded that large quantities of land and resources be reclaimed from the corporations. Thirdly, they declared for government ownership and operation of railroads and telegraph and telephone systems of the country. So far, they declared, the expansion of government powers should go in 1892, and many were prepared for it to go further in the near future.

[. . .]

The political strategy of Southern Populists was based on combinations and alliances along regional, class, and racial lines – first, an alliance between South and West; second, a combination of farmers and city and factory laborers; and third, a political union with Negro farmers and laborers within the South. Every phase of this strategy was a challenge to the New-South system, which had sought to divide all the elements Populists were trying to unite.

[. . .]

More important to the success of Southern Populism than the combination with the West or with labor was the alliance with the Negro. Yet it was the most difficult of the three. That alliance had wrecked the Readjusters and had proved a fatal weakness of the Republicans. In the end, it had been the Redeemers, the party of white supremacy, that had been most successful in controlling the Negro vote. A special difficulty of the Populist-Negro combination lay in the historical position of the upland whites toward the blacks, an antagonism with roots in slavery days. The regions where Populism made its strongest appeal were the very regions that found it most difficult to overcome racial feeling.

℘ ℘ ℘

Paul Gaston

The New South Creed[†]

Perception of the reality of both the past and the present is greatly determined for most people by the myths which become part of their lives. Defeat in the Civil War and humiliation in the Reconstruction that followed provided an atmosphere for the growth of two images of the South that, on the surface at least, appeared to have little in common. The defeat and despondency called forth a collection of romantic pictures of the Old South and a cult of the Lost Cause that fused in the Southerner's imagination to give him an uncommonly pleasing conception of his region's past. Increasingly, he came to visualize the old regime as a society dominated by a beneficent plantation tradition, sustained by a unique code of honor, and peopled by happy, amusing slaves at one end of the social spectrum and beautiful maidens and chivalric gentlemen at the other – with little in between. That this noble order had been assaulted and humiliated by the North was a source of poignancy and bitterness for Southerners; but, in the bleak aftermath of defeat, the recollection of its grandeur was also – and more importantly – a wellspring of intense satisfaction and the basis for an exaggerated regional pride.

No amount of nostalgia, however, could gainsay the fact that the South in the generation after Appomattox was desperately poor, alternately despised, ridiculed,

---

[†]Paul Gaston, *The New South Creed: A Study in Southern Mythmaking* (Baton Rouge: Louisiana State University Press, 1970), pp. 6–7, 54, 63–4, 65–6, 68, 167–8, 171–2, 175–7, 179, 184–5.

or pitied, and saddled with many unwelcome burdens. To find a way out of this syndrome, optimistic young Southerners like Henry W. Grady and Richard H. Edmonds began to talk hopefully of a new scheme of things that would enrich the region, restore prestige and power, and lay the race question to rest. The term "New South" in their lexicon bespoke harmonious reconciliation of sectional differences, racial peace, and a new economic and social order based on industry and scientific, diversified agriculture – all of which would lead, eventually, to the South's dominance in the reunited nation.

Unlike though they were, the picture of the Old South and the dream of a New South were both expressions of the hopes, values, and ideals of Southerners. In time, both became genuine social myths with a controlling power over the way in which their believers perceived reality. The mythic view of the past, already beyond the embryo stage in the antebellum period, was fully articulated in the 'eighties. The New South creed, born to inspire a program of action, expressed faith in the South's ability to bring about its own regeneration in partnership with sympathetic Northerners; but in the 'eighties it began to undergo a metamorphosis and soon came to be a description not of what ought to be or would be, but of what already was.

[. . .]

As they grew up in, and pondered, the depressed state of the South in the postwar years – and as the burgeoning wealth of the North was incessantly thrust before them as evidence of their backwardness – the New South prophets were early persuaded that their plight was not the result of the war itself (as so many Southerners believed) but that it was a natural consequence of those conditions which had led to defeat in the first place. The essential lesson which they learned and then translated into the first plank of the New South program was that wealth and power in the modern world flowed from machines and factories, not from unprocessed fields of white cotton. To make the region rich, then – to bring into existence the opulent South – they became in the first place proponents of industrialism and urbanism.

[. . .]

Assailing the errors of the past and denouncing their perpetuation in the present, the New South spokesmen turned confidently to the positive aspects of their blueprint for an opulent South. The commanding feature of their plan, of course, was the design for an industrial society. But the South in the 1880s continued to be overwhelmingly rural and agrarian, and it required no great insight to see that a program for the reconstruction of the Southern economy could not neglect agriculture. Despite their passion to erect an industrial utopia, then, the New South spokesmen also drafted a program for a renovated agricultural system infused with the values of business enterprise. Moreover, the vital connection between a sound farm economy and dynamic industrial growth was quickly perceived and assidu-ously worked out. The spirit of Hamilton and Clay was much alive in Edmonds when he wrote that a "harmonious relationship between industry and agriculture would make the South, with its vast natural resources and human power, 'the garden spot of the world.'"

[. . .]

Cotton's dominion was the great bête blanche of the New South spokesman and its tyranny occupied a central position in their economic and promotional writings. Edmonds filled column after column in the *Manufacturers' Record* with blasts at "the all-cotton curse" and Grady railed against the "all-cotton plan" with dependable regularity in his editorials and elsewhere.

[. . .]

Cotton's tyranny, according to the New South view, was all-pervasive. For the region as a whole it retarded economic growth and thus per capita income by frustrating industrial development. It put the farmer at the mercy of a capricious international market and tied him to a credit system that drove him deeper into debt each year. With a lien on his crop and a mortgage on his home he failed to realize that much of the profits from the cotton crop went out of the region, never to return, and it never occurred to him to grow crops which might be mar-keted locally; or, if it did, he lacked either the knowledge or the credit, or both, to undertake new systems.

To break this unhappy syndrome, the New South spokesmen early became advocates of agricultural diversification. Over and over again the farmer was told to cut his cotton acreage in half and plant the other half in smaller crops. The possi-bilities for agricultural diversification were without limit, or so it must have appeared to readers of Grady's optimistic essays on the variety of crops suitable for Southern agriculture. In the North, he noted, farmers concentrated on "small grains, grasses, truck farming, fruit growing, stock raising, and dairy farming," among other things, and all of these enterprises, he believed, were eminently suited for the South. Truck farming held special appeal for him, as it offered profits that were "simply wonderful." The truck farm, Grady wrote,

> should also be a fruit farm, and the fruit that cannot be marketed at good rates should be dried by the new processes. This would give employment throughout the entire season, and at the end of it the fortunate farmer would have before him the assurance that diversified crops and a never-failing market alone afford, with no guano bills to settle, and no liens past or to come to disturb his mind.

[. . .]

Important as the agricultural renascence was to the New South spokesmen, it always occupied a minor place in their blueprint for the future. The crusade for an urban, industrialized society was their absorbing concern. Indeed, so extensive was the emphasis on industrial propaganda that one observer, writing at the end of the century, concluded that "the program of the New South . . . has not taken the direction of agriculture. It is through its urban development only that the section has justly earned its sobriquet."

[. . .]

One of the ironies of Southern history lies in the simultaneous rise during the 1880s of both the New South creed and the mythic image of the Old South. Sweet "syrup of romanticism," to use Professor Woodward's term, flowed over the Old South in the same decade that the New South spokesmen's ideal of a bustling, rich, and reconstructed South captured the American imagination. Joel Chandler Harris introduced Uncle Remus to the general public in 1880 and Thomas Nelson Page's idyllic old Virginia became a national treasure after the publication of "Marse Chan" in 1884. Grady's landmark address before the New England Society of New York was only two years later. To compound the irony, most of the New South spokesmen accepted the mythic view of the past, rarely failing to preface a New South pronouncement with warm praise and nostalgic sighs for the golden age that had passed. While Old South idolaters such as Charles Colcock Jones, Jr., shuddered with horror at the mention of the New South, its spokesmen showed no such single-mindedness, and the warm reception they gave the emerging legend further emphasizes the attempt to relate their movement to the values and aspirations of the past.

[. . .]

Thus it was that the romantic view of the Southern past achieved what Gaines calls a "complete conquest" in the 'eighties. An enormous number of authors, the most prominent of whom were Harris and Page, "fed to the public fancy some variety of the plantation material." At the same time, the mythic view of the past was achieving the status of an inviolable shibboleth through other means as well. Schoolbooks and educational curricula carefully guarded the old memories. Religious imagery and political rhetoric were built on appeals to former glory. And numerous organizations devoted their full time to perpetuating the correct view of the past. To Jones's Confederate Survivors' Association there were soon added the United Daughters of the Confederacy, for women, and the United Confederate Veterans for men. All basked in the admiration shown them by *The Confederate Veteran*, a reverent journal established in Nashville in 1893 to represent the various memorial groups. One contributor to the *Veteran* stated simply what had now become the orthodox Southern view of the past:

In the eyes of Southern people all Confederate veterans are heroes. It is you [the Confederate veterans] who preserve the traditions and memories of the old-time South – the sunny South, with its beautiful lands and its happy people; the South of chivalrous men and gentle women; the South that will go down in history as the land of plenty and the home of heroes. This beautiful, plentiful, happy South engendered a spirit of chivalry and gallantry for which its men were noted far and near.

[. . .]

The allegiance given to the myth of the Old South by the propagandists for the New Order is in itself evidence of the extent to which the romantic view prevailed in the South. Further evidence is found in unsuspected places, the most notable of which is in the writings of Booker T. Washington. Normally, one would not expect the most influential champion of Negro freedom of his generation to contribute to a romanticized view of the slave regime into which he had been born. And, of course, there are many aspects of Washington's picture of the Old South which do not harmonize with the Thomas Nelson Page version. Washington's picture differed from the stereotype in his emphasis on the miserable living conditions of the slaves, the torturous flax shirt, the unpalatable rations, and the absence of the kind of "civilized" living that he was later to champion. Important, too, is his contention that the slaves he knew understood and desired freedom, receiving it first with great jubilation and later with a sobering sense of responsibility.

However, much of Washington's picture resembles the stereotyped version. He stresses the loyalty of the slaves to their masters and insists that it was based on a genuine love. When young "Mars' Billy" died there was great sorrow in the quarters and it "was no sham sorrow but real." There is no sense of resentment, and when emancipation brought hard times to a former master the slaves rallied and stood by him in his adversity. Washington explained that "nothing that the coloured people possess is too good for the son of 'old Mars' Tom.'" One is reminded of Irwin Russell's famous lines which began by extolling the virtues of "Mahsr John" and conclude:

Well, times is changed. De war it come an' sot de niggers free,
An' now ol' Mahsr John ain't hardly wuf as much as me;
He had to pay his debts, an' so his lan' is mos'ly gone –
An' I declar' I's sorry for my pore ol' Mahsr John.

Washington's account of Reconstruction is equally congenial to the romantic version. In his autobiography he includes the standard comic view of the newly freed Negro, stating that the principal crazes were for Greek and Latin and public office. He is critical of the precipitous way in which the Negro was pulled up from the bottom rung of society, and he has harsh words to say about Negro preachers, teachers, and politicians. Most important of all is what is not said: nowhere in *Up from Slavery* does one find an indictment of the native white Southerners' behavior during Reconstruction. The Negro suffered in the end, Washington felt, in large part because "there was an element in the North which wanted to punish the Southern white men by forcing the Negro into positions over the heads of Southern whites."

The commitment of both black and white New South prophets to the romantic view of the past was not made without purpose. To some extent, to be sure, there was no alternative for many of them, for their own emotional requirements as well as the need for public acceptance dictated that they operate within the intellectual framework of the time and place in which they lived. But however compelling the emotional and strategic considerations may have been, they were matched in appeal to the New South spokesmen by several concrete, useful functions which the myth of the Old South could perform in the cause of the New South movement. Washington . . . had special reasons for mythmaking. The white leaders in the movement quickly perceived and ably exploited the benefits that the myth offered them. For one thing, they would not have agreed with those later historians who saw the romantic legend exclusively as a source of fruitless ancestor worship and rancorous sectionalism. On the contrary, a close examination shows that it was nationalism rather than sectionalism, an identification rather than a separation, of interests that emerged as benefactors of the myth.

[. . .]

The complex strands that wove together the myth of the Old South – alienation of the Southerner from national values and ideals in the antebellum period; alienation of a few Northerners, both before and after the war, from the strident pace of material progress; innocent love for another, grander civilization on the part of most – did not obscure for the New South spokesmen the incalculably valuable service it could perform in the cause of sectional reconciliation, a basic tenet of the New South creed. If the myth in antebellum days had bespoken alienation on the part of Southerners from national ways, in the postbellum period it worked in precisely the opposite direction, uniting the two sections. To the South it gave a vitally necessary sense of greatness to assuage the bitter wounds of defeat; to the North it offered a way in which to apologize without sacrificing the fruits of victory.

[. . .]

Finally, in the South itself the romance of the past was used to underwrite the materialism of the present. The names and signatures of Confederate generals were everywhere in demand by railroad companies and corporations, for the New South prophets were well aware that the blessing of a "colonel" (if there were no generals handy) would do as much to float bonds and raise subscriptions as a dozen columns of optimistic statistics in the *Manufacturers' Record*. In *Colonel Carter of Cartersville*, a successful third-rate novel of the period, one of the characters observes wisely that "in a sagging market the colonel would be better than a war boom." The marriage of the gentle life of the past and the bustling era of the present was perhaps nowhere better symbolized than in the advertising columns of that journal of worship, *The Confederate Veteran*. There one learned that Confederate flags could be purchased from a New York firm and the aspiring capitalist found notices of potentially prosperous factories up for sale.

ᦒ ᦒ ᦒ

Steven Hahn

The Roots of Southern Populism[†]

"The stock law is the topic in this part of the county now. I want to say to the voters of Carroll county, that we as poor men and negroes do not need the law, but we need a democratic government and independence, that will do the common people good." So thundered the white dirt farmer L. J. Jones in an 1885 letter to the local newspaper. Jones was not alone in viewing the stock law as an instrument of class oppression or as an issue that transcended purely economic concerns. Nor was he alone in challenging the tenets of white supremacy and racial solidarity. Nor, indeed, did he articulate strictly regional sensibilities. Hundreds of small farmers and laborers of both races in the Georgia Upcountry rallied with Jones to protect the grazing rights that the stock law threatened to abridge. For them, the law was the starkest instance of efforts by the emerging postbellum elite to cast petty producers into a state of dependency. And in associating social and economic dislocation with new expressions of political power, they joined industrial workers in Northern cities and farmers in the Midwestern countryside who assailed the corruption of the democratic process in Gilded Age America, in a campaign to defend their own version of the Revolutionary republican heritage.

It has been customary to portray the 1880s in the South as a political hiatus, a period of relative quiescence between the turbulent eras of Reconstruction and Populism. With the end of military rule, it is argued, the Bourbon Democrats crushed indigenous Independent movements, consolidated their hold on the political system, and reigned virtually unopposed until the advent of the Southern Farmers' Alliance. Such a picture does have some plausibility if we focus on the Black Belt or the statehouses, though recent studies suggest persisting contests. But in the Upcountry the 1880s saw the intensification of social and political conflicts that had begun to surface in the years after 1865. A variety of issues stirred local politics and sharpened divisions created by the developing staple economy,

---

[†]Steven Hahn, *The Roots of Southern Populism: Yeoman Farmers and the Transformation of the Georgia Upcountry, 1850–1890* (New York: Oxford University Press, 1983), pp. 239–44.

none more so than the stock, or fence, law. Bitterly fought out over the course of the decade, the fencing controversy galvanized budding antagonisms that the Independents initially tapped, it revealed the cultural, as well as economic, dimensions of political struggles, and it paved the road to Populism.

Efforts to reform fencing statutes which provided for common or "open-range" grazing had been made during the antebellum era. Concerted agitation, however, began only after the Civil War, as part of a series of skirmishes over social relations and property rights. The impetus came from the Black Belt, where the "labor question" first surfaced after Emancipation. Believing black dependency to be the handmaiden of work discipline, the planters moved to circumscribe the freedmen's mobility and access to the means of production and subsistence. The legal and extra-legal actions taken by the planting elite to prevent blacks from owning land, to tie them to the plantation sector, and, with the rise of tenancy, to control their crops were products of such an offensive – one waged by large landowners throughout the Western Hemisphere and continental Europe in response to the liberation of slaves and peasants. Day-to-day matters of work rhythms, provisioning, and leisure also proved to be bones of contention. Complaining of the freedmen's "lack of forethought," their failure to "appreciate the importance of making hay while the sun shines," and their generally "lazy disposition," and attributing these "habits" to innate racial characteristics, the planters nonetheless acknowledged conflicting sets of priorities.

This confrontation was not peculiar to the postbellum period, but it became more salient when the prerogatives of slaveownership and the old plantation forms of management dissolved. By seizing upon privileges they had transformed into rights as slaves, the freedmen tried to stake out spheres of autonomy within a system of unequal economic power. Securing family sustenance was an important one of them. Freedmen, the traveler Edward King observed during his tour through the South in 1874, "are fond of the same pleasures which their late masters gave them so freely – hunting, fishing, and lounging; pastimes which the superb forests, the noble streams, the charming climate minister to very strongly." These "pleasures" may have been viewed as paternal indulgences by wealthy slaveholders; following abolition, they amounted to direct challenges to the planters' authority and claims on the freedmen's labor time.

Hence, when Georgia's landed elite regained political power after Reconstruction, they set their sights on remedying the problem. Commencing in 1872, a series of game laws, localized in nature, fanned out over the Black Belt. Three counties enacted statutes in that year, fourteen did so in 1874, and twenty-four followed suit in 1876. By 1880, fishing and hunting had come under regulation in most of the plantation districts. The laws covered three main areas: they established hunting seasons for a considerable assortment of animals and fowl, prohibited certain methods of trapping, and restricted access to game on unenclosed private land. An act passed for Burke, Taylor, and Jefferson counties in 1875, for example, prescribed it a misdemeanor to "kill or destroy" deer and partridges between April and October, to "trap, snare, or net" partridges, to catch fish by means of drugs or poison, and to "hunt, trap, or fish" on an individual's land without permission. At times these measures were passed separately, and strictures against trespass might encompass no more than specific districts or plantations within a county.

[. . .]

The trespassing ordinances require little explanation, but their implications were the most far-reaching. For by restricting entrance to unenclosed lands, the planters did not simply limit the freedmen's ability to hunt and fish, to obtain a portion of their subsistence independently; they also began a process of redefining use rights, a process of enlarging absolute and exclusive property. While fee simple landownership had always been the abiding principle, pre-Civil War custom and law turned unimproved acreage into "commons." The slaves could not, of course, freely use the forests as hunting and fishing grounds, though individual planters often permitted it. But blacks understood local custom and expected that it would continue to govern social relations, if the liberties they took upon Emancipation are any indication. Poorer whites in the Black Belt also held to their hunting privileges with great tenacity. In response to the new conditions of the postwar era, however, the elite subjected such common rights to an increasingly withering attack.

The fencing issue, which emerged as a central feature of this attack, also saw conservation, as well as agricultural improvement, serve as justifications for curtailing use rights. The antebellum practice of enclosing crops and turning livestock out to forage long commanded widespread support and worked to the special advantage of smallholders, tenants, and laborers. Only in the Upper South did attempts at reform make any headway prior to the war, and limited headway at that. After 1865, though, agitation won a closer hearing and soon a larger following. In Georgia and other states of the Lower South, planter organizations, such as local and state agricultural societies and the Grange, took the lead. Arguing that the "old habits" threatened the supply of timber, exacted undue expense, and encouraged theft, they called for new laws requiring the fencing of stock rather than crops. And they received eager assistance from railroad companies liable for damages if locomotives struck animals straying on the tracks. According to the presidents of several Georgia railways, these disbursements amounted to $70,000 annually, and as one agricultural reformer put it, the open range "impede[d] business" by slowing rail traffic.

The planter class did not close ranks on the fencing question. As with other matters bearing on social relations in the postwar South, some planters clung to the traditional ways. Representatives from many nonplantation counties, particularly in the cattle-raising Wiregrass region, also balked. Consequently, a blanket statewide law failed to pass the assembly. But advocates mustered sufficient strength to see local-option legislation through, and "An Act Relating to Fences and Stock and for the Protection of Crops" obtained approval in 1872. It provided for a county election when fifty freeholders submitted a petition to the county ordinary. All eligible voters, whether they owned property or not, were entitled to cast ballots. If a majority favored the initiative, the law, which forced farmers to enclose their livestock and deemed land boundaries legal fences for crops, would take effect within six months.

Traditionalist planters were not alone in opposing the new fence law in the Black Belt. Small-landholding and landless whites, along with the freedmen, accurately saw the measure as a threat to their ownership of livestock, and in some counties succeeded in defeating, or at least postponing, implementation. As an index of their growing power in the area, however, promoters of the law achieved notable results in relatively short order. By the early 1880s much of the central Plantation Belt had the statute in operation, and it was being pressed vigorously in the south-western section of the state. While sharing with traditional planters the desire to keep the South a "cotton country," these "reformers" inspired a significant meta-morphosis in the character of their class as a whole. For by accepting abolition and searching for new means of labor control, they enabled the landowning elite to withstand the demise of slavery and reassert their authority in the realm of production. In so doing, they contributed to a wider process through which the planters gradually transformed themselves into a type of agrarian bourgeoisie and market relations in agriculture took hold.

❧ ❧ ❧

Jack Temple Kirby

Darkness at the Dawning[†]

In the South, an era of reform called "progressive" by its contemporaries began with a new system of racial control. The craftily devised disfranchisement of blacks and poor whites and the achievement of legal segregation ended a quarter century of uncertainty and white controversy over the place of nonwhites. This great race settlement laid the foundation for most other reforms during the era. Some whites opposed the settlement; literate, middle-class people profited most and became the most articulate reformers. No one class held a monopoly on initiating and executing the settlement; it was essentially the work of a white consensus. From Mississippi in 1890 to Virginia in 1902 and to Oklahoma in 1907 – the disfran-chisers and segregators spoke of reform and of entering a new period of moral and material progress. To them, a generation of chaos had ended. The South left its dark ages, its long unhappy season of troubles.

The Civil War and Reconstruction destroyed a two-centuries-old system of social control and labor supply, lowered land values, and left a critical shortage of farm

---

[†]Jack Temple Kirby, *Darkness at the Dawning: Race and Reform in the Progressive South* (Philidelphia: Lippincott, 1972), pp. 7–9, 12–13, 20–1, 25.

credit. Landless and muleless blacks and whites sought places while landholders sought fieldhands without wages to give them or credit to offer them. Finally, country merchants – themselves deeply indebted to inventory suppliers – bound land and labor together with the crop lien arrangement. Cotton prices were high enough in the late 1860s to warrant the risk of advancing seed, plows, food, clothing and other necessities to sharecroppers during the growing season – all against the expected crop. The merchants midwifed a reborn cotton kingdom. Production advanced to new records, but prices began a long downward slide: from 29¢ per pound in 1868 to about 11¢ in 1890, to 7½¢ in 1892, to a pathetic 4.9¢ in 1898. It cost 7¢ per pound to grow cotton.

Scarce credit and low prices swept farmers into ruin and despair. The costs for fertilizers, jute bagging, and railway shipments remained high. Many croppers, hopelessly indebted to supply merchants, fled in the night to seek new places and fresh liens. Merchants raised prices and lien costs to recoup losses. They insisted that cotton, which always brought cash, be planted to the virtual exclusion of other crops – and these crops might have saved the soil. The same rules prevailed in the tobacco country. Such was the self-destructive economic impasse that afflicted Jefferson's "chosen people of God" and that created the class and racial struggle that stormed throughout the last quarter of the century.

[. . .]

The rural revolt . . . revived the stresses of Reconstruction. Within the state Democratic parties, white men divided along economic and social lines and bid against each other for the black vote. When blacks chose factions, they realistically sided with the white group which offered them office, protection, and the continued exercise of their civil rights. The planter-business – or conservative – faction usually bid higher. Outnumbered planters, large farmers, businessmen and townspeople sorely needed the voting help they gained by "fusions" with blacks. Sometimes conservatives also assumed the old paternal pose of protecting the "helpless darkies" against "nigger-baiting white trash." These planter-business patrons stood for government by the "best people," based upon sound economic principles and minimal governmental services. Such principles – along with a low tax base – helped them to rationalize the paucity of public schools, the infamous convict-leasing system, and inadequate informational services for farmers. Poorer white farmers leaped to the conclusion that black men blocked the pathway to their every goal.

[. . .]

In August 1890, the convention met in Jackson. After considerable disagreement over means, delegates decided to limit the suffrage by a poll tax, long residency requirement, and a literacy test. Chief among the convention's problems was assuring poor whites that they would not lose the ballot along with blacks.

This assurance took the form of the "understanding clause," which gave white Democratic registrars wide discretion in reading aloud sections of the law and judging applicants' ability to explain or "understand" it. In no place did the constitutional amendments mention race. The United States Supreme Court would accept this formula, the famous Mississippi Plan, eight years later in *Williams v. Mississippi*.

[. . .]

During the next dozen years, the genius of the Mississippi formula and the permissive apathy of most Yankees prepared the way for black disfranchisement in one southern state after another. The fateful step was delayed here and there as white political factions continued the contest for black alliances or hesitate – before the *Williams* decision – for fear of federal court intervention. However, variations of the Mississippi theme played again and again.

White southerners divided widely on race policy, with numberless nuances within each broad category of opinion. The poorer whites appear to have been the most militant negrophobes. Closest to the black masses in economic status, the poor usually had the most to fear from the specter of "equality." Thus, it was often they who made physical war on blacks and demanded clearcut, legislated race distinctions. Poorer whites had been the rank and file, if not the leaders, of Reconstruction Ku Klux Klans and other terrorist groups, and it was the spokesmen of this class who pushed the first post-Reconstruction Jim Crow laws in the late 1880s. Economically and socially secure whites, many of them former slaveholders, often took a conciliatory and paternal stand. They seldom felt the compelling personal need to underline their "superiority" with a rigid color line. Thus, some members of the white elite, such as Wade Hampton, actively stood in the way of segregation. Most, however, were passive before redneck fury and gave way when confronted. Sometimes, for reasons of political expediency if not actual conviction, planters and businessmen led the segregators and disfranchisers; such was at least partly the case in Mississippi, Alabama, North Carolina, and Virginia.

A handful of southern whites held beliefs bordering on egalitarianism. In 1884, George Washington Cable of New Orleans, foremost novelist of the Lower South, confirmed gentleman, and a twice-wounded Confederate veteran, penned "The Freedman's Case in Equity," an extraordinary article published in *Century Magazine*. Cable indicted fellow southern whites for their race hatred, segregationist sentiments, discrimination, and their cruel exploitation of blacks in the convict-leasing system. Cable nonetheless insisted that such racist extremism was not actually representative of the white South. There was, he held, a vast, disapproving "silent South." He hoped to scold this silent majority into countervailing action in behalf of blacks: "But is not silent endurance criminal?" he asked. "Speech may be silvern and silence golden; but if a lump of gold is only big enough, it can drag us to the bottom of the sea and hold us there while all the world sails over us."

Cable's nobility of sentiment won for him enduring infamy and immediate reprobation throughout the South. Among the bitter published retorts was that of Charles Gayarré, Louisiana planter-lawyer, Creole historian, and erstwhile friendly acquaintance of Cable. Writing in the New Orleans *Times-Democrat*, eighty-year-old Gayarré termed Cable's *Century* article libelous and impertinent and decried the novelist's "wish to bring together, by every possible means, the blacks and whites in the most familiar and closest friction everywhere, in every imaginable place of resort, save the private parlor and the private bed chamber, into which, for the present, a disagreeable intrusion may not be permitted." Old paternalist Gayarré vied with the poorest whites in his segregationist ardor, and admirers dubbed him "Champion of the South." Henry W. Grady, publisher of the Atlanta *Constitution* and the paladin of southern industry, joined Gayarré in a withering rebuke to Cable. Such attacks influenced Cable to move north, but he was not the last to dramatize white differences of feeling.

[. . .]

Only in the new century . . . did the South – from Maryland to the Southwest – consolidate a final racial settlement and a new orthodoxy. Some variances in whites' opinions and behavior would persist for a while, but the great inconsistencies of the 1870s, 1880s, and 1890s had virtually disappeared by 1906, when Middle Western journalist Ray Stannard Baker began his tour of the region, "following the color line." Shortly before, Professor W. E. B. Du Bois of Atlanta University sadly observed that, in contrast to previous decades and despite continued workaday "physical contact and daily intermingling, there is almost no community of intellectual life or point of transference where the thoughts and feelings of one race can come into direct contact and sympathy with the thoughts and feelings of the other." Blacks and whites "go to separate churches," he wrote. "They live in separate sections, they are strictly separated in all public gatherings, they travel separately, and they are beginning to read different papers and books."

This, however, had been precisely the goal of the white reformers. Now white men of all classes were at least partly freed of their racial obsessions. Putting these aside, they could turn to other matters. This was the spirit of the new century. Jim Crow rescued the white South from the dark uncertainties of heterodoxy. Now, with order and orthodoxy, anything might be possible.

10

Stephen Tuck

LIVING JIM CROW

Among the more consequential developments of southern history was the rise of "Jim Crow," the system of legal segregation and disfranchisement that consolidated itself across the region in the years surrounding the turn of the twentieth century. This legislative assault on the status of African Americans both fed upon and reinforced a wider onslaught, marked by persisting forms of labor coercion, a hardening spirit (North and South) of white racism, and a growing incidence of lynching and mob violence. So completely did the codes and culture of Jim Crow envelop Dixie, that it gradually came to be seen as a timeless, immutable reality, a fixed and essential property of the "southern way of life." The renowned historian C. Vann Woodward would shatter that notion in 1955 with his classic *The Strange Career of Jim Crow*. Since that time, as Stephen Tuck relates in his opening essay, historical scholarship on the origins of Jim Crow has been geared towards replacing reflexive assumptions of inevitability with careful inquiry into why the South adopted this course, and why it did so at the time that it did. Historians have examined the Jim Crow era from a number of angles, including the spread of legal segregation and disfranchisement, the forces and motivations behind these measures, and their actual effects on southern life; the interplay among the concurrent waves of Jim Crow legislation, extra-legal violence against African Americans, and racist imagery in popular culture; the varied ways in which Jim Crow was perceived on each side of the color line; the range of black response, individual and collective, to the system and culture of segregation; the place of gender ideology in the promotion of, and resistance to, Jim Crow; and, the evolution of Jim Crow – and black response to it – through the eras of Populism, Progressivism, the First World War, and the 1920s. The readings in this chapter address the forces behind the rise of Jim Crow, and the ways in which African Americans survived within, and at times mobilized to challenge, this modern incarnation of white supremacy.

Stephen Tuck is University Lecturer in American History at Pembroke College, University of Oxford. Dr. Tuck's research interests include American race relations, black protest, and white supremacy from the Civil War to the present. He is author of *Beyond Atlanta: The Struggle for Racial Equality in Georgia, 1940–1980* (2003) and *We Ain't What We Ought to Be: The Black Freedom Struggle from Emancipation to Obama* (2010), and *The Civil Rights Movement in America* (2010). His current research projects explore religion and Jim Crow, the civil rights movement abroad, and American historical writing in Europe.

The Jim Crow era haunts the history of the South. In the subtitle of his 1954 survey of American race relations, the distinguished black historian Rayford Logan famously called it "the nadir." It was an era when white mobs lynched over 3,000 African Americans; when white men could, and did, rape black women with impunity; when black southerners were disfranchised; and when images of black rapists and jezebels permeated popular culture. Not least, it was a time when southern states adopted a web of segregation (or "Jim Crow") laws, mandating racial separation in one realm of public life after another – from railroads to schools, libraries to hotels, restaurants to residential neighborhoods, hospitals to prisons, theaters to cemeteries, and restrooms to drinking fountains. (And nowhere, of course, was the color line more sharply drawn than in the institution of marriage.) For African Americans, the era was all the more heartbreaking because it betrayed the promise of post-Civil War Reconstruction, which had – for a short but heady time – conferred political rights on former slaves. The Jim Crow era would last until the Second World War and the civil rights movement. Like the Holocaust in Germany, or apartheid in South Africa, Jim Crow is at once repellent and fascinating. And like those other cases of racism (and other forms of oppression) run wild, the dark years of the past extend their shadows into the present.

Little surprise then, that the story of Jim Crow has been the focus of intense and abiding interest. For decades, historians have explored and debated the topic from many angles. What accounts for the wave of segregation and disfranchisement laws that swept the late nineteenth- and early twentieth-century South? How did Jim Crow legislation transform southern race relations (beyond simply codifying long-familiar practices)? How did southerners on each side of the color line experience and perceive Jim Crow? How pervasive were the lines of segregation, and how effectively did such artificial barriers impede any attempts to achieve interracial association? What were the varieties of African American responses – from informal and individual, to organized and collective – to the spread of legal segregation and disfranchisement?

Nor is it surprising how historical analysis of the Jim Crow era has tended to reflect contemporary notions of race. During the mid-twentieth century, a self-serving southern mythology held that white supremacy dated back to the overthrow of Reconstruction. It was, quite simply, a return to the natural way of things: well-bred white gentlemen were in charge, white women were safe, Yankees were north of the Mason–Dixon line, and grateful Negroes occupied their rightful, subservient, place. It was a storyline that dovetailed nicely with the contemporary defense of southern segregation.

But at the very moment the civil rights movement began to challenge the future of Jim Crow, historians began to challenge the origins of Jim Crow. None more so than C. Vann Woodward, the pre-eminent historian of the South. In 1955, one year after the Supreme Court's groundbreaking *Brown* decision (which ruled against segregated schools) – and the very year of the Montgomery bus boycott which introduced Martin Luther King to America – Woodward published a brief history of southern white supremacy: *The Strange Career of Jim Crow*. It turned the conventional understanding of the era on its head.[1]

For Woodward, the strangeness of Jim Crow lay in its twists and turns. It was in fact a recent phenomenon, not an ancient system set in stone. It was imposed only at the end of the nineteenth century, not immediately after Reconstruction. During the post-Reconstruction generation, black men voted and segregation was not yet on the statute books. Before Jim Crow, there were alternative solutions to the "Negro problem" on offer – alternatives that would be "forgotten" by the mid twentieth century. Above all, Jim Crow was the product of a political campaign, not the reflection of immutable "folkways." Indeed, if anything, white supremacy was the by-product of a struggle between white men, over *which* white men would be supreme. According to Woodward, white conservative politicians – and their cronies in the press – summoned the specter of "Negro domination" to split asunder the emerging Populist coalition of poorer whites and African Americans during the economic downturn of the 1890s. So Jim Crow was a story of change and contingency. And with change came hope. For what was contingent and constructed could, under the right circumstances, be *de*constructed – something the Supreme Court and Martin Luther King seemed to be doing with aplomb. Woodward was acutely aware of the electrifying present-day implications of his thesis. As he put it later, the realization that "race relations had a history" meant that "that the status quo was neither invariable, inevitable nor unalterable."[2]

The Woodward thesis soon came to dominate the study of the period. As is the way with dominant theses, this one in time found its critics. Some historians argued that segregation displaced not racial integration but racial *exclusion*; in other words, there had never been any halcyon alternative in the

South. Some pointed out that the imposition of legal segregation was often the codification of existing customs rather than the introduction of new practice. Some suggested it was rural Black Belt elites, not grasping city businessmen, who pulled the strings. And some pointed out that the process of reasserting exclusive white political control began soon after Reconstruction. To use a boxing analogy, the knockout punch at the end of the century followed a much longer softening-up process.

Yet despite – or rather because of – all the criticism, *Strange Career* remained the center of Jim Crow's historiographical universe around which other scholars orbited. Or to use an analogy suggested by one generous critic, *Strange Career* was the host on which the various parasites fed. Much to the annoyance of his critics, Woodward not only weathered the storm, he harnessed its energy to further his story. As Howard Rabinowitz – who had demonstrated the existence of segregation and exclusion during Reconstruction – lamented, "it has often been frustrating for Woodward's critics, since the master continues to absorb what they see as knockout blows and even to incorporate adversaries' weapons into his own arsenal."[3] With typical irony, Woodward celebrated critics of his thesis, "Long may they persevere."[4]

For all the debates, a consensus among late twentieth-century historians emerged in favor of an emphasis on change – the late nineteenth century, according to this perspective, saw a *new* surge of white supremacy in the South. Certainly that was how many southerners understood Jim Crow at the time. Consider the question of the franchise. The Democratic leaders who "Redeemed" the South after Reconstruction did not initially seek, or even envisage, a world without black voters. In a roundtable discussion of black voting in the influential *North American Review* in 1879, Mississippi Senator L. Q. C. Lamar knew of no "southern man of influence" who believed disfranchisement to be a "political possibility." South Carolina Governor Wade Hampton agreed. It was not that he (or other Democrats) thought that newly emancipated male slaves should have been given the vote, just that because of the Fifteenth Amendment, "the disfranchisement of the negro at this or any subsequent period would be more surprising than any political event in our past history."[5] Republican observers supposed that Democrats accepted the Fifteenth Amendment only because it had not stopped the Democratic party sweeping back into power. But even those cynical about Democratic motives could not imagine the black vote disappearing altogether. As late as 1890, Republican Senator John Ingalls reckoned disfranchisement would be "impossible . . . No race has ever been deprived of rights and prerogatives once solemnly conferred."[6] Yet by the opening years of the twentieth century, southern disfranchisement was complete.

The arrival of scholarly consensus meant that "the debate over Woodward's 'Jim Crow' thesis," to quote historian (and Woodward critic) James Tice Moore in 1978, was "already stale." Woodward allowed that he was partly to blame because *Strange Career* had stressed the question of when Jim Crow began over the more interesting questions of where and how.[7] But a generation later, historiographical debate over the Jim Crow South was fresher than ever. As Woodward predicted, the more interesting questions were indeed where and how – and also who and why, and how people responded.

Far from revoking the Woodward thesis, the answer to these questions enhanced it. Turn-of-the-twentieth-century southern historians found more change and contingency than Woodward could himself have imagined. Jim Crow was the product of a wide range of social tensions. It was frequently contested and never stable. As the title of one anthology put it, this was not fixed Jim Crow or immutable Jim Crow but *Jumpin' Jim Crow*. "What lessons can we draw from the defeat of the Readjusters [an interracial coalition in Virginia] in 1883?" asked Jane Dailey. "Before 1902 [when African Americans in Virginia were disfranchised] . . . before Jim Crow – nothing was sure, and it often seemed, anything was possible."[8]

Many of the new historians shared Woodward's passion for the future as they looked at the past. Some – perhaps even more than Woodward – argued it could, and should, be no other way. For Glenda Gilmore, placing oneself in the story was key to unlocking the past. "All of us, white and black . . . must think hard about how [white supremacy] stunted our lives and our imaginations . . . Our pasts – personal and collective – are present within us."[9] Like Woodward, many took heart that white supremacy was constructed rather than innate. In his biography of southern demagogue Ben Tillman, Stephen Kantrowitz concluded that white supremacy was not "so deeply ingrained that it might as well be biologically rooted . . . If that were true, then perhaps the United States was – or even is – condemned to remain two nations, separate and unequal."[10] As with Woodward, some drew strength from the "forgotten alternatives" of the past. To quote Gilmore again: "When white and black southerners search their pasts, they can find reason for hope amid a heritage of violence and racial oppression."[11]

Thus, the new history of Jim Crow followed in an older, engaged tradition that emphasized change and contingency. What was new about it was the introduction of fresh methodological approaches. Any number of developments in the wider academy transferred to the history of the Jim Crow South. But in particular, the rise of gender history (recognizing the power implicit in ideas of manhood and womanhood); the development of cultural history (including the study of ritual, rumor, gesture, and imagery); the influence of "subaltern" studies (including a focus on the hidden history of the masses and their resistance to domination); and the establishment of African American studies (the liberation of black history from being studied only in relation to white society), reoriented the field.

Take the case of gender history. Gender was certainly not something that Woodward considered. Gilmore tells the story that at one meeting, Woodward turned to a colleague and in "a stage whisper of those wearing hearing aids" asked "what *is* Gender?"[12] The answer was, and is, more than simply including women in the story (although the role of women was also ignored during the Woodward wars). Rather, the new history focused on how ideas of manhood and femininity shaped the origins and course of the Jim Crow era. Placing gender at the center of the analysis did more than add a little flourish to the existing story – it *recast* the story. In her highly acclaimed *Gender and Jim Crow: Women and the Politics of White Supremacy in North Carolina, 1896–1920*, Gilmore explained how "rewriting southern politics from the viewpoint of Sarah Dudley Pettey's [a "better-class" African-American woman in North Carolina] made everything look different: the reasons for disfranchisement, its immediate effects on black political life, and its legacy."[13] For example, the demonization of African-American manhood constrained the options of southern black men, while opening up some intriguing possibilities for black women willing to play the game of client politics in the Progressive era.

A number of scholars have shown how the appeal to white manhood became part and parcel of white supremacist politics and racist behavior. A particularly illuminating episode came in 1898 in Wilmington, North Carolina, where a sexually charged (and ultimately successful) campaign to remove African American officeholders unleashed mob passions that could only be satisfied with murderous violence. Detailed in the following selection by Glenda Gilmore, the Wilmington riot demonstrates the inflammatory power of appeals to white manhood to face down the black beast rapist. Like Woodward, scholars such as Gilmore see Jim Crow as a by-product of white elite conflict. But they add a third dimension – gender – to what was previously a two-dimensional story of race and class. In this telling, Jim Crow was not just a struggle by white elites for supremacy but by white *male* elites for supremacy. (Gilmore concludes by connecting these century-old passions with contemporary emotions. Indeed, explain the editors to the fine collection of essays on the Wilmington riot from which Gilmore's essay is drawn, "We look to Wilmington in 1898 . . . not to wring our hands in a fruitless nostalgia of pain, but to redeem a democratic promise.")[14]

Like Woodward before them, the new historians have their critics. Some worry that historians' fascination over the unpredictable dance of Jim Crow might divert attention from the heavy tread of racial oppression. The southern intellectual historian Michael O'Brien commented that the contributors to *Jumpin' Jim Crow* "seem to ask us to look at a glass that was, at best, twenty percent full and take doubtful courage from the sight. But one does not have to be much of a pessimist to observe that it looks eighty percent empty."[15] Some, such as the historian of disfranchisement J. Morgan Kousser, argued that making gender central to the story leads to a "disturbing . . . unwillingness to consider any other explanations of events or trends."[16] For Kousser, "institutions and institutional rules . . . not customs, ideas, attitudes, culture, or private behavior – have primarily shaped race relations."[17] (Interestingly, what fuels some of this criticism is a shared concern with social justice in the present. Kousser's privileging of institutions in his own account of disfranchisement, for example, dovetails with his frequent role as an adviser in present-day voting rights cases.)

But for the most part, historians who have widened the definition of politics to include customs, attitudes, and private behavior have won much praise and many of the prizes the academy has to offer. For example, Ed Ayers, author of the landmark *Promise of the New South*, found that the "challenge facing us now is to combine the brilliant possibilities of this new political history with the proven strengths of the old, fusing language and action, culture and power, boundary and center." For Ayers, the "prospect is exciting indeed."[18]

If gender history revitalized an old question, subaltern studies introduced a new one. Woodward's main focus had been the causes of white supremacy. Yet what of the response of African Americans? In *Strange Career*, African-American activism in the Jim Crow years was conspicuous by its absence. For historians, the most obvious place to look for protest (as Woodward did in later editions of *Strange Career*) was in the Second World War years and beyond. For Woodward, as for many historians, the Jim Crow era was a time of accommodation rather than protest, victims rather than heroes.

Subaltern Studies (so named after a school of Indian history that emerged in the 1980s) turned historians' attention to the ways in which the masses resisted and subverted domination.[19] In particular, the new approach called historians to look for a "hidden transcript" of resistance – a factory worker slowing down the line; a domestic servant stealing from her mistress; a teenager refusing to step off the sidewalk; a tenant farmer invoking the paternalism of the planter to request better conditions; young men and women dressing up for a night out to assert their worth. As Steven Reich indicates in the selection that follows, the historian Robin Kelley was one of the first historians to apply this approach to the Jim Crow South. In a brilliant essay on Birmingham, Alabama during the Second World War, Kelley examines the numerous fights and confrontations over segregated seating on the city buses. In so doing, he encourages historians to broaden their conceptions of working-class protest.[20]

At the height of the Jim Crow era, moments of collective public protest were rare. Indeed, their comparative infrequency might easily lead to the conclusion that the masses mostly accommodated the system. But the presence of the "hidden transcript" suggests otherwise. Thus, the sporadic moments of collective public protest are important because they reveal clearly what might otherwise remain hidden. In a sense, it was as if the seemingly tranquil landscape of Jim Crow sat atop a subterranean magma of resistance. Any rupture in the crust of white supremacy allowed the boiling rage to spew out.

Seldom was there a bigger rupture – or bigger outpouring of collective protest – in Jim Crow society than during the First World War. In the old telling (if there was a telling at all), this moment of resistance was so short-lived that it might seem to be an exception that proved the rule of African

American passivity. But, in the following selection by Steven Reich on the National Association for the Advancement of Colored People in Texas, we are introduced to a network of African Americans – rich and poor, men and women, soldiers and civilians, local people and national civil rights leaders – eager to exploit the opportunities opened by this "war for democracy." Taking advantage of the rhetoric of war, the turmoil in the Southern economy, and the presence of black soldiers, local activists reckoned "the time has come that the white man and the black man to stand upon terms of social equality."

This focus on "hidden transcripts" and isolated moments of open resistance has drawn its share of criticism. Some, noting that the difference between resisting and merely coping can be hard to define, have warned against romanticizing protest. The weak may have had weapons but we should not forget how weak these weapons actually were. Barbara Fields criticized the "near-totemic significance often attached to the notion of powerless people's agency. In a few scholarly interpretations 'the essence of Damocles' predicament, it seems, is the tensile strength of the hair from which the sword hangs, rather than the circumstance that a sword is hanging over him by a hair in the first place."[21] For the most part, though, new studies of resistance have deepened our understanding of black activism during the Jim Crow era – not to mention the explosion of black protest in the post-Second World War years. Recognizing such protest helps us explain the frequency with which southerners felt compelled to update Jim Crow. As Reich shows in the case of the First World War, Texas authorities used violence and imposed new laws to preserve the social order. Such protest also explains how a widespread movement could emerge so quickly in the 1950s and 1960s, when even greater ruptures in southern society allowed the "hidden transcript" to go public.

The long overdue rise in black studies led to the uncovering of African American community life during the Jim Crow era. These local studies reveal the ways that African Americans built their own worlds, and sought to resist those who interfered. As is often the way, the most marginal lives of all were uncovered last – in this case, the lives of poor black women.

Tera Hunter's To 'Joy My Freedom: Southern Black Women's Lives and Labors after the Civil War (from which the last selection is drawn) is a triumph of detective work and storytelling. The book as a whole charts the lives of working black women in Atlanta from slavery into the Jim Crow era. Here are domestics determined to "live out" from their place of work – and thus be free from supervision – even though the long hours working away from home could be extremely inconvenient. Here are washerwomen who use their control over clothing to strike for higher wages. Here are women who have a leisure life of their own, where they can escape the daily grind, express their sexuality, and (en)'joy their freedom. But it is not all 'joy. Here are women, too, who are stigmatized as disease carriers and consequently find their lives

247

regulated further (by well-to-do African Americans as well as by city authorities). And here are women who do indeed suffer disproportionately from disease – if only because of poor diets and healthcare.

Piecing together hidden history lays the historian open to the charge of relying on insufficient evidence to construct a connected narrative. The history of poor black women in the Jim Crow era necessarily draws upon fragmentary sources which have to be read against the grain, such as a snippet from minutes of a council meeting concerned about public morals, or a paragraph in a local newspaper expressing outrage at unreliable domestic workers. Ultimately, though, *To 'Joy My Freedom* is notable not so much for its lack of evidence than for its impressive range and use of sources – from local newspapers to municipal records to interviews with (now) elderly black women. Besides, if a historian is faced with a choice between a best guess and no guess, surely that leaves her with only one – suitably signposted – option.

Another charge commonly leveled at African American history (and at women's history and the history of ordinary people for that matter – so Hunter faces a triple whammy here) is that such accounts amount to nothing more than "me-too" history, one which merely adds new detail, rather than offering new interpretations. Hunter's reply is pithy and on the mark: "the parade of naysayers who wish to deny the importance of local knowledge, ordinary people, and everyday life are [sic] all humbug. Why must we choose to study the elite *or* the plebian, the earth-shattering event *or* the quotidian?"[22] Why indeed, especially when the story of ordinary people transports the reader back to a fascinating world of juke joints and blues bars, seemingly as close to hearing the rhythms of the past as a bystander on Atlanta's Decatur Street.

In any case, while the focus is on the plebian, the story is hardly quotidian. Hunter's private world of poor African American women connects – via white women's homes – with the public world of Atlanta's politics and economy. The resistance of washerwomen and domestics prompted the city to introduce new systems of control. In turn, Hunter's story of Atlanta shows the constraints that Jim Crow imposed on everyday lives. For example, in the extract that follows we see the "better" classes of African Americans alternately seeking to distance themselves from and to "uplift" the riff-raff – and generally failing on each count. Moreover, the story of poor black women reminds us that Jim Crow, for all its domination, had its limits. Even the most downtrodden found ways to carve out a private world where they lived, and loved, and longed for better days. For historians seeking hope from the past, it is an uplifting story. But the longing, of course, is also a reminder of the constraints and impositions of a racist society. It is a reminder, to quote historian Jacquelyn Dowd Hall, that for southerners especially, writing the history of Jim Crow is "a privilege even if it is sometimes laced with pain."[23]

NOTES

1. C. Vann Woodward, *The Strange Career of Jim Crow* (New York: Oxford University Press, 1955).

2. C. Vann Woodward, "Strange Career Critics: Long May they Persevere," *Journal of American History*, 75 (December 1988), p. 861.

3. Howard N. Rabinowitz, "More Than the Woodward Thesis: Assessing *The Strange Career of Jim Crow*," *Journal of American History*, 75 (December 1988), p. 846.

4. Woodward, "Strange Career Critics," p. 857.

5. L. Q. C. Lamar, in roundtable discussion of the question, "Ought the Negro to Be Disfranchised? Ought He to Have Been Enfranchised?" *North American Review*, 128 (March 1879), p. 231. Wade Hampton, in ibid., p. 240.

6. Michael Perman, *Struggle for Mastery: Disfranchisement in the South, 1888–1908* (Chapel Hill: University of North Carolina Press, 2001), p. 38.

7. Woodward, "Strange Career Critics," p. 857.

8. Jane Dailey, *Before Jim Crow: The Politics of Race in Postemancipation Virginia* (Chapel Hill: University of North Carolina Press, 2000), pp. 155, 14.

9. Glenda Gilmore, "But She Can't Find Her (V.O.) Key," *Feminist Studies*, 25 (Spring 1999), pp. 133–53.

10. Steve Kantrowitz, *Ben Tillman and the Reconstruction of White Supremacy* (Chapel Hill: University of North Carolina Press, 2000), p. 9.

11. Glenda Gilmore, *Gender and Jim Crow: Women and the Politics of White Supremacy in North Carolina, 1896–1920* (Chapel Hill: University of North Carolina Press, 1996), p. 228.

12. Glenda Gilmore, "Gender and *Origins of the New South*," *Journal of Southern History*, 67 (November 2001), pp. 781–2.

13. Gilmore, *Gender and Jim Crow*, p. xx.

14. Timothy Tyson and David Cecelski, eds., *Democracy Betrayed: The Wilmington Race Riot of 1898 and Its Legacy* (Chapel Hill: University of North Carolina Press, 1998), p. 11.

15. Michael O'Brien, review of Tera Hunter, *To 'Joy My Freedom: Southern Black Women's Lives and Labors After the Civil War*, *Times Literary Supplement*, May 25, 2001.

16. J. Morgan Kousser, "The New Postmodern Southern Political History," *Georgia Historical Quarterly*, 87 (Fall/Winter 2003), p. 429.

17. J. Morgan Kousser, *Colorblind Injustice: Minority Voting Rights and the Undoing of the Second Reconstruction* (Chapel Hill: University of North Carolina Press, 1999), p. 1.

18. Edward L. Ayers, "Portraying Power," in Jane Dailey, Glenda Elizabeth Gilmore and Bryant Simon, eds., *Jumpin Jim Crow: Southern Politics from Civil War to Civil Rights* (Princeton: Princeton University Press, 2000), p. 303; Edward L. Ayers, *The Promise of the New South: Life After Reconstruction* (New York: Oxford University Press, 1992).

19. The new social history – "history from below" – and the rise of African American studies also turned historians towards protest during the Jim Crow era.
20. Robin Kelley, "We Are Not What We Seem: Rethinking Black Working Class Opposition in the Jim Crow South," *Journal of American History*, 80 (June 1993), pp. 75–112. Other examples of looking at hidden history include Evelyn Brooks Higginbotham, "Beyond the Sound of Silence: Afro-American Women in History," *Gender & History*, 1 (Spring 1989), pp. 50–67.
21. Barbara J. Fields, "Origins of the New South and the Negro Question," *Journal of Southern History*, 67 (November 2001), pp. 820, 822.
22. Tera Hunter, "A Response," *Labor History*, 39 (May 1998), p. 185.
23. Jacquelyn Dowd Hall, "Reflections," in Dailey et al., *Jumpin' Jim Crow*, p. 306.

* * *

FURTHER READING

Cell, John W., *The Highest Stage of White Supremacy: The Origins of Segregation in South Africa and the American South* (New York: Cambridge University Press, 1982).

Dailey, Jane, Glenda Elizabeth Gilmore and Bryant Simon, eds., *Jumpin' Jim Crow: Southern Politics from Civil War to Civil Rights* (Princeton: Princeton University Press, 2000).

Dorsey, Allison, *To Build Our Lives Together: Community Formation in Black Atlanta, 1875–1906* (Athens: University of Georgia Press, 2004).

Gaines, Kevin K., *Uplifting the Race: Black Leadership, Politics, and Culture in the Twentieth Century* (Chapel Hill: University of North Carolina Press, 1996).

Gordon, Fon Louise, *Caste & Class: The Black Experience in Arkansas, 1880–1920* (Athens: University of Georgia Press, 1995).

Higginbotham, Evelyn Brooks, *Righteous Discontent: The Women's Movement in the Black Baptist Church, 1880–1920* (Cambridge, MA: Harvard University Press, 1993).

Litwack, Leon F., *Trouble in Mind: Black Southerners in the Age of Jim Crow* (New York: Knopf, 1998).

McMillen, Neil R., *Dark Journey: Black Mississippians in the Age of Jim Crow* (Urbana: University of Illinois Press, 1989).

Perman, Michael, *Struggle for Mastery: Disfranchisement in the South, 1888–1908* (Chapel Hill: University of North Carolina Press, 2001).

Rabinowitz, Howard N., *Race Relations in the Urban South, 1865–1890* (New York: Oxford University Press, 1978).

Williamson, Joel, *The Crucible of Race: Black-White Relations in the American South since Reconstruction* (New York: Oxford University Press, 1984).

Woodward, C. Vann, *The Strange Career of Jim Crow* (New York: Oxford University Press, 1955).

* * *

Glenda Gilmore

The Flight of the Incubus[†]

In 1897, Wilmington Republicans won a majority on the board of alderman and elected a white Republican as mayor. White Democrats promptly protested, and the previous Democratic city administration refused to yield city hall to the newly elected Republicans. Before it was over, yet a third board of aldermen constituted itself and elected yet another mayor. Ultimately, the state supreme court decided in favor of the duly elected Republicans. Wilmington's white Democrats, accustomed to ruling without majority support by state appointment, would not abide by the decision; they vacated their offices but immediately began to undermine the new government. Thus, in the beginning, the roots of the Wilmington racial massacre grew in political soil, but the Democrats' sexually slanderous depiction of black men rained down on those roots to nourish a mutant growth.

In Wilmington, the discontent of deposed officeholders quickly blended with that of frustrated white workers. Businessmen organized a "white man's labor bureau" to take jobs away from black men. The point was never to drive much-needed black labor out of Wilmington, but rather to skim off the best jobs as an object lesson. As a contemporary put it, "Of course, enough white laborers to supply the demand cannot be secured, but it is thought that after a few negroes have been turned adrift, the rest will need no further warning." The chamber of commerce boldly declared "against Negro Domination," arguing that officeholding by black officials "arrests enterprise, hampers commerce and repels capital." Many characterized the white supremacy campaign as a "business men's movement" arguing that even the "democratic political leaders are simply trailing behind." It did not bode well for the peacefulness of the community when the leading newspaper became a "veritable arsenal, a large closet being stored with revolvers and rifles," or when a "business men's committee . . . purchased a Colt rapid-firing gun with which to protect the cotton wharves and other property from incendiary mobs."

The sources of white men's discontents were political and economic, but the language of "home protection" gave that discontent a powerful psychosexual charge. Without the hysteria that swelled from the belief that their wives and daughters lived in danger, it is unlikely that otherwise average white men could find it within themselves to commit mass murder, as they ultimately did in Wilmington. A white man might protest an election or gripe about the prosperity of his black neighbors while he had trouble finding work, but it took Furnifold Simmons's incubus hovering over the city to incite him to kill. Asserting manhood and protecting womanhood – upholding "family values" one might say – provided a rationale for self-defense. To be remade into killers, white men had to connect gender and race; they had to

---

[†]Glenda Gilmore, "The Flight of the Incubus," in David Cecelski and Timothy Tyson, eds., *Democracy Betrayed: The Wilmington Race Riot of 1898 and Its Legacy* (Chapel Hill: University of North Carolina Press, 1998), pp. 76–90.

believe that one duty – the exercise of patriarchy – prevailed over all other commandments, including the biblical injunction against murder. Manipulated by propagandists elsewhere in the state, encouraged by their own ministers, inflamed by leading white men in their own community, they came to believe that black men's very presence in public affairs threatened white women. The lie of the incubus became their reality.

Looking back on the racial massacre in 1936, a Wilmington resident recalled the compelling power of the incubus. Colonel John D. Taylor, a one-armed Confederate hero, and his son, J. Alan Taylor, allegedly talked in the weeks just prior to the 1898 election. "Alan," the old veteran warned, "we are a conquered people . . . The day is coming, however, when Northerners will regard our cause, 'State's Rights,' as just . . . Meanwhile, we must continue to grin and bear it." To which his son, a rising young man, was said to have replied, "But my little daughter, Mary, and young son, Douglas, now in their 'teens are representative of a new generation; and I am going to do my utmost to make Wilmington a clean, safe, and happy place . . . I do not want them, and their little friends growing up . . . [among] rapists!" Together with eight other white men, J. Alan Taylor organized an armed militia to patrol each of the city's five wards, block by block. This group, known among themselves as "the Secret Nine," refashioned their identities. From the clay of upstanding businessmen, they remolded themselves into murderous "revolutionaries."

Given the lack of real, live black rapists, Wilmington's white men, now organized and armed in secret militias, began to see all around them signs that pointed to tears in the social fabric, that seemed to be portents of the incubus lurking just out of sight. It was in this tense atmosphere that Alexander Manly, editor of the only black daily newspaper in the state, the *Daily Record*, tried to counter the rape scare in August. Manly felt he must answer the unfounded charges that lay thick on the ground, and he took the opportunity to do so when the white-owned *Wilmington Messenger* resuscitated a year-old speech that Rebecca Latimer Felton had given in Georgia. According to Felton, neglectful Southern white men had let things deteriorate to the point that lynching of black rapists was the only remedy, a pronouncement that fit[ted] perfectly with the white supremacists' campaign.

To answer the Democrats' dangerous revitalization of Felton's command to "lynch 1,000 weekly," Manly fought fire with fire. First, he argued that often white women cried rape after illicit affairs across the color line came to light. Then Manly pointed out that white men both raped and seduced black women. Why, he wondered in print, was it worse for a black man to be intimate with a white woman than for a white man to be intimate with a black woman? "We suggest that the whites guard their women more closely, as Mrs. Felton says, thus giving no opportunity for the human fiend, be he white or black," Manly chided. "You leave your goods out of doors and then complain because they are taken away. Poor white men are careless in the manner of protecting their women." Thus, Manly played directly into the "home protection" campaign and brushed up against white men's bruised patriarchy.

It was the sexually charged political climate that gave Manly's words their explosive effect. Manly dared to equate the morals of poor white and poor black people. For Manly, class trumped race; poor white women were no better than poor black women. Manly's best-aimed blow was the suggestion that some white women freely chose black men as lovers, which shook the monolithic power of whiteness. All white women were pure, regardless of their class or circumstances. All black men were animals or children. Therefore, no white woman could prefer a black man over a white man.

Reaction to the August editorial came swiftly. Felton declared: "When the negro Manly attributed the crime of rape to the intimacy between negro men and white women of the South the slanderer should be made to fear a lyncher's rope." The *Wilmington Messenger* reprinted the statement each day until the election, often as the lead-in for a new "outrage" report, and the *Raleigh News and Observer* often ran parts of the column. Manly, very handsome himself, had commented that some black men were "sufficiently attractive for white girls of culture and refinement to fall in love with." To this one editor added, "Here he tells of his own experience, and he has been holding 'clandestine meetings' with poor white women, wives of white men." But others, realizing the problem of alleging that any white women sought trysts with black men, simply called Manly's editorial "a dirty defamation," a "sweeping insult to all respectable white women who are poor," and a "great slur." Tensions ran high as rumors circulated that whites were plotting to burn Manly's press and lynch him.

Ten days before the racial massacre, Furnifold Simmons seized upon Manly's editorial as if it had inspired the home protection campaign rather than answered it. Manly, Simmons told white Wilmingtonians, had "dared openly and publicly to assail the virtue of our pure white womanhood." All other political issues paled by comparison to this attack on the home. Politics "passed out of the public mind, and in a whirl of indignation, which burst forth like the lava from a pent up volcano, there was thrust to the front the all absorbing and paramount question of White Supremacy." The "sturdy manhood" of North Carolina should not "submit" to a "mongrel ticket" backed up by "federal bayonnets," Simmons warned, even as he reminded white men that "the issues involved are pregnant with momentous consequences."

We don't know if Furnifold Simmons read Sigmund Freud, but we can be sure that Simmons read his audience perfectly. His barely concealed sexual references – pent up volcanos, lava bursting forth, thrustings to the fore, federal bayonnets, mongrel tickets, and pregnant issues – struck white men where they lived. Such language linked the most intimate issues of home and family to local politics and federal law in a bond that Southerners would take a century to uncouple.

While Manly's editorial provided fodder for fully sexualizing the home protection campaign, John C. Dancy's vice presidency of the newly formed National Afro-American Council illustrated to Wilmingtonians the direct connections between black political power and home protection. Dancy had been born a slave in Tarboro, North Carolina, where his father thrived as a builder after Emancipation.

He attended Howard University and then taught and worked in journalism. As a lay leader of the African Methodist Episcopal Zion Church, he was a staunch temperance man who had traveled the world in support of the cause. Now, at forty-one, Dancy stood at the peak of his ambition, since the national Republican administration had appointed him collector of customs for the Port of Wilmington, one of the few salaried appointments available in the fledgling federal bureaucracy. At its first meeting in Rochester, New York, the National Afro-American Council adopted a resolution to "secure uniform marriage laws in all the states, and revision of the laws in the twenty four States where inter-marriage between whites and blacks is not allowed."

Here, thought white Democrats, was an astoundingly bold use of black political power to undercut white patriarchy through legal reform. By passing such a resolution, white men could argue, the new organization of black men declared its members' desire to marry white women. The legal right to marry white women, however, was probably not at all what the resolution meant to those present. In truth, black delegates addressed an entirely different but very pressing issue for their constituents. Their proposals sought to extend statutory protection to black women who were in long-term liaisons with white men, a common occurrence, particularly in the South.

In Wilmington, whites used the resolution as an object lesson for the damage that could ensue if blacks held political power. Dancy held one of the highest paid and most coveted appointments in the state. He had enjoyed the respect of many whites. A scant eight months earlier, before the statewide white supremacy campaign, the *Wilmington Messenger* said of him, "He has never been an extremist and numbers his personal friends among both races. He is true to his convictions, but always courteous and conservative in their expression." Suddenly, Dancy represented everything wrong with the Fusion takeover two years earlier; there was no longer such thing as a "courteous and conservative" black leader. Indeed, white Democrats argued, political success had licensed Dancy's personal desire to marry white women, as evidenced by his vice presidency of an organization promoting interracial marriage. The white Democrats argued that "the success of the combination [of Republicans and Populists] in this State . . . has evidently emboldened the race, specially [sic] those in this State led by Dancy." In less than a year, politics had led Dancy straight into white men's homes; soon he would stand beside their beds with the force of law propping him up. Whites ignored Dancy's protest that he personally had opposed the resolution.

In such a heated racial climate, each stroll down the street suggested to white people fresh evidence of the incubus that lurked in their midst. They began to turn incidents that might have earlier gone unnoticed or been seen as individual encounters into evidence of an African American plot on the safety of white homes. Some of these confrontations involved black and white men only. When, for example, Hugh MacRae, a prominent white man, stood in the street several feet from the curb deep in conversation with a friend, he simply expected traffic to move around him. Accustomed to deference, MacRae assumed that he literally owned the street.

When a two-wheeled cart, pulled by "a fast-stepping horse," came toward him, he probably never thought of moving. But the black driver surged "defiantly" onward, and Hugh MacRae jumped up on the sidewalk, grievously offended. MacRae recounted the incident that evening to his uncle, Walter MacRae, who is said to have exclaimed, "If something is not done to put down this surly and rebellious attitude of the Negroes towards the whites, we will have a repetition of the Sepoy rebellion, which ended only after the British had shot some of the mutinous leaders at the very mouths of cannon, to which they were lashed."

[. . .]

If white men could not abide a lack of deference from black men, they certainly were not going to tolerate it from black women.

[. . .]

We have only the flimsiest strands of evidence rendered by white sources to recover black women's outrage at the white supremacy campaign. The white newspapers began to report street confrontations between black and white women as signs of "Negro outrages." The stories suggest that black women struck back in the language of the streets.

The most infamous of these confrontations came in Wilmington. One morning, several white women encountered a black woman standing in their way on the sidewalk. One of the white women, forgetting for a moment her "frail but lovely form," seized the black woman and shoved her out of the way. The black woman raised her umbrella and began to strike back at her assailant. A black man, watching the fight, shouted encouragement to the umbrella-wielding woman: "That's right; damn it, give it to her." A street fight between a black woman and a white woman so confounds our notions of white women's delicacy and black women's deference, it is difficult to know what to make of it. Josephus Daniels knew, however. "Such exasperating occurrences," the editor argued about a similar incident, "would not happen but for the fact that the negro party is in power in North Carolina." Wilmington's white men also read such incidents as political and formed an organization of "Minute Men," vowing to put an end to three things: rising crime, poor policing, and "negro women parad[ing] the streets and insult[ing] men and ladies."

[. . .]

This unfinished "business in the furtherance of White Supremacy" explains why white men ran amok in the streets of Wilmington two days after the election, murdering some black leaders and driving others from town. The massacre testifies both to the larger purposes of the campaign and to the inexorability of hatred unleashed. What happened in Wilmington was about more than party politics or economic jealousy. It was about how political rhetoric can license people to do evil in the name of good.

[. . .]

At the end of the day, no one knew how many had died. Alfred Waddell seized the mayor's office, and his cronies demanded the "resignations" of Republican officeholders, filling the positions themselves. Subsequently fourteen coroner's juries met, and all found that the black victims had died "at the hands of unknown persons." Waddell thought around twenty African Americans had died. George Rountree, J. Alan Taylor, and Hugh MacRae bragged of ninety dead. It is doubtful that the terrified family members of the slain would have presented their loved ones' dead bodies to the Democratic city officials for a coroner's inquest.

Sometimes, murder does its best work in memory, after the fact. Terror lives on, continuing to serve its purpose long after the violence that gave rise to it ends. During the massacre, hundreds of Wilmington's African Americans left and huddled in the woods surrounding the city. In the next month, 1,400 blacks left Wilmington. Six months later, prosperous African Americans were still departing by the scores in special rented cars attached to regular passenger trains going north and west.

Some who lacked the means to flee appealed to the federal government for assistance. Three days after the Wilmington massacre, an anonymous African American woman sent a letter to Republican president William McKinley begging for help. Why had he not sent troops? Why had he left Wilmington's black citizens unprotected "to die like rats in a trap"? "We are loyal, we go where duty calls," she said, noting that many of Wilmington's young black men served in the 3rd North Carolina Volunteer Regiment mobilized for the Spanish-Cuban/American War. Now, with the damage done, McKinley could at least send a ship for the survivors, perhaps working out a way to take them to Africa, where "a number of us will gladly go." Then she hurled the rhetoric of patriotism back at the president of the United States: "Is this the land of the free and the home of the brave? How can the Negro sing my country tis of thee?" "Why," she asked her president, "do you forsake the Negro?"

[. . .]

The likelihood of an acquittal is what ultimately convinced the men in Washington to drop the matter. Within living memory, a war had been fought to establish federal authority. But thirty-eight years later, that "authority" still did not include enforcement of the US Constitution's guarantee of civil rights – even though the same authority was often used to check labor union uprisings. From the end of the Civil War until Dwight D. Eisenhower sent federal troops into Little Rock in 1957, no president dared to prove the power of the Reconstruction amendments on Southern soil. The federal government's failure to act in the aftermath of the Wilmington racial massacre became a pattern it followed for another fifty years.

Since the federal government refused to take action to punish Alfred Waddell, George Rountree, J. Alan Taylor, Hugh MacRae, and others of their ilk, the cultural work of the Wilmington racial massacre spread from its intensely local context to serve as an object lesson for African Americans across the nation. Publicity washed over Wilmington. The white supremacists who led the riot bragged in the national press about their success and justified their actions. As far away as Omaha, Nebraska, African Americans held a mass meeting to condemn "the criminal collusion of the Government and State authorities" with the leaders of the massacre.

[. . .]

As complicated as life is, we are rarely able to untangle our own cultural legacies; rather, we tend to accept them as a matter of course, to call them our "feelings," sometimes to name them our "prejudices." First, the politics of the massacre faded; then even its memory faded. But the most powerful legacy of the Wilmington racial massacre lived on: the idea that black men represent the greatest danger against which white women must be constantly vigilant. Now, as one hundred years ago, this simply is not true. All statistics show that rapes and assaults are overwhelmingly more likely to be committed on women by men of the same race and the most likely perpetrator is someone known to the victim.

Of course, white women are not taught to fear their acquaintances, lovers, and family members. They are taught to fear black men. Growing up as a white girl in the South, I learned an intricate racial etiquette that served to isolate me from black men even as I moved around them in public places. Never look a black man in the eye. Never sit down on a park bench beside a black man. Move to the other side of the sidewalk, or better yet the other side of the street, if a black man comes toward you. If the elevator doors open and a black man is inside, stand there and look distracted – do not enter. The racial choreography to which I moved served to prevent me from coming face to face with black men, but the dance itself always reminded me of the danger. I might never see the incubus, but everywhere I went, I could feel the brush of his wings.

[. . .]

Collectively and individually, white and black Southerners have tried to shed the horrors of their past and build an integrated society. We have not succeeded completely, but then we have powerful memories to face. Once we face them, their lessons bear down on us, causing us to question ideas that seem apolitical, and sometimes, at first glance, unrelated to race.

ᴦ ᴦ ᴦ

Steven A. Reich

Soldiers of Democracy[†]

On the night of December 8, 1918, Black residents of Kildare, an unincorporated hamlet nestled in the northeast corner of Texas, gathered at the local African Methodist Episcopal Church to hear a lecture "on the War and after the War." The audience, composed mostly of farmers and sharecroppers who struggled to make a living out of the stubborn piney woods soil, listened to the preacher describe how, despite their bravery abroad and sacrifice at home, Blacks were "still being treated badly by the White man." The United States, he grieved, "forced the Negro to go 3,000 miles away to fight for Democracy when they should have been fighting for Democracy at home." Now that the war was over, Blacks must no longer "close ranks" with whites but demand their rights as citizens, even if it meant opening "another war for Democracy, right here at home." Black veterans, he envisioned, would lead this fight for citizenship. Although whites drafted "our boys against their will," they also armed them and taught them lessons of combat. "When our boys return," he warned, a disciplined army of "trained officers, of men not afraid to die" and experienced "in killing white men," would invade the South. He urged his listeners to "arm themselves with Winchester rifles" and join the returning soldiers of democracy in a united stand against white supremacy.

This call to arms stands out as neither an isolated incident nor the wishful fantasy of a deluded preacher. On the contrary, African Americans echoed these themes in churches, fraternal societies, union halls, and social settings across Texas and throughout the South from 1917 to 1919, the years during and immediately following American involvement in World War I. They took such ideas seriously, seizing upon the idealistic rhetoric of President Woodrow Wilson's Fourteen Points to claim new rights at home. In a multitude of ways – withholding their labor, fleeing the state, evading the draft, stockpiling arms, forming local chapters of political organizations such as the National Association for the Advancement of Colored People (NAACP) – African Americans resisted their oppression, posing a formidable threat to the status quo.

[. . .]

The story of African American resistance during the war and immediate postwar years challenges prevailing interpretations of Black politics in the age of Jim Crow. Much race relations scholarship posits that the system of Jim Crow was powerful enough to preclude any substantive challenges to it. In an era of declining electoral rights, growing segregation, and rising negrophobia, African Americans, according to this view, remained politically apathetic.

[†] Steven A. Reich, "Soldiers of Democracy: Black Texans and the Fight for Citizenship, 1917–1921," in *Journal of American History*, 82 (August 1996), pp. 1478–85, 1490–2, 1496, 1498, 1500–1.

Other historians, however, insist that African Americans did not remain politically passive under Jim Crow. Black workers in the South, for example, recognized that demands for higher wages and shorter hours rang hollow without the attainment of full citizenship rights.

[. . .]

In a recent pathbreaking article, Robin D. G. Kelley argued for an expansive definition of Black political action. Southern Blacks did not separate politics "from lived experience or the imagined world of what is possible." In fact, political action and resistance among African Americans was going on all the time. Through countless "unorganized, evasive, seemingly spontaneous actions," Kelley writes, Black workers battled "to roll back constraints, to exercise power over, or create space within, the institutions and social relationships that dominated their lives." Such everyday struggles informed African American participation in moments of broader political insurgency.

American participation in World War I proved such a moment. Subterranean resistance briefly erupted into above-ground, organized political action. Local activists understood the implications of a worldwide struggle for democracy and self-determination. The metaphor of a war for democracy, the heroics of Black troops in France, and the anticolonial struggles of Africans served as a powerful basis for organized political action, empowering Blacks to expand their vision of what was possible. They linked their everyday challenges to white supremacy to those of Blacks not only in other parts of the South but in Chicago, New York City, the Caribbean, and Africa. The possibility that daily, unorganized challenges to white supremacy might cohere into something national, even global, in scope threatened the nation's white establishment, who mustered legal and extralegal authority to smash the emergence of such a movement.

[. . .]

Mobilization for the Great War in 1917 and 1918 presented southern Blacks an unprecedented opportunity to escape white control. African Americans fled Texas in droves, seizing new opportunities in wartime industries and military service. Elijah C. Branch, a Black minister from Galveston, established the International Relief Company in 1917 to secure loans for Blacks who wished to leave. Northern Black newspapers such as the *Chicago Defender* enjoyed a wide circulation in Texas and informed readers of the opportunities available in the North. The letters of the migrants reveal the energy and determination of southern Blacks to improve their lives, not only economically but socially and politically as well. Most migrants likely agreed with the Houston freight handler who wrote to the *Houston Observer* that he would move anywhere north "so long as I Go where a man is a man." Others willingly joined the army, as military service promised relief from repressive conditions at home. By the summer of 1918 the Dallas Exemption Board announced that "more negroes . . . responded to the calls than could be sent to camp." Black enlistees expected to receive good clothes, three meals a day, shelter, some money, and the chance for travel and adventure.

Migration to the North and the draft precipitated an intense labor shortage, giving those who remained greater leverage in negotiating wages. On some plantations, farm laborers, by withholding their labor, compelled planters to increase daily wages from $1.50 to as high as $4.50. Unregulated by government price controls, cotton prices soared to 35 cents a pound in 1919, as compared to 8 cents and less in 1914. For rural Blacks, the prospects of moving up the tenure ladder and of escaping debt and dependence on oppressive landlords never seemed brighter. Nate Shaw, an Alabama tenant farmer, recalled that "the war was good to me because it meant scarce cotton; and scarce cotton, high price." In 1918 Shaw raised enough money from selling cotton to pay off a five-year debt to his landlord. Other Black workers organized collectively to exploit the labor shortage. At Jefferson, in Marion County, Texas, washerwomen refused to take in laundry for less than two dollars, prompting white women to complain "that it is practically impossible to secure domestic help" because Black women are "so organized and demand so much." Employers in the state's railroads, sawmills, logging camps, and shipyards complained often of labor shortages during these years.

African Americans wedded their aspirations for higher wages and better working conditions to broader demands for civil and political rights. In a letter to the *Fort Worth Record*, an anonymous Black man announced, if "you think that we are going to war, bleed and die and come back here and still be a step stone for you unthankful people, not so." The Black press in Texas and elsewhere across the South celebrated Black soldiers as symbols of a new, more militant race pride. "'Black Devils' Are Sounding Death Knell to Trench Warfare – Germans in Deadly Fear of Our Black 'Boys'" ran one typical headline. Such stories carried an implicit message: Blacks at home should exhibit the same assertiveness as did the troops abroad. The *Galveston New Idea*, a Black paper, echoed this theme, declaring that "patience will cease to be a virtue" if lynch law and prejudicial juries continued to tyrannize Blacks. Now that America needed to stand united, Blacks should press "to rectify the wrongs done us" by "the bloody, savage vampires of the white race."

Such declarations fed white fears that Black soldiers would return from France to start a social revolution across the South. Indeed, few images haunted the white supremacist's imagination more than a Black man in uniform. African American soldiers exposed potent contradictions within the Jim Crow social order and raised critical questions about the very foundations of citizenship. Could United States soldiers stationed in southern cities be denied seats on a bus, at a lunch counter, or in a theater? What authority did civilian police have over servicemen who violated Jim Crow laws? Could a liberal democratic government compel citizens to sacrifice their lives in battle yet continue to deny them the franchise? Would Black soldiers who faced the horrors of death on the battlefield, asked the *New Republic*, "accept the facts of white supremacy with the same spirit as formerly?" And did not white opposition to Black conscription confirm that the southern social order rested on nothing more than fear? The *Houston Chronicle* thought so. In defending the military's decision to station Black battalions at Houston's Camp Logan, the editor wondered, "Can we conscientiously ask our allies to quarter soldiers whom we ourselves profess to be afraid of?" To ban Black troops from the city, he concluded, would be an open admission that Texas governed through an indefensible form of discrimination.

[. . .]

From the beginning of the war, white Texans acted swiftly with a campaign of terror and violence to restrict the social implications of military service. In August 1917 Black soldiers stationed at Houston's Camp Logan, responding to reports of police brutality against a Black soldier, clashed with armed civilians and police in a riot that left seventeen whites and two Black soldiers dead. The military moved quickly to punish Black suspects. In a court-martial in December 1917, thirteen Black soldiers were found guilty, sentenced to death, and hanged without public notice or opportunity to appeal.

Southern whites also tried to deny returning Blacks the right to continue wearing their uniforms for three months after discharge.

[. . .]

In response to this spreading racial violence, African Americans across the state, beginning in San Antonio in 1918, started organizing branches of the NAACP. As a branch organizer from Matt explained, "we are in need very much of strong organization" so "that we might be protected." Activists quickly enlisted a broad base of support for this organization dedicated to civil rights. The *Dallas Express*, a Black weekly, urged readers, "JOIN NOW AND FIGHT FOR JUSTICE – Lynching, Jim Crowism and Denial of Civil Rights Must Cease." The Fort Worth Branch circulated leaflets and handbills and advertised its meetings in Black-owned grocery stores and drugstores. The Dallas Branch sent representatives to the city's Black churches, where they spoke on the benefits of membership and enrolled new members. Activists distributed the *Crisis* and the *Branch Bulletin*, the NAACP's monthly journal of chapter news, placing them in Black-owned businesses and churches and selling them at association meetings where they reportedly "went like 'hot cakes.'"

Through these and other tactics, branches aroused mass support, enlisting recruits outside of the Black business and professional classes. At Galveston, Blacks of the International Longshoremen's Association No. 807 organized a branch, recruiting not only waterfront workers but other laborers as well. Elsewhere, janitors, laborers, letter carriers, housekeepers, laundresses, seamstresses – even the butler at the governor's mansion – joined the ranks of the NAACP. "The people are worked to a 'fever heat,'" exulted the San Antonio Branch secretary. That branch grew from an initial membership of fifty-two in March 1918 to over 1,700 by the summer of 1919, making it the second largest branch in the South, behind only that in Atlanta. Given the size of some of these branches and the occupational profile of the African American population, the Black working class likely constituted the core of the membership.

The national NAACP office assisted in boosting the Texas movement. In the fall of 1918, Mary B. Talbert, president of the National Association of Colored Women's Clubs (NACW), toured Texas and Louisiana to organize NAACP branches. Talbert dedicated her life to the eradication of mob violence, Jim Crow, and colonial domination of Africa, and she agitated for penal reform, education, and protective legislation. An acclaimed orator who "held the undivided attention" of audiences, Talbert delivered her trenchant message to some forty thousand people during her three-month trip, sparking enthusiasm for the NAACP. She raised several thousand dollars, formed eight new branches, and led membership drives at existing ones. Texas "is thoroughly aroused," she wrote; "everywhere they are anxious to join the Association." Thanks to Talbert's "two sterling addresses," she "will long be remembered in Beaumont," reported Aaron Jefferson; "her convincing argument gained many whom we could not interest." In addition to organizing branches, Talbert recruited volunteers to continue building the Texas NAACP after she returned to New York. "Texas will have 50 branches," she predicted; "of the people I talked with, [many] do not go to sleep."

The work of Mary Talbert demonstrates the centrality of women in building branches. Women took the lead in organizing several branches and constituted the core of the membership in many of them, and at least ten served on branch executive committees. Talbert expanded branch membership by appealing to women through the Texas Federation of Colored Women's Clubs. As president of the NACW, Talbert strengthened the relationship between the national organization and its state branches through frequent visits, creating a nationwide network of women who supported and implemented NACW initiatives. Talbert called upon such contacts to build the Texas NAACP.

[. . .]

Letters from rural branches reveal an eagerness for political activity and a faith in democracy among poor people. Not since Reconstruction had an organization emerged that connected Blacks in these isolated regions to the larger struggle for citizenship. Through the NAACP, rural Blacks learned of civil rights battles occurring beyond the confines of their community.

[. . .]

The advent of the NAACP in Texas generated vigorous debate among the state's African Americans. Some questioned the value of organizing. Skeptics charged that the NAACP would heighten, not ease, racial tensions and that it would isolate, not redress, Black grievances. Within branches, members quarreled over strategies and tactics. Some preferred to steer a cautious course. Others advocated a more militant approach.

[. . .]

This resistance among Blacks fed white fears that outside agitators and Black Texans had allied to overthrow the state's racial order.

[. . .]

By the end of 1921 all but seven of the thirty-three branches had disbanded. Fear of violence frustrated attempts to reorganize branches.

৯ ৯ ৯

Tera Hunter

To 'Joy My Freedom[†]

When Alice Adams, a domestic worker, moved to Atlanta in the early 1900s, her family members warned her about the perils of unseemly places that she should avoid. As she recalled years later, they said to "stay off Decatur Street, and I did just that." But as Adams admitted, despite the street's notorious reputation for "vice" and crime, she was drawn to experience its attractions for herself. "They had one restaurant on . . . Decatur Street and Central Avenue. We would go in that restaurant and go from there to Eighty One Theater." Mary Morton, also a domestic worker, had a similar story to tell. "Decatur Street was terrible, momma didn't allow us on Decatur Street," she reported of her youth. "One night my sister and me went over to spend the night with a girl that lived out in that section, and momma didn't allow us to go in no shows or nothing like that, but we went to a picture show and so – and this girl took us."

Despite familial admonitions, working-class women like Adams and Morton found relief from their workaday lives in Atlanta's central amusement district. Though old forms of leisure persisted, African Americans increasingly turned to commercial outlets for pleasure amid the rigors of their daily labors. Lugenia Burns Hope had created the Neighborhood Union, in part, to provide "wholesome" alternatives to Decatur Street's "hurtful" amusements for young women like Adams and Morton. Henry Hugh Proctor expanded the community outreach programs in his church with a similar goal in mind. But thanks to rapid urbanization, advances in technology, and electricity, many new and controversial amusements had become

[†]Tera Hunter, *To 'Joy My Freedom: Southern Black Women's Lives and Labors after the Civil War* (Cambridge, MA: Harvard University Press, 1997), pp. 145–6, 161–7.

accessible to a wider public by the turn of the century. The changing rules and expectations of public decorum and social conviviality as strangers encountered one another more casually and intimately on this new terrain heightened the tensions that accompanied modernization throughout urban America in the Victorian era. The imperatives of de jure segregation exacerbated anxieties in the South even further. Blacks in Atlanta vigorously created and defended a separate and unequal, but vibrant and distinctive, world of entertainment that was at once removed from and subjected to the limitations imposed by Jim Crow. Alice Adams and Mary Morton would encounter this rich, contradictory, and contested domain at its most typical on Decatur Street, the center of urban leisure.

[. . .]

When blacks in Atlanta entered amusement establishments they sought, and to a large degree achieved, respite from the trials and tribulations of their workaday lives, yet they traversed a terrain as hotly contested as wage labor or electoral politics. The proximity of legal entertainment and the underground world of vice in the era of prohibition and social purity crusades exacerbated tensions over physical pleasures and indulgences. The red-light districts in Atlanta were the crossroads for the intersection of these two worlds, and it was here that a subterranean nightlife originated and fostered opposition to the demands and values of the dominant culture.

While white pimps such as George Jones, Pretty-boy Redmond, and Fashion-plate Charley held sway over the illicit trade on Courtland Street, black gangsters such as Joe Slocum, Lucky Sambo, and Handsome Harry controlled the sporting action and barrooms on Decatur Street. Rowdiness, violence, and gangsterism were common occurrences. As Perry Bradford recalled from his childhood: "It was a tame Saturday night in the notorious Decatur Street section if there were only six razor operations performed, or if only four persons were found in the morgue on Sunday morning."

Decatur Street's reputation for colorful characters, violence, and illicit sex led moral reformers to confront the sinful and extend "the right hand of fellowship" to wayward souls. One group of women organized open-air religious meetings at the height of merrymaking on Saturday nights "to bring the frequenters of that thoroughfare to a higher moral plane." But despite its notoriety, Decatur Street patrons were typically not the larger-than-life pimps or mobsters but ordinary women and men in search of social diversions and alternative financial prospects denied to them elsewhere in their lives.

The saloon, in its multiple guises, was one of the most common and most controversial sites where these expectations were met. The emergence of industrial capitalism in the late nineteenth century stimulated the popularity of the saloon as a distinctly class-based institution. Mechanized labor, tighter work discipline, shorter workdays, relatively higher wages, and intensified regulation of public recreation were all factors that led workers to drink in saloons. Though saloons were dominated by men, women visited them as well. Some workers went to saloons and clubs after work in the evenings. Others who were unemployed because of the seasonal nature of many jobs patronized the bars during the day as well. Still others took time off from jobs that offered no vacations.

Drinking was not the only appeal of saloons in Atlanta, nor was it necessarily the main attraction. Prostitution and gambling also thrived in the tenderloin bars. The blues and ragtime melodies, played by pianists like Thomas Dorsey, brought in patrons to listen and dance. As Dorsey described the music and the atmosphere, it was a "lowdown type music, they put any kind of words to it they wanted . . . In these places, they'd shine out with anything, say 'Yeah!', you know, so I think that's why they called it barrelhouse, you'd go down to where they'd opened a keg, and you'd hear anything, did anything, you could get arrested." It was precisely the "doing anything" that disturbed city officials, who decided that the music was as much of an "improper" stimulus as alcoholic drinks.

Drinking was a pastime widely enjoyed and a habit difficult to break; as Spelman College students discovered in the 1890s in their proselytizing missions across the state, wage-earners were not easily persuaded to give up drinking or other "hurtful" amusements. Though religious faith and biblical teachings had the strongest influence in deterring the use of alcohol, devout Christians did not necessarily think of drinking per se as evil. Still, not all working-class people chose to indulge, since drinking created or exacerbated family stress and diverted hard-earned wages away from family coffers toward fleeting gratification. Temperance societies, sponsored by the American Missionary Association, were popular among black working-class people shortly after the Civil War in Atlanta. Under the banner of the "Lincoln Brigades," the "Bands of Hope," and the "Morning Stars," freedpeople dedicated themselves to abstaining from liquor, tobacco, and swearing. Woman's Christian Temperance Union branches, such as the Sojourners of Truth, were active in the early twentieth century and picked up where the early leagues left off. Some secret societies also enforced morality rules among their members that prohibited drinking and other vices. Bettie Dacus was expelled from the Household of Ruth, for example, after it was discovered and verified by official records that she had been arrested, fined, and jailed for "disorderly and immoral conduct."

Middle-class reformers and city officials led the most intense campaign against alcohol and sounded the loudest alarm against the heterogeneity of drinking crowds. "White men and black men, white women and black women, and even children, are now seen at the bars of the beer saloons, drinking together," one source reported. The city tried to prevent this intermingling across color and gender lines by requiring "near beer" saloons to designate one race of customers exclusively and to prohibit women altogether. Working-class blacks and whites defied the law in saloons and "dago bar joints," which led many whites, and some blacks, to fear the violence – or, what was more troubling, the affection – that could develop between these two groups. Rumors of an interracial crime ring operating on Decatur Street in the 1910s made these fears palpable. But even when segregation was adhered to, many of the saloons designated as "colored only" were owned and managed by whites. At times, a semblance of "social equality" prevailed between the white owners and the black customers: "Some of the saloon men allow the negroes to curse them, applying the vilest epithets, while they in turn call the negroes 'mister' and speak of them as gentlemen," one source reported. On the other hand, some white saloon owners, in the spirit of Jim Crow, charged their black customers inflated prices for diluted drinks.

The electorate in Atlanta debated the pros and cons of public drinking in highly visible political campaigns beginning in the 1880s. Voters flip-flopped from one election to the next, variously passing and rejecting prohibition, with blacks carrying critical swing votes. Prior to 1908, when prohibition against the manufacture and selling of alcohol was enacted throughout the state, the city made efforts to regulate the liquor trade through licensing saloonkeepers, restricting their hours of operation, and barring women and children. Alcohol was a substance that could not be easily regulated through the law, however. After 1908, suppliers from Chattanooga, Tennessee, and Jacksonville, Florida, regularly delivered gallons of bootleg whiskey and beer to barrooms and residences. Saloonkeepers resorted to a quasi-legal selling of "near beer." In reality, critics argued, "near beer" was a clever euphemism for the real thing and was more widely available than undisguised alcoholic beverages prior to prohibition. "Near beer" could be bought at some soda-fountain stands, and since it was presumably a nonintoxicating substance, it was difficult for city officials to justify special regulations or taxes on it.

Despite the interracial character of saloon customers, police officers disproportionately targeted African Americans in their raids and arrests. The Atlanta riot of 1906 was ample demonstration of the sinister power of racial paranoia that fantasized a biological disposition for inebriation based on race. The Georgia Anti-Saloon League alluded to memories of the riot in its campaign against "near beer" saloons. These attitudes led to simultaneous raids throughout the city to empty black bars, poolrooms, and other such places of "idlers" and "vagrants."

The victims of barroom raids were predominantly men, which reflected the fact that the saloons attracted a mostly male clientele drawn to other by-products of the saloon, such as gambling and prostitution. The coupling of sex and drinking was not merely coincidental to the disproportionate number of attacks on black men in particular. White fears of black male sexuality running rampant under the influence of alcohol and leading to attacks upon white women were exacerbated by the casual attitudes toward racial etiquette shown on Decatur Street.

Black women were also the target of complaints, however; they were criticized for violating both prohibitions against consuming intoxicating drinks and gender restrictions. And though black women were arrested less frequently than black men, they were picked up, far more than white women, for drinking, gambling, using or selling cocaine, and running "blind tigers" of their own.

The moral implications of women consuming intoxicating substances troubled many middle-class blacks and whites. Women not only evaded laws prohibiting them from entering saloons, they frequented barroom "annexes," they drank alcohol in alleys and streets, and they sold beer from their homes. Jackson

McHenry, one of the leaders in the prohibition campaign during the 1880s, complained to city officials in 1904 about women evading anti-liquor edicts. Some restaurants were simply charades for "women bars" designed expressly to cater to women of all ages who were carousing all day and late at night "when they ought to be at work," he argued. As McHenry urged the "better element" among Negroes to fight against the "women bars" and close them up, an avowed Christian joined the chorus of alarm against the downfall of the women of the race who frequented Decatur Street: "Just see them with glasses and quarts of beer! Hear the language that they use! See them almost beastly drunk! It is a shame. It is a disgrace to the race. It is a scandal on moral and civil men." Various groups of preachers and "colored citizens" petitioned the city council before and after prohibition to "break up places where women congregate and drink."

The outrage expressed against women who drank was part of a larger discourse on the virtues of subordinate women in an urban setting. The sheer number of black women in cities like Atlanta magnified their visibility on the street and reinforced the perception that they were out of control – beyond the grip of black men as well as white authorities. Women's behavior became a trope for the race, their public deportment and carriage the basis by which some assumed the entire race would be judged. The journalist E. B. Barco was among the most consistent critics of female indulgence in a variety of urban amusements. His descriptions of women strolling the streets in the red-light district evoked images of seasoned sexual predators and pubescent hormones run amok: this "class," he wrote, "can be seen prowling around on the streets seemingly seeking whom they may or can devour, instead of being in their homes, helping their poor mothers to earn bread." Barco explained their delinquency as a racial deficiency: "Self pride in white women is natural instinct, but in the great majority of negro women self pride is much needed." His solution was disciplinary and blunt: "Let the city authorities enact an ordinance forcing this class of women off the streets after a certain hour, or lock them up."

Working-class women and men largely refused to abide by the simplistic polarities between "wholesome" and "hurtful" amusements. Although women like Alice Adams and Mary Morton displayed some ambivalence about reconciling parental admonitions with youthful curiosity, they ultimately found respite in a wide range of recreational activities in small, private circles in their homes and neighborhoods and also in mass, popular events in the burgeoning red-light district. The division between decency and indecency that dominated the middle-class discourse on leisure reflected the tenor of debate throughout urban America as popular culture modernized. But the anxieties manifest everywhere about crowds of strangers indiscriminately engaging in festive social intercourse were magnified in the Jim Crow South, where whiteness was literally reinscribed through play – in grandiose landscaped gardens, mechanical amusement parks, shopping promenades, and in the theaters on stage and off. Decatur Street, the richest and most contested terrain, staunchly upheld the color line and at the same time openly defied it. Consumers, performers, and small entrepreneurs were multiracial and often engaged in interracial social, cultural, and material transactions. But middle-class reformers refused to abandon the sights, sounds, and visceral experiences of revelry to the whims of consumer preferences and demands. The irony of this situation was that playing was hard work for everyone – for the officials and reformers, who worked hard to control, contain, and impose order on leisure time and space, and for working-class people, who worked hard at having fun.

11

Eric Arnesen

WORLDS OF SOUTHERN LABOR

Southern history is, in no small measure, the story of working folk. From the farmlands and timberlands, to the waterfronts and mines, to the cotton mills and private homes, to many other points between, labor has been an essential aspect of the lives of most southerners. Not so long ago, however, Dixie's working-class past remained a woefully neglected branch of southern historiography. That began to change in the 1970s, and by the 1980s the "new labor history," then in full bloom, was finally making its presence felt below the Mason–Dixon line. By the last decade of the twentieth century and the opening decade of the twenty-first, labor history had emerged as one of the busier areas of southern historical scholarship.

With growing depth and subtlety, historians have been investigating how the circumstances, options, and strategies of southern workers have varied between male and female, black and white, rural and urban, agricultural and industrial, service and artisanal, settled and transient, free and coerced. Propelling this research has been a series of intriguing questions. In what ways is the history of southern labor distinctive; in what ways, merely a variant on the wider patterns of working-class experience in America? How valid, historically, is the classic portrayal of the southern common folk as passive, individualistic, fatalistic – as more receptive to paternal control than to collective action? How, in the relations between southern workers and their employers, has a common sense of regional identity held up against the chronic tensions of class? What accounts for the oft-noted weakness of organized labor in the South compared with that in the North? In settings where it did take root, how far did labor unionism go in challenging the racial order of the New South? In what measures, that is, did organized labor serve as a brick in the wall of segregation, as a battering ram for racial equality, or as the testing ground for a diversity of agendas, arising on each side of the color line? Likewise, in what ways did southern unionism challenge, and in what ways reinforce, the gender hierarchies of the New South? The opening essay by Eric Arnesen, and the diverse set of selections he has chosen for this chapter, bring illuminating attention to all these questions.

Eric Arnesen, Professor of History at The George Washington University, has published extensively on black union activism, workplace race relations, civil rights, and organized labor in America. In addition to dozens of articles and essays, he is author of *Waterfront Workers of New Orleans: Race, Class, and Politics, 1863–1923* (1991), and *Brotherhoods of Color: Black Railroad Workers and the Struggle for Equality* (2001). He is also editor of *Black Protest and the Great Migration: A Brief History with Documents* (2002), *The Human Tradition in American Labor History* (2003), *The Encyclopedia of U.S. Labor and Working Class History* (2006), and *The Black Worker: Race, Labor, and Civil Rights since Emancipation* (2007); and co-editor (with Bruce Laurie and Julie Greene) of *Labor Histories: Class, Politics, and the Working-Class Experience* (1998). He is currently working on a political biography of the civil rights and labor leader, A. Philip Randolph.

At the dawn of the twentieth century, few Americans, black or white, would have questioned the centrality of the "race question" in the states of the former Confederacy. The demise of Reconstruction, the restriction of African Americans' political rights, the rise of legalized segregation, and the ubiquity of a shrill anti-black political discourse served as constant reminders that whatever the promises of emancipation, its outcome fell far short of equality. Yet "notwithstanding the many political disadvantages which the race must face," the black New Orleans weekly the *Southwestern Christian Advocate* concluded in 1902, "the great question of to-day is the labor question." To emphasize the point, it insisted the following year that the labor question "overshadows all other questions" confronting African Americans.[1] Given the saliency of *race* in scholarly treatments of the New South (chronologically defined here as the period between 1880 and 1930), these claims seem surprising. Yet the paper's editors were hardly alone in highlighting the prominence of what contemporaries called the region's "labor question" – or "labor problem" – for blacks and whites alike.

Today, historians have come to recognize the centrality of labor, both on and off the land, to the lives of southerners – and to the history of the region itself. "No strand of southern life can be fully grasped without regard to issues of labor," Daniel Letwin observes in his own assessment of labor relations in the industrializing South. "[N]o serious chronicle of working-class America can slight the South."[2] In so arguing, Letwin is speaking to relatively recent developments in historical scholarship. Until the 1970s and 1980s, the history of southern workers was but a minor current in both southern history and American labor history. Earlier generations of southern historians expressed more interest in the region's politics and economic development (or lack thereof), while US labor historians focused somewhat narrowly on skilled craft workers and trade unionism outside of the South. Even as the "new labor historians" of the 1960s to the 1980s reoriented the field away from its institutional focus toward an exploration of the "local world" (in Herbert Gutman's phrase) of workers at the grass roots, their focus remained on the North. "For decades," Melton McLaurin pointed out in 1978, "labor historians virtually ignored the South," assuming that the region was an "agrarian society" with "no class struggle to relate, no industrial labor force to examine."[3] For their part, historians of the New South black experience concentrated on the transition from slavery to freedom, exploring the agricultural systems of sharecropping and tenant farming that ensnared the vast majority of black workers at the bottom of the economic ladder. When researchers focused on non-agricultural pursuits, they tended to highlight the operation of a discriminatory labor market that kept black workers out of skilled, higher-paying jobs. For many scholars, the dismal features of the New South – its higher levels of poverty and racial division, and its lower levels of industrialization, labor conflict, and union density – reconfirmed the image of a weak working class, docile, fragmented, and isolated. It was not a setting likely to attract the attention of scholars eager to recover lost traditions of resistance to an emerging industrial capitalism. It was as if southern workers were an amorphous – perhaps anonymous – mass, ground down under the heel of capital and a racially oppressive social order.

To be sure, from time to time those same workers defied their stereotype in ways that caught the historian's eye. The Grand and Noble Order of the Knights of Labor had taken firm root in the South, as it had in much of the nation, during the 1880s. An ideologically heterogeneous organization – one which deplored the growing concentration of wealth in the hands of the few and advocated cooperation over competition – the Knights opened its doors to all bona fide producers, regardless of gender or race (with the notable exception of Chinese in the United States). Such unprecedented (if limited) inclusivity meant black participation, even if, for most, within racially separate local assemblies. The Order engaged in high-visibility conflicts, conducting boycotts, waging strikes in textile mills, coal mines, and sugar fields, and, not infrequently, challenging the color line. Although the Knights faded by the end of the 1880s, renewed labor conflict erupted in the early 1890s. Through their spirited organizing and strike efforts, historian C. Vann Woodward noted, workers from the coal fields of Tennessee and Alabama to the waterfront of

New Orleans "gave notice . . . that Southern labor was not going to accept the Old-South labor philosophy of the New-South leaders – not without a fight, anyway."[4]

Still, labor conflict remained more sporadic and less widespread than in the North. That was precisely the way New South industrialists wanted it. Among the advantages advertised by proponents of New South industrialization were the region's low wages and overall labor peace. Investors weary of labor strife and union power up North, they insisted, would find a more congenial atmosphere down South, where a calmer, more cooperative labor situation prevailed, and where wage rates were markedly lower. For decades, the image of a union-free, low-wage region prevailed in both the popular imagination and in the historiography of the New South. On one level, this picture captured basic truths: In the North and West, industrialization was, indeed, accompanied by far higher levels of labor conflict, unionization, and wages. "Labor unionism in the South," George B. Tindall observed in 1967, experienced merely "a feeble growth before the 1930s."[5] Unionism did persist among some skilled craft workers, reawakening more broadly at particular moments – most dramatically, for this period, during the First World War era, when a wave of "new militancy" swept through the Texas oil fields, Alabama coal mines, Louisiana lumber camps, and Tennessee and North Carolina tobacco factories. But this upsurge was short-lived. "By the end of 1921," Tindall noted, "the upthrust of unionism was over. In not a single case had it brought an important union recognition, and the feeble locals soon disappeared."[6]

Why the historical weakness of unionism in Dixie? Here, historian Bryant Simon observes, "is the 'big' question [that] stalks every examination of the history of working people and industrialization in the South." "So what is it that makes the South so antiunion?" he continues. "Is it something in the red-clay soil; something that grows like kudzu, swallowing up trade unions like it does patches of land along the highway? Does antiunionism hang in the air like the lint in a textile mill?" Simon rejects more traditional explanations – that there was something distinctive about southern culture or experience – their "*southern-ness*" – that proved incompatible with labor organizing; that southerners' individualism, religiosity, or (in the case of whites) racism produced an ingrained anti-union disposition. He finds similarly unconvincing the assumption that a paternalistic managerial culture – particularly on the part of textile operators – generated worker loyalty, or at least apathy, in place of rebellion. Southern politicians' "virulent antiunionism" – and their willingness to resort to force to repress strikers – "no doubt . . . stood in labor's path, but the propensity of elected officials to play the strikebreakers' role was common in the more pro-union North as well."[7]

Ultimately – if speculatively – Simon attributes the relative weakness of southern unionism to two inhibiting factors. The first lies in the structure of key southern industries. By the 1930s, "gigantic vertically and/or horizontally integrated firms dominating large, lucrative markets" found themselves organized by the Congress of Industrial Organizations in the North. But these were "exactly the industries" that were the "least common in the South." Perhaps, he concludes, "the dearth of these industries" helped render the South less hospitable to unionization than the rest of the country. (That said, there is, he reminds us, a "largely unwritten and unrecognized history of craft unionism in the South." As in the North, southern skilled white workers established unions that endured, yielded significant benefits for themselves, and at times achieved a degree of political influence.) Second, "unending hard times" and "unremitting poverty" in the agricultural sector tended to afford industrial employers large pools of labor ready – particularly in the large textile sector – to cross picket lines and learn the job, thus darkening the prospects of union efforts.[8]

Yet, as Simon and others point out, the South's failure to match the North in rates of unionization does not in itself confirm New South boasts of labor docility. Indeed, for two generations, scholars have been uncovering long-forgotten traditions of workplace resistance, community organization, and union mobilization among southern workers – white and black – from Reconstruction through the twentieth century. If the explosion of inquiry in America's labor past (the so-called New Labor History of the 1960s and 1970s) was slow to turn its attention to the South – leaving intact Dixie's reputation as a region without a labor movement heritage – it has made up for lost time since the early 1980s. Upon closer inspection, it became evident that the main labor organizations in the United States – the Knights of Labor, the American Federation of Labor, the Industrial Workers of the World, and the Congress of Industrial Organizations – all had a meaningful presence in the South. Whether they affiliated with national unions or remained independent, southern workers demonstrated repeatedly that the "labor question" was a vital issue in the New South.

But with the emergence of the "new labor history" in the 1960s, scholars no longer strictly equated their subject with organized labor. While hardly ignoring such classic forms of labor conflict as strikes and riots, they broadened their focus to incorporate familial relations, individual survival tactics, and multiple forms of workplace- and community-based resistance – not to mention the myriad effects of ethnicity, gender, and race. While the South's history of labor may have diverged markedly, often dramatically, from that of the North, it has nonetheless proven a fertile field for the study of working-class activism and culture. By the 1980s, a sufficient body of scholarship had appeared to herald the arrival of a "new southern labor history." Among the issues debated by historians are the extent to which the experiences of southern workers have been distinctive, the character of the southern workforce, the nature of migration within, and out of, the region, and the role unions played in upholding, or challenging, the racial order.

One of the earliest and most influential of the works is *Like a Family: The Making of a Southern Cotton Mill World*, extracted in this chapter. Drawing upon archival sources as well as extensive oral histories, author Jacquelyn Dowd Hall and her five collaborators explore the lives of the men and women whose labor in the textile mills "fueled the South's industrial revolution" that literally "built the New South." In the late nineteenth century, the South's textile industry was touted as an economic salvation – for the region generally, and not least, for poor whites whose fortunes on the land were in decline. Promoters of a "New South" in the 1880s proclaimed that a growing textile industry would usher in the "dawn of a new era." For them it promised, in Patrick J. Hearden's words, to "blaze the trail for the introduction of related business concerns" and create "local markets for diversified agriculture."[9] While such claims proved somewhat overstated, textile manufacturing in Georgia, Virginia, and the Carolinas would eventually provide employment to hundreds of thousands of poorer whites (along with a small number of African Americans). During what Allen Tullos calls the "mill-building fever of the last quarter of the nineteenth century,"[10] manufacturers "seized upon the labor of distressed farmers and the tradition of family work" to populate their new villages. In a paternalist vein, they constructed company towns, providing housing for workers, administering schools and local governments, and even building churches.

Informed by the political currents of the new labor history as well as the recollections of former mill workers, Hall and her collaborators effectively challenge long-standing assumptions about the nature of the Piedmont's textile labor force. For decades, mill villages had been portrayed as company towns ruled by powerful owners who paternalistically and benevolently ministered to a simple-minded and docile labor force. "They *are* like children," historian Frank Tannenbaum wrote of mill workers in the reform journal *Century* in 1923. "Their faces seem stripped, denuded, and empty . . . and their eyes drawn and stupid . . . [T]hey are men and women who have been lost to the world and have forgotten its existence."[11] That derogatory image endured for years.

The authors of *Like a Family* overturn this portrait. There was little question that work conditions in the Piedmont's mills were difficult – wages were low, work arduous, and hours long. Machinery could be dangerous to operate, the noise unpleasantly loud, and cotton dust damaged many a worker's health. Sustaining a family often required the labor of all of its members – fathers, mothers, and children. But these oppressive conditions, Hall et al. insist, simply did not produce Tannenbaum's empty-faced workers. Contemporaries and scholars alike had missed much that was going on, both on the shopfloor and in the community.

For all of their power, Hall et al. conclude, mill owners "never held full sway over the shop floor"; the "mill village system was never a foolproof instrument of labor control." Over the years, millhands "themselves helped fashion the social world of work in a way that blunted the shock of their encounter with bosses and machines." However difficult their working lives, millhands derived a "measure of self-esteem and a feeling of accomplishment" from their toil as they "sought to wrest from the mills some of life's rewards" through their own "initiative, creativity, and dexterity." They engaged in "[p]ersonal strategies of resistance and accommodation," weaving them into "the fabric of everyday life in the mills." They were not, for that matter, "peculiarly individualistic or untouched by the uprisings of laboring people across America." At times, their dissatisfaction was reflected in high rates of labor turnover and mobility. At other times, they "fashioned [their own] customary ways of thinking and acting" that subtlely undermined managers' efforts at paternalistic control. And, crucially, they relied upon close family ties and "tight-knit" local and even regional communities to provide them with a modicum of independence and material security. If southern textile workers did not always behave in the heroic and class-oriented manner that some historians may fancy, they nonetheless forged a distinctive world for themselves that defied the negative pictures drawn by mill owners, reformers, and even scholars.[12]

Given the regional division of labor by race, black workers often found themselves segregated from white workers and excluded from better-paying and skilled jobs. In *Making Their Own Way: Southern Blacks' Migration to Pittsburgh, 1916–30*, extracted here, Peter Gottlieb explores the seasonal migration of black workers seeking work within a racially segmented labor market. Earlier scholarship on the Great Migration to the North focused on push factors – those conditions in the South that prompted African Americans to migrate north – and on pull factors – those conditions in the North that drew migrants out of the South. A labor historian, Gottlieb sees black migration as part of a "worldwide country-to-city migration that has paralleled the rise of commercial and industrial economies." He advances a number of related arguments. First, the "kind of work, culture, and society" black southerners engaged in "before moving north" influenced the "kind of urban laborers" they would become in the North. And second, black laborers' lives were changed not solely by "impersonal social and economic forces" – push or pull factors – but by a "process of self-transformation." Their "historic aspiration for freedom, justice, and opportunity," as well as their "southern rural way of life," shaped this process.

Gottlieb's portrait of the pre-migration experience reveals not a static world of work – with former slaves and their descendants simply locked into a form of neo-slavery – but rather a dynamic one – oppressive, to be sure, but accompanied by mobility and some opportunities. The migrants he studies did not move directly from the agricultural countryside to the urban, industrial North; many acquired significant experience as wage laborers within the South, taking advantage of the seasonal rhythms of farm life to procure temporary employment in sawmills, railroad and turpentine camps, coal mines, and brickyards. Such work, whose cash wages proved indispensable for many families, often required black men (and, in the case of domestic work, black women) to leave their homes and families for a time. These "repeated shifts from farm to nonfarm work," and the independence such labor afforded rural African Americans, "readied" southern blacks "to grasp new opportunities when they arose." When First World War-era labor shortages prompted northern industrialists to seek black employees in significant numbers for the first time, southern blacks responded with enthusiasm. Thus, their northward migration was "not a sudden, sharp departure" from their lives in agriculture; on the contrary, their "lives in the rural South amounted to an education in migration and alternating seasons of farm and industrial labor."

In emphasizing the "self-transformation" of black southerners and treating migrants as conscious architects of their own destinies, Gottlieb further extends the spirit of the new labor history into the New South. There is no disagreement among scholars today about the central role played by black southerners' aspirations, prior life and work experiences, and familial networks in shaping migration.

One issue that has proven most contentious, on the other hand, is the role of race in the history of southern unionism. Over half a century ago, C. Vann Woodward laid out the choices open to white labor in biracial settings: "Two possible but contradictory policies could be used: eliminate the Negro as a competitor by excluding him from the skilled trades either as an apprentice or a worker, or take him in as an organized worker committed to the defense of a common standard of wages. Southern labor wavered between these policies."[13] Although he acknowledged that southern miners and longshore workers did cross the color line to organize jointly, these efforts appeared to be the exception to a broader rule of exclusion. For years, few American labor historians tested Woodward's claim; instead, most simply ignored the South, the racial practices of white workers, and working-class race relations.

Starting in the 1980s, that changed dramatically. In his narrative of a 1906–08 coal miners' strike across the Birmingham district of Alabama (extracted in this chapter), Brian Kelly offers one reading of the character of interracial labor activism, of the openings that made it possible even amid the hostile environment of Jim Crow, and of the often fierce resistance it still encountered from employers, government, and voices of public opinion. In Kelly's view, the Alabama district of the United Mine Workers (UMW) promoted a genuine interracialism among the state's downtrodden miners. In his telling, the mine operators and their allies in state government and the press fomented racial discord in order to thwart miners' challenges to their power. White miners, he makes clear, do not emerge from this larger study as "egalitarian knights," but rather as a "complicated and varied mass," one whose views on race, while drawing upon the broader currents of white supremacy, remained "subject to change in the protracted social crises that industrial confrontation produced." He concludes that black and white Alabama miners "advanced a vision that – while falling short of thoroughgoing racial egalitarianism – nevertheless had to be snuffed out," in the eyes of its opponents, "lest it become infectious among others at the bottom of southern society." Daniel Letwin's findings in his 1998 monograph on Birmingham district miners support Kelly's claims. While the UMW neither "wholly eliminated racial strains or hierarchies . . . [n]or overcame a persistent aversion among many miners to organizing across the color line," he argues, it nonetheless "stood as a conspicuous and, to many, unnerving exception to the rising tide of Jim Crow."[14]

Kelly's emphasis on southern labor activism – including that of black workers – is by no means novel. Peter Rachleff and Tera Hunter, among others, have also charted significant levels of southern black union activity (in Richmond, Virginia, and Atlanta, Georgia, respectively) in the late nineteenth and early twentieth centuries, contradicting the old portrait of black workers as apathetic about unionism, if not downright hostile.[15] In his famous speech at the 1895 Atlanta Cotton Exposition, Booker T. Washington hailed the "fidelity and love" of some "eight millions of Negroes" who have, "without strikes and labor wars," tilled white southerners' forests, built their railroads and cities, and "brought forth treasures from the bowels of the earth."[16] Without question, many African Americans *were* hostile or indifferent to unions, an understandable response considering the broad exclusion of blacks from white unions. Yet the fact remains that tens of thousands of southern blacks enlisted in organized labor's ranks – whether in interracial or in all-black unions – as a way to attain higher wages and better working conditions, to resist abusive treatment, and to assert a stronger voice at the workplace. In developing a tradition of labor activism, they showed that the union movement was never solely the property of whites.

Kelly's insistence on the existence of a heritage of union interracialism, however qualified, has proven contentious. Drawing upon Herbert Gutman's pioneering 1968 article on black UMW official Richard L. Davis, Kelly, along with Daniel Letwin, Daniel Rosenberg, Eric Arnesen, Steven Reich, Clifford Farrington, and others, have unearthed a variety of biracial union efforts in coal fields, timber camps, and on southern docks.[17] None claims that these movements were wholly egalitarian or that white participants entirely repudiated the tenets of white supremacy. Yet even the implication that a small number of white workers could serve as anything other than a vehicle for the exclusion or subordination of black workers was too much for some scholars. Leading the attack on Gutman and those following his lead was Herbert Hill, a former labor secretary of the National Association for the Advancement of Colored People. As a professor of industrial relations, Hill charged new labor historians with reducing "race consciousness to class consciousness," denying "race as a crucial factor," ignoring "racism as a system of domination," and creating a "myth" of the UMW – and, by extension, of other unions – as an "advanced model of interracial working class solidarity."[18]

By the end of the first decade of the twenty-first century, the sheer volume and complexity of the scholarly literature on southern race and labor have considerably tempered these passionate debates. Those who insist on the significance of interracial unions in the New South make no claim that these enterprises were paragons of egalitarian virtue, and readily acknowledge the exclusionary tendencies that characterized much, if not most, of organized labor. More importantly, perhaps, increasing numbers of historians are professing less interest in race relations among white and black workers, and more in the efforts of black workers – in and out of unions, in the workplace and in the community – to address issues of economic and racial inequality.

New South workers, Daniel Letwin has recently written, "were a study in diversity," toiling "across a mosaic of farmlands, railroads, forests, factories, coalmines, docks, laundries, homes, craftshops, and offices."[19] The "worlds of Southern labor," not surprisingly, were never reducible to a common denominator. The region's heterogeneous labor force – divided by race, skill, and gender – never spoke with one voice. But neither did its northern counterpart. Southern workers may have generally lagged behind northern workers when it came to organizing and advancing their agendas. But through their words and their actions, individual and collective, they kept their region's labor relations unsettled and ensured that the labor question, however defined, remained unresolved.

NOTES

1. "The Importance of the Labor Question," *Southwestern Christian Advocate*, January 16, 1902; "The Labor Situation in New Orleans," *Southwestern Christian Advocate*, May 21, 1903.
2. Daniel Letwin, "Labor Relations in the Industrializing South," in John Boles, ed., *A Companion to the American South* (Malden: Blackwell, 2002), p. 424.
3. Melton Alonza McLaurin, *The Knights of Labor in the South* (Westport: Greenwood Press, 1978), p. 3.
4. C. Vann Woodward, *Origins of the New South, 1877–1913* (Baton Rouge: Louisiana State University Press, 1971 [orig. 1951]), p. 234.
5. George B. Tindall, *The Emergence of the New South, 1913–1945* (Baton Rouge: Louisiana State University Press, 1967), p. 331.
6. Tindall, *Emergence of the New South*, p. 338.
7. Bryant Simon, "Rethinking Why There Are So Few Unions in the South," *Georgia Historical Quarterly*, 81 (Summer 1997), pp. 465, 455, 466–9.
8. Simon, "Rethinking Why There Are So Few Unions," pp. 472, 475–6, 480–1.
9. Patrick J. Hearden, *Independence and Empire: The New South's Cotton Mill Campaign, 1865–1901* (DeKalb: Northern Illinois University Press, 1982), p. xiii.
10. Allen Tullos, *Habits of Industry: White Culture and the Transformation of the Carolina Piedmont* (Chapel Hill: University of North Carolina Press, 1989), p. 9.
11. Frank Tannenbaum, "The South Buries Its Anglo-Saxons," *Century*, 106 (June 1923), pp. 204–15.
12. Jacquelyn Dowd Hall, James Leloudis, Robert Korstad, Mary Murphy, Lu Ann Jones, and Christopher B. Daly, *Like a Family: The Making of a Southern Cotton*

Mill World (Chapel Hill: University of North Carolina Press, 1987), pp. 356, 44, 45, 100, 139, 146.

13. Woodward, *Origins of the New South*, p. 229.

14. Daniel Letwin, *The Challenge of Interracial Unionism: Alabama Coal Miners, 1878–1921* (Chapel Hill: University of North Carolina Press, 1997), p. 2.

15. Peter J. Rachleff, *Black Labor in Richmond 1865–1890* (Urbana: University of Illinois Press, 1988 [orig. 1984]); Tera W. Hunter, *To 'Joy My Freedom: Southern Black Women's Lives and Labors after the Civil War* (Cambridge MA: Harvard University Press, 1997).

16. Washington quoted in "Booker T. Washington Delivers the 1895 Atlanta Compromise Speech," at http://historymatters.gmu.edu/d/39/.

17. Letwin, *Challenge of Interracial Unionism*; Daniel Rosenberg, *New Orleans Dockworkers: Race, Labor, and Unionism, 1892–1923* (Albany: State University of New York Press, 1988); Eric Arnesen, *Waterfront Workers of New Orleans: Race, Class, and Politics, 1863–1923* (Urbana: University of Illinois Press, 1994 [orig. 1991]); Steven A. Reich, "The Making of a Southern Sawmill World: Race, Class, and Rural Transformation in the Piney Woods of East Texas, 1830–1930" (PhD dissertation, Northwestern University, 1999); Clifford Farrington, *Biracial Unions on Galveston's Waterfront, 1865–1925* (Austin: Texas State Historical Association, 2007).

18. Herbert Hill, "Myth-Making as Labor History: Herbert Gutman and the United Mine Workers of America," *International Journal of Politics, Culture, and Society*, 2 (Winter 1988), pp. 132–3.

19. Letwin, "Labor Relations in the Industrializing South," p. 424.

* * *

FURTHER READING

Arnesen, Eric, *Waterfront Workers of New Orleans: Race, Class, and Politics, 1863–1923* (Urbana: University of Illinois Press, 1994 [orig. 1991]).

Arnesen, Eric, ed., *The Black Worker: Race, Labor, and Civil Rights since Emancipation* (Urbana: University of Illinois Press, 2007).

Case, Theresa, *The Great Southwest Railroad Strike and Free Labor* (College Station: Texas A&M University Press, 2009).

Flamming, Douglas, *Creating the Modern South: Millhands and Managers in Dalton, Georgia, 1884–1984* (Chapel Hill: University of North Carolina Press, 1995).

Hunter, Tera W., *To 'Joy My Freedom: Southern Black Women's Lives and Labors after the Civil War* (Cambridge, MA: Harvard University Press, 1997).

Jones, William P., *The Tribe of Black Ulysses: African American Lumber Workers in the Jim Crow South* (Urbana: University of Illinois Press, 2005).

Letwin, Daniel, *The Challenge of Interracial Unionism: Alabama Coal Miners, 1878–1921* (Chapel Hill: University of North Carolina Press, 1998).

Rachleff, Peter J., *Black Labor in Richmond, 1865–1890* (Urbana: University of Illinois Press, 1988 [orig. 1984]).

Shapiro, Karin A., *A New South Rebellion: The Battle against Convict Labor in the Tennessee Coalfields, 1871–1896* (Chapel Hill: University of North Carolina Press, 1998).

Simon, Bryant, *A Fabric of Defeat: The Politics of South Carolina Millhands, 1910–1948* (Chapel Hill: University of North Carolina Press, 1998).

Spero, Sterling and Abram Harris, *The Black Worker: The Negro and the Labor Movement* (New York: Atheneum, 1969 [orig. 1931]).

Zieger, Robert H., *For Jobs and Freedom: Race and Labor in America Since 1865* (Lexington: University Press of Kentucky, 2007).

* * *

Jacquelyn Dowd Hall et al.

Like a Family†

Textile mills built the New South. Beginning in the 1880s, as the South emerged from the wreckage of the Civil War, business and professional men tied their hopes for prosperity to the whirring of spindles and the beating of looms. Agriculture continued to dominate the southern economy until well into the twentieth century. But in the Piedmont, a region of gentle hills and rushing rivers that stretches from southern Virginia through the central Carolinas and into northern Georgia and Alabama, a new society rapidly took shape. By the mid-1920s this land of farms and farmers had been crisscrossed by railroad tracks and dotted with mill villages, and the Piedmont had eclipsed New England as the world's leading producer of yarn and cloth. World War I marked a turning point in this regional transformation, setting the stage for two decades of modernization and rebellion that culminated in the General Textile Strike of 1934. In the aftermath of that conflict, manufacturers began to abandon the mill village system, and a distinctive form of working-class community gradually disappeared.

[. . .]

Whatever their origins, mill builders and their supporters thought they offered salvation even as they helped create a new economic and cultural order based on acquisitiveness and individual accumulation. Fusing the profit motive and a philanthropic impulse, mill promoters often cast themselves as public benefactors who

---

†Jacquelyn Dowd Hall, et al., *Like a Family: The Making of a Southern Cotton Mill World* (Chapel Hill: University of North Carolina Press, 1987), pp. xi, 31, 77, 80–1, 100–2, 104–6.

were creating jobs for the growing number of rural poor. Textile work, reserved almost exclusively for whites, was supposed to free white farmers from poverty and teach them the virtues of thrift, regularity, and industrial discipline. Such reasoning obscured the fact that mills rested on a paradox: the same conditions that made life on the land precarious contributed to the accumulation of capital by merchants and other professionals. Amid stalks of cotton and tobacco in the Piedmont and on worn-out mountains in the Appalachians grew the pool of cheap labor that southern industrialists counted as one of the region's chief assets. Under these conditions, farm families were confronted by a powerful push off the land and an increasingly attractive pull into the mills.

[. . .]

For some people, of course, mill work was just a job. They did just enough to earn a living and to keep from being fired but refused to apply themselves whole-heartedly. John Wesley Snipes, for one, shared Chester Copeland's contempt for the "robot life." "I never had no use for a cotton mill. Look at it run twelve hours a day, and the same old thing in the morning, and the same old thing next morning. I didn't like it at all, but I had to do it. I had to make bread and butter."

Wherever they labored, and however they felt about their jobs, all mill workers endured the long hours and low wages that characterized the industry. Six twelve-hour days represented a normal work week in the late nineteenth century. The shift started at 6.00 a.m., with quitting time around 6.00 p.m. The piercing sound of the steam whistle replaced the rooster as the herald of the new day. In summer, winter, spring, and fall, in hot weather or in cold, rain, sleet, or snow, "they'd blow their whistle to wake everybody up and then about fifteen minutes later they'd blow it again to make sure that you was up." At Bynum the notice came from a bell, but the message was the same: "time to go to work."

From the early days of the industry, millhands complained about the long hours. "Twelve hours a day is too long for any one to work in a mill," wrote a worker from Gaston County to the North Carolina Bureau of Labor Statistics. Beginning in the 1880s, the Knights of Labor and the National Union of Textile Workers agitated for change. By 1903 North Carolina, South Carolina, and Georgia had laws limiting the work week to sixty-six hours. South Carolina, a pacesetter among southern states on labor legislation, went further, mandating a sixty-hour week in 1907 and a fifty-five-hour week in 1922. But passing laws was one thing; enforcing them was another. Without vigilant inspection or serious penalties, these regulations meant little. Mills continued, by and large, to set their own schedules. When John Wesley Snipes began work at Bynum in 1929, the workday was still twelve hours, with a half-day on Saturday. Southern textile workers did not enjoy the eight-hour day until 1933, when the federal government began regulating hours under the National Industrial Recovery Act.

[. . .]

Wage rates for southern workers did increase over time, particularly when labor was scarce, but compared to northern textile workers, southern millhands were grossly underpaid. Indeed, cheap labor was the foundation of the southern textile industry. Between the 1880s and the imposition of a national minimum wage in the 1930s, southern workers could expect to receive roughly 60 percent of the wage paid for the same job in the North. Manufacturers advanced a number of justifications for this differential. Above all, they cited the lower cost of living in the Piedmont – cheaper food, fuel, and housing – which supposedly made real wages comparable to those in the North. Although there was some truth to the argument, studies done in the 1910s and 1920s showed only a slightly lower cost of living in the South – nowhere near enough to justify the wage differential. The other rationale rested on the fact that the South produced coarser goods than the North, with a lower "value added" in manufacturing; therefore, it was said, the southern mills could not afford to pay wages as high as those in the North. While this argument, too, had some validity, southern manufacturers also paid a smaller percentage of their value added to workers, thus retaining for themselves a greater share of the profits.

Southern manufacturers could pay less because they purchased labor in a regional market where the general level of economic development kept wages low. Lower labor costs, in turn, made southern products more competitive in national and international markets, and mill owners, rather than workers, reaped the rewards. From the outset, textile entrepreneurs realized generous returns on their investments. "It was not unusual for mills in [the early] years," according to historian Broadus Mitchell, "to make 30 per cent to 75 per cent profit." Earnings leveled off after the initial boom, but until the textile depression of the 1920s mill stocks continued to pay substantial dividends.

Workers' health was another casualty of the drive for profits in a region that placed no restrictions on capital and offered workers no protection. Without unions, and without the legal and administrative apparatus that now provides a basic level of industrial health and safety, millhands were at the mercy of dangerous machinery. The threat to a worker's health could be as sudden and violent as the snapping of a bone or as insidious as the relentless clouding of a lung.

Cotton dust was a killer in the card room. "Some of that dust was terrible," Carl Durham remembered. "Whew! That dust would accumulate and you had to strip them cards out every three hours, get all that stuff out. It would get to where it wouldn't do its work, it would be so full of particles and dust. When I was coming along, and for a long time, that was all in the air. It's a wonder I can breathe, but somehow or another it didn't affect me like it did some folks. It just killed some folks."

[. . .]

Personal strategies of resistance and accommodation defined the fabric of everyday life in the mills. But it would be wrong to conclude that mill folk were peculiarly individualistic or untouched by the uprisings of laboring people across America in the late nineteenth century. Millhands' first attempts to develop a lasting organization came in the 1880s. The stimulus was a national depression that threatened workers' already meager standard of living; the vehicle was the Knights of Labor. The Noble and Holy Order of the Knights of Labor was a loose coalition of America's "producing classes" – predominately farmers, laborers, craftsmen, and small businessmen – that captured the imagination of thousands of workers in the 1880s. The Knights concentrated their efforts on politics and the formation of producer cooperatives but in many locales also served as a labor union for newly industrialized workers. The Knights' criticism of the increasing concentration of political and economic power by a financial and industrial elite resonated with the experiences of southern workers. By the end of 1885 hundreds of millhands had joined skilled urban laborers to establish local assemblies of the Knights throughout the textile heartland.

In the South, however, the Knights were poorly situated to battle the emerging industrial order. Manufacturers took immediate steps to "nip in the bud" the spread of labor organization. Mill owners in South Carolina reportedly conspired to "crush the Knights beyond resurrection" by discharging any operatives who joined. A weak national organization could provide little help in such cases, and local government – despite some electoral success by Knights of Labor candidates – could not, or would not intervene on workers' behalf. Equally decisive was the youthfulness – in terms of age and industrial experience – of the southern work force. Millhands who had just arrived in town were unlikely candidates to lead a revolt against an increasingly powerful manufacturing class. Nevertheless, several years of agitation – highlighted by a three-month strike by thousands of textile workers in Augusta, Georgia, in 1886 – served notice that millhands' discontents were not to be taken lightly.

If the Knights were the trailblazers of organized protest in the South, the National Union of Textile Workers brought the ideals of permanent trade unionism into the region. The NUTW originated in 1890 among craft workers in northern mills, but quickly welcomed skilled and unskilled alike into the organization. Internal conflicts led to the election in 1897 of a weaver from Columbus, Georgia, as president of the union, and the headquarters subsequently moved south. With the financial support of American Federation of Labor (AFL) president Samuel Gompers and the experience of organizers from southern craft unions, the NUTW mounted a sustained organizing drive among southern millhands. Between 1898 and 1900 organizational meetings were held in every important textile center in the Piedmont. Workers responded enthusiastically, and the union reported the formation of ninety-five different locals by late 1900. The NUTW's strength lay in urban manufacturing areas such as Columbus and Atlanta, Georgia; Horse Creek Valley and Columbia, South Carolina; and Danville, Virginia. But there were also locals in the small mill villages of North Carolina.

Although the NUTW passed quickly across the horizon of southern history – by 1902 there was only a scattering of active locals – this brief insurgency revealed much about the consciousness of southern mill folk in the late nineteenth century. The ideals and discontents that stirred hundreds to join the union stemmed from a combination of immediate concerns and long-standing resentments. Low wages, long hours, and child labor were the leading complaints. W. W. Oakes, president of the local at Altamahaw, in northern Alamance County, denounced wages that were "too low for the average man, woman and child who are toiling day by day for their daily bread," and long hours that were turning women to "skin and bones" and the children to "dwarfs." "We need better wages," wrote another union leader, "shorter hours, better schools, and above all we need a child labor law and a compulsory school law."

[. . .]

The owners' decision to ban union labor from their mills confirmed workers' worst fears about the emerging social order. "The privilege of all free men of belonging to anything . . . that's honorable and lawful" was not to be extended to millhands. This action raised serious questions about the meaning of democracy and citizenship in the New South. "Is it right," asked a union committee, "that mill owners shall organize, meet together, fix prices on their yarns, their loom product, and regulate wages, and then say to the laborer: 'You take what we give you, do what we tell you, and say nothing.'" T. A. Allen concluded that the attacks on the NUTW showed "that freedom of thought and action is not allowed among the common people. When a body of citizens are [sic] denied the right and privilege to unite for the common good into a lawful organization, we may then say our liberty is no longer our own, but is to be utilized for the benefit of some one who controls the purse strings of hundreds of men and women."

Despite widespread support, the NUTW lacked the power to force the owners to accept union labor. At most of the mills a small contingent of nonunion workers kept up minimum production. In any case, manufacturers seemed in no hurry to return to normal. Autumn was the "dull season" in textiles; and they were happy to await a return of higher prices. Once evictions began, workers who had declared earlier that the strike would go on "until we win out or are starved out" began to realize that their only choice was to quit the union and go back to work or to leave; there was no hope that they could work in the Alamance mills as union men and women. Some renounced the union and went back to work. But "the great majority," reported the *Alamance Gleaner*, "remain firm and are moving away."

The NUTW's campaign dovetailed with the efforts of the Southern Farmers' Alliance and the Populist Party to shape the contours of the new social order. This broad movement, which embraced blacks and whites, farmers and factory workers, crested at the turn of the century with the victory of "fusion" parties – parties that linked black Republicans with white Populists in attempts to wrest control from the Democratic Party. Between 1895 and 1902 southern Democrats turned to race baiting, fraud, intimidation, and violence to destroy this challenge to their power. The passage of state constitutional amendments disfranchised blacks, and the accompanying flurry of Jim Crow laws guaranteed that they would have little to say about the political contours of the New South. Politicians wooed the support of white workers and farmers for black disfranchisement with promises of prosperity and protection against black competition. But they quickly turned the weapon of disfranchisement on whites themselves. Literacy tests, short voter registration periods, and high residency requirements kept large numbers of millhands from the polls. The result was a one-party South in which political opposition was stifled.

As prospects for collective protest diminished, Piedmont millhands opted for a personal strategy as old as the industry itself – relocation. In Alamance County alone, hundreds of union stalwarts left after the 1900 strike to find jobs in South Carolina and Georgia. "Among them," reported the *Alamance Gleaner*, "are a great many excellent people who prefer to go elsewhere rather than surrender rights and privileges which they as citizens deem their own and should enjoy." Striking workers in Augusta, Georgia, voiced a similar response when they were unable to force concessions from local manufacturers. "The only way we can whip the master now," explained one man, "is by lighting out for other districts. They don't mind having their mills closed . . . because with cotton so dear they can't make much money anyhow just now – and that's our bad luck – but they don't like to see the skilled help going away." In choosing to leave in search of better conditions, these workers set a pattern for the next two decades. Until the end of World War I quitting was textile workers' most effective alternative to public protest or acquiescence. According to one student of the southern textile industry, a millhand's "ability to move at a moment's notice was his Magna Carta, Declaration of Independence, and Communist Manifesto."

The movement from job to job could be touched off by any number of factors – curtailed production, a promise of higher wages elsewhere, or a simple desire to move on – but it could also be a response to a perceived abuse of authority, and thus a means of voicing discontent. "A lot of people in textile mills come and go," Josephine Glenn of Burlington remembered. "They're more or less on a cycle. They're not like that as a whole, but a lot of them are. They're dissatisfied, you might say, restless. They just go somewhere and work for a while, and, if everything don't go just like they think it should, why, they walk out. They'd just [say], 'I've had it,' and that was it." Alice Hardin explained the millhands' predicament. "Some of the overseers wasn't real good to people. [But] there wasn't anything [workers] could do about it. They could quit or work, because they didn't have any union to go to. If they were mistreated, they just had to work or quit." Under such circumstances, many people chose to follow George Dyer's advice. "I think if you can run your job, ain't no use to be scared of it – ain't no use to be scared of the boss either. Sometimes some boss don't like you, gets it in for you. It's best then just to quit. Don't work under conditions like that. I don't want to work for a man that don't respect me."

֍ ֍ ֍

Peter Gottlieb

Making Their Own Way[†]

The mass migration of southern blacks to northern cities that began during World War I had deep roots in the New South. Ever since Emancipation freedmen and their descendants had moved frequently in search of a better living. This geographic shifting that preceded the wartime movement to the North was not random, however. It stood in a particular relationship to the patterns of landholding and labor and to the organization of family and community life. Specifically, black migration in the pre-World War I South was strongly related to the seasonal character of work and leisure in cotton cultivation and to the life cycle of rural blacks. We can discover in these facets of black life the beginnings of the trails that thousands eventually followed to Pittsburgh and other northern cities.

It was the combination of a traditional agriculture with emerging industries of the New South that created a matrix from which black migration emerged. The light and heavy industries spreading across the South were places from which rural blacks could garner cash wages to add to their farm incomes and raise their standard of living. Like preindustrial peoples everywhere from the eighteenth century to the present, southern blacks learned how to adjust their customary styles of work, their household organization, and their family responsibilities in order to derive the benefits of wage employment and still maintain their rural homes. Through a pattern of seasonal migration and temporary industrial work within the South, they prepared themselves for geographic movements further afield.

[. . .]

Farm families enjoyed two lengthy reprieves from intensive field labor, during which either light work or no work at all was done. The first break came during July and August, when the cotton had been "laid by" and no longer needed plowing or hoeing. The second rest period followed the completion of the harvest. When the cotton had been picked, ginned, baled, and sold, the farming community enjoyed a respite from fieldwork until after New Year's Day. Comparing these interludes of light work with the periods of intensive labor on the index of seasonal labor demand, the July–August period declined to 90 and the November–January period to 70. Alternating periods of light and intensive work defined life in all rural regions of the United States and all types of agriculture. The seasonality of life in the cotton South differed from that of other regions in the sharpness of the fluctuation in labor demand.

Alternating periods of intensive and slack work tended to regulate many other aspects of the lives of the black rural population, including market relations,

---

[†]Peter Gottlieb, *Making Their Own Way: Southern Blacks' Migration to Pittsburgh, 1916–30* (Urbana: University of Illinois Press, 1987), pp. 12, 19–20, 22–5, 30–3.

consumption patterns, forms of socializing, education, and temporary migration. Significantly, the mutual obligations of tenant and landlord changed over the twelve-month cycle roughly in step with the phases of the work calendar. Agreements between sharecroppers or tenants and landowners were initiated after Christmas and just before the beginning of the next growing season. In the experience of Ed Brown, a Georgia sharecropper in the 1920s, the time for making the new contracts was well defined. "Unless it's Sunday everyone hired on shares meet the overseer at the barn by sunup January 1." Food, clothing, and medicine, provided on credit by landlords or merchants, could be cut off with the coming of the July–August break. Tenant families during these months were expected to support themselves from home-grown vegetables and meat or wild game. In November or early December, after all of the cotton had been harvested and sold, landlords, storekeepers, and tenants settled accounts. With wry humor, Ed Brown recalled how the progress of the cotton crop shaped his landlord's attitudes: "Along about April the bossman would say, 'Ed, is *your* cotton gettin ready to chop? . . . [Around July] I plow my cotton for the last time. It's laid by till time to pick. Furnish money ends. Now the boss ask, 'Is *our* cotton doin pretty good? . . .' By the latter part of September it's all picked . . . Now Mr. Addison can handle it and just as sure as you're livin he'll call it his'n. '*My* cotton, *my* corn, *my* crop.'"

[. . .]

As responsibility for the family's fortunes increased in step with their age, the black children's attendance at school tapered off. The proportion of black children in single age groups enrolled in school throughout the South in 1910 showed steady increases up to age eleven. Then the percentage of black children in school began to drop, with a sharp decline after the age of thirteen. It was just at this point in their lives that black rural youth turned to plowing, driving wagons, cooking meals, and looking after younger siblings.

[. . .]

Another pattern of geographic mobility among rural blacks was seasonal movement from farms to industrial sites, towns, or cities. Many rural blacks who migrated in this fashion got temporary jobs in expanding southern industries. They became wage earners during the periods when there was little fieldwork to do on the cotton crop, returning to their farms to plow, plant, or harvest. Though such temporary migration fit well into the cycle of fieldwork and leisure, it also bore the seeds of permanent cityward migration.

Some rural blacks seeking temporary wage work turned to small-scale industries that, because they were closely related to agriculture, operated seasonally. Fertilizer plants, cotton gins, and cottonseed presses were busiest both before and after the growing season, when labor from farm families in the surrounding areas was available for hire. An investigator reported that a fertilizer plant in Clarke County,

Georgia, during World War I divided its annual work into two periods. One began in February and ended in April and the other went from May to January. The plant was busiest in the early spring months, hiring up to 155 workers to manufacture fertilizer and ship it to merchants and landlords. During the slack months of the year, much lower rates of production and lighter shipments took place. The payroll of unskilled labor, mostly blacks hired from the local area, was cut by 40 percent. "They are what are termed 'field hands,' or field laborers, and most of them, when they have completed the work of the busy season at the fertilizer plant, go back to the farm."

Black men also sought temporary employment in other industries that were not so closely connected with southern agriculture and that offered relatively steady work year round. In the interludes of light farm work rural blacks moved to sawmills, logging camps, railroad construction and tie-cutting camps, turpentine camps, brickyards, coal mines, steel mills, and river or ocean docks. A historian of lumber workers found that part-time farming and part-time logging were common in Mississippi, northern Georgia, and South Carolina. Mississippi landowners lost their black hands to logging camps and sawmills during the summer lay-by period. But apparently the off-farm employment was strictly seasonal, because "the black man would choose cotton picking every time in preference to sawmill work. On the cotton plantation, rations were furnished, and with very little labor the Negro could make a crop." In Georgia a survey of "home employment" – industrial or semiindustrial jobs provided to black tenants and laborers by white landowners – showed that a decisive majority of landlords offered sawmill work during the July–August period.

The seasonal shifting from agricultural to industrial or semiindustrial labor made work roles within black families more flexible and more complex. Some family members had to remain at home in the periods of light field labor while others were away earning wages, since there was still much work to do in the house, vegetable garden, and animal pens. In families with very young children, only the husband or wife could move in search of temporary jobs. But as sons and daughters reached their adolescence, their parents could take them along as extra hands or helpers at the seasonal jobs or assign them employment at neighboring farms and nearby towns. Gender as well as age determined where each family member worked, for how long, and at what wage rate. Beyond a certain point in his or her life cycle, however, each rural black was likely to spend the year at both farm and nonfarm labor, supplying a money income to the family when help on the farm was not needed, supplying field labor when making the crop demanded work from everyone.

[. . .]

The way in which seasonal tasks, work roles, and family resources combined also depended on the local economy and the jobs available to potential wage earners. The proximity of cities or towns to black farms could mean that parents and children lived under the same roof throughout the year, whether some members of the family worked off the farm seasonally or year round. The wider choice of occupations in the more densely populated areas of the South also allowed black rural families in these regions greater flexibility in assigning wage employment among members according to age and sex. In the more remote country districts the narrower range of options for increasing the black family's income could mean harder choices: accepting poorly paid jobs provided by the white landowner from whom the family rented land or migrating comparatively long distances over longer periods of time for better-paying seasonal work.

[. . .]

The custom of seasonal migration and the coming of age among southern blacks . . . clarify how impoverished, semiliterate inhabitants of an economically backward region could respond quickly to changes both in their own rural settlements and in distant urban centers. The repeated shifts from farm to nonfarm work and the attainment of an independent status allowed rural blacks to link their routine lives to the urbanizing world of the South and the nation. By doing so, they readied themselves to grasp new opportunities when they arose, to exploit to their own advantage even the crises, reversals in their agricultural fortunes, or disruptions to their family lives. Consequently, rural blacks were already partially inducted into industrial and urban modes of labor by 1916, well prepared to seek the best-paying line of work they could find.

[. . .]

As in many other parts of the world, the South's urbanization and industrialization nourished the process of cityward migration among rural blacks, allowing them to extend the geographic range of their movements gradually and bringing thousands of men and women more or less in contact with the cities and workshops beyond their places of origin. Though southern blacks remained largely a rural group on the eve of World War I, they had already contributed greatly to the growth of cities in the South. Between 1880 and 1910 the black populations of the major cities increased each decade by the following averages: Atlanta, 48.7 percent; Memphis, 57.2 percent; Birmingham (1890–1910), 131.5 percent; New Orleans, 15.8 percent; Richmond, 20 percent. While large cities in the South rapidly enlarged their black populations, the number of blacks in smaller southern cities also grew. Between 1880 and 1910 the black population of Mobile increased on an average of 23 percent each decade; Jacksonville, an average of 105 percent every ten years; Savannah, 29 percent per decade; Columbia, South Carolina, 28 percent; and Chattanooga, 63 percent.

At the same time that blacks were entering southern cities, they were also moving into industrial occupations. Most jobs in newer industries of the South like textile manufacturing and railroad shop work were denied to blacks. But a narrow range of occupations specifically designated as "Negro jobs" provided work opportunities. The 66 percent increase in black nonfarm employment between 1890 and 1910 was funneled into railroad track construction and maintenance, coal mines, sawmills, and turpentine camps. By 1910 black men dominated this unskilled work. They also made up most of the dock workers in New Orleans, the tobacco workers in North Carolina, and the teamsters in major southern cities. There were thousands of skilled black workers in southern towns and cities, but the black farmers seeking temporary jobs could find them most easily in the common labor positions of the rapidly growing sectors of the southern economy. Though physically exhausting and frequently very danger-ous, these jobs provided wage earnings for short periods to rural blacks who could work only briefly.

Some southern blacks also moved to the North before 1916, despite their limited chances for good jobs in major industrial centers. Pittsburgh's black popula-tion more than doubled between 1890 and 1910, and that of major northern cities increased substantially between 1900 and 1910. Though the relative growth in these cities' black groups was impressive, the overall impact of northward migra-tion from 1890 to 1910 on the distribution of the US black population was not great. The proportion of blacks born in the South but living in the North and West rose from 3.5 percent in 1890 to 4.8 percent in 1910. The real importance of this early northward movement lay more in the strategic position it gave the pre-World War I black migrants in northern cities in relation to those who followed them from 1916 to 1930. The earlier migrants in many instances became Pittsburgh gate-keepers to the southern blacks who arrived after them.

When viewed against this background of black urbanization and industrial employment in both the North and South, we can see that the mass migration beginning in 1916 was not a sudden, sharp departure from agriculture. It was instead an attempt to garner the benefits of new types of employment while maintaining foundations in the only way of life many blacks knew. The accumu-lated experience of thousands of southern blacks in seasonal cityward migration and temporary nonfarm employment showed up clearly in the ways that the grandchildren of the freedmen advanced toward Pittsburgh and other northern cities. Their lives in the rural South amounted to an education in migration and alternating seasons of farm and industrial labor. The rapid social changes set off by World War I did not immediately change all that they knew. Instead it quickly enlarged the field of geographic movement and work opportunities in which they could apply the lessons in seasonal migration that they had already mastered.

Brian Kelly

Race, Class, and Power[†]

"It was a third of a century ago," Frank Evans reminded readers of the *Birmingham Age-Herald* in August 1908,

> that the people of Alabama by rigid force . . . stopped the advance of a threatening peril which endangered our social fabric [–] the inculcation in the minds of blacks [of] the idea of social equality. [This] terrible poison . . . was . . . applied for political purpose by carpetbaggers from the north, and for a time the cloud seemed ominous, but the Caucasian blood of this state was aroused to resentment and to the defense of the home fireside.
>
> When today this correspondent saw the comingling [*sic*] of whites and blacks at Dora, where he beheld the sympathetic arms of a negro . . . embrace a white speaker to impart to him a secret of his bosom, in the very presence of gentle white women and innocent little girls, I thought to myself: has it again come to this?
>
> One interesting feature of this meeting . . . was the singing of a hymn by the assembly. As [UMW President] Fairley took his seat a "square note" music teacher led the sacred warning hymn, "Are You Ready for the Judgment Day," and white and black, male and female joined in concert.
>
> Just what bearing the musical introduction of this all-important question has upon the present status of affairs at Dora I do not fully understand, but I thought as I looked upon the assembly of idle men, heard of dynamite fury and beheld the presence of armed officers, civil and military, and saw the glittering of handcuffs here and there, that the question is not inappropos at this time.

Measured against other men of his race and social standing in turn-of-the-century Alabama, Frank Evans was not a particularly rabid race-baiter. Nor was he normally inclined to public grieving over the Lost Cause, the dark, bygone days of Reconstruction, or the tragedy of black Republican rule. Less than a decade earlier, in fact, Evans had "openly welcomed" black support for his mayoral bid, and the desertion of prominent Birmingham "race leaders" to the Democratic Party ticket had been key to his electoral success. Evans's peers in Birmingham's business elite would have scoffed at any suggestion that his was a reactionary, backward-looking creed; like him, they considered themselves "progressives," harbingers of a new, enlightened social order in the region. But the odious dispatches he penned to the Birmingham press in the fall of 1908 – for which Evans was handsomely rewarded by district coal operators – reflected the state of panic that he and Birmingham's

---

[†]Brian Kelly, *Race, Class, and Power in the Alabama Coalfields, 1908–21* (Urbana: University of Illinois Press, 2001), pp. 17–24.

white elite had been thrown into by the remarkable insurrection gathering force before them.

On July 6, 1908, four thousand black and white Alabama coal miners had gone on strike after commercial operators in the Birmingham district demanded a 17 percent reduction in wages. The strike was an all-or-nothing affair for District 20 of the United Mine Workers (UMW), a last-ditch attempt to hold on to some semblance of organization in the Alabama coalfields after a half-decade of debilitating, increasingly defensive skirmishes with local operators. Formed out of the remnants of a statewide miners' organization in 1898, Alabama's District 20 had never enjoyed any real stability in the Birmingham district coalfields. From a peak of some ten thousand members just after the turn of the century, the union found its very existence challenged from the outset by local operators. The district's largest employer, the Tennessee Coal, Iron, and Railroad Company (TCI), had balked at renewing its contract with the union in 1903, and in May 1904 it led the other major captive mine operators, including Sloss-Sheffield and the Republic Iron and Steel Company, in announcing their refusal to sign a contract and their determination to operate the mines on an "open-shop" (nonunion) basis. These three companies alone employed nearly half of all miners in the Birmingham district, and the UMW had little choice but to respond with a district-wide strike.

That strike lasted over two years, exacting a heavy toll on the UMW's power in the Birmingham district and sapping the morale of its members. Relying heavily on convict labor to guarantee a steady supply of coal, the mine owners managed to maintain their operations without any serious disruption in output. At many mines the notorious "contracting system" – through which operators contracted with individual foremen for the labor of predominantly black work gangs under their control – was successfully reintroduced after having been discontinued under union contract. The major companies forced their employees to sign "yellow dog" contracts, which stipulated that they would not join unions. By the time the strike ended in August 1906, UMW influence was confined to some thirty or forty of the small, commercial companies, covering less than a quarter of all miners in the district.

The business depression that followed the financial panic of 1907 reinforced the inclination of those operators still holding contracts with the UMW to follow the example set by the captive operators. Their July 1908 demand for a sharp wage reduction was understood by the UMW as a final effort to dislodge the union from Alabama. Both sides geared up for a major confrontation. Faced with extinction, District 20 called a strike on July 6 and launched a major effort to reorganize the coalfields, dispatching organizers across the district and attempting to revive the union in mines where it had been dormant for years. On July 12, twenty-three of the major coal companies published a statement in the local press declaring their "adherence to 'open-shop' principles" and vowing to rid the district of coal unionism.

The UMW recognized early on that the union's very existence was at stake in the confrontation. To prevail they would not only have to bring their existing membership out on strike but also make substantial inroads at those mines that had been conducting themselves on an open-shop basis, including especially those run by the major captive operators. The UMW's early success must have stunned the employers: thirty union locals were organized within the first week and some seven thousand miners joined the four thousand already out on strike. By the end of July District 20 claimed twelve thousand members, and they had planted UMW organization at a number of nonunion mines. Their success in building a local among the five hundred black miners at Blue Creek, who only several years earlier had been imported to the district as strikebreakers, illustrates the ready reception that UMW organizers met across the district.

Though mine operators refrained from publicly acknowledging the strike's effectiveness, their panicked response reflected deep bewilderment at the turn of events. They organized a major effort to import strikebreakers into the district, dispatching labor agents as far away as Ellis Island to bring relief. At the larger mines, operators constructed stockades around their operations. At Mary Lee mines, the *Age-Herald* reported, "a space ha[d] been cleared" that was "brilliantly lighted" at night, "making it almost impossible for anyone to get close to the place without the guards seeing them." As the strike wore on, however, it became unclear whether such precautions were being taken to fend off intrusions by "agitators" or to prevent imported strikebreakers from deserting. When authorities visited the Banner mines to investigate charges that men were being forced to work against their will, none of those queried replied that they were, "though 15 decided to leave."

From the beginning of the strike, heavily armed "deputies" were deployed throughout the district, and by the end of the month some sixty "Texas sharpshooters" had been imported from the west and deputized by the companies. Despite these measures, however, the operators' efforts to replace striking miners in the first few weeks were frustrated by the strikers' impressive militancy and organization. A *New York Times* correspondent lauded the miners' remarkable ability "to anticipate arrivals of strikebreakers hours ahead of time," attributing it to "their excellent detective system." Frequently, crowds of up to a thousand striking miners rallied at the rail depots to "welcome" incoming strikebreakers, appealing to them for support. "Get off and join us and we'll feed you and give you five dollars a week!" a gathering of black strikers yelled out to strikebreakers at the Adamsville rail depot. "We were out there day and night," one striker later recalled, asking the people "did they know where they was going? Well, they said they was going on a farm [but] we told them no you are not . . . you are going over here to a coal mine to break a strike."

As company-paid deputies and later soldiers intervened to prevent such interactions, union miners resorted increasingly to violence to stop the influx of scabs. Reports from a range of sources agree that their efforts were effective. By mid-July, the *New York Times* reported that "at least a half dozen lives had been lost, and the well-armed, well-fed, and well-housed strikers are in command of the situation." Following a fierce gun-battle near Brookside on July 17, described by one newspaper as "the most exciting battle . . . since the Civil War," a "train load of thirty deputies escaped through a tunnel in the mountain," leaving the area "in the hands of nearly a thousand sympathizers of the striking miners." At Pratt City "hundreds of strikers gathered about the convict mines . . . and threatened to turn loose the convicts as they were being conveyed back to prison." From Wylam came a report that the air shaft at the number 5 mine had been blown up. Strikers dynamited the houses of nonunion miners throughout the district, and at Pratt City they targeted the home of the TCI mine boss Thomas Duggan. In early August, twenty-seven people were arrested in connection with an attack on a train at Blocton, among them "8 negro men, 1 negro woman, and the balance Slavs," most of whom had been strikebreakers themselves during an earlier strike. Surveying the situation developing in the coalfields, one prominent Birmingham citizen insisted that events had overstepped the boundaries of a mere strike: "It is simply a revolution!" he declared indignantly.

As the strike's effectiveness began to impress itself upon the operators, their penchant for vigilante methods began to dominate public discussion about resolving the dispute. Backed by powerful allies in Birmingham's business community, operators called on Governor Braxton Bragg Comer, himself an owner of the state's largest textile mills at Avondale, to intervene with troops. "If the state has no law to deal with the strike the citizens should make one," the real estate magnate Robert Jemison asserted. The owner of the Shelby Iron Company, J. E. Shelby, concurred, prodding an audience at the city's Commercial Club with the suggestion that "If the governor is not going to take steps to declare martial law, the public ought to get together and let him know what they want." The industrialist J. W. Bush went further, promising that he could "gather a force of Confederate veterans who could disarm the strikers if only given the power to do so," and from south Alabama came the taunt that "If [UMW President] Fairley and his black co-conspirators had invaded [here] nothing further would be needed but the coroner." In the end, however, no such measures would be necessary: Comer obliged the business community with troops and a declaration of martial law.

From the beginning, public discussion of the events had focused prominently upon the union's racial composition. One of the most troubling aspects of the strike from the perspective of the operators and their allies in the business community was the sharp challenge it posed to the area's rigid racial order. The operators Walter Moore and Guy Johnson penned a letter to the *Birmingham Age-Herald* characterizing the UMW's interracial policy as "a direct insult to our southern traditions." Frank Evans, the former mayor of Birmingham, under contract from the Alabama Coal Operators' Association (ACOA), fed his readership a steady diet of racial hysteria, complaining that "the chief white leaders of this strife" had "fired the minds of ignorant and vicious blacks with the statement that under the contract system the negro was doing all the work and the white man getting the pay." Elsewhere he protested the remarks of a "negro speaker" who had stirred up black miners by telling them that "they were as good as white men, and should demand high places of honor and trust." The editor of the society page, Dolly Dalrymple (whose "specialty" it was to "put witty sayings into the mouths of darkies"), transformed her gossip-filled column into a diatribe against the UMW. Horrified by the union's attempt to organize women's auxiliaries among miners' wives, Dalrymple mounted an aggressive rearguard defense of the color line: "White women and black women meeting on the basis of 'social equality' indeed! White men holding umbrellas over negro speakers! Black men addressing white men as 'brother'! The women of our fair southland resent it."

Daily reports from the coalfields added to the perception, widely embraced by Birmingham elites, that their social order and the racial hierarchy it embodied was threatened with imminent collapse. Evidence mounted that the strike had punctured the aura of invincibility that enshrined white supremacy in the district. In spite of the racial conservatism of its leadership and many white rank-and-file miners, the UMW's militancy had conferred a degree of legitimacy upon black resistance that it never enjoyed in more placid times. The strike had upended racial protocol and with it the ritual deference that allowed white paternalists to convince themselves that theirs was a harmonious society. Black strikers were "armed to the teeth and . . . everywhere in predominance," warned Major G. B. Seals of the Alabama Guard, and press accounts left little doubt that the weapons were for practical rather than decorative purposes. When deputies challenged two armed blacks at Blue Creek in mid-July and "told them to stop parading the roads with their weapons," the strikers "stood up and gave the deputies a fight, firing at them with considerable precision." One striker was killed in the battle, "literally punctured with shot." Another serious gun battle was narrowly averted at the Adamsville rail depot, where deputies attempted to disperse a crowd of seven hundred miners who had gathered to "attempt to entice [strikebreakers] to join their ranks." "Twice a negro in the crowd raised his gun, preparing to fire," a reporter recounted, and "as many times the deputies drew a bead on him . . . but the snapping of a trigger would have resulted in a fight." Of seventeen miners arrested for dynamiting houses at Acton, thirteen were black. Two black men and a black woman were the only strikers arrested for setting the charge to the TCI foreman's house at Pratt City. Clearly black strikers suffered the brunt of repression in the coalfields; but by all accounts they were also the most determined strikers.

Black unionists did not hesitate to deal harshly with strikebreakers of either race. A white strikebreaker at Pratt mines was startled on his way to work in mid-August when two heavily armed black strikers "step[ped] out from behind some bushes in front of him." Racial solidarity may have reinforced whatever sympathies black unionists felt for those packed onto the trains arriving daily from the Cotton Belt, but it seemed to offer little protection to those who had willfully defied the UMW's strike order. At Short Creek, a black union stalwart "entered the mine through a private, unused narrow passage . . . and told the negro miners that they had better cease work immediately . . . that the strikers had sworn vengeance upon all who continued to work." When a black miner at the Banner mines declared in early August his determination to break ranks and return to work, Ned Harris, a black UMW member, "cursed at this, and replied that any man who would do that ought to be killed . . . then pulled a pistol and shot [him]."

For operators accustomed to extolling black loyalty, the specter of a social challenge that overstepped the bounds of industrial conflict seemed a prospect too appalling to tolerate, and from early August onward the race issue figured prominently in their attempts to win public support for suppressing the miners. Operators calculated that their best chances for undermining the strike lay in driving a wedge between the "ignorant whites and blacks who have been idling away these many weeks" and the "better class of white union miners," who they supposed "would return to work at once but are afraid of assassination."

Dividing the union along racial lines was more difficult than its adversaries might have imagined, however. If black strikers' militancy was a source of deep despair for Birmingham elites, they could take little comfort from the union's flagrant disregard for racial protocol. Though it never lived up to the lurid egalitarianism ascribed to it by its enemies, the UMW's interracialism represented an implicit challenge to the racial status quo, and the bonds being forged between black and white miners threatened to permanently derail Birmingham from its path to industrial prosperity. The willingness of black and white strikers to join forces – frequently in arms – against the operators seemed to many to signal an unwelcome blurring of racial lines. The spectacle witnessed by one correspondent at Jasper, where "a brass band led a parade through the streets" in which "negroes as well as whites bore red flags, and black men were among the principal speakers," seemed to Birmingham's men of wealth to portend certain disaster.

The operators' turn to the race card coincided with a steady escalation of violence in the coalfields. At Brighton in early August two company deputies were charged with murder after they snatched the black union militant William Millin from jail and lynched him. Just over a week later the union miner Jake Burros was hanged from a tree after being arrested for allegedly dynamiting the house of a strikebreaker. With tensions mounting, a delegation of prominent Birmingham citizens threatened the UMW vice president John P. White that unless the strike was ended they would "make Springfield, Illinois [where a vicious race riot had taken place only weeks earlier] look like six cents." Governor Comer became increasingly adamant that the strike must be defeated, dispatching troops to the strike zone and concentrating his remarks on the danger it posed to white supremacy.

With the threat of racial conflagration looming over them, the UMW leadership began to fold under the pressure. Comer summoned UMW officials to his office on August 25 and informed them that "members of the legislature in every sector of Alabama" were very much "outraged at the attempts to establish social equality between black and white miners." Declaring that he would not tolerate "eight or nine thousand idle niggars [sic] in the State of Alabama," Comer threatened to convene a special session of the state legislature unless officials ended the strike immediately. In a maneuver that revealed the efficacy of the operators' race-baiting campaign and its own accommodation to racial conservatism, the UMW attempted to deflect the "social equality" charge rather than confront it directly. At one point the national UMW offered to "transport out of the state every Negro who was on strike and make it a white man's fight," but to no avail. Invoking public health concerns as a pretext for a final assault on the union, Comer ordered the military on August 26 to cut down the tents erected by striking miners throughout the district.

Four days later, union officials declared the strike over. Judgment Day had arrived, though decidedly not in the form that operators had dreaded early in the strike. The UMW had suffered a colossal defeat in Alabama, a debacle that sealed the fate not only of industrial unionism in the coalfields but of any possibility that black workers might extend their challenge to the racial status quo. In attempting to explain the defeat some weeks later, John P. White attributed the loss to the deliberate manipulation of racial prejudice. "Finding themselves defeated on the industrial battlefield," he claimed, operators "resorted to drastic methods . . . the columns of the press began to teem with appeals to [prejudice], and they injected the race question . . . Any one who is a student of Dixie Land knows what effect this has . . . The entire South is slumbering with racial hatred, ready to break out in widespread racial conflagration . . . Yet it was necessary in order that the operators would not be defeated. We find ourselves in a very precarious condition." The truth of White's somber assessment would be revealed in the weeks and months ahead. The UMW was shattered beyond recovery, at least in the here and now. For as far into the future as anyone could see, Alabama operators would have things their way.

12

Paul Harvey

MINDS OF THE SOUTH

The South of the early twentieth century was a region awash in paradox, flowing not least from the friction between the cherished mythologies of the Old South and the very different sensibilities of the New. In various corners of cultural and intellectual life – including the realms of literature, the arts, politics, religious life, and scholarly exchange – southerners engaged in a lively discourse over questions of regional character and values, identity and history. How did contemporary southerners think (and argue) about the historical meanings and legacies of the Old South, the Civil War, Reconstruction, and the ongoing tensions between tradition and modernity, countryside and city, farm and factory, region and nation? How did they define and debate regional notions of "manhood" and "womanhood," race relations, social class, community, honor, and religion? These are the kinds of questions explored by intellectual and cultural historians of the early twentieth-century South.

The readings in this chapter illuminate a key strand of this discourse: the Modernist critique of the old sentimental Victorian-era verities (known as the "Cavalier Myth"), a critique embodied in the works of W. J. Cash and William Faulkner. As Paul Harvey suggests in his opening essay, the three selections – including an extract from Cash's own classic, *The Mind of the South* – "provide excellent entrées into the complexities of the various minds of the South."

Paul Harvey is Professor of History at the University of Colorado-Colorado Springs, where he specializes in the religious, cultural, and racial history of the American South. In addition to his many essays and articles, he is author of *Redeeming the South: Religious Cultures and Racial Identities Among Southern Baptists, 1865–1925* (1997), *Freedom's Coming: Religious Culture and* the Shaping of the South from the Civil War through the Civil Rights Era (2005), and Through the Storm, Through the Night: A History of African American Christianity (2011). He is also co-editor (with Philip Goff) of Themes in Religion and American Culture (2004) and The Columbia Documentary History of Religion in America Since 1945 (2005). Forthcoming volumes include Jesus in Red, White and Black (with Edward J. Blum) and Moses, Jesus and the Trickster in the Evangelical South. He is currently working on a book project entitled "Trouble the Waters: Religion in the South from Jamestown to Katrina."

The South is a land of paradox and contradiction. What place is not? But surely the American South qualifies more so than many places for this appellation. How else can we grasp the coexistence of barbaric rituals such as lynching and the efflorescence of literature as represented most notably by William Faulkner? How else can we explain that racial violence seemed especially vicious in counties dominated by evangelical piety? How else can we plumb a "southern" identity defined for so many by whiteness – by that "single resolve indomitably maintained," according to early twentieth-century historian Ulrich B. Phillips, that the South had been and would remain a "white man's country" – together with Wilbur J. Cash's observation that "Negro entered into white man as surely as white man entered into Negro – subtly influencing every gesture, every word, every emotion and idea, every attitude?" How else can we match up the brilliance of southern arts both "high" and "low" – Faulkner's novels, Tennessee Williams's plays, Robert Penn Warren's poetry, blues music, early country music, Appalachian mountain culture – with the despair of contemporaries who, like Cash, characterized the "mind of the South" precisely as having no mind but rather a "savage ideal?"[1]

Through the first part of the twentieth century, the South was "modernizing," in a sense, as industrially organized workers laid railroad track, cleared lumber, mined coal, and worked in textile mills. Mass migration of white and black people out of the region through much of the twentieth century – numbering in total some twenty-eight million people (twenty million or so white and Latino, about eight million African American) – accelerated as agricultural land was taken out of production and as farm work grew more and more mechanized. On the other hand, at the very time when southern literary and cultural modernism appeared nearly fully grown, the region appeared in other ways to be regressing, appearing notably in President Franklin Delano Roosevelt's addresses as the nation's number one economic problem. Increasingly, it came to stand for everything that was backward, for futile energy and wasted lives, stuck in an economic system that was almost perversely unproductive. As Cash wrote:

> The mind of the section . . . is continuous with that past. And its primary
> form is determined not nearly so much by industry as by the purely agri-
> cultural conditions of that past. So far from being modernized, in many
> ways it has actually always marched away, as to this day it continues to
> do, from the present towards the past.[2]

At this same historical moment, from the 1910s to the 1940s, William
Faulkner, Robert Penn Warren, the Fugitive poets at Vanderbilt, and many
others were experimenting with modernist forms in ways that would revolutionize literature and the arts around the country. So was Cash, whose work
The Mind of the South stands today both as a secondary source, with useful
historical interpretation, *and* as a primary source, a voice of the generation
of southern Modernists who were delivering a "knockout blow . . . to the
Cavalier myth," as scholar Daniel Singal notes about Cash's attack on the
southern myth of the high-born nobility of the slaveholding class. They did so,
Singal suggests, "in far more concentrated fashion, with fewer false starts on
the one hand, but with greater tension and drama on the other."

This chapter contrasts three selections which illuminate this "tension and
drama" of southern identity, the "split psyche" that Cash plumbed in *The
Mind of the South*. First, Grace Hale's "Deadly Amusements" introduces the
reader to "spectacle lynchings," a prototypical example of what Cash referred
to as the "savage ideal" of the South. In Hale's selection, the reader encounters
southern racism and violence at its most grotesque, seemingly primitive in its
blood lust, and yet chillingly modern in its organization. Next, the chapter
revisits some passages from Cash's classic *The Mind of the South*, and explores
how he demolished the "Cavalier myth" of the South even while decrying
what he saw as the region's desiccated social and intellectual life. Ironically,
as Singal points out in the selection from *The War Within: From Victorian to
Modernist Thought in the South*, the publication of Cash's book itself served
as a refutation of his exaggerated attack on the region's philistine tastes. Singal
summarizes the wrenching transition from southern Victorianism to southern
Modernism, an achievement remarkable for its occurrence at the very time
that the region seemed to many the most vexed by its unproductive economic
system, its unjust racial order, and its intellectual torpor.

"Racial violence was very modern," argues Grace Hale in her stimulating
interpretation of lynching, a practice which, while not unique to the South,
became particularly identified with the region during this era. In particular,
Hale conveys how roads, railroads, the press, cameras, and other modern
forms of transportation and communication made the communal nature of
spectacle lynchings both terrifyingly possible and unforgettably visible.

As Hale makes clear, crimes of racial hatred were common in the segregated
South. More often than not, they were private affairs. But in the late nineteenth century, a vividly public and ritualized version of lynching emerged,
one that was well documented by the participants who posed for photographs

and purchased body parts as souvenirs. The fear of race mixing, particularly between white women and black men – the symbol of virginal purity encountering the black beast rapist – was a pernicious and brutally effective justification for segregation and racial violence, and a pervasive specter haunting southern folklore. By its very nature, tangible proof was irrelevant. Race purity was at stake. Spectacle lynchings could be purposeful rituals, like solemn purification rites; hence, the frequency with which lynching victims were *burned*, and the invocations pronounced at such events by clergymen. At other times, they could be commodified carnivals. The black intellectual W. E. B. Du Bois discovered this when he saw one lynching victim's fingers for sale at a store. He later wrote about his coming to grips with this irrational horror in a moving essay in his classic work, *The Souls of Black Folk*. As Du Bois witnessed and Hale explains in her piece, lynching brutally marked and reinforced the boundaries between whiteness and blackness.

Well over four thousand lynchings (4,786 by one count) occurred in the United States from 1880 to 1950. The injustices perpetrated within the legal system simply added to the violence meted out to black Americans outside the legal system. In either case, for southern blacks there was no respite, no safe space, no real means of recourse.

As northern academics and social reformers came south to investigate lynchings, they connected the relative prevalence of Baptist and Methodist churches in a given area with the incidence of the grossest forms of racial violence. The correlation was chilling. Timid white parsons feared dividing churches by calling for the prosecution of perpetrators in their midst; bolder white clerics were immobilized in the face of "an almost fierce resistance to anything that resembled recognition of Negro equality," as Joseph Martin Dawson, a pastor in Waco, Texas put it. Present at the notorious, mass carnivalesque lynching of Jesse Washington in 1916, Dawson felt "entirely helpless because five thousand monsters participated and who was I, a lone individual, to do anything about it." The lynching victim in this case was innocent of the crime; the guilty party was soon thereafter found. When Dawson introduced a resolution at a pastor's association denouncing the act of lynching Washington, he later recalled, "to my utter surprise, when they discovered they had burned an innocent man, they found the guilty, the only comment I heard around town . . . was 'Well, it's fine. At last, they got the right Nigger.'"[3]

White voices of moderation idealized a time of relative racial harmony in an older South, one supposedly undisturbed by the rising influence of lower-class whites or impudent Negroes. What they failed to account for, as Hale shows, was the very modernity of racial violence, its synergy with the same forces – railroads, better roads, more extensive media – so praised by advocates for the New South. A "progressive" South could more effectively enforce apartheid, both through the legal system and through an economic order that provided circumscribed opportunities for poorer whites while repressing the subordinated class of black rural laborers.

As a brilliant young journalist, Wilbur J. Cash watched the conditions which made such happenings as spectacle lynchings possible. He wrote *The Mind of the South* as an attempt to overturn the sentimentalities about the "old South" that were then being unforgettably rehearsed in the film *Gone with the Wind*. He witnessed the premiere of the Technicolor extravaganza in Atlanta in 1939, and described it as a "high ritual for the reassertion of the legend of the Old South," with Margaret Mitchell's story becoming "a sort of new confession of the Southern faith."

Born in North Carolina of southern Baptist stock, Cash was alert to confessions of faith, and our selection from *The Mind of the South* memorably portrays the rise of southern evangelicalism in the early nineteenth century. During the antebellum era, the evangelical faith, most notably represented by Baptist and Methodist believers, exploded through the region, tracing almost exactly the westward and southward movement of slavery. From its earliest days, then, southern evangelicalism was tied up with sin and subordination, and with "a personal God, a God for the individualist, a God whose representatives were not silken priests but preachers risen from the people themselves."

Southern historians have searched for a central theme to bring together the difficult contradictions of the region's past – in particular, the paradox of slavery and freedom. Scholarship on religion in the American South has engaged in little such argument. The central theme of southern religious history in scholarly works remains the rise of evangelicalism, symbolized in the term Bible Belt. According to this view, the focused moment of salvation has constituted the bedrock of southern religious belief and practice. This evangelical individualism stifled any social ethic, leaving white southern churches captive to the cultural norms of racism and dogmatic literalist theology. Musicians, poets, and novelists of the South have recognized the centrality of evangelical Protestantism in a region "haunted by God." William Faulkner, hardly renowned for adherence to evangelical morality, acknowledged how he "assimilated" the South's religious tradition, how he "took that in without even knowing it. It's just there. It has nothing to do with how much I might believe or disbelieve – it's just there."[4]

Writing in the same period, social critic Lillian Smith suggested that "God and Negroes and Jesus and sin and salvation" were "baled up together" in the minds of southerners. Both Cash and Smith understood emotional evangelicalism of the Baptist and Methodist variety – with its itinerating preachers delivering fiery exhortations on sin and redemption – as fundamental to a southern psyche torn between hedonism and guilt, as likely to take up the bottle or the knife as to break down in tears at a revival meeting. "What our Southerner required . . . was a faith as simple and emotional as himself," Cash wrote in one of his characteristically exaggerated but trenchant summaries.[5]

Having traced the roots of southern evangelicalism, Cash then portrays how a more business-oriented, coldly calculating religion settled into the established churches in the twentieth century. When the German sociologist Max Weber traveled to North Carolina in the early twentieth century, he observed the same phenomenon that Cash notes here. Weber witnessed bankers going to the river to be baptized, in an act of cultural solidarity that he saw as essential to their prosperity.

Like Cash, most southern intellectuals of the modernist generation derided the established regional evangelicalism that had long since made its peace with the reigning authorities, be they slaveholders (in the nineteenth century) or mill owners, landlords, and bankers (in the twentieth). Like Cash, later scholars and intellectuals depicted religion in Dixie as being in a state of "cultural captivity," reduced to giving divine imprimatur to the region's peculiar institutions. The same might be said of Cash's dismal portrayal of southern intellectual life in his era. The few doing worthy work, he suggested, were utterly lacking in social influence. "There was," he explained, "no articulation between the new intellectual leaders and the body of the South, and it is in this that the tragedy of the South as it stood in 1940 centrally resided."

Writing squarely in the middle of the era of southern modernism (and, tragically, committing suicide just after the publication of *The Mind of the South*), Cash could not see that the intellectuals, writers, and artists of his very era were far more powerful than most of the transitory political figures of the time. From the publication of *The Report on Economic Conditions of the South* (by a commission appointed by Franklin Delano Roosevelt), to Howard Odum's sociological studies, to Walker Evans's powerful modernist photographs, to the legions of other photographers combing the South (and the country) on behalf of the Farm Security Administration, to novelists such as William Faulkner and Zora Neale Hurston and playwrights such as Tennessee Williams, to a generation of musical geniuses emanating from the Delta flatlands (Robert Johnson, Son House, Muddy Waters, and scores of others) and the upland and mountain South (the Carter family, Charlie Poole, and countless others), southern literary, intellectual, and cultural life was varied and vibrant. But that is more clear in retrospect than at the time, when southern politics seemed inert, utterly unable to respond to the catastrophe of the Depression, and when millions of southerners found their best opportunities in the North and West, and set out to improve their lives outside the region altogether.

Daniel Singal's selection provides a historical analysis of southern cultural and intellectual life between the world wars, one which both draws from Cash and sets his work in a different context. For Singal, *The War Within* raged between an entrenched Victorian culture that had stifled the South, and an emerging modernist one that threatened every received verity and shibboleth of the region. Singal defines the Modernist mind as one that explores and even relishes human irrationality, a

> willingness, even eagerness, to plumb the nether regions of the psyche . . .
> the recognition of man's irrational nature, the acceptance of an open and
> unpredictable universe, the notion of conflict as inherently virtuous, the

tolerance of uncertainty, and the drive toward probing criticism – all are part of the Modernist effort to reintegrate the human consciousness and thus to liberate man from the restrictive culture of enforced innocence with which the century began.

Cash was a classic model of the Modernist generation, for he destroyed the "Cavalier myth" and any notion of southern innocence, substituting for it a "near-schizophrenic split within the southern psyche, between a voracious hedonism and an equally powerful Puritan guilt, a split that led to all sorts of pathological behavior from miscegenation to lynching."

During these years, while Cash was composing *The Mind of the South*, William Faulkner was revolutionizing American literature in a series of works that remain central to the American literary canon. Cash's and Faulkner's versions of southern history come together almost telepathically in Faulkner's murky but brilliant novel *Absalom, Absalom*. In tracing this story of the rise and fall of the central protagonist, Thomas Sutpen, from lowly origins in the Virginia backcountry to a faux plantation gentility in Faulkner's fictional Yoknapatawpha County in Mississippi, Faulkner told a story which mirrored that described in non-fiction form by Cash. As Singal explains, "Cash presented the Old South as a frontier society dominated by the 'hard, energetic, horse-trading type man' who attempted to disguise his crudeness by posing as an aristocrat." Likewise, Faulkner's Thomas Sutpen, having appeared in Yoknapatawpha County bearing guns and dragging along slaves, then

> skuldugged a hundred miles of land out of a poor ignorant Indian and built the biggest house on it you ever saw and went away with six wagons and came back with the crystal tapestries and the Wedgwood chairs to furnish it and nobody knew if he had robbed another steamboat or had just dug up a little more of the old loot.

Although described by other characters as a "demon," we learn from Sutpen's own story that "his trouble was innocence." His "design" for creating a plantation, one that would salve the ever-living wound of having been denied entrance into a front door as a poor white boy approaching a plantation house in Virginia, was an American dream that he had to follow. He had no choice; his design controlled him: "All of a sudden he discovered, not what he wanted to do but what he just had to do, had to do it whether he wanted to or not, because if he did not do it he knew that he could never live with himself for the rest of his life."

Sutpen's design ultimately is foiled by the return of Charles Bon, his secret son from a previous liaison with an octoroon woman in the Caribbean. Bon now wreaks his vengeance by courting Sutpen's daughter, provoking Sutpen's son to murder Bon to avert family dishonor. And this dishonor, it becomes clear, is not incest, not the marriage of half-siblings, but rather miscegenation, the tainting of Sutpen's daughter with a tincture of Negro blood, however untraceable that blood may be in Charles Bon's fair-skinned features. "Let flesh touch with flesh," a character pronounces upon the history the novel recounts, "and watch the fall of all the eggshell shibboleth of caste and color too." Faulkner's modernist fable, published in 1936, serves as an exaggerated allegory of slavery, race, miscegenation, the Civil War, and the rise and fall of the planter class. Cash in history, and Faulkner in literature, typify a modernist generation determined to explore and then explode the treasured myths of southern history, and probe more deeply into the southern psyche.[6]

For Singal, the modernists were so successful that, in yet another irony of southern history, intellectual life in the region was actually less vibrant and far-reaching in the coming decades, just as the segregated South was crumbling, than it was previously, when the culture of apartheid held its firmest grip on the region. Just a few years later, the dean of southern historians, C. Vann Woodward, would outline his own version of the irony of southern history. "The experience of evil and the experience of tragedy," he would write, "are parts of the Southern heritage that are as difficult to reconcile with the American legend of innocence and social felicity as the experience of poverty and defeat are to reconcile with the legends of abundance and success." The three selections below provide excellent entrees into the complexities of the various minds of the South.[7]

NOTES

1. Wilbur J. Cash, *The Mind of the South* (New York: Alfred A. Knopf, 1941), p. 51; Ulrich B. Phillips, "The Central Theme of Southern History," *American Historical Review*, 34 (1928), pp. 30–43.
2. Cash, *Mind of the South*, p. x.
3. Joseph Martin Dawson Oral History, Texas Baptist Historical Collection, Baylor University, pp. 53, 65.
4. Interview in Frederick L. Gwynn and Joseph L. Blotner, *Faulkner in the University: Class Conferences at the University of Virginia, 1957–1958* (Charlottesville: University of Virginia Press, 1959), quoted in Charles Wilson, "William Faulkner and the Southern Religious Culture," in Doreen Fowler and Ann Abadie, eds., *Faulkner and Religion* (Jackson: University Press of Mississippi, 1991), pp. 27–8.
5. Lillian Smith, *Killers of the Dream* (New York: W. W. Norton, 1994 [orig. 1949]), p. 103; Cash, *Mind of the South*, p. 58.
6. Quotations from William Faulkner, *Absalom, Absalom* (New York: Vintage Books reprint ed., 1991), p. 112.
7. C. Vann Woodward, "The Irony of Southern History," in *The Burden of Southern History* (Baton Rouge: Louisiana State University Press, 1993), p. 21.

* * *

FURTHER READING

Blum, Edward J., *W. E. B. Du Bois: American Prophet* (Philadelphia: University of Pennsylvania Press, 2007).

Clayton, Bruce, *W. J. Cash: A Life* (Baton Rouge: Louisiana State University Press, 1991).

Cobb, James C., *Redefining Southern Culture: Mind and Identity in the Modern South* (Athens: University of Georgia Press, 1999).

Escott, Paul D., ed., *W. J. Cash and the Minds of the South* (Baton Rouge: Louisiana State University Press, 1992).

Harvey, Paul, *Freedom's Coming: Religious Cultures and the Shaping of the South from the Civil War through the Civil Rights Era* (Chapel Hill: University of North Carolina Press, 2005).

Kirby, Jack Temple, *Media-Made Dixie: The South in the American Imagination* (Athens: University of Georgia Press, 2004).

Litwack, Leon F., *Trouble in Mind: Black Southerners in the Age of Jim Crow* (New York: Knopf, 1998).

Williamson, Joel, *William Faulkner and Southern History* (New York: Oxford University Press, 1993).

Wilson, Charles Reagan, *Judgment and Grace in Dixie: Southern Faiths from Faulkner to Elvis* (Athens: University of Georgia Press, 1997).

Wood, Amy, *Lynching and Spectacle: Witnessing Racial Violence in America, 1890–1940* (Chapel Hill: University of North Carolina Press, 2009).

* * *

Grace Hale

Making Whiteness[†]

Despite the parchment paper pronouncements of separate but equal and the bright block-lettered signs loudly proclaiming "For Colored" and "For White," at the heart of the culture of segregation lay a profound ambiguity. Separation, after all, did not necessarily mean racial inferiority. It could also signify the creation of relatively autonomous black spaces, even autonomous black bodies. In fact, even as African Americans fought disenfranchisement and legal segregation in the courts across the South, many black southerners sought to separate themselves as fully as possible from the white southerners who had been their former masters. Segregation certainly meant shabby or nonexistent waiting rooms and train cars where African American passengers were jumbled together with smoking whites and engine soot.

[†]Grace Hale, *Making Whiteness: The Culture of Segregation in the South, 1890–1940* (New York: Pantheon, 1998), pp. 199–203.

W. E. B. Du Bois made the intended indignity clear in revising his 1925 article on Georgia for *The Nation* while traveling through the state: "I am in the hot, crowded, and dirty Jim Crow car where I belong . . . I am not comfortable." Yet segregation also created spaces for black doctors, black colleges, and increasingly black business districts – from Auburn Avenue in Atlanta to Beale Street in Memphis – as southern African Americans moved into growing southern cities. The creation of a separate white southern world, a culture of segregation, implied that somewhere there existed a separate black one. As whites strove to create an all-encompassing system of separation, then, they also risked aiding African Americans in the very struggle for more autonomy that white supremacy sought to deny.

The culture of segregation was always a process, never a finished product. Despite the dizzying multiplication of the spaces of consumption, white southerners sought to found their own racial identity within the maintenance of an absolute color bar. Yet black southerners continued to fight separation and exclusion, pushing against each new boundary. And despite Du Bois's discomfort in the Jim Crow car, the expansion of transportation systems across the region rapidly increased spatial mobility, for black as well as white southerners. As threatening to whites as the development of a separate black world were the ways changes in leisure, consumption, and travel threatened to blur the edges of those carefully constructed white and black spaces. Indeed, southern whites found what the film historian Miriam Hansen has described as "the simultaneous liberation and commodification of sexuality that crucially defined the development of American consumer culture" particularly dangerous and yet also titillating. And threats came from within as well. The shift from an agrarian toward a more industrialized and urban economy and increasing activism among white industrial workers as well as Populists made class lines more visible. Southern white women, too, demonstrated a growing interest in reform and joined the temperance and suffrage movements in large numbers. Would a whiteness founded in a culture of segregation, then, be able to hold white southerners together?

Though Allen Tate referred to an older, antebellum southern white tradition in his essay for the Agrarian manifesto *I'll Take My Stand*, he was right about the methods white southerners were using to defeat perceived threats to the racial line they had drawn in the sand. And as Tate participated in yet another recycling of Lost Cause themes of past southern glory and pastoral utopia, he surely would have appreciated the long history of the answer at which he arrived. Unfortunately, white southerners' best-known acts of violence, lynchings, became increasingly bound up between 1890 and 1940 in the very practices of a modern culture of consumption that Tate hoped his region in 1930 would use violence to reject.

It was an uneasy landscape, the early twentieth-century South, a small-town, small-city world of ice companies and beauty parlors, soda fountains and gas stations. It was a world where people who went to church some days watched or participated in the torture of their neighbors on others. In the decades following 1890, many lynchings no longer occurred in places untouched by the technological advances of the larger world. Lynchers drove cars, spectators used cameras, out-of-town visitors arrived on specially chartered excursion trains, and the towns and counties in which these horrifying events happened had newspapers, telegraph offices, and even radio stations that announced times and locations of these upcoming violent spectacles. Although after the peak decades of the 1890s the number of lynchings decreased even in the South, the cultural impact of the practice became more powerful. More people participated in, read about, saw pictures of, and collected souvenirs from lynchings even as fewer mob murders occurred. In the twentieth century white southerners transformed a deadly and often quiet form of vigilante "justice" into a modern spectacle of enduring power.

Yet not all southern lynchings fit this new and evolving pattern. More often, small groups of white men hunted down and shot or hanged their African American victims after an argument over the year-end sharecroppers' settle or to send a message to other timber or turpentine camp laborers not to demand any better. These lynchings in the night claimed many more victims than the open-air spectacles of torture that drew such large crowds. And white violence against southern blacks was not limited only to lynchings – white men continued in more private settings to rape black women and assault African Americans for "reasons" ranging from black resistance and economic success to white hatred, jealousy, and fear. "Private violence," as W. J. Cash explained in 1941, stemmed from the same circumstances that made spectacle lynchings "socially defensible" from a southern white perspective; "to smash a sassy Negro, to kill him, to do the same to a 'nigger lover' – this was to assert the white man's prerogative as pointedly, to move as certainly to get a black man back in his place, as to lynch." Southern whites did not need Tate to encourage them to use violence to secure what he conceived as their more "private, self-contained, and essentially spiritual" way of life – it had been a chosen method of empowerment since colonial Jamestown.

But something was new about lynchings in public, attended by thousands, captured in papers by reporters who witnessed the tortures, and photographed for those spectators who wanted a souvenir and yet failed to get a coveted finger, toe, or fragment of bone. More was at stake than putting African American southerners brutally in their place, as Cash understood, for "private violence" succeeded in limiting and often eliminating African American political activity and achieving significant white control of black labor. Explanations of the practice of lynching in the twentieth century, however, have focused on the persistence of the "barbaric" practice of the past rather than its transformation, in the case of spectacle lynchings, into a peculiarly modern ritual.

Southern whites, according to both contemporary observers like H. L. Mencken and Arthur Raper and present-day scholars like James McGovern and Joel Williamson, lynched African American men and occasionally women in the absence of "modernity" – because they lacked a "modern" economy, a "modern" white male sexuality, or even a "modern" theater. Even Jacquelyn Dowd Hall, in the best analysis of lynching to date, saw the region's extreme racism as existing in conflict with southern modernizing efforts. And while the historians Fitzhugh Brundage and

Edward L. Ayers have convincingly argued that lynching was central to the New South and particularly the structuring of its labor markets in areas experiencing rapid increases in their African American populations, they have focused mainly on the more common private lynchings and their role in the New South economy.

African American anti-lynching activists, too – some of whom had barely escaped lynching themselves – saw lynching as central to the New South, and they examined the function of violence in structuring a changing southern economy and culture. From Ida B. Wells, who founded both the study of lynching and anti-lynching activism, to Frederick Douglass, W. E. B. Du Bois, Mary Church Terrell, James Weldon Johnson, and especially Walter White, they understood that whites' practice of ritualized violence, what Terrell called "this wild and diabolical carnival of blood," was central not only to the white economy but to white identity as well. Yet even the liberal W. J. Cash condemned Walter White as an extremist for denouncing the "rape complex" as a "fraud." African American activists were more often simply ignored.

A practice dependent on modern transportation and printing technologies, increasingly intertwined with the practices of an emerging consumer culture, was not some frontier residue and soon-to-be-lost small obstacle to "Progress," then, but a part of the southern present and future, a key medium for resolving the contradictions within the culture of segregation in which these brutal spectacles took place. "Lynch carnivals," as a popular book on the subject written in the 1930s described them, were rituals increasingly bound up with the way southern whites shaped the practices of modern consumption to their own ends, communal spectacles of torture that helped ease white fears of a raceless consumer society even as they helped structure segregation, the policy that would regulate this new southern world. Publicly resolving the race, gender, and class ambiguities at the very center of the culture of segregation, spectacle lynchings brutally conjured a collective, all-powerful whiteness even as they made the color line seem modern, civilized, and sane. Spectacle lynchings were about making racial difference in the New South, about ensuring the separation of all southern life into whiteness and blackness even as the very material things that made up southern life were rapidly changing. Racial violence was modern.

∾ ∾ ∾

W. J. Cash

The Mind of the South[†]

What our Southerner required . . . was a faith as simple and emotional as himself. A faith to draw men together in hordes, to terrify them with Apocalyptie rhetoric,

[†]W. J. Cash, The Mind of the South (New York: Vintage Books, 1991 [orig. 1941]), pp. 56–8, 222–3, 418–21.

to cast them into the pit, rescue them, and at last bring them shouting into the fold of Grace. A faith, not of liturgy and prayer book, but of primitive frenzy and the blood sacrifice – often of fits and jerks and barks. The God demanded was an anthropomorphic God – the Jehovah of the Old Testament: a God who might be seen, a God who *had* been seen. A passionate, whimsical tyrant, to be trembled before, but whose favor was the sweeter for that. A personal God, a God for the individualist, a God whose representatives were not silken priests but preachers risen from the people themselves.

What was demanded here, in other words, was the God and the faith of the Methodists and the Baptists, and the Presbyterians. These personal and often extravagant sects, sweeping the entire American country with their revivals in the first half of the nineteenth century, achieved their greatest success in the personal and extravagant South. And not only among the masses. Fully nine-tenths of the new planters – of the men who were to be masters of the great South – were, and, despite some tendency to fall away to Anglicanism as more high-toned, continued to be, numbered among their adherents.

But the spirit of these sects, of course, was essentially Hebraic – their ideal theocratic. And it was characteristic of them all that they asserted, and that their communicants unquestioningly believed, the voice of their ministers to be literally the voice of God.

Thus, as the *nouveaux* came to power, this spirit and this ideal came to power also, and the evangelical ministers armored all too often in ignorance and bitter fanaticism, virtually always in a rigid narrowness of outlook, entered upon that long career of always growing and generally inept sway over public affairs, over the whole mind of the South . . . By the time Andrew Jackson had got to be President, the old easy tolerance was quite dead. Skepticism of any sort in religion was anathema, and lack of frenetic zeal was being set down for heresy.

[. . .]

The triumph of the evangelical sects also naturally involved the establishment of the Puritan ideal. From the first great revivals onward, the official moral philosophy of the South moved steadily toward the position of that of the Massachusetts Bay Colony. Adherence was demanded, and, with the exception of a handful of recalcitrant colonial aristocrats and stubborn sinners, willingly and even enthusiastically given, to a code that was increasingly Mosaic in its sternness.

And this, mind, coincidentally with the growth of that curious Southern hedonism which was its antithesis. The two streams could and would flow forward side by side, and with a minimum of conflict. The Southerner's frolic humor, his continual violation of his strict precepts in action, might serve constantly to exacerbate the sense of sin in him, to keep his zest for absolution always at white heat, to make him humbly amenable to the public proposals of his preachers, acquiescent in their demands for the incessant extension of their rule; his Puritanism might at a pinch move him to outlaw the beloved fiddle from the church as an instrument of Satan, would indeed lead him habitually to regard pleasure as in its very nature *verboten*. Yet, in the long run, he succeeded in uniting the two incompatible tendencies in his single person, without ever allowing them to come into open and decisive contention.

Hypocrisy? Far from it. There was much of Tartarin in this Southerner, but nothing of Tartufe. His Puritanism was no mere mask put on from cold calculation, but as essential a part of him as his hedonism. And his combination of the two was without conscious imposture. One might say with much truth that it proceeded from a fundamental split in his psyche, from a sort of social schizophrenia. One may say more simply and more safely that it was all part and parcel of that naïve capacity for unreality which was characteristic of him.

[. . .]

By 1914 we can begin distinctly to discern that calculation was . . . seeping more and more into the great fabric of the Southern loyalties of the captains of industry and commerce, and indeed of the ambitious classes as a whole, though not, to be sure, of every individual in these classes.

The matter was most obvious in the case of the religious pattern. On every hand men of business position and aspiration were showing a continually more rigorous zeal for going to church and having everybody else go to church; for passing the collection plate, teaching Sunday school, and leading and multiplying prayer meetings. Terms like "salvation" and "grace" and "soul-winning" occupied their grave lips on Sundays and Wednesday nights as absolutely as talk of making money occupied them for the rest of the week. Furthermore, they were growing remarkably more liberal with their purses. No few of them were ostentatiously adopting the Hebraic law and dedicating the tithe of all their income to the service of heaven, and were engaging in campaigns to dragoon everybody else into doing the same. Out of their pockets missionaries to the heathen of China and Europe were multiplying. And so were new churches. In fact, new churches were building in Dixie almost as fast as factories, the old simple chapels giving place in all the towns to ornate piles in early Dayton Romanesque or a kind of Gothic it was easy to believe the Goths had actually invented.

And nobody who looked closely into all this could have escaped the unpleasant feeling that one very potent element in it was the sense that it paid, materially and immediately – that interest was figuring here more definitely than it had in the past. Nor was it only the laymen who were being infected. The old-fashioned Southern minister was gradually giving ground to men who had the stamp of Babbitt upon them as clearly as any of their parishioners – brisk, unctuous, and greatly given to grandiose schemes for the creation of an always more elaborate "organization" and ever larger "plants" – men as obsessed with the passion for large figures as any factory-builder, and as full, too, of the competitive spirit, noisily anxious to have a greater church and a greater enrollment than the parson on the next street or in the next town.

And interest was all too obviously beginning to play strange tricks with the judgment of such parsons. Let a parishioner only have sufficient money and a willingness to gratify their passion for building and outdoing, and let him only be sufficiently unbending in his public declarations of adherence to the moral code laid down by the evangelical sects, and he was increasingly likely to find himself a steward or a deacon or a presbyter, in spite of the fact that it was notorious that he was a pirate in commerce and that he passed his free evenings in making most unholily merry.

But if the growth of the spirit of calculation was most evident in the religious field, it was surely not confined to it. Nearly all these men of business belonged now, of course, to that Yankee-izing party which we have seen as appearing before 1900; professed loudly to being militant apostles of change. But in reality the changes they were talking about were only such relatively minor ones as would plainly serve to further their chances of making money. When it came to a question of the fundamentals of the Southern pattern, they were in fact growing distinctly more conservative, if that were possible – precisely because of the gathering knowledge within themselves that the Southern status quo presented a nearly perfect stage for the working out of their personal ambitions – precisely because of the gathering perception that the Southern mind was a mighty bulwark for its preservation.

[. . .]

Here was the final great tragedy of the South as it stood in 1940 – not that it had no intellectual leadership. In those elements at which we have already looked with some closeness – in its schoolmen, its literary men, its more enlightened editors, and so on – it had the best intellectual leadership it had ever had, the first which really deserved the adjective. The tragedy was that this leadership was almost wholly unarticulated with the body of the South. If the people of the region were not entirely unaffected by what the men who represented the new analytical and inquiring spirit were doing, they were still affected by it only remotely and sporadically.

This was true all along the line. Take the strictly cultural field for example. If the South now had more writers of a literary sort than any other part of the country, it was still overwhelmingly the nation's poorest book-buying area. And this was true not merely with reference to the population as a whole – was not to be explained simply by reference to the presence of the Negroes and the large numbers of poor whites – but strictly with reference to the wealthier classes and to those who had been to college.

A private library of any dimensions was the exception rather than the rule in the big and beautiful houses in the fashionable suburbs, and often when they were found there they represented simply a collection made by some secretary and kept purely for exhibition purposes. The body of business men, including those of high rank, read no book heavier than Dale Carnegie's manuals on how to make more money by false geniality; and perhaps the majority read no book at all. The same often held for their wives and daughters. Many houses in the twenty-thousand-dollar class and up were to be found completely bare of books save for half a dozen disposed as ornaments on a table in the drawing-room.

The South read a good deal more now than in the past, to be sure. But the total number of those who read anything worth reading was still incredibly small. And among those who read, if a few greeted such writers as Thomas Wolfe, Faulkner, and Caldwell with tolerance and even sympathetic understanding, the prevailing attitude toward them was likely to be one of squeamish distaste and shock, of denial that they told the essential truth or any part of it – in many cases, of bitter resentment against them on the ground that they had libeled and misrepresented the South with malicious intent.

It was the measure of something that, after fifteen years of the new spirit in Southern writing, Margaret Mitchell's sentimental novel, *Gone with the Wind*, which had curiously begun by a little offending many Southerners, ended by becoming a sort of new confession of the Southern faith. The scene at Atlanta when the motion picture made from the romance was given its first showing in the nation was one of the most remarkable which America has seen in our time. Primarily, of course, the showing, and its accompaniment of parades and balls, represented a purely commercial scheme arranged by the producers of the picture. But in the event it turned into a high ritual for the reassertion of the legend of the Old South. Atlanta become a city of pilgrimage for people from the entire region. The ceremonies were accompanied by great outbursts of emotion, which bore no relationship to the actual dramatic value of a somewhat dull and thin performance. And later on, when the picture was shown in the other towns of the South, attendance at the theaters took on the definite character of a patriotic act.

In other purely cultural spheres the tale was much the same. Most of the larger Southern towns, for instance, now paid at least perfunctory respect to the kind of music which is usually called classical. Volunteer symphony orchestras or local concert- or chamber-music groups were maintained in some instances. And musical festivals, with important concert and opera artists on the program, were general. But it was noteworthy that Southern radio stations regularly carried fewer "class programs" than those of any other American region. Members of the staff of one of the largest of these stations tell me that this is due wholly to the fact that there is no effective demand for such programs. And what is to the same purpose is that I am told by the largest music dealer in a Southern city of a hundred thousand people, which serves as trading center for a million people, that he has only four customers who regularly buy phonographic-record albums of the more serious composers.

I digress a little, of course. But I have set these matters down as a proper part of the story as a whole, and as leading naturally back to the matters with which we were originally engaged. If Southern people of the ruling orders read the Southern novelists but little and often repudiated their findings when they did read them, they read the studies, such as those emanating from the University of North Carolina Press, which were concerned with the questions directly involved in the cotton-population-unemployment quandary of the South hardly at all. Indeed, they were usually dismissed contemptuously and bitterly as the work of busybody theorists bent on raising disturbing issues which had better not be thought about at all and upsetting conditions which were quite well enough if let alone.

But the core of the tragedy lay deeper than this. It was, after all, not surprising that any body of people should prefer the comforts of complacency and illusion to facing highly unpleasant facts for which the remedy was far from being obvious – least of all that the Southern people, so long trained to believing what they liked to believe, should prefer them.

If, as I have said, the South now had the best intellectual leadership it had ever possessed, it has to be borne in mind that intellectual leaderships are by themselves always helpless. Invariably they are quite incapable of taking their facts and ideas directly to the people, persuading them of their validity, and translating them into action. What is necessary is an active and practical political and economic leadership which is able and willing to serve as a liaison force to these ends. The South simply had no such political and economic leadership, or at least it had far too few men who had been brought under the influence of the new intellectual leadership much to change the result. That is what I meant in saying that there was no articulation between the new intellectual leaders and the body of the South, and it is in this that the tragedy of the South as it stood in 1940 centrally resided.

Daniel Joseph Singal

The War Within†

[The] Victorian concept of culture was based ultimately on a world view of radical innocence and that Modernist thought represents a deliberate flight from that innocence. The point is not that Victorians were in fact innocent people (or that Modernists have entirely escaped innocence), but that they established innocence as their cultural goal. Their impulse was to strive for purity in all things, to refuse resolutely to accommodate the presence of conflict or evil within the perimeter of civilization. Such was the purpose of their dichotomy between civilized and savage – to wall off as far as possible those irrational tendencies in the human personality that could lead to cruelty, excess, and pain. In truth their actual behavior saw frequent lapses from this lofty standard, most evident in that "other" life of prostitution and pornography that Victorian gentlemen commonly led. On the "spiritual" level, moreover, there were constant struggles of the moral will to keep the more acceptable domesticated emotions from degenerating into the forbidden passions,

†Daniel Joseph Singal, *The War Within: From Victorian to Modernist Thought in the South, 1919–1945* (Chapel Hill: University of North Carolina Press, 1982), pp. 7–10, 373–7.

and the battle was often lost. The key point, though, is that these outbreaks of "animalism" were viewed precisely as lapses. The ideal of the Victorians remained a world governed by moral purity, and they tried hard to attain it.

Modernists, it is clear, have pursued the exact opposite course. They launched their rebellion with the express intention of countering what they felt was an unnatural repression of human vitality ordained by Victorian culture. Following the insights of Darwin and Freud, they insisted on seeing man as the human animal and turned their attention to those darker reaches of his being that the Victorians sought to evade. For contemporary novelists especially, the human capacity for evil has become, not a source of shame, but rather the force that gives life its texture and significance.

[. . .]

Although the battle between Victorian and Modernist culture raged throughout Western society, nowhere can it be seen with greater clarity than in the American South. There Victorianism had settled in with a vengeance during the late nineteenth century, merging with the distinctive cultural patterns that had formed prior to the Civil War. The war had devastated southern society, wiping out the political and economic base, along with most major social institutions. By the end of Reconstruction all that southerners could salvage from their history was the sustaining conviction that, in its day, theirs had been an aristocratic culture infinitely superior to the crass materialistic culture of their enemy. This Cavalier myth, moreover, embodied traits of order, stability, and cohesion that southern society stood in desperate need of. The result was what Paul Gaston has called the New South Creed, a transposition of Cavalier mythology onto the framework of Victorian belief in morality and industrial progress, a fusion of ideological elements so formidable that it effectively blocked the arrival of intellectual Modernism in the region through the First World War.

Thus when a new generation of southern intellectuals emerged after the war, theirs was a task of deliberately and rapidly catching up. Modernism, they soon discovered, was an accomplished fact in most of the Western world, of which the South had become a backward province. To escape that backwardness, they would have to assimilate a veritable galaxy of new ideas with unusual speed, recapitulating as they did the experience of their northern brethren during the previous half century. Far more self-conscious than the northern pioneers of Modernism had been, and operating, one might say, with the script already written, they were to follow a smoother and straighter path. As a consequence, by the time the United States entered the Second World War Modernism had been firmly installed as the predominant style of literary and intellectual life in the region.

That is why the South offers a special opportunity for studying the shift from nineteenth- to twentieth-century culture and for determining what the latter truly entailed. When it finally arrived, change proceeded there in far more concentrated fashion, with fewer false starts on the one hand, but with greater tension and drama on the other – making the process of transition easier to observe. The question of southern culture itself, past and present, became the most emotional issue of debate, sufficiently charged to make those who approached it critically fearful of retribution. When W. J. Cash, for instance, wrote in 1941 that the "intellectual and aesthetic culture of the Old South was a superficial and jejune thing . . . not a true culture at all," his were fighting words, aimed at the most sensitive beliefs of his opponents. In addition, nowhere else was the topic of race, a prime concern of Modernists, more explosive than in the South. Ever since the Civil War the Victorian dichotomy had supplied a principal bulwark for southern white supremacy, with blacks cast customarily as savages (or undisciplined children) and whites as the foremost paladins of civilization. Those hoping to alter southern racial thought through the concept of environmentalism would first have to deal with this residual belief in the dichotomy, rendering the struggle for Modernism still more dramatic and conspicuous.

Lastly, not only was the clash of cultures fiercest in the South, it was also comparatively self-contained. The script was played out on a smaller stage than elsewhere, with far fewer characters and a more limited plot. Participants normally couched their arguments in terms of the region's specific dilemmas, leaving matters of national policy and abstract theory to their northern counterparts. The version of Victorian culture propagated by southern intellectuals was far simpler than that found in the North or in England. The subtlety, complexity, and contradictory tendencies of English Victorianism generally did not survive transplantation into the thin soil of southern bourgeois life . . . As a result, the basic framework of Victorian thought stood exhibited in the South in sharper relief than elsewhere, and, to a lesser extent, the same can be said of Modernism. For our purposes, in sum, the South may serve as an arena large enough to contain the chief contending forces, but small enough to make manifest what in essence was involved.

[This process of change can be traced] in three rough stages, corresponding to the emergence of a Modernist intellectual generation in the South. The first stage, which might be called "post-Victorian," was made up of those southerners born in the wake of Reconstruction who tried consciously to break with the strictures of Victorianism, but whose underlying loyalty to nineteenth-century values dominated in the end. Next, there was a small contingent of transitional figures who managed to straddle both cultures, coming down ultimately on the side of Modernism, but by the barest margin. These "Modernists by the skin of their teeth" provide a chance to assess the special potentialities and pitfalls facing intellectuals who live at a time of rapid cultural change. Finally, a group of southerners unquestionably in the twentieth-century camp and displaying several of the varieties of southern Modernism will be considered. In examining them, one may gain a sense not only of what was won in the transition to Modernism but also of what was lost.

[. . .]

For any who still doubted it, the triumph of southern Modernism was demonstrated in 1941 with the publication of Wilbur J. Cash's *The Mind of the South*.

Surely the great significance of that work lay in the knockout blow it delivered to the Cavalier myth. Gathering the insights of the new generation of southern writers, Cash presented the Old South as a frontier society dominated by the "hard, energetic, horse-trading type of man" who attempted to disguise his crudeness by posing as an aristocrat. For Cash, the post-Reconstruction South was even more cutthroat and individualistic. Indeed, ugliness, conflict, and brutality abounded in his portrait. Relying heavily on his understanding of Freud, Cash posited a near-schizophrenic split within the southern psyche, between a voracious hedonism and an equally powerful Puritan guilt, a split that led to all sorts of pathological behavior from miscegenation to lynching. The final impression left was not that of a civilized society, but rather of one governed, to use Cash's own phrase, by a "savage ideal." *The Mind of the South*, in short, represented a complete reversal of the vision of the region's history once offered by New South writers – it read like a compendium of those aspects of the South they had deliberately screened out.

What was remarkable was the rapidity with which this distinctly unflattering description of the region found general acceptance, not only in the North but among southern intellectuals as well. Save for Donald Davidson's harsh attack in the *Southern Review* and one other unfavorable notice, no dissenting voices were raised against Cash's work. On the contrary, the book became an instant classic, thereby testifying to the firm hold the Modernist viewpoint had gained among the South's educated elite. What would have been regarded as an unpublishable scandal a quarter century earlier was now largely accepted as a conventional truth.

In fact, it is probably not unfair to say that Cash's South of conflict and depravity was, ironically, coming to enjoy the mythological status that had once characterized the innocent and genteel South of the nineteenth century. From Erskine Caldwell to Tennessee Williams, from C. Vann Woodward to Marshall Frady, southern authors carried the critical spirit to its logical extreme, until Americans living outside the region formed a picture of southern society as one immense Tobacco Road. In doing this writers were simply following one of the basic dynamics of Modernist culture, with its rebellion against the practice of deliberate evasion. Cash himself was shrewd enough to recognize that the debunking he and others were engaged in represented a "sort of reverse embodiment of the old sentimentality." There should be no surprise in this: cultures typically take their shape in reaction to the culture being rejected, and their excesses often arise by way of correcting the excesses of their predecessors. Beyond doubt the false optimism and complacent self-deception of Victorianism needed correction, and that is precisely what the new generation accomplished.

Perhaps the clearest articulation of these tendencies in the 1940s appeared in the writings of Lillian Smith, who, more than anyone else, brought the issues of race and segregation into the open. With her, the assault against the Victorian ethos reached maturity. Her account of the psychic forces sustaining segregation identified the Victorian dichotomy, with its separation of mind and body, as the chief culprit:

Not only Negroes but everything dark, dangerous, evil must be pushed to the rim of one's life. Signs put over doors in the world outside and over minds seemed natural enough to children like us, for signs had already been put over forbidden areas of our body. The banning of people and books and ideas did not appear more shocking than the banning of our wishes which we learned early to send to the Dark-town of our unconscious.

Smith's entire crusade was pitched against this compartmentalization that her inherited culture had depended upon. Her goal was to establish a new culture based upon the opening of "doors" and the recapture of previously forbidden human energies. For her, "integration" meant more than a racial strategy; it meant the effort to restore man's "wholeness" in the deepest Modernist sense.

Yet the striking thing is that, as bold as these pronouncements sounded in the late 1940s, today they have about them the ring of the commonplace. At the time Lillian Smith wrote, the Supreme Court's historic decision on school desegregation was still more than five years away, and the ensuing civil rights movement was beyond the imagination of most southerners. Now the so-called Second Reconstruction appears to be over; legal segregation has been banished, and the cultural battle Smith waged has largely been won. As a result, her description of southerners as repressed, violent, and perverted strikes readers of the 1980s as extravagant and overdramatic, much as Cash's critique of the South does. Her contention that blacks possess a unique culture that permits them a "marvelous love of life and play, a physical grace and rhythm and a psychosexual vigor," is now greeted with suspicion. Above all, her prescriptions for psychic health and liberation, radical as they seemed at first, evince a certain stilted quality for the present-day reader. We have long since passed this stage of the cultural debate, with the result that Smith's insights have become stale.

Perhaps the fact that the main battle was over, that the transition to Modernist culture was essentially completed among southern writers, helps account for the noticeable drop in the intensity of intellectual activity in the region since the 1950s. One almost senses that southerners had little new to say about their society. Those sociologists who focused on the region continued the work of the Odum school, but their work, however competent, was not original or exciting. A high level of craftsmanship also distinguished southern journalism, with many newspapers earning Pulitzer Prizes during the civil rights struggle. However, from the standpoint of intellectual content their editorials in most instances repeated the themes set forth by the Regionalists. And in literature the shadows of Faulkner, Tate, and Warren loomed mightily over their successors: the Modernist mode had become a tradition. Tragedy, paradox, heroic endurance – those flashes of literary fire that had lit up the southern landscape during the interwar era – all became the staples of the new established mythology.

[. . .]

This was the quandary to which Modernist culture had brought southern writers by the mid-1960s. If one followed its mode of perception consistently and looked relentlessly beneath "appearances," one was lost in a world of paradox and moral relativism. Returning to the apparent stability of the nineteenth century was not an option: we are reminded of this by the plight of Barrett's father, a man of imposing self-certainty who blasts his head off with a shotgun, thus revealing the impasse of concealed agony the Victorians had come to. The twentieth century had at least brought these tensions into the open. Yet the price for liberation has been high, and perhaps it is now time for a liberation from liberation itself. Having freed the individual from the old moral code and reinstated the animal part of his being, Modernist culture may have reached its furthest limits. A new source of guidance has to be found. Surely the South, with its acute sense of loss of the old certainties, will have a role to play in that quest.

13

Kari Frederickson

THE NEW SOUTH IN TRANSITION: NEW DEAL, WORLD WAR II, AND COLD WAR

The American South of the 1920s was widely regarded as a world apart; a region marked by economic underdevelopment, cultural intolerance, intellectual sterility, reactionary politics, a calcified social hierarchy, and overall stasis – an insular, backward place, largely removed from the material and cultural dynamism associated with the "Roaring Twenties." Even the economic collapse of 1929 seemed not so much to transform the region, as to reinforce the widespread poverty and stagnation that had long belied the promise of the "New South."

Few at the close of the Twenties could have imagined the series of challenges that would transform the region in the quarter of a century to come. The readings in this chapter address the sweeping changes brought to Dixie by the arrivals, in rapid sequence, of the New Deal, the Second World War, and the Cold War. Of the successive crises that beset the nation, from the Crash through the post-war decade, each would affect the South in its own way. Yet throughout these phases ran certain common dynamics. Chief among these was the assertion of an activist federal state – emerging as a response to the Great Depression, and sustained amid America's conflicts with the Axis powers and the Soviet bloc. At each of these stages, the expansion of federal power opened up material opportunities around the South. But as these readings show, federal intervention also opened up potential challenges to the southern social order – welcome to some, alarming to others. In what measures could the scheme of power relations that had long prevailed in Dixie – marked by white supremacy, labor repression, and anti-democratic politics – weather the egalitarian and social democratic thrusts of the New Deal, or the democratic ethos of the wars against Nazism and Communism? What openings did federal intervention offer workers and African Americans to challenge the class and racial orders of the South, and what kinds of resistance did such challenges encounter? Such questions have been a focus of considerable research and debate. Some highlight the extent to which federal intervention subverted the regional status quo; others, the extent to which such intervention reinforced it. The opening essay by Kari Fredrickson, and the three selections that follow, bring out the fluidities of the southern social order, the ambiguities of federal intervention, and the varied ways in which each has been assessed in the historiography of the New Deal-, wartime-, and postwar-era South.

Kari Frederickson is Associate Professor of History at the University of Alabama. Her first book – *The Dixiecrat Revolt and the End of the Solid South, 1932–1968* (2001) – placed the conservative "Dixiecrat" campaign of 1948 in the context of the turbulent changes sweeping the South during the 1930s and 1940s, and suggested how the movement helped set the stage for the eventual demise of the New Deal coalition. She is also co-editor (with Jack E. Davis) of *Making Waves: Female Activists in Twentieth-Century Florida* (2003). Her current book project is entitled, "The Cold War in Dixie: Militarization and Modernization in the American South, 1945 to the Present."

In 1938, President Franklin D. Roosevelt declared the South the "Nation's No. 1 economic problem." Chief among the region's economic woes were its over-dependence on cotton, its outmoded sharecropping system, and the proliferation of low-wage industries that almost guaranteed the majority of its citizens a lifetime of unremitting toil and poverty. To complete the picture of the region's backwardness, one would also have to add the suffocating bonds of Jim Crow which relegated African Americans to second-class citizenship, third-rate education, and meager economic opportunities. Undergirding Dixie's economic and social structures was a Byzantine political system characterized by an undersized electorate and one-party rule.

Although interlocking and mutually reinforcing, these patterns were not insurmountable. The Great Depression and the New Deal had inaugurated a new era for the South. To begin with, they set the region on the road to economic modernization. Beginning in the 1930s, the national state became a crucial actor in southern life. Federal programs gave southern states the investment capital they sorely lacked for economic development. Over the decades, federal spending changed the South's economic base and demographics to such a degree that, by the early 1980s, the region had become one of the nation's leading industrial producers.

Set in motion by the New Deal, accelerated by the onset of the Second World War, and sustained into the Cold War era, these trends affected not only the southern economy but power relations within the region as well. How these dynamics played themselves out is the focus of this chapter.

The mobilization of the federal state to confront national and international crises provided marginalized groups the opportunity to press their claims to resources, protection, and rights. Historians debate the extent to which the expansion of the federal state changed economic, social, and political relations in the South. Some, such as Patricia Sullivan, argue that the impulses unleashed by the New Deal brought about "days of hope," a period in which a nascent biracial liberalism worked to democratize the region's politics. Others, such as Tony Badger, point out that the weak members of southern society often lost critical struggles, and that the New Deal left the South's conservative political structure basically untouched.[1] The essay by Bryant Simon extracted in this chapter suggests a new way to examine the impact of the New Deal: namely, its ability to expand the horizon of political possibilities for disempowered southerners. His essay illustrates how profoundly federal recognition of labor rights transformed the political identities of textile workers. Shackled for decades to an antistatist politics by bitter memories of Reconstruction, South Carolina workers adopted a new identity grounded in their distinctive conception of "New Deal Americanism," one that was based on a recognition of their rights and the protective role of an expanded national state.

The inclination of southerners to regard the federal government as an agent of economic prosperity and a guarantor of equality grew stronger during the Second World War and the Cold War years. Wartime contracts brought badly needed jobs to southern cities and ports, while the escalating hostilities with the Soviet Union in the postwar era kept southern training bases open and defense dollars flowing into southern communities. African American servicemen, who had fought in the recent war for democracy, returned home less willing to accommodate Jim Crow. But as the following selections by Jennifer Brooks and Bruce Schulman remind us, the reach of federal power was not boundless; throughout this period, white southerners consistently put limits on its influence, particularly when federal intervention into the region threatened the racial order. As Brooks shows, African American men bristled at the hypocrisy of fighting Nazism abroad while suffering the indignities of racial discrimination at home. Like Simon's Depression-era textile workers, Brooks's wartime blacks found in an activist federal state fresh prospects for empowerment and equality. Returning to their communities determined to democratize the South, black veterans encountered white veterans equally determined to maintain white supremacy. Proponents of an expanding federal state dedicated to enacting meaningful economic and political change in the South confronted new obstacles in the Cold War era; the power of the state to redistribute resources in a meaningful way, as well as the state's protection of civil rights, became severely compromised by the specter of anticommunism. As Schulman illustrates, shorn of its more radical potential, southern liberalism became a pro-growth philosophy, a middle way of development that was ill-equipped to address the region's grinding poverty and racism.

Tracing the impact of the expanding state on the American South from the 1930s through the 1950s is a useful way to integrate, and better understand, what have often been treated as separate eras. Historians of these years have showered the greatest attention on the impact of the Second World War on southern race relations. While most agree with Brooks that wartime service and the war's ideological component instilled in African Americans a determination to win freedom at home, they continue to differ over the degree of continuity – in terms of personnel, goals, and tactics – between the wartime civil rights efforts and the post-1954 civil rights movement. Of the three periods under examination here, the Cold War has received the least attention. Historians have been concerned primarily with the degree to which both civil rights activists and defenders of the racial status quo endeavored to harness the ideological power of the international conflict to their best advantage. Civil rights proponents hoped that the exposure of inequality at home would embarrass US officials on the world stage and thus work as a lever of power in the civil rights struggles. White supremacists, on the other hand, capitalized on the nation's anticommunist mood to discredit civil rights advocates by linking them with radicalism. By considering these eras collectively through the prism of the expanding state, we can appreciate not only changes to the region's race relations but gain a greater understanding of the reach of the state into a multitude of other power relationships.

When the Great Depression hit, the South was already wallowing in intractable poverty. A predominantly rural region, the South by 1929 had been ravaged by a prolonged agricultural depression and a series of natural disasters. By 1932, one in four Americans came from a family with no discernible income. In the South, the proportion was one out of every three; southern cities were even more desperate, with half of all residents out of work. Life on the farm was little better. The Great Crash only compounded the privation endemic to the region's outdated system of agriculture. During the 1930s, approximately one-quarter of all southerners and one-half of all southern farmers were tenants and sharecroppers. The Depression hit them the hardest. Hurt by low commodity prices as farm income fell by half, many landlords discontinued the sharecrop furnish system, displacing hundreds of thousands of tenants and swelling the ranks of the landless.

By the end of the 1930s, New Deal relief programs had poured more than four billion dollars into the desperate region. Although they did not come close to ending the Depression, these measures relieved what one Mississippian referred to as "the sharp pockets of poverty" in many southern communities. New Deal jobs programs brought some hope to a chronically underemployed region. In Alabama, one quarter of all eligible young men between the ages of eighteen and twenty-five were employed by the Civilian Conservation Corps. The Tennessee Valley Authority and Rural Electrification Administration brought power and the promise of industrial development to underserved rural regions. New Deal works programs, such as the Works Progress Administration, dramatically changed the landscape of southern towns by providing funds for the creation of roads, swimming pools, and schools.

The nation's most desperately poor and impoverished region became a laboratory for New Deal reformers hoping to revolutionize, modernize, and diversify southern agriculture. Indeed, the president himself hoped eventually to use New Deal legislation to transform the region's landless tenants into independent landowners. But restoring economic stability in the agricultural sector was Roosevelt's most immediate priority, and tenants were often victimized by New Deal legislation designed to achieve recovery: witness the centerpiece of New Deal farm legislation, the Agriculture Adjustment Act (AAA), which was crafted to create scarcity and parity pricing. Under the commercializing thrust of the AAA, southern rural labor practices were not so much reformed as destroyed. The AAA rescued tobacco and cotton farm owners but left tenants to bear the burden of scarcity. Denied their share of the benefit checks, they were unceremoniously swept from the land.

For industrial workers, the New Deal inaugurated a new era in labor relations, a period in which economic justice became the battle cry of federal reformers and the state asserted itself as the guarantor of workers' rights. The National Industrial Recovery Act (NIRA) in 1933 endorsed the nation's first minimum wage, advocated maximum hours for a standard work week, called for the abolition of child labor, and supported workers' rights to organize. American labor was quick to seize upon the opening: within weeks after the passage of the NIRA, the United Mine Workers of America had organized 92 percent of the country's coal miners. As Bryant Simon illustrates in the extract below, the protections outlined in the NIRA instilled textile workers – the largest category of industrial workers in the South – with a new sense of their rights as American citizens.

Although the NIRA lacked strong enforcement mechanisms and was ultimately declared unconstitutional by the Supreme Court, future legislation resurrected and fortified the rights working people had initially enjoyed under its provisions. The National Labor Relations (Wagner) Act of 1935 reaffirmed workers' rights to organize, engage in collective bargaining, and participate in strikes. More forceful than the labor provisions of the NIRA, the Wagner Act outlawed unfair labor practices, provided for referendums among workers to determine their collective bargaining agents by majority vote, required that employers bargain with these agents in good faith, and set up a National Labor Relations Board to administer these provisions. The Fair Labor Standards Act (FLSA), passed by Congress in 1938, set maximum hours and minimum wages. For most of the South's industrial workers, this meant a raise. New

Dealers hoped that the FLSA would increase consumer purchasing power and offset the depression, and that ultimately it would make workers more productive and modernize the region.

With the new protections for union organizing offered first by the NIRA and later by the Wagner Act, southern workers flocked to the union banner – although in numbers much smaller than their counterparts across the nation. Employers fought them every step of the way. Throughout the New Deal era, southern workers engaged in strikes to fight employers' violation of those rights; many of these strikes were bloody failures. In one instance, textile mill guards in Honea Path, South Carolina, killed six picketers and injured more than twenty others. Local law enforcement in Gadsden, Alabama, working on behalf of the Goodyear company, beat and kidnapped United Rubber Workers organizers and broke up picket lines. Although the gains made by workers through New Deal legislation did not conclusively change industrial power relations in the South, workers' continued militancy represented a belief in labor's claim to full citizenship that had been fostered by the New Deal.

What federal programs did not deliver to the South in terms of economic salvation, they brought in increased expectations on the part of ordinary people and a popular willingness to push claims for protection and benefits from government. The New Deal changed forever the relationship between southerners – both black and white – and the state. This expectation and commitment were reflected in the region's politics. The decade's economic crisis, together with a growing interest on the part of the federal government in class issues, awoke a slumbering grass-roots populism, and stoked the fires of political reaction within the South.

Throughout the region, new faces appeared on the political scene. In 1934, Bryant Simon's white working-class voters elected former mill worker Olin D. Johnston to the South Carolina statehouse. A strong advocate of the rights of labor, Johnston worked hard for the election of state legislators supportive of liberal economic reforms. Georgia voters in 1936 replaced anti-Roosevelt governor Eugene Talmadge with E. D. Rivers, who proceeded to launch a "little new deal" for the Peach State. In Mississippi, voters resurrected the disgraced former governor and "redneck liberal" Theodore G. Bilbo, electing him to the United States Senate, where he became one of the New Deal's most reliable supporters. Promising to "raise more hell" than Louisiana's senator, Huey P. Long, Bilbo ran on a platform that appealed to farmers and laborers, calling for wealth redistribution and unemployment insurance. But if Bilbo's election highlighted the distress of Mississippi's poor – and their willing embrace of New Deal legislation – it also highlighted the New Deal's limitations. A virulent white supremacist, Bilbo railed against any federal legislation that threatened the region's rigid racial hierarchy. Not necessarily as rabid in their defense of white supremacy as the Mississippi senator, the majority of southern New Dealers nevertheless remained committed to the racial status quo.

The coming of the Second World War brought the economic recovery that had always eluded the New Deal. The South benefited substantially from the preparedness program, which fostered both industrialization and urbanization. As the region gorged itself on defense contracts, new shipbuilding, aircraft, and munitions plants dotted the landscape, increasing the South's industrial capacity by approximately 40 percent. Although many of these new industries would not survive the transition to peacetime, the degree of growth was nevertheless unprecedented. The number of manufacturing establishments grew by 20,000; jobs for production workers more than doubled; and the average worker saw a yearly salary increase of 40 percent. After reconversion, the South retained about half the wartime addition to its factory force.

If the war brought economic recovery, the fruits of that recovery were not evenly spread. Nor, in the South, did wartime growth mean an end to discriminatory hiring practices. Although the war brought greater opportunities and material rewards for African Americans than they had enjoyed in the past, they did not reap their share of the economic benefits within the Arsenal of Democracy, suffering discrimination within industry, the military, government training programs, and labor unions. Those blacks able to secure employment in defense industries were confined to segregated crews and relegated to the least desirable, lowest-paying jobs.

No longer willing to endure starvation wages on the region's farms, millions of blacks simply left the South altogether. They were joined by even greater numbers of southern whites seeking wartime opportunity up North and out West. Whole communities were drained of manpower; some never recovered. White landowners complained of chronic labor shortages. Tenants who stayed proved less disposed than ever to tolerate ill treatment, much to the chagrin of local whites.

For many white and black southerners, their encounter with the state's power of conscription had a particularly transforming effect. When questioned by the Army Research Branch in 1944 and 1945 about their understanding of the war aims and their contributions to it, nearly half of all black GIs "believed that they would 'have more rights and privileges' after the war." Declaring that "men who faced bullets overseas deserve ballots at home," more than one hundred black veterans marched on Birmingham's courthouse in January 1946 for the right to register.

Equally determined to change the South's political culture was a small but vocal circle of white veterans returning to the region. They created new political coalitions and fomented "GI Revolts" aimed at turning out entrenched political machines. Their experiences in other parts of the country and overseas had underscored for them the backwardness of southern society. While not necessarily inclined to challenge Jim Crow, they dedicated themselves to promoting clean, efficient government as a vital precondition for economic growth.

Just as wartime service opened new political possibilities to southern veterans, so too did the Second World War let loose forces that changed the nation's racial and political landscape. Black migrants to northern cities found not only greater economic opportunity but also the chance for political participation denied them in the South. This increasingly important voting bloc did not escape the attention of the Democratic and Republican parties, both of which moved forward, however haltingly, on civil rights. The contradictions of fighting a war for equality while suffering Jim Crow discrimination at home gave African Americans a powerful weapon in their fight for civil rights. Altogether, these dynamics opened a new dialogue concerning the proper role of the state in ensuring equality. The federal government took the first, tentative steps toward eliminating discrimination in hiring. But it had to be pushed. Angered by the exclusion of African Americans from industry and the discriminatory treatment of black soldiers, and frustrated by federal officials' willingness to turn a blind eye to these abuses, African American leaders threatened in 1941 to stage a massive march on the nation's capitol to dramatize their plight. Hoping to avoid an embarrassing protest, Roosevelt issued Executive Order 8802, which forbade employment discrimination in defense industries and created a Fair Employment Practices Commission (FEPC) to investigate complaints and monitor compliance. While this move initially garnered praise from black citizens around the South, the committee lacked any real enforcement powers and had to rely primarily on publicity to achieve its objectives.

These wartime pressure tactics illustrated African Americans' new militancy and assertiveness. Alarmed by this new attitude, southern whites retaliated. Racial clashes erupted on military bases throughout the region. Nor did the end of the war bring peace to the South. Much of the racial violence that scarred the postwar years pitted returning black veterans, eager to claim their full citizenship, against whites determined to preserve racial hierarchy. Outraged by attacks on black veterans, pressured by civil rights groups, and anxious to court African American voters for his upcoming election campaign, President Truman in 1946 created the President's Committee on Civil Rights (PCCR), charged with exploring how federal, state, and local laws might be strengthened to protect the civil rights of all Americans. The committee issued its seminal report, *To Secure these Rights*, in October 1947. In February 1948, Truman delivered to Congress a speech devoted entirely to civil rights, the first of its kind in American history. Following the recommendations outlined in the PCCR's report, the president called for the creation of a permanent peacetime FEPC, along with the establishment of a civil rights division within the Department of Justice, anti-lynching and anti-poll tax legislation, and the desegregation of interstate transportation.

The conflicting experiences of wartime played out in the politics of the postwar South. Buoyed by their military service – along with developments like the creation of the FEPC and the PCCR, and the Supreme Court's landmark *Smith* v. *Allwright* decision declaring the white primary unconstitutional – black southerners made insistent claims to the ballot. As the following selection by Jennifer Brooks illustrates, black voter registration and political activity increased dramatically in the postwar era. Alarmed by these grass-roots developments and by the Democratic party's embrace of civil rights, conservative white southerners refused to support Truman's presidential campaign in 1948, bolting to create their own States' Rights Democratic Party (or Dixiecrats), with South Carolina governor Strom Thurmond as their candidate.

As the nation entered the Cold War, political leaders and industrial boosters throughout the South hoped to continue the economic growth that had taken off during the Second World War. Southern state leaders aggressively pursued federal projects as part of a long-term strategy to modernize the region. Their efforts paid off handsomely. Southern leaders were especially successful in acquiring money for infrastructure, such as highways and airports which, in turn, helped them compete for industry, particularly in defense-related sectors.

The intense regional focus on growth mirrored the shift in liberalism nationally during the Cold War from a philosophy dedicated to economic redistribution to one committed to "growing the economic pie." Smacking to many of socialism, redistributive New Deal policies became anathema in the early Cold War era. The Democratic party's commitment to economic justice wrecked on the shoals of anti-communism. Ultimately, as Bruce Schulman shows in his selection, southern development was funneled into a moderate direction – one that minimized conflict, particularly racial conflict. War plants and military bases benefited the South as a whole but did little to eradicate poverty within the region.

Despite their often supercharged rhetoric to the contrary, white southerners did not reject all types of federal intervention. In Aiken County, South Carolina, the turmoil that accompanied the creation of the Savannah River Plant, an Atomic Energy Commission facility built to produce materials for the hydrogen bomb, revealed the level of comfort white southerners found in securing federal benefits. Thousands of new and temporary residents poured into the region within months of the plant's announcement in November 1950, overwhelming neighborhoods, placing further stress on an already-inadequate infrastructure, and swamping schools. For locals, the creation of the plant came with an implicit quid pro quo: in exchange for the disruptions involved with living in a community that was an essential component of the Cold War military-industrial complex, residents expected good schools and improved services in return, and they lobbied consistently for the goods and services they felt were due to them.

Although it did not hinder southerners' comfort with the growth of the state altogether, anti-communism sufficiently poisoned the political atmosphere to render any attempt at biracial cooperation difficult, if not impossible. Civil rights legislation was one of the early victims of cold war hysteria, as Truman's program was defeated in 1949. The prospect of a peacetime FEPC aroused the wrath of white southern conservatives in these years perhaps more than any federal program. Opponents argued that a permanent FEPC would usurp the rights of employers and drain low-wage labor from the countryside. Strom Thurmond warned that Communists would use the FEPC to force "their agents and saboteurs into every tool and die room, every machine shop and every industrial plant and laboratory, atomic or otherwise, in America." As the civil rights movement picked up momentum in the mid-1950s, ardent white supremacists stepped up their rhetoric, charging that integration was a communist plot.

In this atmosphere, southern moderates' beliefs that a rising tide raises all boats proved elusive. During the 1960s and 1970s, the South would lead all regions in economic growth. But, as Schulman argues, growth there took its own peculiar form. Southern leaders sought funds for airports, infrastructure, and schools, but were less aggressive in developing welfare programs. The resulting surge in development, funded largely by federal contracts, did little to eradicate poverty and injustice. Blunted by anti-communist concerns, the potential of the state to engender dramatic change was severely compromised. For the next several decades, economic help for the downtrodden would remain a secondary concern.

As the following selections demonstrate, in a multitude of ways, the encounter of southern citizens with the expanded power of the federal state in the years from the Great Depression through the Cold War had a dramatic impact on the region as a whole. The growth of federal jobs programs in the 1930s, the unintended consequences of some New Deal agricultural programs, and the arrival of the military-industrial complex transformed the economic life of the South to the point where it was almost unrecognizable by the 1980s. Likewise the growth of the welfare state and black men's service in the Second World War instilled in the white working class and in African Americans a belief in their rights as citizens and a new confidence with which to demand equality. That these rights were not always granted or even acknowledged in no way diminishes the importance of the state's role in the fostering those expectations.

NOTES

1. Anthony J. Badger, *New Deal/New South: An Anthony J. Badger Reader* (Fayetteville: University of Arkansas Press, 2007); Patricia Sullivan, *Days of Hope: Race and Democracy in the New Deal Era* (Chapel Hill: University of North Carolina Press, 1996).

* * *

FURTHER READING

Badger, Anthony J., *New Deal/New South: An Anthony J. Badger Reader* (Fayetteville: University of Arkansas Press, 2007).

Bartley, Numan V., *The New South, 1945–1980* (Baton Rouge: Louisiana State University Press, 1995).

Biles, Roger, *The South and the New Deal* (Lexington: University Press of Kentucky, 1994).

Cobb, James C., *The Selling of the South: The Southern Crusade for Industrial Development, 1936–1980* (Baton Rouge: Louisiana State University Press, 1982).

Cobb, James C. and Michael V. Namorato, eds., *The New Deal and the South* (Jackson: University Press of Mississippi, 1984).

Daniel, Pete, *Breaking the Land: The Transformation of Cotton, Tobacco, and Rice Cultures Since 1880* (Urbana: University of Illinois Press, 1885).

Dudziak, Mary L., *Cold War Civil Rights: Race and the Image of American Democracy* (Princeton: Princeton University Press, 2002).

Egerton, John, *Speak Now Against the Day: The Generation Before the Civil Rights Movement in the South* (Chapel Hill: University of North Carolina Press, 1995).

Frederickson, Kari, *The Dixiecrat Revolt and the End of the Solid South, 1932–1968* (Chapel Hill: University of North Carolina Press, 2001).

Goldfield, David R., *Cotton Fields and Skyscrapers: Southern City and Region, 1607–1980* (Baton Rouge: Louisiana State University Press, 1982).

Sullivan, Patricia, *Days of Hope: Race and Democracy in the New Deal Era* (Chapel Hill: University of North Carolina Press, 1996).

Tindall, George Brown, *The Emergence of the New South, 1913–1945* (Baton Rouge: Louisiana State University Press, 1967).

Tyson, Timothy B., *Radio Free Dixie: Robert F. Williams and the Roots of Black Power* (Chapel Hill: University of North Carolina Press, 1999).

* * *

Bryant Simon

A Fabric of Defeat[†]

For South Carolina workers to become New Deal supporters they had to reinterpret history. In the early 1930s white southerners read history books and watched films that presented a singular version of Reconstruction. In this view, the postbellum years were a "tragic era" of fraud, corruption, racial chaos, and sexual disorder.

[. . .]

This is how Reconstruction was portrayed in the white South. Well into the twentieth century, it continued to shape people's thinking. Federal action of any

---

[†]Bryant Simon, *A Fabric of Defeat: The Politics of South Carolina Millhands, 1910–1948* (Chapel Hill: University of North Carolina Press, 1998), pp. 80–9.

sort was easily branded a "second invasion of the carpetbaggers." No one had to say what would happen next: a return to Reconstruction would unleash the filthy passions of African American men. Vulnerable white women would again be sexually victimized. Buried between the lines of these Reconstruction narratives about lust and thievery, whiteness and blackness, was a coded message. For white southerners, Reconstruction represented disorder of any kind, not just racial upheaval. Whenever the status quo was challenged, some white person invariably raised the specter of Reconstruction, warning that change would produce chaos. In the end, this discourse hindered reform, especially federal initiatives.

[. . .]

Speedups, strikes, layoffs, wage cuts, the mobilization of the National Guard, and legislative setbacks, however, opened the minds of many South Carolina millhands. Slowly and unevenly from the late 1920s through the early 1930s, workers moved away from . . . racially, sexually charged politics . . . toward government intervention in the economy on their own behalf.

[. . .]

By the time Roosevelt came to power in March 1933, the Great Depression had reached its lowest point. People were tormented by hunger and uncertainty. Indeed, they were so desperate that they were willing to consider new ideas, new policies, and a New Deal. Without explicitly challenging the white South's interpretation of Reconstruction, workers began to see the federal government less as an alien force and more as a powerful protector of freedom and economic rights . . . By the close of the decade, millhands pushed for the centralization of authority in Washington, even if it came at the expense of states' rights.

Workers' support for the centralization of power – the antithesis of the mythology of Reconstruction – was smoothed over by their personification of the nation-state. For South Carolina millworkers, the government was Roosevelt and Roosevelt was the government. Piecing together snippets from pictures, radio broadcasts, newsreels, rumors, and FDR's carefully crafted public persona, millhands constructed their own image of the New Deal presidency. Roosevelt's confident smile gave them confidence. When they listened to his fireside chats and heard him explain complicated government programs in straightforward terms like their favorite teacher or preacher, workers felt connected to the president. Roosevelt strengthened the tie with his use of inclusive language. "My friends," he began his addresses, seeming to speak directly to each person in the audience. Often in the middle of a talk, he would stop and ask listeners to write to him at the White House about their troubles and triumphs. No president, at least none that South Carolina laborers could recall, had ever solicited their opinions. Here was evidence that the president cared about their personal problems.

[. . .]

A South Carolina weaver showered FDR with the highest praise, telling him that he was "the first man in the White House to understand that my boss is a son of a bitch."

. . . [I]t took more than these qualities to persuade South Carolina workers to put aside their Reconstruction-inspired fears of federalism and join his New Deal. But labor laws, relief programs, and recovery measures would demonstrate that the administration was committed to ending the depression, that the president was a strong ally in the long-standing fight of working people to transform their daily lives, to end their ceaseless toil for low pay under dirty, risky conditions. With the government's help, one millhand told the novelist Sherwood Anderson, "we might be able to make the South into something gorgeous."

[. . .]

Roosevelt's actions and choreographed gestures showed wage earners that a determined and partisan federal government could end "industrial slavery." At the same time, he said little about race. Fearful of scaring off southern lawmakers, FDR left white supremacy alone, concentrating on economic issues. His tactical decision about race allowed white millhands to back federal action, confident that it would do nothing to undercut the privileges of whiteness.

[. . .]

As Roosevelt men and women, South Carolina workers identified their interests with the nation and the federal government. In waving the American flag and signing their letters "an American citizen," they announced that they now saw themselves as American citizens first and foremost. In the early 1930s U.S. citizenship, or what Gary Gerstle has called Americanism, had multiple meanings. For some it conjured up patriotic glories of military conquest and national superiority. For others, race, gender, and ethnicity defined the nation in exclusive terms. America was male, white, and Protestant. Women and African Americans were shuttled off to the sidelines of citizenship. Immigrants could join the nation only by flattening their foreign accents and shedding their Old World religious and cultural practices. Industrialists put forth yet another vision of Americanism. Anchored in constitutional safeguards for private property, factory owners trumpeted the creeds of individualism and unfettered economic competition. Theirs was a land of vigorous, sustained capitalist growth.

South Carolina millworkers fashioned an alternative, progressive, although still racist, brand of Americanism. Rooted in the Declaration of Independence, the Bill of Rights, and the glories of consumption, their Americanism highlighted the notion of "life, liberty, and the pursuit of happiness" for all white people. As U.S. citizens, white millhands claimed not only the right to vote but also economic rights to a job set at a reasonable pace that paid a fair wage. They also demanded the right to join a union free from the interference of "autocratic" mill owners.

[. . .]

They pressed the government to build a safety net beneath them without putting a ceiling over their heads. Someday, they or their children might make it out of the mills, and then they wanted nothing to get in the way of their progress.

As South Carolina millhands began to speak the language of New Deal Americanism, they described themselves less as besieged white South Carolinians.

[. . .]

The more South Carolina workers asserted themselves in the vernacular of New Deal Americanism, the more they highlighted their economic concerns over their racial anxieties, and the more they did this, the faster their fears of the federal government dissolved.

The New Deal's first sign of federal action to assist the working class came in the summer of 1933 with the National Industrial Recovery Act (NIRA). During the 1932 presidential campaign, FDR had blamed the economic collapse on "self seekers" and spotlighted the plight of the "forgotten man." His rhetoric ignited workers' expectations for change. Roosevelt's inaugural address heightened their anticipation of a better future. On that crisp March day in 1933, the president pledged to run the "money changers" out of Washington. Most working people welcomed FDR's remarks, but still they wanted proof that a New Deal was on the way.

[. . .]

Signed into law on June 16, 1933, ninety-nine days after FDR took office, the NIRA was a "crazy patchwork quilt of . . . ideas" that "had a little for everyone." The legislation suspended antitrust statutes, allowing business leaders to fix prices and regulate output in their industries. In exchange for industrial self-rule, manufacturers' groups had to agree to abide by a "code of fair competition." Every code of fair competition had to include Section 7(a).

Perhaps the most controversial and potentially explosive part of the plan, Section 7(a) appeared to guarantee workers the right to "organize unions of their own choosing." Each code also had to set minimum-wage and maximum-hour guidelines. Finally, the NIRA authorized the formation of the National Recovery Administration (NRA) to oversee the rebuilding of the nation's economy.

Normally plainspoken – some would say bland – [American Federation of Labor] President William Green gushed over the NIRA's labor planks, heralding them as a "Magna Carta" for workers.

[. . .]

President Roosevelt, however, never intended to declare a new age or deliver workers from industrial slavery. When he signed the NIRA into law, he had more prosaic and more narrowly political concerns on his mind.

Mill owners saw the law differently as well. Battered by endless rounds of punishing competition, many textile manufacturers, especially the larger ones, considered the NRA their last chance for financial salvation.

[. . .]

Hailed by New Deal officials as a "patriotic thing," the textile code, as it came to be called, was "code #1" – the nation's first code of fair competition under the NRA. Like all the NRA codes that followed it, the textile code loosened antitrust constraints for management, while vaguely spelling out labor's right to organize. It mandated a maximum workweek of forty hours and, taking into account the customary regional wage differential, it set up a minimum pay scale of $12 per week in the South and $13 in the North. But "learners," a loosely defined category, could be paid far less. Seeking to limit output, the code also outlawed the night shift. In addition, it barred the use of child labor. Finally, Section 15 of the textile code addressed machine loads and the implementation of newer and faster equipment.

[. . .]

Most laborers thought that the textile code represented the start of a new era. How else could South Carolina workers interpret a law that overnight handed them, and legitimized, almost everything they had been fighting for on the shop floor, on the picket line, and in state politics for eight or so years? As textile workers saw it, the code guaranteed them a decent, albeit modest, paycheck; protected their right to join a union; and, with Section 15, ended the stretchout. It also offered them a firm yardstick with which to gauge the owners' actions . . . [A]fter July 1933, they argued that if their bosses forced them to work more than forty hours a week or paid them less than twelve dollars, they would be violating the law, or even worse, Roosevelt's will.

Family life would also improve as a result of the code. Freed from the rigors of a sixty-or-more-hour workweek, women and men looked forward to a new life at home. "The men want to fish, play baseball, do odd jobs around the house," a reporter heard. "Most mothers say they want to spend more time tending their children.'"

[. . .]

"A new era has dawned," shouted a South Carolina millhand after hearing about the textile code. Just after dusk on July 17, a thousand people from Greenwood and the surrounding areas gathered on the edge of town. For the next four hours, they snaked through the streets of the city dancing and singing. Long past midnight, the party ended with millhands "making merry" in front of the Greenwood Cotton Mill.

[. . .]

"The industrial recovery act," a Horse Creek Valley man declared, "is our industrial declaration of independence."

[. . .]

With the enactment of the NIRA, [UTW official John Peele] concluded, "Labor is upon the threshold of industrial freedom."

The NRA rhetoric of the president and New Dealers strengthened the link between working people and the federal government.

[. . .]

With the formation of the NRA, the Roosevelt administration declared war on the industrial depression. "We Do Our Part" became the New Deal's battle cry. The president compared the blue eagle – the NRA's symbol – to "bright badges" worn by soldiers "in the gloom of a night attack . . . to be sure that comrades do not fire on comrades" . . . Meanwhile, the NRA chief held what seemed like an endless series of flag-waving parades to rally the nation to recovery, calling on Americans to sacrifice equally in the war against the depression. Over the radio and in person, Johnson voiced disdain for the selfish few who defied the blue eagle. "[M]ay God have mercy on the man or group of men," he cautioned, "who attempt to trifle with this bird."

Millhands were convinced that the president and his lieutenants waged this war against the depression on their behalf . . . For millhands, no aspect of the New Deal was more compelling than the idea that the president and the machinery of the national government were squarely behind them in their struggle for better conditions. They believed that the mill owners, far more than structural flaws in the economy or the ruinous effects of overproduction, stood between them and a return to the prosperity of the 1920s. Now the president was ready to force the manufacturers to slow down the machines to a humane pace and to pay decent wages. Who better, workers thought, to have on your side? The president was, after all, more powerful than all of the supervisors, foremen, and mill owners combined. At least that was what they thought in 1933.

Faith in a better future can sustain people through a dark day. But hope can also distort things. Deeply religious, often evangelical, millhands understood faith almost without thinking about it. During the 1930s South Carolina workers put their faith in Franklin Roosevelt. In their eyes, he could not, would not fail them. He was "a god-sent man," "a modern day Moses," determined to lead them "out of the Egypt of depression to the promised land of prosperity." The problem was that FDR, though eager to have labor's vote, did not see himself as a working-class savior. Faith, however, was hard to shake. When the stretchout did not end and industrial democracy remained a distant dream, millworkers still believed in Roosevelt. In the end, faith seemed to stamp out any critical appraisal of the president, the New Deal, and the nation-state. In the yellow, four-room company houses on the mill hills of South Carolina, ordinary people were, for a time, blinded by faith.

୨୦ ୨୦ ୨୦

Jennifer E. Brooks

Defining the Peace[†]

Georgia's African American men answered the call to military duty in World War II for a variety of reasons, including patriotism. More often, though, service in the war offered an escape from the dead-end lot most black men faced in the Depression-era South. Nevertheless, black veterans found that participation in the war tended to magnify the importance of individual citizenship, strengthening the connection between political, racial, and male identity. On the one hand, the highest act of citizenship was to fulfill the call to military duty in defense of the nation, an act that put a premium on one's identity as a male and as a citizen.

[. . .]

[S]outhern black veterans returned with a new moral claim on the American democratic conscience, a claim they readily used to justify their activism after the war.

[. . .]

Who could now legitimately deny them at least a voice in postwar political affairs and the chance to establish the economic independence and family security that they believed men and veterans had a duty to provide?

[. . .]

Yet . . . the rights of citizenship could not be invoked by black men, especially veterans, without also inducing the age-old political-racial-sexual anxiety of many southern whites, who remained as wedded as ever to the notion that majority rule

---

[†]Jennifer E. Brooks, *Defining the Peace: World War II Veterans, Race, and the Remaking of Southern Political Tradition* (Chapel Hill: University of North Carolina Press, 2004), pp. 16–22, 24–9, 32–3, 35–6.

meant whites only. Anything less threatened white supremacy and the very sanctity of white womanhood.

Thus, black veterans also confronted a strong phalanx of resistance in postwar Georgia, as fearful and resentful whites worked hard to circumscribe the veterans' economic and political ambitions. Taken together, service in the war *and* this persistent discrimination served to heighten both black veterans' expectations for a new day and their frustration with the racial barriers and injustices that still kept that day from dawning.

[. . .]

Whether in the United States or overseas, military service provided skills and training to which few black southerners had ever had access. The army's Quartermaster, Transportation, and Engineering Corps in which many black GIs served . . . for example, proved to be schools of occupational education. Even though most black GIs labored in semi- and unskilled jobs in these outfits, including stevedoring, road building, laundering, fumigation, and truck driving, it would be misleading to assume that they gained little in the way of useful training.

[. . .]

Not surprisingly, black soldiers anticipated parlaying this wartime training into better jobs when they returned home. Sixty-one percent of black soldiers interviewed by the Army Research Branch during the war believed that military training would help them find a better job than they had held before the war. Only 39 percent of white soldiers proved to be as optimistic.

[. . .]

Nor were black soldiers' aspirations purely economic. The army's wartime research data, for example, indicated that "there was a tendency among Negro soldiers to expect or hope for an increase in rights and privileges, improved treatment, or better economic status after the war," with southern black soldiers tending to be more optimistic than those from the North.

[. . .]

Doyle Combs, who later became a leader of the Toccoa, Georgia, chapter of the National Association for the Advancement of Colored People (NAACP), aptly illustrated the direct influence that the expectations, ambitions, and racial consciousness born in the war exerted on the political and racial identity of many black veterans. Combs did not take lightly the cruel irony of being seriously wounded while fighting to defeat an intolerant and undemocratic enemy in defense of an unjust and unequal country: "Since I lost a portion of my body to protect my own rights," Combs declared, "I would die for my rights, and I would kill for my rights. And I was going to vote if I had to kill somebody to vote."

A clearer sense of the dynamic relationship between service in the war and postwar activism could hardly be stated. The war tended to create highly motivated black men cognizant of their own rights . . . What they discovered when they returned, however, was that few white southerners valued black servicemen's contribution to American victory . . . Rather than the improved opportunities, full citizenship, and respect black veterans had hoped to find, they encountered a level of discrimination and violence that seemed all too familiar.

[. . .]

As soon as the war ended, white southerners initiated a widespread campaign of discrimination aimed at impeding black veterans' utilization of their wartime skills and GI Bill benefits.

Of the 246 approved on-the-job training programs in Georgia in March 1946, the American Council on Race Relations observed, black veterans participated in only 6 . . . Such discrimination, wrote "L.M.S." of Atlanta, was "a big slap in the face" to veterans who had gone "to the front for the right of the pursuit of liberty and happiness."

[. . .]

Difficulty in readjusting to the traditional parameters of southern race relations was a dangerous thing. Indeed, racial violence permeated the immediate postwar years, as one scholar concluded, "cast[ing] a shadow of dread over the postwar South."

[. . .]

Not surprisingly, many black veterans beat a fast track out of their communities and region to the North and West in search of safer conditions and better economic and educational opportunities.

[. . .]

Not all black ex-servicemen, however, chose to leave. For those who stayed, the injustices they continued to encounter in Georgia added a critical dimension to the impact of the war on their postwar political activism.

[. . .]

[E]xamples of black veterans organizing for change and engaging in political activism immediately upon their return home are ubiquitous throughout the postwar

South, particularly in Georgia. And black veterans such as Doyle Combs routinely explained their political activities as a direct outgrowth of participation in the Second World War. An important part of the story of the war's impact on the South, then, was the determination of Georgia's black veterans to resist white racial control.

[. . .]

Although black veterans sometimes chose to wage . . . individual battles, most recognized the obvious wisdom in organized group action. In Georgia this political mobilization started with the establishment of all-black veteran services organizations . . . Groups such as the [Georgia Veterans Leagne] GVL, a statewide association headquartered in Atlanta, assisted black veterans in cutting through the inevitable red tape that applying for any government benefits entailed.

[. . .]

Right from the beginning, however, veterans quickly learned that "there was no need of applying for [certain jobs] . . . You weren't going to get [them] . . . You had to stay within these artificial barriers." And these barriers would never begin to crumble, veterans surmised, without the pressure of black political influence. Regulatory measures passed throughout the southern states in the late nineteenth and early twentieth centuries and enforced by electoral fraud, intimidation, and even violence had effectively disfranchised southern blacks for decades. Along with literacy tests, the grandfather clause, and other creative and legal tools of disfranchisement, one of the most effective and widespread practices to bar black voting had been to maintain a lily-white membership in state Democratic parties.

In the one-party South, the only elections that had real meaning were the Democratic primaries . . . Since southern Democratic parties barred black members, black citizens generally could not vote in Democratic primary elections, which meant, effectively, that they could not participate in the electoral process. Although progressives within and outside the South often condemned this practice as a violation of the Fifteenth Amendment to the Constitution, state primary elections remained under the purview of state power. That is, until the *Smith v. Allwright* decision in 1944.

In the *Smith* decision, the U.S. Supreme Court overturned the all-white primary in Texas as a violation of the Fifteenth Amendment, which prohibited infringing on a citizen's right to vote because of race or color.

[. . .]

This decision galvanized black civil rights activists in the postwar 1940s, heartened progressives within and outside the South, and unnerved many southern whites. Southern Democrats, particularly in the Deep South . . . rushed to remove all state regulation of primary elections. Their strategy was to subvert the *Smith* ruling by claiming that the Democratic Party had the status of a private club that could determine its own membership and was independent of state regulation.

At the same time, black activists also took immediate action, developing voter registration campaigns and attempting to vote in the first Democratic primaries that followed the *Smith* decision. When black citizens were still denied the right to vote, these individuals and groups brought suit against the state Democratic parties for these violations, which led to a series of related cases that went before the Supreme Court. In Georgia the Reverend Primus E. King of Columbus attempted to vote in the July 1944 primary, immediately after the *Smith* decision came down, but recalcitrant whites turned him away. With the assistance of the NAACP, King sued in federal court. In early 1946 the U.S. Supreme Court refused to overturn federal district court judge T. Hoyt Davis's decision in the *King v. Chapman* case that the *Smith* decision outlawing an all-white primary did apply to Georgia. Governor Ellis Arnall, who could not run for reelection in 1946, then refused to call a special session of the state legislature to find a way to subvert this decision. As a result, blacks could vote in Georgia's 1946 primary elections.

The *King* ruling and Arnall's subsequent stance underscored the value of adopting a conventional political strategy that was aimed at expanding black voter registration. The demise of the all-white primary provided at least the potential opportunity for black participation in southern Democratic politics for the first time since the disfranchising period of the late nineteenth and early twentieth centuries. Southern white resistance, combined with a lack of federal enforcement of black voting rights, ultimately would negate this potential in the postwar 1940s. That outcome, however, was not apparent at the time. Moreover, the *Smith* and *King* decisions instilled hope that change might be initiated within the regular channels of conventional electoral politics. Given the rhetoric of democratic victory against the totalitarian Axis powers, along with the developing anticommunist sentiment that infused the postwar era, conventional political activism probably had more ideological and pragmatic appeal immediately after the war than the sort of militant direct action tactics more common in the civil rights movement of later decades. Moreover, voter registration and electoral politics conformed with the reform strategy adopted by the national NAACP, its many local community branches, the national and state [Congress of Industrial Organizations], and other progressive reform organizations. Finally, veterans had just fought a war that had emphasized the importance of the processes and values of American democracy versus the exclusivity and intolerance of totalitarian regimes. It made sense to at least try those processes as a means of initiating reform, given veterans' special claim to having earned a right to that participation through their war service.

For all of these reasons, voter registration drives in support of moderate or progressive candidates, or against reactionary ones, became a primary goal of black veteran organizations, in cooperation with other civic groups such as the Urban League and local NAACP chapters.

[. . .]

The most successful of these initiatives occurred in Savannah, Augusta, and Atlanta. All were responses to unusual opportunities in 1946 to elect candidates with more moderate racial views and to defeat Eugene Talmadge in the state gubernatorial race. Black World War II veterans played pivotal roles in turning out a historic number of black citizens to register and vote in all three cities.

Savannah's voter registration drive emerged in the context of a developing reformist campaign of businessmen, labor, and white veterans against the corrupt urban machine headed by John Bouhan, Savannah's county attorney and long incumbent Democratic political boss. The insurgent campaign launched by the Citizens Progressive League in the spring of 1946 immediately attracted black veterans who seized the chance to augment black political influence by helping to defeat the Bouhan-supported candidates for the state legislature. A new organization called the World War II–Veterans Association (WWII–VA) announced its formation as a "nonpartisan" association that, nonetheless, also promised to "take a leading role in politics" in order to improve "the political and economical positions of all of its colored citizens." The WWII–VA immediately launched an enthusiastic voter registration drive.

[. . .]

Meanwhile, black veterans in the GVL in Atlanta joined an equally vigorous registration campaign for the gubernatorial and Fifth District congressional primaries. A new umbrella civic organization called the All Citizens Registration Committee (ACRC) initially had registered black voters earlier in the year in support of the candidacy of moderately liberal Helen Douglas Mankin in a special election to fill the Fifth District congressional seat. When that effort succeeded, ACRC leaders decided to expand the registration drive. They planned to support both Mankin's reelection in the regular primary and the gubernatorial candidacy of James V. Carmichael, who was perceived as being a racial moderate, against Eugene Talmadge, known to be a racial reactionary. Black veterans in the GVL assumed a leading role in organizing and carrying out this effort.

[. . .]

The voter registration drives in which these veterans participated did produce significant results, registering between 135,000 and 150,000 black voters in Georgia in 1946 alone. Between 85,000 and 100,000 of these actually managed to vote that year, 98 percent for gubernatorial candidate James V. Carmichael against Eugene Talmadge. Black voters helped to defeat entrenched political machines in Savannah and Augusta and to elect a new mayor in Macon in 1947. Around 200,000 black citizens registered statewide for the gubernatorial race between Melvin E. Thompson and Herman Talmadge the following year.

Other southern states made significant, if less striking, progress. In Mississippi, for example, black veterans' efforts to oust Senator Theodore G. Bilbo failed to get rid of that state's most noted reactionary, but their courage in testifying against

"The Man" at a later congressional hearing encouraged other black Mississippians to take action. By 1950, some 20,000 African Americans had registered to vote in Mississippi, a significant start in a state known for its rabid racism. By the time of the *Brown v. The Board of Education* decision in 1954, over one million African Americans were registered to vote in the South.

These successes, however, hardly tell the whole story. Ultimately, the voter registration drives of the postwar 1940s failed to evolve into ongoing grassroots movements.

[. . .]

[T]he potential for progressive racial change that seemed so promising within the first couple of years after the war quickly dissipated. Leading civil rights organizations generally remained wedded to gradualist strategies emphasizing conventional legal and political avenues for change, but these channels narrowed considerably as the developing Cold War complicated the postwar political context for progressive campaigns of all sorts. The new war on communism sapped the momentum for reform, in part, by redefining progressive social causes as inherently un-American and even communistic. Moreover, the international fight for the "Free World" paradoxically drew national and world attention to the southern system of apartheid *and* made federal officials and national party leaders, anxious to secure broad support for Cold War policies, reluctant to challenge the southern white defensiveness that resulted. The national postwar climate for progressive racial change in the South thus quickly soured.

Scholars also have emphasized the lack of commitment to the cause exhibited by many black southerners, including veterans, who, like many Americans, chose to focus on personal advancement over political mobilization after the war.

[. . .]

Certainly, all of these factors help to explain why the modern direct action phase of the black freedom struggle took at least a decade to develop after World War II ended. The intensity of the white backlash that black activists faced in states like Georgia in the postwar 1940s, however, also undermined black political participation. Each protest against Jim Crow and each black citizen who registered and voted weakened the confidence many white southerners had in the immutability of southern racial tradition. They responded accordingly. From purging registration lists of black voters to outright acts of violence . . . racial conservatives reacted to the political activism that black veterans encouraged with a stalwart defense of white supremacy.

[. . .]

Despite veterans' bravery and determination, this backlash caused black voting in the immediate postwar years to fall below expectations. Although the number of African Americans who registered quadrupled between 1945 and 1950, 80 percent of eligible black citizens in the South remained unregistered. The NAACP hoped to enroll two million black citizens for the presidential election of 1952 but managed to meet only half of that goal. A [Southern Regional Council] survey in 1953 found that the registration of African Americans of voting age in the entire South amounted to only 50 percent of white registration. Such statistics led historian Steven F. Lawson to conclude that the voter drives of the 1940s "had skimmed the cream off the top and succeeded with those most receptive to their message," namely, African Americans in the urban South. Enfranchisement proved slowest in the rural black belt where African Americans outnumbered whites and, consequently, met the stiffest white resistance.

[. . .]

Defining the postwar era in the South only in terms of lost opportunities, nevertheless, neglects taking the events of the period – and the black and white southerners who lived through them – on their own terms. Indeed, the story of black veteran activism in Georgia compels us to understand the postwar 1940s not as an era of failure alone, but as one of significant ferment touched off, at least in part, by the Second World War. If black veterans and citizens had not challenged and threatened the political and racial status quo in Georgia after the war, whites would not have found it so necessary to mount a reactionary backlash. The intensity of their efforts to repel black veterans' advancement testified to the level of racial instability induced by the war. Although this backlash effectively stalled the momentum for progressive racial reform at the time, black veteran activism signaled the real racial discomfort that would only grow for southerners of both races as the twentieth century progressed. The willingness of black veterans to confront the racial injustices that denied them the dignity and freedom they had earned exposed the racial fault line in the foundations of the one-party South, a structural weakness from which massive resistance to integration *and* the black civil rights movement would subsequently emerge.

৶ ৶ ৶

Bruce J. Schulman

From Cotton Belt to Sunbelt[†]

The women and men who had entered the federal government to reform the South during the 1930s left government service soon after FDR's death. They had advocated

[†]Bruce J. Schulman, *From Cotton Belt to Sunbelt: Federal Policy, Economic Development, and the Transformation of the South, 1938–1980* (Durham: Duke University Press, 1994), pp. 127–9, 131–3, 136, 151.

far-reaching socioeconomic change – unionization, industrial development, public power, resettlement of tenants, federal relief programs, minimum wages. They also believed that such reforms would ameliorate the economic distress at the root of racial tensions. Still, most southern liberals, whatever their personal feelings about white supremacy, thought segregation impregnable. They generally opposed integration and feared, in Jonathan Daniels's words, that the nation seemed "to be back to the extreme abolitionists and the extreme slaveholders in the lines of discussion."

[. . .]

Such a halting, indirect program for improving race relations became obsolete under the onslaught of the civil rights movement. Northern liberals, black rights organizations, and the national administration rejected the southern liberals' conservative course on race relations. Many southern New Dealers continued to emphasize economic underdevelopment as the source of black discontent, but this view became increasingly outmoded. It was soon associated with a conservative, even a recalcitrant reactionary position.

At the same time, however, the advancing Cold War shifted the economic program of American liberalism to the right. Southern liberals found themselves behind national opinion on matters of race, but far in front of it on economic issues. The emergence of militant pro-civil rights sentiments coincided with a declining constituency for New Deal-style economic reform.

[. . .]

In the 1940s and 1950s, American liberalism stressed economic growth rather than redistribution, consensus rather than conflict between the "economic royalists" and the working man. Liberal policymakers no longer felt an emotional bond with the masses or distrusted the capitalist system . . . This renewed faith in American capitalism, like support for civil rights, was linked to the era's pervasive anti-communism. Liberals sought to demonstrate the superiority – economic, political, and spiritual – of democratic capitalism to totalitarian communism. They lacked the desire to rebuild institutions and to remold the economy that had animated liberals of the New Deal generation.

Not surprisingly, then, the southern liberals who seemed poised to take on a pivotal role in national policymaking in the late 1930s found themselves virtually without influence a decade later. Seeing the war as a main chance for the economic rehabilitation of the South, some southern liberals knit their objectives too closely into the defense program.

[. . .]

War plants and military bases followed, as did public works justified by military necessity. But such boodle had little peacetime justification and came without liberal politics, unions, or public welfare services. It benefited the South as a region, not its ill-housed, ill-nourished, ill-clad people, and it drained some of the reformist energy from southern liberalism. After 1945, those southern liberals who resurrected the old economic agenda faced charges of truckling with communism.

[. . .]

Old Guard conservatives felt besieged by the national Democratic party and the civil rights movement, and so did the southern New Dealers. Into this chaotic land-scape, then, stepped the new Whigs, southern politicians who numbered economic development as their first priority and who looked to the federal government to underwrite the effort. These new Whigs diverged from the established leadership in their recognition that social change would accompany economic development. They differed also from such New Dealers as Claude Pepper and Frank Graham in that they sought assistance for the downtrodden only as a secondary means to promote regional industrialization and to remove the stigma of southern backward-ness. Accordingly, they favored development-related expenditures like airports and education more intensely than welfare programs, a preference revealed on the ledgers of the state governments they ran during the 1950s and 60s.

These "Whigs" eventually became the pivotal figures in southern politics. The "Other South" of the twentieth century – white voices that dissented from the savage ideals of unbending segregation, massive resistance, and a return to com-plete political and economic isolation from the rest of the nation – was composed not so much of the small coterie of white southerners who actively opposed the racial caste system, as by the much larger and growing faction of development advocates.

[. . .]

[T]he Whigs recognized the South's interdependence with the rest of the nation – its dependence on federal largesse and on the private investment that invariably followed. They realized that industrialization combined with economic and political isolation – the recipe of the business progressives – would fall flat in the post-World War II South.

Still, these development-oriented politicians almost never overtly challenged white supremacy. They simply opposed self-defeating resistance to desegregation, especially visible resistance, arguing that economic progress either required or was certain to accomplish some changes in race relations. The increasingly familiar sight of southern governors personally recruiting new industrial installations and campaigning for increased federal aid demonstrated not only their commitment to industrial growth, but also the increasing potency of economic development as a campaign issue. A candidate had to avoid being "out-segged," as many victims of the everpowerful race issue learned, but they could no longer afford to be out-developed either. That new political imperative offered potential opponents of the established leadership an escape route, a tunnel out of the tyrannous grip of the race issue that had so long afflicted southern politics, thwarted reform efforts, and isolated the region from the rest of the nation.

[. . .]

Even after the Supreme Court's decision in *Brown v. Board of Education* temporarily arrested the trend toward moderation, making political conflict over segregation unavoidable, this Whiggery survived, waking from its dormancy with enhanced potency. While *Brown* initially weakened candidates who were unwilling to advocate massive resistance, the ensuing strife, with its closed schools, boycotted businesses, and deployment of federal troops dramatized the benefits of moderation. Resistance also threatened the region's dependent relationship with the federal government. Cutoffs of federal funds to recalcitrant states loomed closer after desegregation became the law of the land. In that charged atmosphere, many pro-development racial moderates won election at the height of the desegregation conflict.

[. . .]

But already by 1950, a race-free southern politics did not promise a liberal future. The victories of Whig politicians testified to the emergence of a conservative, business-oriented politics.

[. . .]

They did not concern themselves with the problems of the downtrodden or expand welfare services. And over the long run, regional economic development would only augment southern Whigs' political strength.

[. . .]

The success of southern politicians came to rest on their ability to advance industrialization. That task in turn hinged on the region's provision of reliable services, adequate schools, and other public goods. And the South's capacity to provide those facilities depended on both the funding and the approval of the federal government. Federal funds guaranteed a minimum level of social services so that localities could commit their entire resources to industrial recruitment.

[. . .]

Federal intervention, stripped of the reform motives of southern liberals, was more in harmony with the new Whig ruling class of the South. The nagging problem of civil rights remained, of course, but as long as southern states muted their resistance to integration, they could usually count on continued federal largesse. No federal spending was more desirable, no tune was sweeter to southern ears, than defense-related programs.

[. . .]

[M]ilitary spending, understood broadly, offered development without political reform and social change . . .

Social welfare activities waned as the defense intervention waxed. The South aggressively sought military spending, including those civilian programs that fell under the rubric of national security or promised development without direct aid to the impoverished. It paid homage to and reaped benefits from the defense establishment in the forms of prime contracts, the space program, highway and airport funds, and research grants. But at the same time the South ceased to be the prime target or the principal beneficiary of federal social programs. With the exception of the minimum wage, the effects of which were largely absorbed by 1960, the national welfare state had little impact on southern poverty.

[. . .]

Federal action, then, forged a new sort of southern political economy. It permitted the South to pursue development through federal investments, as southern New Dealers had envisioned, but without liberal politics or redistributionist economic policy – without support for welfare, labor, blacks. The alliance between the South and the defense state brought with it highways and airports – old favorites of southern business progressives – but also funds for research facilities and higher education. It provided little in the way of welfare, job training, or primary education.

14

Adam Fairclough

THE CIVIL RIGHTS ERA

Jim Crow was alive and well at mid twentieth century. As the 1950s began, however, segregation was about to be challenged by one of the most dramatic social movements in American history. Black resistance to Jim Crow dated back to the origins of the system itself. But the "modern" civil rights movement can be said to have been born on that iconic moment in 1955 when Rosa Parks of Montgomery, Alabama, defied an order to surrender her seat on a bus to a white person. So began a decade-long crusade, crowded with local campaigns across the South, to put an end to Jim Crow, and to make real the promise of racial equality in the United States.

In retrospect, the civil rights movement is generally regarded as a clear-cut morality tale – a progression of uplifting triumphs that seem all but inevitable. But, as the readings in this chapter show, the civil rights revolution was far from a simple affair. Like any turning point in history, it was marked by complexity, uncertainty, and myriad internal divisions. It is no surprise, then, that the civil rights movement remains a subject of unflagging scholarly interest. Searching questions about this epoch abound. What accounts for the emergence of the modern civil rights movement, and the demise of Jim Crow, during the 1950s and 1960s? In what measure did the initiative come from local, grass-roots activists, and in what measure, from regional or national organizations? How did participants prioritize, and debate over, such aims as desegregation, the right to vote, equal education and employment opportunity, better material conditions, fair treatment in the justice system, and an end to the racist attitudes that pervaded popular culture? How did federal action (or inaction) affect the struggle for civil rights? How did women figure in the ranks and leadership of the movement, and what were their distinctive experiences within it? What explains the movement's eventual success in eradicating Jim Crow laws? What ultimately has been its legacy, for the South and for the nation as a whole? The opening essay by Adam Fairclough, and the selections he has chosen for this chapter, illustrate how questions like this continue to animate the study of this landmark movement.

Adam Fairclough is the Raymond and Beverly Sackler Professor of American History at Leiden University, where he has published widely on the civil rights movement, black education, race relations in the Jim Crow era, and Reconstruction. Among his book publications are: *To Redeem the Soul of America: The Southern Christian Leadership Conference and Martin Luther King, Jr.* (1987); *Martin Luther King* (1990); *Race and Democracy: The Civil Rights Struggle in Louisiana, 1915–1972* (1995); *Teaching Equality: Black Schools in the Age of Jim Crow* (2001); *Better Day Coming: Blacks and Equality, 1890–2000* (2001); and *A Class of Their Own: Black Teachers in the Segregated South* (2007). He is currently working on a study of Reconstruction in the town and parish of Natchitoches, Louisiana.

When Rosa Parks disobeyed a white bus driver, who commanded her to give up her seat so that a white passenger could sit down, she did not plan to launch a protest campaign that would unite 50,000 African Americans. Nevertheless, when the police arrested her on December 1, 1955 – taking her fingerprints and "mugshot" – she hoped that her defiance might lead to bigger things. Rosa McCauley Parks, who worked as a seamstress in a department store, was a well-known and widely respected member of the black community in Montgomery, Alabama. A fighter for civil rights, she was a longtime member of the National Association for the Advancement of Colored People (NAACP), which, since its founding in 1909, had campaigned against racial segregation and discrimination. Upon learning of Parks's arrest, therefore, other civil rights activists, including NAACP leader E. D. Nixon and college teacher Jo Ann Robinson, seized upon the incident to instigate a boycott of Montgomery's buses. After a hard-fought year, the boycott ended in victory. The buses were integrated; blacks could sit wherever they chose.

The Montgomery bus boycott soon became the template for the civil rights movement. It set a new example of mass protest – "nonviolent direct action" – and exemplified the boldness and fervent determination with which black southerners now attacked segregation. Beyond making Rosa Parks a household name, it created a new black leader in the person of Martin Luther King, Jr., and gave birth to a new organization, the Southern Christian Leadership Conference (SCLC). Organized in 1957, SCLC gave King a platform from which he could spread the gospel of nonviolent direct action and inspire black southerners to challenge Jim Crow. It is small wonder, then, that this mass protest shaped the popular image of the civil rights movement as a singing, praying, marching crusade of ordinary people, led by a black Baptist minister who personified its courage and articulated its idealism.

Just as it is fashionable to regard the men and women who fought fascism during the Second World War as America's "greatest generation," we have come to view the people who took part in the civil rights movement as exceptionally heroic. Between 1955 and 1965 black southerners surmounted all the odds to regain the rights – the right to vote, the right to be treated equally under the law – which they had lost after the collapse of Reconstruction. Thanks to their sacrifices, Congress passed five civil rights acts between 1957 and 1968. The civil rights movement also inspired other groups – women, Hispanics, Native Americans, gay people – to protest against discrimination. Black southerners, assisted by white allies and co-workers, accomplished all this by putting their own lives and bodies on the line. Defying the police and flouting court injunctions, they went to jail by the thousands. Many suffered beatings. Some were shot dead by law enforcement officials or murdered by the terrorists of the Ku Klux Klan. King himself died from a bullet fired by a white racist.

This heroic narrative, however, can hinder our understanding of the civil rights movement. The movement achieved so much not because its participants were braver than previous generations – whose struggles, though less remembered, often entailed greater risks – but because historical circumstances now favored them. The long campaign waged by the NAACP and other groups to end lynching, for example, had made life significantly less dangerous for blacks in the South. The gradual improvement of black schools and colleges over many decades had produced a better-educated, more ambitious population, and made black college students important participants in the struggle for civil rights. Federal court decisions had chipped away at laws and practices that prevented blacks from voting; by 1955, more than a million were casting ballots in federal, state, and local elections. In addition, the Cold War had made the federal government acutely sensitive to the charge of racial discrimination, and since 1946 it had begun moving away from its old policy of tolerating, even encouraging, racial segregation. The integration of the armed forces at the behest of President Truman, and the Supreme Court's 1954 ruling in *Brown* v. *Board of Education* that laws must no longer segregate schoolchildren by race, epitomized this sea change.

Alterations in the nation's economy had also, over time, weakened white supremacy. The decline of cotton production in the South pushed millions of black sharecroppers off the land. Farm mechanization – especially the mechanical cotton picker – caused further displacement. Once scattered across the countryside in small farms, by the 1950s most southern blacks lived in towns and cities, where they were more likely to vote, and where they could band together more easily and effectively. Millions streamed to northern cities and, by 1960, half of America's blacks lived outside the South. Northern black voters exercised growing political influence, especially in the Democratic party. Black votes helped to elect John F. Kennedy in 1960.

In short, tactics that a few years earlier would have been considered suicidal – boycotts, marches, sit-ins, "freedom rides" – could now be utilized with growing confidence. Federal power, progressively strengthened by the New Deal, the Second World War, and the Cold War, steadily eroded the power of southern whites to employ violent methods of oppressing the black population. As the civil rights movement unfolded, the federal government intervened repeatedly to help and protect it. Judges struck down segregation laws, overruled state courts, issued injunctions against obstructive white officials, and reversed the convictions of civil rights activists. Presidents Eisenhower, Kennedy, and Johnson deployed troops, marshals, and FBI agents to protect blacks from mobs and terrorists. Although federal assistance was reluctantly and spottily applied, it sent a powerful signal to southerners on each side of the struggle. When, in 1965, President Lyndon Johnson invoked the anthem of the civil rights movement, promising in his Texas drawl that "we shall overcome," he made it crystal clear that the national government stood behind the advocates of racial equality. It would be wrong to underestimate the strength of the white opposition or to minimize the dangers faced by people who stood up for integration. Nevertheless, the fact remains that the civil rights movement suffered relatively *few* casualties. A few days of rioting in Newark and Detroit in 1967 claimed more black lives than a decade of protests in the South.

As the civil rights movement recedes from living memory, the heroic narrative sketched above is being challenged, often by younger scholars who have no personal connection with the story. One school, probing the roots of the movement, emphasizes the continuities with earlier decades, pointing to the persistent agitation of the NAACP and the eruption of black militancy during the Second World War. The waning of the Cold War prompted another argument for continuity. As historians reassessed the "Old Left" of the 1930s and 1940s in a more favorable light, they pointed to the anti-racist policies of the Communist party, and the formation of interracial labor unions, as important precursors of the civil rights movement of the 1950s and 1960s. Indeed, some concluded that the civil rights movement, in its anxiety to deflect allegations of Communism, failed to match the radicalism – and, perhaps, realism – of those earlier crusades. The alleged conservatism of the civil rights movement, especially its reluctance to question capitalism, has led some historians to question its achievements. Did it really represent a decisive breakthrough, finally resolving the problem of racism? Or, was it simply one phase of a struggle that is still being waged? Some historians write about a "long civil rights movement" that is still in progress; others speak of a decades long – even centuries old – "black freedom struggle." However valid their points may be, such terms tend to play down the distinctiveness of the 1955–65 period.

The very notion of the civil rights struggle as a coherent "movement" is also being questioned. The idea that it was a highly organized affair dominated by a single charismatic leader – King – has always been simplistic. Although King remains stubbornly fascinating to many scholars, most prefer these days to study local movements and lesser-known leaders. The accumulated effect of this research is to deny that King was central, or even that important, to the civil rights movement. According to this argument, local activists, operating to a large extent independently of the big civil rights organizations – and of each other – constituted the movement's driving force. No single leader, or small group of master strategists, directed the course of events. The dominance of King was an illusion, and the influence of his ideas quite limited. Few black southerners shared the full measure of King's commitment to nonviolence; many more believed that the most appropriate response to white violence was armed self-defense.

The first reading presented here offers an original and provocative analysis of the civil rights movement. Focusing on the three campaigns that are most closely associated with the leadership of Martin Luther King – the Montgomery bus boycott, the Birmingham protests of 1963, and the Selma demonstrations of 1965 – J. Mills Thornton III asks why civil rights activists utilized nonviolent direct action in these cities but not in so many others around the South. His explanation challenges both the "heroic" narrative of the civil rights struggle and the idea of the movement as a concerted force with an overall strategy. Thornton is not particularly interested in showcasing the religious enthusiasm or high-minded idealism of the movement. He does not describe the singing, the preaching, and the praying. Instead, he treats the movement as a contest for political power between two antagonistic communities. In addition, Thornton sees the movement as a series of locally anchored, largely disconnected struggles, in which the big civil rights organizations played a supportive rather than a primary role.

According to Thornton, those blacks who embraced direct action were influenced not so much by leaders like King, or national events, as by local circumstances. Through a detailed examination of political developments in Montgomery, Birmingham, and Selma, he shows that the actions of white politicians strongly influenced the manner in which blacks pursued their goals. Building upon the old insight that revolutions usually occur when things are getting better, not worse, he argues that blacks took to the streets when, and only when, they saw a realistic chance of wresting concessions from the white power structure. That usually happened, he concludes, when a previously unified political establishment began to reveal internal divisions. In cities like Mobile, where white politicians proved amenable to negotiation and compromise, blacks saw no need to resort to direct action; old-fashioned political horse trading secured satisfactory results. Blacks also shied away from direct action when white politicians appeared implacable in their opposition and willing to use overwhelming force to quash public protests.

A third type of situation, on the other hand, encouraged blacks to organize boycotts, sit-ins, and demonstrations. These situations arose, argues Thornton, when whites appeared divided on the race issue, with moderate and conservative factions fighting for dominance. Blacks calculated that such splits made the white ruling class vulnerable to pressure, and employed direct action to strengthen their bargaining position. Once blacks took to the streets, these campaigns took on a life of their own, developing in unexpected directions. In Montgomery, for example, white officials responded to the bus boycott not by offering concessions, as blacks had hoped, but by digging in their heels and harassing King. Such behavior had the reverse effect from the one intended: white intransigence prolonged the boycott, reinforced black unity, and turned King into a popular martyr. But this does not affect Thornton's contention that blacks, at the outset, regarded direct action as a means of influencing white politicians. Their goals and visions were mainly local in scope. The civil rights movement was thus an extension of local politics, not a grand scheme of moral regeneration or national reform.

Such a limited view of the civil rights movement leaves little room for the soaring idealism of King. According to Thornton, King's vision of reconciliation between blacks and whites – his famous "dream" of a "beloved community" – masked the nitty-gritty of political power on the ground. To be sure, King's idealism had a profound appeal to many, especially white liberals, who supported the movement from outside the South. Blacks themselves, however, had lived too long with the lion to act like lambs. If they lapped up King's words, few embraced his invocation to love the oppressor or believed that unmerited suffering had the redemptive qualities ascribed to it by King. This helps to explain why the goals of local activists, whom Thornton describes as the "movement's heart and soul," often diverged from those of national leaders like King. Thornton labels King a visionary who "profoundly misunderstood the events of which he was a part." The failure of the civil rights movement to realize King's "dream," therefore, was only to be expected. King's "Christian romanticism" stood no chance in the real world.

Yet in making a valuable point, Thornton stretches it too far. His insistence that local political conditions determined the tactics employed by blacks leaves little room for larger factors. Blacks were not unaware of the wider world. Civil rights activists belonged to organizational networks that influenced and supported them: labor unions, professional associations, and the NAACP. Not a few had served in the armed forces – many fighting in the Second World War and the Korean War – experiences that strengthened their determination to oppose segregation and reclaim their right to vote. Blacks were also well aware of how the Cold War helped legitimize the cause of civil rights. They knew about the *Brown* decision and took heart from it. Thornton's treatment of local campaigns as disconnected enterprises also understates the role of national and regional organizations. Local activists may have provided the civil rights movement with its motive power, but organizations like SCLC and the Student Nonviolent Coordinating Committee (SNCC) played a vital role in shaping and steering it. Their experienced, full-time organizers supplied training in nonviolence, political education, legal representation, and national publicity. They linked local movements in the South to sources of support up North. They forged the political contacts that brought these movements to the notice of the president and Congress. In short, the civil rights movement was far more than the sum of its parts.

Thornton's treatment of King is also too limited. To say that King was atypical is something of a truism. Great leaders are by definition exceptional in their ability to articulate ideals and inspire their followers. It does not follow, however, that blacks generally were devoid of the idealism that King expressed. If some of his words soared over their heads, church-going blacks could readily understand his biblical language, as well as his appeals to freedom and democracy. Although nonviolence may have been a difficult concept to convey, King framed it within the religious traditions of black Christians, emphasizing more Jesus than Gandhi. If relatively few blacks embraced nonviolence with the depth of King's own commitment, those who did formed a disciplined cadre that profoundly influenced the overall movement.

Still, Thornton has injected a healthy dose of realism into the study of the civil rights movement. For far too long historians portrayed it as a morality play between heroes and villains, accepting at face value the movement's own image of itself. Thornton cautions us not to overlook local variations, overstate moral idealism, or place too much emphasis on an extraordinary individual such as King.

Our second reading poses an interesting contrast to Thornton's piece. Writing about the oldest and largest civil rights organization, the NAACP, Manfred Berg emphasizes the national rather than the local. Although the NAACP had branches throughout the South, its local activities tended to reflect an overall strategy developed by a small group of national officials. The surest way to fight racial discrimination, these officials believed, was to exert political pressure on the federal government. Adopting unrestricted access to the ballot as its main priority, the NAACP instigated lawsuits against white registrars, mounted voter registration campaigns, and lobbied the president and Congress for the passage of voting rights legislation. By charting the NAACP's long pursuit of the ballot – dating back to the early twentieth century, and intensifying over the 1940s, 1950s, and 1960s – Berg's study provides strong evidence of continuity in the civil rights struggle.

Berg's conclusions reflect a growing recognition that the importance of the NAACP's activities in the South has been overlooked. In the 1960s American culture became fixated by youth, and the leaders of the NAACP were not young. Indeed, the guiding hands of the NAACP were *much* older than the activists of SNCC and even the leaders of SCLC. Roy Wilkins, the executive secretary, had joined the staff in 1931, when King was but a toddler. Moreover, the NAACP lacked a charismatic leader who could capture the attention of the news media. In addition, the NAACP generally eschewed boycotts and sit-ins, disparaging nonviolent direct action as a waste of time and money. Demonstrations, however, appealed to the press because they were so visually dramatic. A photograph of a young demonstrator being attacked by a police dog had far greater news value than a picture of a voter registration worker knocking on a door. As a consequence, much of the NAACP's work went unreported.

As Berg makes clear, the NAACP had an uneasy relationship with the rest of the civil rights movement. Having been around for so long, and having acquired so much experience, the venerable association tended to treat younger organizations with arrogant condescension. Indeed, it often implied that the NAACP and the Civil Rights movement were one and the same. In the view of the association's national officials, additional organizations simply led to wasteful duplication; SCLC, SNCC, and the Congress of Racial Equality (CORE) were thus surplus to requirements. This view stemmed as much from organizational self-interest as from a concern for the common good. The NAACP wished to protect its "turf." Rather like an empire, the more the association grew in size, the more vulnerable it felt to attack. Such feelings could become intensely personal. Roy Wilkins's attitude to King, for example, was strongly colored by his jealousy of the younger man's rise to fame.

Hence the NAACP, although indisputably important, reflected the *spirit* of the civil rights movement far less than did SCLC or SNCC. The fact that the association made its headquarters in New York, while both SCLC and SNCC based themselves in the South, made it less able to interpret, and respond to, the growing militancy of black southerners. Its aging leaders – always ultrasensitive to matters of rank and seniority – found it difficult to treat brash young students as equal partners. Its bureaucratic structure, though more democratic than those of SCLC and SNCC, hampered its ability to deal creatively with crisis situations on the ground.

The third reading, by Belinda Robnett, concerns the role of women in the civil rights movement. Influenced by the feminist ideology of the late 1960s and 1970s, early treatments of this subject exposed the sexist practices and attitudes that were common within the civil rights movement. Indeed, the movement's male chauvinism helped to spark the earliest stirrings of "second wave" feminism. Robnett, however, is not so much interested in tracing the roots of women's liberation as in investigating what women – especially African American women – actually contributed to the civil rights movement. A sociologist, she applies a structural analysis that sorts women's leadership roles into several distinct categories. Although her typology of leadership is rather complex, her basic argument is clear. Robnett rejects the notion that the movement was "led by men but organized by women," an idea originally advanced to explain the fact that, although women comprised most of the movement's rank and file, nearly all the best-known leaders were men. In reality, she argues, women filled all kinds of leadership positions. Women were especially important as "bridge-builders," linking local people to the various civil rights organizations. In some cases, they held formal positions within those organizations; in others they functioned informally. Taken together, women's leadership served as a kind of glue that held the movement together.

It is undeniable that men monopolized the top leadership positions in the civil rights movement: the heads of SNCC, CORE, SCLC, the NAACP, and the Urban League were all men. It is also clear that this male monopoly was a postwar development: from the 1890s to the 1940s, women like Ida B. Wells, Mary Church Terrell, and Mary McLeod Bethune had gained national prominence in the civil rights struggle. After the Second World War, however, the influence of women's organizations and female leaders declined. Why this happened is not entirely clear, but it surely had something to do with the postwar idealization of woman as mother and housewife. In any case, it is indicative that the men who organized the 1963 March on Washington added Dorothy Height to the list of speakers – Height was president of the National Council of Negro Women – only when they belatedly realized that that list included no women.

The social structure of the black community contributed to the dominance of men in formal leadership positions. To survive economic retaliation by whites, black leaders required a degree of economic independence, and most of the jobs that carried that kind of security – minister, postal worker, Pullman car porter – were male preserves. Hence the presidents of NAACP branches and SCLC affiliates were nearly always men. Women, on the other hand, comprised the great majority of black schoolteachers who, because of their economic vulnerability, had to be more circumspect, working behind the scenes and avoiding high-visibility leadership positions. Nevertheless, women who did enjoy economic security – such as Daisy Bates, the wife of a newspaper publisher in Little Rock, Arkansas, or Winson Hudson, a landowner in Holmes County, Mississippi – often assumed positions of formal, open leadership. In addition, women were often more community-minded than men: they attended church more regularly and were on the whole more socially active. This meant that when civil rights workers arrived in rural communities, they often relied upon local women to rally support. Some of these informal "bridge leaders" played such an important role that they acquired formal leadership positions. Mississippi sharecropper Fannie Lou Hamer, for example, ended up joining the staff of SNCC.

The news media, with their relentless quest to identify "the" black leader, underestimated the role of women, encouraging historians to make the same mistake. In reality, women functioned at every level of leadership bar the very highest. Constance B. Motley, for example, served as one of the NAACP's top legal strategists, second in rank only to Thurgood Marshall. Septima P. Clark headed SCLC's important, though little-heralded, Citizenship Education Project. Ruby Doris Smith sat on SNCC's executive committee and served as the organization's executive secretary. Women's own modesty, however, sometimes contributed to their relatively low profile. In a movement that often seemed to be dominated by competing male egos – especially among the ministers of SCLC – women tended to be more interested in "getting the job done" than in personal glory or organizational empire building.

A small selection of readings like this can provide only a taste of the burgeoning scholarship about the civil rights movement. For years to come, scholars will continue to flesh out, and revise, this remarkable chapter in southern history. Their quest for originality, however, should not obscure the fundamental outlines of the story. We can accept the notion of a continuous "black freedom struggle," while still recognizing the events of 1955–65 as an exceptionally important phase of that struggle. Not since the fight to abolish slavery had a campaign for racial justice garnered such a degree of international support. Never before had so many blacks intentionally defied policemen, judges, and politicians, willingly going to jail to promote the cause of democracy and equality. No black leader before King had taken it upon himself to lead such a struggle by personal example. In the scope of its achievements – measured by laws passed and attitudes changed – the civil rights movement remains unique. It was, above all else, a *movement*, a coming together of people and ideals that proved unstoppable. It did not eliminate racism or inequality. It did, however, transform the South beyond recognition, and for the better.

* * *

FURTHER READING

Chafe, William H., *Civilities and Civil Rights: Greensboro, North Carolina, and the Black Struggle for Freedom* (New York: Oxford University Press, 1980).

Cook, Robert, *Sweet Land of Liberty? The African-American Freedom Struggle in the Twentieth Century* (London and New York: Longman, 1998).

Dittmer, John, *Local People: The Struggle for Civil Rights in Mississippi* (Urbana: University of Illinois Press, 1994).

Eskew, Glenn T., *But for Birmingham: The Local and National Movements in the Civil Rights Struggle* (Chapel Hill: University of North Carolina Press, 1997).

Fairclough, Adam, *To Redeem the Soul of America: The Southern Christian Leadership Conference and Martin Luther King, Jr.* (Athens: University of Georgia Press, 1987).

Garrow, David J., *The FBI and Martin Luther King, Jr.: From "Solo" to Memphis* (New York: W. W. Norton, 1981).

Lee, Chana Kai, *For Freedom's Sake: The Life of Fannie Lou Hamer* (Urbana: University of Illinois Press, 1999).

Meier, August and Elliott Rudwick, *CORE: A Study in the Civil Rights Movement, 1942–1968* (New York: Oxford University Press, 1973).

Ransby, Barbara, *Ella Baker and the Black Freedom Movement: A Radical Democratic Vision* (Chapel Hill: University of North Carolina Press, 2003).

Rieder, Jonathan, *The Word of the Lord Is Upon Me: The Righteous Performance of Martin Luther King, Jr.* (Cambridge, MA: Belknap Press of Harvard University Press, 2008).

Tushnet, Mark, *Making Civil Rights Law: Thurgood Marshall and the Supreme Court, 1936–1961* (New York: Oxford University Press, 1994).

Wendt, Simon, *The Spirit and the Shotgun: Armed Resistance and the Struggle for Civil Rights* (Gainesville: University Press of Florida, 2007).

* * *

J. Mills Thornton III

Dividing Lines[†]

The key to appreciating the role of municipal politics in the civil rights movement is to ask ourselves twin questions. Why did the civil rights movement manifest itself as mass direct-action campaigns in certain southern cities and towns, and not in others in which social conditions were apparently so closely comparable? Why were there sustained demonstrations in Birmingham rather than in Mobile, in Montgomery rather than in Columbus or Meridian, in Selma rather than in Valdosta, Bainbridge, or Dothan? And too, why did the direct-action campaigns happen in these places when they did, rather than earlier or later in the period? The history of the civil rights movement as it is customarily told, as an episode in the history of the United States, has not been able to deal effectively with such questions. Indeed, they are usually not even broached. The implication in many popular accounts is that the cities in which confrontations would be staged were consciously selected by national civil rights organizations. It is true that the Southern Christian Leadership Conference (SCLC) frequently selected cities in which it would organize demonstrations with an eye to whether or not the city was likely to gain favorable national publicity for the cause. In every case, however, there was an existing local civil rights organization in the city already engaged in protests; the SCLC was always invited to give its help by the local leaders, though it accepted or rejected the invitation for its own reasons. And this explanation is still less applicable to the activities of other components of the movement. The National Association for the Advancement of Colored People (NAACP) had local branches throughout the nation and ordinarily became involved in litigation when a case came to the attention of local branch officials; it almost never lent its support to demonstrations or direct action. The Student Non-violent Coordinating Committee (SNCC) was committed to long-term community organizing at the local level throughout the

---

[†]J. Mills Thornton III, *Dividing Lines: Municipal Politics and the Struggle for Civil Rights in Montgomery, Birmingham, and Selma* (Tuscaloosa: University of Alabama Press, 2002), pp. 3–13, 569–70, 582–3.

region; and except for the Freedom Rides, the Congress of Racial Equality (CORE) attempted, less successfully, to follow the same pattern. The National Urban League was not generally active in the South. The reality about the civil rights confrontations in southern towns during the period, then, is that they were everywhere local in origin, even when they received assistance from sympathetic outside forces.

I suspect that all careful students of these events would grant that much. At any rate, the three direct-action efforts on which this investigation will focus – those in Montgomery, Birmingham, and Selma – were beyond question indigenous in their origins. Though all three received significant assistance from national organizations, and the campaigns in Birmingham and Selma would undoubtedly have been considerably less successful without it, the campaigns were not produced by the national organizations. Rather, the national organizations – the NAACP in Montgomery, the SCLC in Birmingham and Selma – built upon movements initiated locally; indeed, they used the local movements for their own purposes, which in each of the three cases were not entirely consonant with local intentions.

It remains nevertheless much too easy for historians of the civil rights movement to think of its several local collisions as having built upon each other, in a mounting crescendo from Montgomery to Selma. Indeed, the very concept of a civil rights movement, when viewed from the perspective of its impact upon national history, encourages us to do so. And a focus upon the movement's regional and national leaders seems to confirm it; the SCLC did attempt, for instance, to use lessons derived from Montgomery to understand the challenge of Albany, did worry about the errors committed in Albany when it undertook to assist in Birmingham, and did employ in Selma the strategies it had developed earlier in Birmingham. Students of a maturing "movement culture," moreover, are necessarily compelled by the concept itself to emphasize the linkages from one incident to another. In fact, the abstraction is sufficiently powerful that it sometimes betrays its enthusiasts into assuming the importance of prior influences without bothering to establish that they were really at work. Some investigators, for instance, have erroneously attributed to the Baton Rouge bus boycott of 1953 a causative role in the Montgomery bus boycott of 1955–56 . . .

The notion that the various direct-action efforts in the South after 1955 were particular manifestations of a coherent black protest movement against the southern social system – generated in large part by the U.S. Supreme Court's 1954 decision declaring school segregation unconstitutional, and southern white resistance to that decision – was pervasive among northern journalists and observers at the time. Moreover, in the eyes of most commentators, it was precisely this belief that lent the various local demonstrations broader social significance. And it was what came therefore to seem, in the press reports on it, a swelling regionwide tide of protest that in great part eventually compelled national political institutions to take the movement seriously. Nor, of course, was this perspective devoid of truth. Certainly black hostility to racial discrimination was virtually universal, and the Supreme Court's decisions that the Constitution forbade any governmental enforcement of such discrimination had for the first time in many years placed this long-standing hostility into a powerfully national context. Yet a sensitive examination of the local movements themselves allows us to see them from a different, and no less valid, point of view.

The black Selma attorney J. L. Chestnut, Jr., gives us in his memoirs, for instance, this description of attitudes among his black fellow townsfolk at the time of George Wallace's election as governor of Alabama in 1962[:]

[. . .]

> In Selma in 1962, no black institution or organization, with the exception of the little Dallas County Voters League, was promoting civil rights or organizing black people around any goal except going to heaven, providing a decent education, or having a good time – not the clubs or fraternities, not the churches, not Selma University, not the black teachers' association. The NAACP was banned statewide, and the local chapter already was demoralized by the fallout from the unsuccessful petition to integrate the schools.
>
> At the bootleg houses, the clubs, the Elks, Selma University, we would occasionally discuss the public issues of the day. It was frustrating to listen to the pessimistic theme song: "These [black] folk here won't get together. They won't take a chance."

[. . .]

And even though Chestnut was fully informed about the rapidly developing body of national civil rights law, he was actually not much more sanguine himself than were his more parochial neighbors. "My concern was whether federal power would be exercised against Southern whites on behalf of blacks, and on this score, in 1962, I was only slightly less pessimistic than the people I was arguing with . . . I didn't think anything of great consequence would come out of the White House or the Justice Department."

. . . [T]he principal source of the White Citizens' Council's strength in Montgomery and Selma at this period was its confident conviction that, by preventing local white dissent, it was on the verge of winning the battle with the civil rights forces and their federal allies. Nor did black leaders at the heart of the local struggles therefore possess any greater sense of the vast changes that were just about to sweep through their communities. In the summer of 1963, nearly three months after the end of the demonstrations of that spring, Birmingham city councilman Alan Drennen, while campaigning for merger with the city's suburbs, commented that without it, "Birmingham by 1980 could be politically controlled and operated by members of the colored race." Emory O. Jackson, the editor of the *Birmingham World*, the voice of the black community and one of black Birmingham's best-informed spokesmen, greeted this assertion with astonishment and ridicule: "Mr. Drennen knows better than this. At the present rate of Negro voting [registration], it would take over 40 years for the Negro group to get its potential vote on the poll lists." And even when it had done so, "The Negro population is only 38 per cent of the total." In the end, of course, Drennen's prediction proved quite accurate; Birmingham elected its first black mayor in 1979. But the notion seemed so outlandish to Jackson in 1963 that Drennen's mere expression of it caused Jackson to rage, "The issue of merger is now enmeshed with racial bigotry, it seems to us." Jackson simply could not imagine at that time the capacity of the civil rights movement to sweep aside Alabama's restrictions on registration completely within two more years, and the social transformations that the achievement would shortly thereafter engender in his city.

It is precisely this aspect of the events of the period that the assumption of a coherent regionwide civil rights movement obscures: the capacity of what seemed always to have been to limit understandings of what could be. Very few participants in the civil rights movement were able to conceive the shape of thoroughgoing reform. The movement actually proceeded through tiny revelations of possible change. The Montgomery bus boycott initially sought only to obtain the pattern of seating segregation in use in Mobile; the Albany movement was inaugurated simply in an effort to compel the city's bus and train stations to abide by the Interstate Commerce Commission's nondiscrimination order, issued in response to the Freedom Rides; the Birmingham demonstrations had as their goal just the desegregation of the lunch counters in the five downtown department and five-and-ten-cent stores; the Dallas County Voters League asked merely for an evenhanded administration of the state's literacy standard for registration, not its elimination. It is not that blacks in these cities would not ideally have wished for more. It is that even the belief that this much was attainable was itself a momentous achievement – an achievement that may not be presumed, but instead requires an explanation.

[. . .]

Part of the answer, of course, is that the South in the decades after World War II was caught up in an immense economic transformation, one that brought new prosperity and new opportunities and institutions to black communities as well as – if on a rather more modest scale than – white. Viewed from this long-term perspective, the civil rights movement was unquestionably a revolution of rising expectations; blacks were able to believe that reality could change for them because it actually was changing, and very rapidly too, throughout these years. But again, this observation, however accurate, is no less true for towns in which direct-action campaigns did not develop than for those in which they did. Another part of the answer is that integration in other places, once it occurred, proved that it was possible; there is no doubt, for instance, that Fred Shuttlesworth was moved to seek the integration of Birmingham's buses because of the successful integration of the buses in Montgomery. But no such answer can be fundamental, because in that case it would obviously be circular. And probably of even greater significance than the logical objection is the historical one: as a matter of fact, an achievement by blacks in any one town was ordinarily taken up by blacks in other towns, if at all, only very slowly, haltingly, and with enormous hesitation and difficulty.

[. . .]

In sum, then, if we are to understand why specific towns developed direct-action movements when others that were apparently similarly situated did not, our explanation must attend to local perceptions, assumptions, and interests. Something in one city must have given a crucial number of blacks there a sense that blacks elsewhere did not share, of the immediate malleability of their world. That something, I argue, was the structures of municipal politics.

[. . .]

Let me begin with a simple statement of the causes of the three direct-action movements, as I understand them. In Montgomery, the disintegration of the Gunter machine after World War II in response to the rising political consciousness of lower middle-class whites in the eastern precincts, the election of the stridently anti-machine east Montgomerian Dave Birmingham with black support in 1953, Commissioner Birmingham's hiring of black policemen, and his resultant defeat in the racially charged city election of 1955 form the essential background to the decision of black leaders to call for a boycott of the buses following the arrest of Rosa Parks. In Birmingham, the increasing doubts among business progressives after World War II about the very significant economic and social costs of the stable municipal political order that the business community had itself played a principal role in putting in place in 1937 culminated, after the Freedom Rider riot of May 1961 and the decision to close the city's parks and playgrounds at the end of that year, in a direct assault on the city commission form of government. The business progressives' attack on the city commission led to interracial contacts that exacerbated the deep rivalries between black activist and moderate leaders and triggered the specific events that produced the demonstrations of 1963. In Selma, the dominance of the Burns–Heinz machine and the success of the White Citizens' Council in discouraging any divisions among whites were both challenged in the fall of 1962 by the creation of the Committee of 100 Plus and its attempt to gain control of the board of the chamber of commerce. The insurgent business progressives carried their campaign into politics in 1964, when they united behind the candidacy of Joe Smitherman to defeat Mayor Heinz. In the meantime, the emerging division among prominent whites had already encouraged Edwin Moss and his allies in the Dallas County Improvement Association to seek in August 1963 to use the Retail Merchants Association to outflank Heinz's adamant refusal to consider alterations in the status quo. And the willingness of the new Smitherman administration to discuss racial reform so emboldened black leaders that their impressive courage and enthusiasm was able to convince the SCLC to agree to assist them in renewing voter registration demonstrations.

[. . .]

It is precisely for this reason that the handful of black leaders in the three cities whose experiences and personality permitted them to some degree, at least, to transcend these limits and to envision alternatives not discernible in the imaginations of their fellow townsfolk – Edgar D. Nixon and Jo Ann Robinson in Montgomery, Fred L. Shuttlesworth in Birmingham, and S. William and Amelia P. Boynton in Selma – are such striking figures. But however remarkable these men and women and the few other leaders like them may have been, if circumstances had not created the union of a substantial part of the black citizenry behind their views, their insights by themselves could have had no social consequences. The ability of a tiny number of outstanding residents at a given time to see beyond the limitations imposed by local conditions therefore requires less explanation from history than does the infinitely rarer capacity of thousands not so gifted suddenly to find the impulse to use such perceptions. It is to this latter problem that our observations are intended to speak. An authentic alteration in what had long seemed the fixed structure of local political power – because such an alteration necessarily drew into question also the deeper, and apparently natural, assumptions that had been founded upon that structure – therefore had liberating implications far beyond the ordinary bounds of politics.

[. . .]

In the earlier period [1955–65], the principal figure in the knitting together of what we have called the national and the local understandings of the movements had, of course, been Martin Luther King. The conjunction of the national and local was no mere strategy for him; it was an ardent faith. In fact, it had been precisely his ability to see the connection between the immediate frustration at authorities' refusal to spell out the bus company's seating requirements and the resultant arrest of Rosa Parks on the one hand, and the general claims of justice and democracy on the other, and to express that connection so powerfully, that had quickly elevated him beyond the other boycott leaders in Montgomery to such unchallenged preeminence. He had displayed that ability from the very outset. At the initial mass meeting on the night of the boycott's first day, he had insisted, "Now the press would have us believe that [Mrs. Parks] refused to leave a reserved section . . . [B]ut I want you to know this evening that there is no reserved section . . . I think I speak with legal authority behind me that the law, the ordinance, the city ordinance has never been totally clarified." And he had added, "We are not afraid of what we are doing, because we are doing it within the law . . . When labor all over this nation came to see that it would be trampled over by capitalistic power, it was nothing wrong with labor getting together and organizing and protesting for its rights . . . Not only are we using the tools of persuasion, but we've come to see that we've got to use the tools of coercion. Not only is this thing a process of education, but it is also a process of legislation." However, he had also thundered, "If we are wrong, the Supreme Court of this nation is wrong. If we are wrong, the Constitution of the United States is wrong. If we are wrong, God Almighty is wrong . . . If we are wrong, justice is a lie . . . We, the disinherited of this land, we who have been oppressed so long, are tired of going through the long night of captivity. And now we are reaching out for the daybreak of freedom and justice and equality."

The disposition King evidenced in this, his very first movement speech, to identify the particular and the political with the emphatically moral and eternal would be characteristic of his conception of all his other movement activities for the remainder of his life. It would fundamentally shape the way that many other Americans, of all races, would understand the movement. And it would prove crucial, as we have said, to making the local direct-action campaigns components of a national crusade. Exactly because King so readily and so honestly transmuted questions of power into questions of morality, he succeeded from the beginning in permitting the local campaigns to speak to a broader audience. Observers who came to Montgomery virtually uniformly concluded that King, much more profoundly than most of his colleagues, understood the boycott's larger significance. In fact, it was simply that King, more often than his colleagues, tended to talk about the boycott in terms of fundamental principles rather than in terms of its specific origins and goals. And this pattern of thought and expression proved entirely typical of him in his future battles. He therefore continually depicted the local campaigns in just the form in which observers elsewhere also conceived them. It is almost certainly for that reason that Americans so generally came to regard King – far more than other, equally important national black leaders such as Roy Wilkins, Thurgood Marshall, James Farmer, Whitney Young, or John Lewis; and infinitely more than the local leaders who were arguably the movement's heart and soul, such as C. Kenzie Steele, Fred Shuttlesworth, Dr. William G. Anderson, Amelia Boynton, Amzie Moore, or Aaron Henry – as the great expositor of the movement's principles.

[. . .]

Nevertheless, it is also clear that he [King] profoundly misjudged the events of which he was a part. For the immediate cause of black rights, it is probably a good thing that he did so, since he was therefore able in deepest sincerity to clothe the direct-action campaigns with ennobling constitutional and moral ideals. But in the longer term, his expectation that he and his followers could by their efforts initiate the beloved community could only condemn his enterprise forever to appear to have fallen short of its promise. The truth is otherwise; direct action conceived in terms of its local goals succeeded in placing the contests of blacks and whites on an immeasurably more equitable footing. And yet it is a fact that the political leaders who too often have most benefited from this achievement are the racial polarizers whose community power depends upon the exploitation of racial antagonisms, because it is these leaders who have founded their appeals upon social realities rather than upon dreams of fraternity. It is an ironic outcome indeed, but one very likely dictated by the nature of community itself.

On the other hand, the realism of the racial polarizers need not therefore be regarded as meritorious, and certainly not as noble. Nobility often – perhaps more often than not – lies precisely in the refusal to admit reality. The quest for harmony must perhaps forever be doomed by the structure of community to no greater than partial success.

ༀ ༀ ༀ

Manfred Berg

"The Ticket to Freedom"†

In its 1954 decision *Brown v. Board of Education of Topeka, Kansas*, the U.S. Supreme Court at long last repudiated the "separate but equal" doctrine in the field of public education. Although *Brown* sparked a furious backlash among the white South and did not bring about the fast desegregation of southern schools, the leaders of the National Association for the Advancement of Colored People (NAACP) nevertheless felt that their faith in legal action had finally been vindicated.

[. . .]

[Executive Secretary Ray] Wilkins knew quite well, however, that there was little reason for complacency. In particular, he worried that the association was in danger of losing touch with the aspiring younger generation of blacks.

[. . .]

The challenge was both strategic and organizational. With the Montgomery, Alabama, bus boycott of 1955–56, southern blacks revived the concept of nonviolent direct action and successfully challenged racial segregation head-on rather than in the courtrooms. Moreover, the Montgomery boycott propelled Martin Luther King Jr., a young Baptist minister from Atlanta with a charismatic personality and a gift for mesmerizing oratory, to national prominence. In early 1957, King and his followers formed the Southern Christian Leadership Conference (SCLC) in order to coordinate nonviolent protest in the South. And the SCLC did not remain the only new civil rights group. Following the spontaneous sit-in movement of early 1960, southern black students, with the help of former NAACP director of branches Ella Baker, organized the Student Nonviolent Coordinating Committee (SNCC), pronounced "SNICK." A year later, the Congress of Racial Equality (CORE), a pacifist civil rights group that had been founded in Chicago during the

†Manfred Berg, *"The Ticket to Freedom": The NAACP and the Struggle for Black Political Integration* (Gainesville: University Press of Florida, 2005), pp. 166–75, 177, 253–6.

Second World War but become largely defunct in the 1950s, launched its campaign of "freedom rides" throughout the South in order to test a recent Supreme Court ruling banning racial segregation in interstate travel.

Hence, by the early 1960s the NAACP faced a paradoxical situation: black civil rights activism was soaring, but the association seemed to be falling into the rearguard of the movement and its methods began looking outdated.

[. . .]

The attitude of the NAACP leadership toward the SCLC, SNCC, and CORE . . . was shaped by a combination of paternalism and suspicion that sometimes bordered on outright hostility. Although the SCLC had decided not to form a large organizational structure and saw itself as an umbrella group for various local initiatives, the NAACP feared that the ministers planned to fill the void that had been opened up by the ban against the association in several southern states following the *Brown* ruling.

[. . .]

NAACP activists . . . had no use for unsolicited help and were determined to protect their turf. John Brooks, the tireless registration worker, looked with utter disdain at the fledgling SCLC: "They hold emotional mass and prayer meetings, take up money and do nothing on the civil rights front," he wrote in one of his reports. According to Brooks, the NAACP continued to enjoy strong support among southern blacks and was in no danger of being superseded by a bunch of preachers. Roy Wilkins also did not conceal his mistrust. Martin Luther King Jr. himself might not harbor the idea of replacing the association, he wrote to Dr. Benjamin Mays of Morehouse College, one of King's closest advisers, "yet the very items that he announces are traditional NAACP items and it is natural that many of his followers would assume not that he is attempting to help the NAACP or supplement its efforts, but that he is supplanting the organization."

[. . .]

In addition to the inevitable organizational competition, the personal rivalry between Martin Luther King Jr. and Roy Wilkins, although never openly admitted, complicated matters between the NAACP and the SCLC. In public, the two leaders went out of their way to demonstrate an amicable relationship.

[. . .]

In fact, the relationship between King and Wilkins was far from friendly and deteriorated in subsequent years. The NAACP leader, despite his sober demeanor, was no stranger to personal vanity, and he watched with growing disenchantment as the upstart preacher almost thirty years his junior outshone him as America's most prominent spokesman for civil rights.

[. . .]

While Roy Wilkins saw his seniority challenged by King, the generational conflict within the civil rights movement was even more pronounced in the relations between the NAACP leadership and the young activists of SNCC, many of whom were barely past their twentieth birthday. When the SNCC founders publicly criticized the association for its alleged legalism at their kick-off conference in April 1960, Wilkins fumed at the "doctrinaires" and "upstarts" who were still "little boys" when "the NAACP was battling tooth and toenail . . . to knock out Jim Crow." Subsequently, the NAACP patriarch, born in 1901, kept on complaining about the "ignorance" and "arrogance of youth" who had "absolutely no knowledge of anything prior to February 1, 1960" – the day the sit-in movement began in Greensboro, North Carolina.

[. . .]

As with the SCLC, the NAACP officials did not see any good reason for creating a new organization. Its moderate and constructive element might as well join the association, while the rest were dismissed as noisy troublemakers. The NAACP's attitude toward CORE was similar[ ]

[. . .]

In terms of membership and organizational strength, none of the three new civil rights groups posed a serious threat to the association . . . The crucial reason, however, why the NAACP never ceased to regard the smaller groups as rivals rather than allies was their reliance on nonviolent direct action. This strategy did not require many organizational resources but could be implemented by a small band of dedicated activists. Shrewdly staged confrontations between peaceful protesters and brutal racists involved spectacular drama and threatened to steal the public eye away from the legal and political action preferred by the association. When CORE launched its "freedom rides" in the spring of 1961, the NAACP staff at first dismissed the action as a publicity stunt to boost the group's fund-raising efforts.

This derision was patently unfair because the interracial freedom riders acted out of a deep moral commitment and stoically suffered brutal abuse by white mobs in the Deep South. The practitioners of nonviolent direct action were inspired by the Sermon on the Mount and by the role model of Mohandas Gandhi, whose nonviolent struggle against British colonial rule had helped bring about independence for India. The imperative to love one's enemies perhaps was proclaimed most emphatically at SNCC's founding conference in April 1960: "Love is the central motif of nonviolence . . . Such love goes to the extreme: it remains loving and forgiving even in the midst of hostility. It matches the capacity of evil to inflict suffering with an even more enduring capacity to absorb evil, all the while persisting in love." The central message was that in the end nonviolent action would lead to the liberation of both the oppressed and the oppressors.

[. . .]

[N]onviolence was also a shrewd strategy to claim legitimacy for the civil rights movement. Incidents of black counterviolence against racist assaults, as it flared up during the SCLC's 1963 desegregation campaign in Birmingham, Alabama, jeopardized the movement's moral aura and had to be contained at all costs. Moreover, if conservative critics charged the civil rights movement with provoking violence, they were not entirely mistaken. Violent reactions to nonviolent protests were an integral part of the protesters' strategy to put pressure on the federal government and the American public at large.

[. . .]

[N]onviolent direct action was no invention of the 1960s but had a long history reaching back into the antebellum period. However, according to August Meier and Elliott Rudwick, there was no continuous tradition or ideology of nonviolent protest among African Americans, which led every new generation of activists to believe that they had discovered an entirely new strategy. Once again the historical context of black protest had changed dramatically when the struggle entered into a new phase during the 1960s. Most importantly, the United States claimed to be the champion of international democracy, while at the same time American society was undergoing a process of rapid modernization. Perhaps no other single factor was more important for the civil rights movement than the sweeping advance of television. In 1950, less than two hundred thousand households in the United States had a television set, but ten years later the new medium had been introduced into 90 percent of all American homes. While it remains difficult to gauge the impact of television on diverse audiences, the fact that images of hateful racist mobs and frenzied police descending on peaceful black demonstrators were broadcast nationwide and internationally can hardly be overestimated. President John F. Kennedy had a point when he told civil rights leaders not to "be too hard on Bull Connor," Birmingham's irascible police commissioner, since he had "probably done more for civil rights than any one else." Where local authorities refrained from excessive violence against civil rights protesters, as in the 1962 desegregation campaign by SNCC and the SCLC in Albany, Georgia, the media coverage remained low profile and the movement scored few tangible results.

[. . .]

[T]he line between direct action and voter registration often became blurred because it did not matter much to violent racists whether African Americans challenged white supremacy at a "whites only" lunch counter or by trying to register and vote. Its adherents also did not advocate nonviolent direct action as an alternative to voter registration. At least until the mid-1960s, the voting rights rhetoric espoused by the SCLC, SNCC, and CORE was not different from the NAACP's. For Martin Luther King the suffrage was the "Civil Right No. 1," and the SCLC placed voter registration, not direct action, at the core of its fund-raising efforts. SNCC even chose the catchy slogan "One Man – One Vote" for its letterhead.

[. . .]

However, a closer look reveals significant conceptual differences between the NAACP and its new allies with regard to the vote. The advocates of direct action viewed the ballot not primarily in instrumental terms but focused on voting as a way to build a collective identity. "We register both to secure better community services and to assert our own essential dignity," James Farmer said, describing the goals of CORE's voter education program. Moreover, they were not willing to accept that voter registration should enjoy precedence over direct action, as the NAACP argued. In the 1964 presidential campaign, CORE joined in an all-out registration effort to mobilize black voters in order to defeat Senator Barry Goldwater, the ultraconservative Republican presidential candidate, but refused to obey a temporary halt of demonstrations demanded by the association's leadership.

Finally, even if the adherents of nonviolent action vowed that they did not wish to jettison the NAACP's time-honored ways altogether, they did not conceal their dissatisfaction with the association's legalism and incrementalism.

[. . .]

In a television interview of late 1960, King praised the impatience and courage of the sit-in demonstrators in clear-cut words that were unmistakably addressed to the NAACP: "They require action, and they do not merely wait and deal with a century of litigation, and they do not involve themselves in endless debates, but we see here real action, working to bring about the realization of the ideals and principles of democracy."

Such criticism did not sit well with NAACP officials, who pointed out that the association had never confined its activities to the courtroom and political lobbying.

[. . .]

Nevertheless, spending time in a southern jail had become a badge of honor that the NAACP leadership would not do without. In June 1963, Roy Wilkins went to Jackson, Mississippi, to picket the city's Woolworth department store. Together with local NAACP activists Medgar Evers and Helen Wilcher, the executive secretary was promptly arrested and charged with "conspiring to prohibit free trade and commerce," but soon released on a $1,000 cash bond. With Martin Luther King's Birmingham campaign going on at the same time, one is tempted to dismiss this action as a publicity stunt. This would not be fair, however, as the Jackson NAACP youth chapter had been waging a boycott against the city's downtown merchants since late 1962, combined with picketing and demonstrations to desegregate the public accommodations in the state capital. By May, the campaign was stepped up, resulting in violent assaults by white mobs, mass arrests of black proteers, and a firebomb thrown at Medgar Evers's home. The racist violence reached its horrifying peak on June 11, 1963, when the NAACP field secretary was murdered in his front yard by a sniper. In the heat of the Jackson campaign, Roy Wilkins had employed stark rhetoric to put Mississippi authorities on the spot. The oppression of blacks in the Magnolia state, he asserted, was "an American phase of Hitlerism" leaving only "the establishment of the ovens to complete the picture of Nazi terror." At the same time, however, the NAACP leadership worked to de-escalate the situation by toning down demonstrations and direct action. The campaign had already cost $50,000 in bond money and legal fees. As a committee of NAACP officials had decided the year before, the association sought "success, by negotiation if possible, but demonstrations, if necessary.

[. . .]

[F]rom a long-term perspective we have to ask whether the association's unwavering belief in the ballot and the political process turned out to be justified. To begin with, it is obvious that laws to abolish segregation and other forms of racial discrimination did not come as a direct consequence of black electoral power, as the NAACP had preached for decades. Desegregation was primarily brought about by a series of legal victories, beginning in the 1930s, and by the dramatic mass protests of the civil rights movement. It was nonviolent direct action, more than anything else, that forced the U.S. Congress to enact the Civil Rights Act of 1964 and the Voting Rights Act of 1965, two laws that most Americans considered to be radical departures from the traditional federal–state relationship of the American political system.

Its many accomplishments in the struggle for the ballot notwithstanding, the great breakthrough for which the NAACP continued to hope took painfully long to occur. The ban on the grandfather clause, the end of the white primary, the decline of the poll tax, and the untiring registration work of the association and other civil rights groups all weakened but could not destroy the political system of white supremacy in the South. In the North, the association's ritualistic balance-of-power rhetoric did not have much of an impact on politicians hostile to black interests. Indeed, very few of them could be successfully punished at the polls. To be sure, the growth of the black electorate in the North made the liberal wing of the Democratic Party more responsive to African American voters, but even when they provided the crucial margins for Harry Truman and John F. Kennedy to win the White House, their rewards were rather meager. As long as the southerners held a de facto veto power in the U.S. Senate, all meaningful federal civil rights legislation was doomed. Only when the civil rights movement staged a major national crisis in the early 1960s did this situation change.

Although the ballot was no magical political weapon, the NAACP's struggle for the right to vote had many important long-term consequences. During the first half of the twentieth century, white supremacy was deeply entrenched in the South and enjoyed much support in the rest of the nation as well. That the NAACP – and many other organizations and individuals – firmly asserted and defended the African American claim to first-class citizenship and democratic participation against this hegemonic culture of racism can hardly be overstated, even though the concrete results were often wanting. Its interracial character and integrationist creed allowed the association to reach sympathetic white audiences and to confront white Americans with the blatant contradiction between their self-congratulatory celebration of democracy and the ugly reality of racism.

Equally important were the NAACP's incessant efforts for the political education and mobilization of African Americans. Voter registration, in particular, became a major field of action for the association and its local branches. No other organization had a greater part in increasing black registration in the South from a minuscule 150,000 in 1940 to more than 1.2 million in 1952. This groundwork set the stage for the growing politicization of southern blacks in the late 1950s and early 1960s, when the civil rights movement launched its crucial assault on Jim Crow. Even during the nonviolent action phase of the civil rights struggle the vote remained the movement's second strategic pillar. That many activists were willing to risk life and limb in working for first-class citizenship is impressive testimony to their belief in the transformative power of the ballot. At the same time, the demand for the franchise communicated a "constructive" message to the white majority: Black reenfranchisement held the promise of a peaceful and orderly solution to the race issue.

[. . .]

The hopes for a swift pacification of the racial conflict through civil rights reforms evaporated in the riotous "long hot summers" of the late 1960s. Nevertheless, desegregation and the protection of the right to vote led to profound changes in the political and social status of African Americans in the South and in the rest of the United States. Most obviously, the political system of white supremacy that had prevailed in the South for almost a hundred years began to fade away, even though attempts to prevent blacks from registering and voting did not cease immediately. Often grudgingly, white southerners learned to accept the end of public segregation and to respect the right of their black fellow citizens to political participation. Racial demagoguery, the lifeblood of southern politics for many decades, was no longer a dominant discourse. The region saw the rise of moderate progressives, such as Georgian Jimmy Carter, who promised a better life for all citizens in a truly

New South of prosperity and opportunity. When Carter ran for president of the United States in 1976, the unanimous support of black voters in the South pushed him over the top in ten of the eleven states of the former Confederacy. After a close lead in Mississippi eventually sealed Carter's victory, civil rights leader Andrew Young jubilated: "The hands that picked the cotton finally picked the president."

In the seven southern states covered by the 1965 Voting Rights Act, black registration increased from 31.4 percent in 1964 to 57.7 percent in 1982; in Mississippi it went up from 6.7 percent to 75.8 percent. This not only meant that white politicians were actively seeking black support, but also that African Americans could be elected to public office, often for the first time in the twentieth century. In many places these victories built on the registration work of the NAACP, as, for example, when the first African American was elected to the Virginia legislature in 1967. These "firsts" quickly added up to sizeable numbers, although from a very low baseline. In 1964, the total number of black elected officials in the entire South had been lower than 25, but by 1970 it had increased to roughly 700; over the next decade it grew to 3,140 in 1982. With 426 elected black officeholders, Mississippi led all other states of the Union. Moreover, beginning with Maynard Jackson's election as mayor of Atlanta in 1973, a good number of the major southern cities elected black politicians to their top executive post, including New Orleans, Birmingham, Charlotte, North Carolina, and Richmond, Virginia. As voters and as candidates, African Americans have become widely accepted actors in southern politics.

ഔ ഔ ഔ

Belinda Robnett

How Long? How Long?[†]

While the civil rights movement gained momentum in the upper South, it became increasingly clear that this heightened movement activity did not extend to smaller cities and isolated pockets of the rural South. Following the 1955 Montgomery bus boycott civil rights movement organizations – primarily the National Association for the Advancement of Colored People (NAACP) and the Congress of Racial Equality (CORE) – targeted southern cities for direct action – that is, sit-ins and organized protests. The Freedom Rides, precipitated by CORE, resulted in several successes in the upper South. In the Deep South, this challenge to segregation in interstate travel resulted in bloodshed and left the racist order intact. Strategies were needed to link movement organizations to these otherwise isolated areas. Bridge leaders would fill this need.

[†]Belinda Robnett, *How Long? How Long? African-American Women in the Struggle for Civil Rights* (New York: Oxford University Press, 1997), pp. 140–1, 143–8, 153, 155–6.

What became increasingly clear was the need to penetrate the very core of these southern communities. Mobilization of Black populations in the deep pockets of the rural south and in smaller cities had been weak, yet their participation was critical for the demise of the powerful and ruthless southern order. Civil rights organizations, especially CORE, the Southern Christian Leadership Conference (SCLC), and Student Nonviolent Coordinating Committee (SNCC), sought to mobilize these areas, but they were well aware of the dangers such tactics posed for both organizers and community members.

[. . .]

The mobilization of smaller communities was more difficult in many ways than previous efforts in larger cities. Direct-action efforts in the latter, while certainly dangerous, were at least visible to the media. Violent reprisals in rural areas of the South were less likely to receive such attention. Moreover, in rural areas and in small towns, outsiders were more visible and the contacts between movement organizations more cumbersome and tenuous. Rural people tended not to trust outsiders and many wanted no part in "stirrin' up trouble." Mobilization of these sectors required recruitment tactics that built specifically upon trust and interpersonal community ties. Most rural people, no matter how inspired by the charisma of movement leaders or how impressed by an organization's financial resources, would not risk their lives without powerful motivation.

[. . .]

While . . . student volunteers, ministers, and movement halfway houses provided many resources for rural and small-town mobilization, that mobilization could not have succeeded without the efforts of indigenous bridge leaders, who facilitated the connection between these communities and movement organizations. Even Bob Moses, the SNCC leader who has been credited with initiating SNCC's movement into the deepest pockets of the South, relied on the contacts Ella Baker had cultivated while traveling as the NAACP's director of chapters.

[. . .]

SNCC workers would enter a community and contact local, indigenous leaders, often one or more women or men, and sometimes a minister as well.

[. . .]

These men and women had been local leaders long before the arrival of SNCC or CORE activists. Moreover, the strategy of community and secondary bridge leaders to bypass the formal local leadership in lieu of their assistance or resistance and instead to seek support from informal local leaders began to pay off. Unita Blackwell illustrates this as she describes the beginning of her involvement.

How I became an organizer was that one day I was out there trying to get registered to vote myself. And I spoke up and guess I was spotted as one of the potential leaders by [John] Lewis . . . I could get up and stand in a church and tell people that nothing from nothing leaves nothing, and we're going to all have to get up and try to do something here by ourselves because none of us have anything.

Absorption into SNCC provided local women with considerable support and direction, strengthening the organization's connection to the local community at the same time. That such women benefited from outside tactical support – a common enough practice among field commanders – should not be confused with deference. These women were the critical links, mobilizing the massive community support it took to effect change, and they would become movement bridge leaders in their own right.

[. . .]

Women not only secured meeting places but provided outsiders with insights into the interworkings of the local community. In a report from the headquarters of Mrs. Annie Raines in Lee County, Georgia, an unidentified worker writes:

Mama Dolly [Mrs. Raines] is definitely a leader in this community and looked up to by the Negroes here. She has always remained dignified and a woman of high principal and sagacity. She has instincts about the "movement" and strategy which has not as yet proved wrong. In her own quiet way she trys to force her people to realize that "a new day's a come!" and for them to take action and take a stand. She talks with everyone and in her own way tries to educate and lift them to new heights. Her understanding of situations is unusual and her perception seldom equalled.

[. . .]

This independence is discussed by Victoria Gray, who considered herself a "local person": "I worked with every organization that was working in the state." She considered herself to be an interpreter between the old and the young. Many older people in the community believed in the local media, though they were "just distorting every thing." Negative media appraisals of the movement kept these people afraid to trust movement organizers. Victoria Gray convinced them that the organizers were the same "young people as your daughters and sons." In this way she could encourage them to trust the workers, and convince them to register to vote.

[. . .]

These women were an inspiration to SNCC workers as well as to the community. Charles McLaurin, a SNCC worker wrote:

> In 1962, I was in Ruleville to do voter registration work or to get Negroes to go to the courthouse to register to vote. I lived with a Negro man and his wife who for all of their family and lives had lived and worked on the plantation. The Negroes had already made attempts to register and the whites was upset. The police had started to harass the Negroes to keep them from trying to register to vote. Six brave ladies had taken it upon themselves to go to the courthouse to register and now they was like sore thumbs (meaning they were out there). These six ladies was the start of a fire that is still burning one year later.

[. . .]

Those who provided local support for movement workers incurred terrible physical and economic risk to themselves and their loved ones. Annelle Ponder recalls that "many of them have experienced reprisals and intimidations either personally or through their families, friends, or students." These reprisals took the form of jailings, beatings, and loss of jobs for themselves and/or their loved ones.

[. . .]

Registering to vote, housing SNCC workers, or becoming involved in any way with civil rights activities meant risking one's life. Even young children who became involved in protest activities were beaten and arrested . . . Economic reprisals were also not unusual. Peter Cummings, a SNCC worker, writes:

> Mrs. Reaves was a teacher at Old Salem High School until she lost her job this spring due to her civil rights activities. She was the only teacher in the school with an M.A. (from the U[niversity] of Chicago).

[. . .]

These indigenous leaders who risked their lives and the lives of their family members acted as crucial bridges between movement organizations and members of their respective communities. Without their day-to-day mobilization work and the trust that grew from their methods of operation, deeply frightened rural people could not have risked their lives. Although SNCC community and secondary bridge leaders provided the indigenous leadership with the tools to transfer their prefigurative politics to movement activism, they did not have the community connections and local know-how to motivate the rural masses to act. And in many cases, ministers as formal local leaders did not provide the leadership necessary to inspire their congregations or to assist the organizations' activists. The bridge between community and secondary leaders and indigenous leaders, the bridge between the latter and the rural community, and the preexisting community ties and networks nurtured by bridge leaders facilitated connections between rural life in the Deep South and the ideals of movement organizations.

Equally important is the fact that people in rural communities, in the face of extreme repression and violence, were able to overcome their fears through individual acts of courage . . . It was the cumulative efforts of these emotionally charged, small but powerful, spontaneous, and sometimes planned responses that gave momentum to the movement. Local-level mobilization was the base upon which the civil rights movement rested, and it was no less important to the success of the movement than were the primary and secondary formal organizations and their formal leaders.

15

Clive Webb

THE SOUTH TODAY

Where has the South been heading during the late twentieth and early twentieth-first centuries, and where does it stand today? If some stretches of southern history lend themselves to neat labels (the "Antebellum era," the "Civil Rights era," and so forth), the period since the 1960s is not so readily classified. It may be that we are simply too close to this era (indeed, still within it) to discern its defining issues; perhaps a clear appraisal must await the kind of distance available only to later generations.

Be that as it may, what presently stands out about the newest of New Souths is not so much a central theme as a kaleidoscope of trends, alternately economic and cultural, demographic and political. Out of a swirl of disparate developments – say, the continued expansion of the urban "Sunbelt," or the rising political influence of southern Baptists, or the region's growing integration into the global economy – who is to say which best captures the age? Reckoning what such developments signify, how they interrelate, and what in the end they all add up to – these are the challenges awaiting current and future students of the contemporary South. As they go about this task, historians are bound to seek a certain coherence by framing these trends within the classic tensions – continuity versus discontinuity, tradition versus modernity, regional distinctiveness versus American-ness – that have defined the region throughout its history.

The opening essay by Clive Webb reconfirms both the diversity of topics and themes in recent southern history that vie for our attention and their connection to those dualities so familiar to the southern past. Illustrating these points are the selections he has chosen for this chapter, exploring in turn: the ongoing convergence of southern and national cultures; the continuing relevance of historical representation to popular consciousness; the wellsprings of southern social conservatism; and, the swelling of Hispanic immigration during the 1980s and 1990s. Brought together, these readings comprise what might be called an early draft of the history of the late twentieth- and early twenty-first-century South. Those seeking a final, definitive treatment may have to wait some time.

Clive Webb is Reader in North American History at the University of Sussex. His research has focused on the history of race and ethnic relations in the United States, the civil rights movement, and racial violence. His published books include: *Fight against Fear: Southern Jews and Black Civil Rights* (2001); *Race in the American South: From Slavery to Civil Rights* (with David Brown, 2007); and *Rabble Rousers: The American Far Right in the Civil Rights Era* (2010). He is also editor of *Massive Resistance: Southern Opposition to the Second Reconstruction* (2005).

Over the last half century, no region of the United States has undergone greater transformation than the South. To be sure, its tortured and often violent history of racial, economic, and political inequality has a residual influence on the popular image of the region. Still, in the opening years of the twenty-first century the South boasts a degree of stability and prosperity that has affected its people not only materially but also temperamentally, their traditional defensiveness having been turned into a more optimistic outlook.

Change has nonetheless had an ambiguous impact on the region. Academic debate about the contemporary South has turned on a series of questions about these changes. How broadly have southerners shared in the affluence generated by economic modernization; or, put another way, how far have these advances gone in overcoming the old cleavages between the haves and have-nots? To what extent does racial inequality continue to shape, and reflect, material disparities in the region? Do such problems as urban squalor and environmental spoliation demonstrate that material growth has diminished as much as improved southern life? And what of the South's distinctive identity? To what degree does – or for that matter *should* – the region retain those cultural practices and traditions that set it apart from the rest of the nation?

Historically, the issue that has most set the South apart from the rest of the United States was race. Here, too, the contemporary situation is complicated and eludes simple conclusions. Although the civil rights movement eliminated legal segregation, the legacies of Jim Crow endure in myriad ways – most conspicuously perhaps in the realm of political debate. While racially charged disputes demonstrate the persistence of historical tensions between blacks and whites, new ethnic fault lines have also opened up, as thousands of Latino immigrants settle in the region. This demographic change shows how the familiar dialectic of continuity and change continues to characterize life in the South today.

For generations, the rest of the nation regarded the South as blighted by economic backwardness and poverty. Although the region had abundant natural resources, its people were the poorest in the nation. In 1938, President Franklin D. Roosevelt identified the South as "the Nation's No.1 economic problem." Since the Second World War, Dixie has nonetheless experienced an economic renaissance. The second half of the twentieth century saw the vision of a New South outlined decades earlier by *Atlanta Constitution* editor Henry W. Grady finally come closer to reality. With the exception of the West, the South has undergone faster growth and greater diversification than any other region.

The modernization of commercial agriculture has transformed the rural economy, displacing the tenant farmers and sharecroppers who once dominated the landscape. During the 1960s alone, declining opportunities contributed to a 50 percent fall in the farming population, while the urban centers of the newly dubbed "Sunbelt" boomed.

The emergence of the Sunbelt is attributable to a number of factors. First, the South benefited substantially from federal defense spending, pulling in a disproportionate number of new military bases and industrial plants during both the Second World War and the Cold War. As political commentator Dick Morris observed, the Pentagon had become "A Five-Sided Building That Faces South."[1] Interstate highway construction and urban redevelopment programs further facilitated infrastructural advances. For their part, state and local governments offered numerous incentives to northern investors, including low corporate tax rates, anti-union laws, and environmental loopholes. Through improved municipal services and public relations, civic and business leaders endeavored to counter the negative images that had long deterred northern investment in their communities. The spread of air conditioning also made the region more inviting to northerners otherwise repelled by its sweltering summer climate. By the mid-1970s – with the Sunbelt waxing and the industrial economies of the Northeast and Midwest on the wane – per capita income levels in the South had drawn even with the rest of the country. Its population was also on the rise, owing largely to an influx of northerners, many of them managers or skilled workers, frustrated by declining opportunities in their native region.

Urban expansion has nonetheless seen the coming of new social problems, as southern cities – like their counterparts in other areas of the country – confront environmental damage, congestion, and rising crime. The harsher realities of urban life were starkly exposed when Hurricane Katrina hit the Gulf Coast in August 2005. The storm damage brought to light the depth and persistence of black poverty. Three decades of industrial decline and white flight to the suburbs have created a black underclass trapped within decaying inner-city neighborhoods. The disaster also demonstrated how blacks still often lack political representation. With little or no voice in the recovery program,

African Americans were powerless to withstand proposals that their neighbor-hoods be bulldozed rather than rebuilt.

No less significant than economic change has been the political transforma-tion of the postwar South. The disfranchisement of African Americans and failure of the Populist challenge in the late nineteenth century had heralded an era of Democratic party hegemony in the South. The 1950s, however, saw the start of a process of electoral realignment in the South, as white voters disaf-fected with the civil rights policies of the national Democratic party switched their support to the Republicans. White southern estrangement from the Democrats intensified during the late 1960s. The Republicans implemented what became known as the "southern strategy" to exploit the anger and alien-ation of white southerners, in language laden with racial undertones. By the 1980s, this strategy had made the Republican party the predominant electoral force in the region.

What brought about this sea change of southern politics? Historians have long attributed the resurgence of Republicans in the region to their manipula-tion of white racial prejudice. (One oft-cited illustration of this tactic is the opening speech of Ronald Reagan's 1980 presidential campaign in which the candidate gave a staunch defense of states' rights; and in Philadelphia, Mississippi, no less – site of the 1964 murders of three voter registration workers.) Recent scholarship has nonetheless cast doubt on the significance of the southern strategy to Republican electoral success. Instead, they emphasize the importance of economic change to the growth of the New Right. Matthew Lassiter, for instance, highlights the response of southern whites to Republican policies of fiscal conservatism and limited federal involvement in local and state affairs. The manipulation of racial code words was not, concludes Lassiter, the chief factor behind the rise of southern Republicanism; rather, the growth of suburbs in the Sunbelt South created a racial and class barrier that insulated its inhabitants from the poorer and less privileged. Their desire to protect their social and economic status led them to oppose such "liberal" policies as busing. In this sense, the southern white middle class differed little from suburbanites elsewhere across the nation.[2]

In addressing the rise of southern Republicanism, the following selection by Joseph Crespino puts a further spin on this revisionist interpretation. While not disputing the role of racism, Crespino nonetheless asserts that the traditional emphasis on the "southern strategy" overlooks the influence of economic change on electoral politics. In recounting the struggle over tax exemptions for private educational institutions, Crespino complicates our understanding of southern white conservatism. Although these academies were almost exclusively white, those who supported their tax-exempt status did so not simply to preserve educational segregation but also to protect reli-gious freedom from government interference. To their way of thinking, these champions of private religious academies were seeking to safeguard traditional values from an aggressively liberal secular culture.

The transformation of southern politics is only one aspect of a broader process that has seen the region remolded in the image of the rest of the nation. This political, cultural, and economic convergence has raised debate over the extent to which the region retains (or for that matter *should* retain) its historically distinct identity. Although many of the changes to southern society have arguably been for the better, some critics contend that, as the region becomes absorbed into a blandly homogenized national consumer culture, it is in danger of surrendering even its more positive traditions. One of the first and most influential jeremiads on the decline of southern distinctiveness came from journalist John Egerton. In his 1974 book of the same name, an extract of which appears here, Egerton lamented what he described as "the Americanization of Dixie." Southern culture, he concluded, had become indistinguishable from that of New England, the Midwest, or the Pacific Coast. Southerners ate at the same fast food restaurants, shopped at the same chain stores, and watched the same movies and television shows as other Americans.

Measured in material terms, there was considerable merit in this diagnosis of southern regional identity. Culturally, however, there are numerous ways in which southerners are still set apart from their fellow Americans. Southerners retain their own cuisine, their obsession with certain sports, and a distinctive inflection when they speak.

Moreover, as many authors have observed, the South remains not only a physical but also a psychological entity. Southerners perceive that they are different from other Americans. Drawing on public opinion polls, sociologist John Shelton Reed produced a study in the 1970s that emphasized what he identified – in contrast to Egerton – as *The Enduring South*. According to Reed, southerners maintained a keen association with their region. This abiding sense of identity could no longer be laid to ignorance of other regional cultures. It is actually better-educated and more widely traveled southerners, Reed found, who tend to have a stronger sense of regional identification, since their broad exposure throws into sharper relief all that is distinctive about their own upbringings and attitudes.[3]

It is also important to recognize that cultural change has been a reciprocal process. National culture may have reshaped the South but the region has also redefined the attitudes and habits of the rest of the nation. Egerton acknowledges this dynamic by giving his book the subtitle, *The Southernization of America*. He did not, however, welcome this development, any more than he did the reverse. Noting, for example, the increasing national popularity of country music, he argued that uprooting this genre from its regional context had rendered meaningless its formerly resonant themes of poverty, loneliness, and religious faith. Whether or not one accepts this criticism, the spread not only of country music but also of religious fundamentalism and conservative political culture attests to the continuing influence of the South on national life. (A more optimistic perspective on this trend is conveyed in the title of Peter Applebome's 1996 book, *Dixie Rising: How the South is Shaping American Values, Politics, and Culture*.)[4]

Egerton also appreciated that the realignment of the South with the rest of the United States was in other ways a positive force. The civil rights movement, in particular, effected the most fundamental transformation of postwar southern society, the destruction of Jim Crow. Securing the full rights of citizenship has enabled African Americans in many respects to overcome discrimination and exclusion. As historian W. Fitzhugh Brundage observes, however, blacks have not always seen the impact of racial integration as being entirely beneficial. In the following selection, Brundage documents how the desegregation of the public school system led to the shutting down of African-American educational institutions, and resultant job losses for many teachers. Lost as well were their distinctive curricula, which had for decades been instrumental in promoting a sense of racial pride among African Americans. The ambiguous legacy of desegregation described by Brundage is reflected in the recent works of some black authors who wistfully reminisce about aspects of the pre-Civil Rights era. According to these writers, the color line imposed by whites – however offensive in its own right – fostered a profound feeling of solidarity and cultural identity among African Americans, a spirit largely dissipated in the wake of desegregation.

Still, the greater inclusion of southern blacks in public life has heightened recognition of their role in shaping the region. School and college curricula, museum exhibitions, and historical markers facilitate a more comprehensive understanding of the southern past, one that not only celebrates its triumphs but also acknowledges the brutal injustices of slavery and segregation. As Brundage shows, this process has not been without controversy. If the South is a state of mind, then a sense of history is one of the forces that shape that psychology. Historical revisionism inevitably challenges the self-perception of southern whites. One of the most potent illustrations of the contested nature of southern history is the contemporary debate on the Confederate battle flag. Defenders of the flag insist that it is not a symbol of white supremacy but rather one of Confederate valor during the Civil War – or of some gauzy spirit of regional "heritage." Critics counter that race is integral to the meaning of the flag, since slavery was the root cause of the sectional conflict. Within living memory, the flag also served as an emblem of massive resistance to the civil rights revolution. The racially polarizing impact of the debate was revealed in 2001 when Mississippi voters rejected a proposal for a new state flag shorn of Confederate symbols. While blacks overwhelmingly voted for the new flag, most whites wanted to preserve the old one. This racial divisiveness underlines one enduring aspect of southern distinctiveness. In no other region do disputes over the meaning of the past so profoundly influence contemporary public debate.

Examining relations between blacks and whites is not the only way to assess the shifting character of the contemporary South. One of the most noticeable changes to the region at the turn of the twenty-first century has been the influx of immigrants from Latin America and Asia. Historically, immigrants have made relatively little impression on the region. Although Jews can trace their southern roots back to the colonial era, they have never constituted more than a small fraction of the population. Immigrants such as the Irish who arrived during the antebellum era had a similarly negligible impact on the regional culture. Even during the era of mass immigration to the United States in the late nineteenth and early twentieth centuries, comparatively few foreign arrivals settled below the Mason–Dixon line. According to scholar James A. Dunlevy, the relatively backward economy and strength of religious and ethnic prejudice created an "avoidance of the South syndrome."[5] Those immigrants that did find their way to the region – such as the Italians of New Orleans and the Chinese of the Mississippi Delta – may have complicated the color line but were too few in number to represent a serious threat to the southern racial order.

In contrast to the past, the South is now changing rapidly into a multiethnic society. Spurring this change has been the integration of the region into the modern global economy. New immigration and economic policies, such as the 1986 Immigration Reform and Control Act and the 1994 North American Free Trade Agreement, have facilitated increased labor migration from Latin America. The following selection from Raymond A. Mohl considers the current and future effects of these immigrants on the economic, cultural, and political life of the South. The arrival of Latin American and Asian immigrants is redefining the racial dynamics of a region long shaped by a binary division between black and white. Where race relations once set the South apart from the rest of the nation, it has now come to share the same issues associated with a multiethnic and multicultural society.

This reconfiguration of race relations is emblematic of the transformation of the American South over the last half century. A history of racism, violence, and poverty still casts a long shadow over the region. Yet few southerners who contemplated the future fifty years ago, whatever their hopes or fears, could have imagined the scale or speed of regional change. The forces that reshaped the South have come alternately from within – most conspicuously through the black freedom struggle – and without – especially through federal government reform and globalization. This latter factor will also have a profound future influence. Southern culture has historically been a synthesis of black and white folkways. The unprecedented influx of foreign migrants will create multiple new meanings of what it is to be a southerner in the twenty-first century.

NOTES

1. Richard S. Morris, *Bum Rap on America's Cities: The Real Causes of Urban Decay* (Englewood Cliffs: Prentice-Hall, 1980), p. 147.
2. Matthew D. Lassiter, *The Silent Majority: Suburban Politics in the Sunbelt South* (Princeton: Princeton University Press, 2006).

3. John Shelton Reed, *The Enduring South: Subcultural Persistence in Mass Society* (Lexington: Lexington Books, 1972).
4. New York: Times Books, 1996.
5. James A. Dunlevy, "Regional Preferences and Migrant Settlement: On the Avoidance of the South by Nineteenth-Century Immigrants," in Paul Uselding, ed., *Research in Economic History: A Research Annual* (Greenwich: JAI Press, 1982), pp. 217–51.

* * *

FURTHER READING

Black, Earle and Merle Black, *The Rise of Southern Republicans* (Cambridge, MA: Belknap Press of Harvard University Press, 2002).

Cobb, James C., *Redefining Southern Culture: Mind and Identity in the Modern South* (Athens: University of Georgia Press, 1999).

Fite, Gilbert C., *Cotton Fields No More: Southern Agriculture, 1865–1980* (Lexington: University Press of Kentucky, 1984).

Goldfield, David R., *Cotton Fields and Skyscrapers: Southern City and Region, 1607–1980* (Baton Rouge: Louisiana State University Press, 1982).

Grantham, Dewey W., *The South in Modern America: A Region at Odds* (New York: HarperCollins Publishers, 1995).

Horne, Jed, *Breach of Faith: Hurricane Katrina and the Near Death of a Great American City* (New York: Random House, 2006).

Lassiter, Matthew D., *The Silent Majority: Suburban Politics in the Sunbelt South* (Princeton: Princeton University Press, 2006).

Lassiter, Matthew D. and Joseph Crespino, eds., *The Myth of Southern Exceptionalism* (New York: Oxford University Press, 2010).

Lowndes, Joseph E., *From the New Deal to the New Right: Race and the Southern Origins of Modern Conservatism* (New Haven: Yale University Press, 2008).

Patterson, James T., *Brown v. Board of Education: A Civil Rights Milestone and Its Troubled Legacy* (New York: Oxford University Press, 2001).

Reed, John Shelton, *The Enduring South: Subcultural Persistence in Mass Society* (Chapel Hill: University of North Carolina Press, 1986 [orig. 1972]).

Shulman, Bruce J., *From Cotton Belt to Sunbelt: Federal Policy, Economic Development, and the Transformation of the South, 1938–1980* (New York: Oxford University Press, 1991).

* * *

Joseph Crespino

In Search of Another Country[†]

The fight over tax exemptions and private education in Mississippi reveals the strange intersection of racial and religious politics in the Deep South by the 1980s. From one angle, the fight for tax exemptions for religious schools seems like another chapter in a long history of segregationist subterfuge.

[. . .]

Southern segregationists who used religious associations to try to protect private, white-flight schools from government regulation carried on in this tradition. Civil rights activists argued that the church schools of the 1970s were mere extensions of the segregation academies of the previous decade.

[. . .]

Church school defenders . . . however, saw themselves not as the bearers of an earlier fight for Jim Crow but as pioneers in an effort to protect fundamental American rights of religious freedom.

[. . .]

Not all church school defenders fit the caricatured image of racist, rural, fundamentalist Christians. They were, in some cases, successful white-collar professionals, the children of segregated small towns who were moving in large numbers to growing metropolitan areas where they joined newly expanding Protestant evangelical churches.

[. . .]

Before 1964, private schools in Mississippi were scarce.

[. . .]

The growth of private schools began sluggishly after 1964; growth was slow because school desegregation was slow.

[. . .]

[†]Joseph Crespino, *In Search of Another Country: Mississippi and the Conservative Counterrevolution* (Princeton and Oxford: Princeton University Press, 2007), pp. 239–40, 245, 247–9, 253–6, 261–3, 265.

The real turning point came with two landmark decisions by the Supreme Court in the late 1960s. *Green v. New Kent County* (1968) undermined the use of freedom-of-choice desegregation plans – the preferred method of recalcitrant southern school districts – and *Alexander v. Holmes County* (1969) called for an immediate end to segregation in thirty-three Mississippi school districts.

[. . .]

By September 1970, the number of private non-Catholic schools had increased to 155, with an estimated enrollment of 42,000 students, virtually all of whom were white.

These new schools were private in name only.

[. . .]

By 1969, a total of 6,130 students attending fifty-two private schools benefited from state tuition grants.

[. . .]

The impact of the private school movement on public schools in Mississippi was clear: the growth of segregation academies drained financial and human resources from a public school system that was already hard-pressed for both.

[. . .]

But fears that whites across the state would abandon the public schools en masse were never realized. White enrollment in private schools statewide peaked in the 1971–72 school year at 18.9 percent. Private schools would continue to crop up in Mississippi in the 1970s and 1980s, and they continued to appeal almost exclusively to whites, but those that did were often more explicitly religious in their orientation, and they appeared not as re-creations of local public schools but as smaller, religious-oriented supplements to them.

[. . .]

In the 1970s . . . new private schools in the South were organized increasingly as Christian schools. Sponsored by evangelical churches and located in suburbs or metropolitan areas, these schools had a curriculum heavily influenced by conservative, evangelical theology.

[. . .]

Church school defenders . . . argued that while many of the schools were founded coincident with public school desegregation, church schools had their true origins in a broader set of conservative social and religious beliefs.

[. . .]

They argued instead that in their schools racism was negligible compared with the broader disenchantment with a liberal, secular culture that rejected the traditional values that had long sustained family and community life in the United States.

[. . .]

In May 1978, an investigation by the U.S. Commission on Civil Rights determined that at least seven private academies in Mississippi that had been cited by the federal court as having a discriminatory admissions policy were still tax-exempt.

[. . .]

[U]nder the 1978 guidelines, schools not only had to have minority students enrolled but also needed a "significant" number of minority students . . . [T]he IRS defined an insignificant minority enrollment as one where the proportion of minority students was less than 20 percent of the percentage of the minority school-age population in the community served by the school.

[. . .]

Church school defenders fastened on the formula as evidence that federal bureaucrats were creating racial quotas that threatened church schools.

[. . .]

More than 120,000 letters flooded the IRS in protest of the new guidelines. The response was, by one official's estimation, "more than we've ever received on any other proposal." Some 400,000 more protest letters were sent to members of Congress.

The tumult over the new procedures led the IRS to hold four days of contentious hearings in Washington. The furor was fueled as much by Christian conservatives as by southern segregationists, though distinguishing between the two was not always easy.

[. . .]

The specter of the secular government "persecuting" Bible-believing Christians motivated fundamentalist and evangelical Christians like few other issues.

[. . .]

Conservatives in Congress were eager to build on the grassroots reaction against the new IRS guidelines.

[. . .]

The private school controversy also figured prominently in presidential politics.

[. . .]

In January 1980, Ronald Reagan gave a speech before a cheering crowd of more than six thousand students and faculty at Bob Jones University, a fundamentalist Christian school still involved in a suit against the IRS after having had its tax exemptions revoked because of racially discriminatory practices.

[. . .]

"You do not alter the evil character of racial quotas simply by changing the color of the beneficiary." He received three standing ovations and was interrupted by applause some fourteen times.

[. . .]

[I]n January 1982, the Reagan administration revoked the eleven-year-old practice of denying tax exemptions to segregated private schools and abandoned its case against Bob Jones University and Goldsboro Christian Schools.

[. . .]

The decision opened the door to the reinstatement of some 111 private schools that the IRS had listed as ineligible for tax deductions because of their discriminatory practices[.]

[. . .]

On May 24, 1983, the Supreme Court . . . determined that the IRS was justified in denying tax exemptions to private schools that discriminated against African Americans. The Court ruled that the national interest in eradicating racial discrimination in education "substantially outweighs whatever burden denial of tax benefits places on petitioners' exercise of their religious beliefs."

[. . .]

The church schools controversy in Mississippi shows both the continuities and the discontinuities in conservative white politics in the state by 1980. Some segregationists who in the 1960s fought to preserve white supremacy against what they saw as an invasive and meddling federal government continued that fight through the private school movement well into the 1980s. But the argument that all private school supporters in Mississippi were carrying on essentially the same fight that had sustained the generation of massive resistance fails to appreciate both the complex social and religious context in which some of these church schools emerged as well as the multiplicity of sources for modern conservative politics in the Deep South.

☙ ☙ ☙

John Egerton

The Americanization of Dixie[†]

Industrial growth is setting new records in virtually every Southern state.

[. . .]

The South's industry is constantly diversifying. It is not just food products, wood and paper products, textiles, and tobacco, as in the past, but also petrochemical products, electronics and aerospace facilities, and major financial institutions. And the region's airports, its seaports, its interstate highways, and its railroads are moving goods and supplies and people as never before.

[. . .]

A burgeoning new middle class, laden with the largess of an affluent society, clogs the highways and airports, bound for weekends in the mountains, summers on the seashore, Saturdays and Sundays in the stadiums[.]

[. . .]

The free-enterprise system, with a benevolent boost from government and the ironic stimulus of the war in Southeast Asia, has brought economic boom time to the American South, and almost everyone who is benefiting from it seems more preoccupied with the profits to be made than with the price to be paid.

Yet in the midst of all this growth and consumption, some troublesome questions intrude: what about all the people who are not sharing in the South's newfound

---

[†]John Egerton, *The Americanization of Dixie: The Southernization of America* (New York: Harper & Row, 1974), pp. 105–6, 168–9, 175–6, 198–207.

affluence – who are, in fact, becoming further removed and separated from it? And what about the people who *are* getting theirs – what does the sudden availability of wealth and affluence do to people's values?

[. . .]

In the biggest Southern cities, runaway growth has already propelled them to the point where they resemble the giant American metropolis in almost every particular. Houston and Dallas and Atlanta sweep and sprawl in every direction, consuming countryside like a prairie fire[.]

[. . .]

[I]n America, where the motto might well be "Grow or Die," urbanization is unavoidable, irresistible, unstoppable, inevitable. It may also be uncontrollable.

[. . .]

Southern cities are favorably different from their counterparts elsewhere: the region as a whole is still less metropolitan than other sections, its cities are comparatively smaller, they have less heavy industry, they are less decayed and deserted at the core, they have a thinner bureaucratic overlay, they are less densely populated, they are on the whole younger. These advantages are being eroded, says [Joel] Fleishman [of Duke University], by two powerful national trends: the suburbanization of people (mostly whites) and jobs, and the ghettoization of racial minorities and the poor in the central cities.

[. . .]

The South still has a little time, he says, and it still has an element of choice. How much time?

[. . .]

[T]he South is . . . not a cultural wasteland. For good and ill, it resembles the rest of America more and more with each passing year. There is developing an increasingly dominant and singular American culture, overlaying myriads of subcultures that struggle constantly for their identity and survival. The subcultures are like the people who comprise them – new ones are born of purposeful union or accidental conjugation, old ones die of neglect or old age. Any examination of elements of the larger culture, or of some of the smaller ones, is apt to show how powerful the process of Americanization has become – and Southern contributions to that process are by no means lacking.

[. . .]

The vessels in which culture is created and transmitted and homogenized grow and multiply like hothouse tomatoes. Disney World, the Southern version of Disneyland, is predictably bigger, costlier, and more fantastic than its parent, a monument to gargantuan artificiality, and its imitators sprout everywhere. One of Disney World's neighbors near Orlando, Florida, will be Bible World, a sort of prefabricated New Jerusalem that will feature a walled city, a six-story mosque, museums, shops, acres of parking spaces, an Easter "Passion Week Panorama," and "the only minaret in the Western hemisphere." Fred C. Tallant, president of a land development company with holdings in Georgia and Florida, says Bible World "will be designed for everyone," and its purpose will be to "inform, entertain and inspire." Tallant, who comes from a Baptist family but describes himself as being not particularly religious, says he and a group of religious Atlanta businessmen hope to make a million dollars in profits from Bible World after its first year of operation.

Movies are another medium shaping cultural styles and patterns, and the trends there, reflected in every region of the country, are now dominated by a mixed bag of black films, by hard-core pornography, and by ever more explicit and sophisticated presentations of violence. The moneymakers are films like *The Godfather, A Clockwork Orange, Straw Dogs, Oh, Calcutta!, Shaft, Super Fly,* and *Deep Throat,* and most of them have enjoyed long runs not only in New York and Los Angeles but in the cities of the Midwest and South[.]

[. . .]

As the single most widely used instrument for the continuing education of adults – and for the initiation of children into society – television molds the culture and values and life styles of Americans more than any other thing. And that shaping process is more or less the same everywhere, for the ubiquitous TV screen glows in almost every mansion, apartment, cottage, and cotton-field hovel, and its lights and shadows look the same in New York City and Des Moines and Albuquerque and Holly Springs, Mississippi.

[. . .]

The South's obeisance to provincialism and piety – the mindset that long kept Prohibition in force, blue laws on the books, *Catcher in the Rye* out of the libraries, and New York magazines off the newsstands – is rapidly eroding. *Jesus Christ Superstar* has packed theaters all over the South, and *Hair* is everywhere; the largest work of art ever created by the late and renowned Pablo Picasso – a 100-foot sculpture entitled *Bust of a Woman* – is being erected at the University of South Florida in Tampa; and *Rolling Stone* gathers no moss among its avid following in the South.

The cultural rites of white Anglo-Saxon Protestants still dominate, but you can find Mexican influences all over Texas, African and Afro-American cultural festivals on dozens of college campuses, a Chinese New Year's parade in Nashville, and a Brazilian Carioca Carnival in Miami, where the Spanish-speaking population now numbers a half-million.

[. . .]

Even Mississippi has relaxed its border guard: a delegation of Soviet Communist party members visiting Greenville in 1972 was so charmed by Southern hospitality that they chose that Mississippi delta community as their favorite American city. "Here we feel absolutely at home," their leader said.

The magnolia curtain that used to shield the South from cultural breezes is pinned back now, and all sorts of once exotic influences are floating in.

[. . .]

The diversity is welcome; certainly it is better to have variety, however mixed its quality may be, than to have a closed and conforming society that regards every stranger as an intruder. But exhilaration would be too strong a response to it all. What is happening to mass culture in the South is what is happening nationwide, and if there is diversity in it, there is also an element of sameness, of homogenization, of artificiality and shallowness and transience.

And finally, there is music. In the perpetuation and diffusion of the many strains of Southern culture, no other instrument carries more force and vitality. The South has been the incubator for most of the indigenous elements in the treasury of American music. It produced jazz and blues and all of their derivations; it spawned country-and-western music, bluegrass, gospel, spirituals; it was a source of rock 'n' roll, and it has contributed its share of pop and folk and contemporary rock.

[. . .]

And country music, Southern to the core, is warmed by the echoes of ringing applause and ringing cash registers, not only at the Grand Ole Opry in Nashville but on the West coast, the East coast, the vast reaches in between[.]

[. . .]

As it has risen in popularity and spread across the country, country music has been modified by new performers, new audiences, and new instruments.

[. . .]

The lines that separate country from pop and rock are not always clearly drawn, and as country goes more and more to the city, there is about it a little less twang and a little more slickness.

392

[. . .]

One of the most distinctive things about country music has been the closeness that has existed between the pickers and singers and their audiences. They have shared an intimacy in the music because they also shared a personal knowledge of the experiences it described – poverty and loneliness and all the rest. How much of that intimacy, that authenticity, can be retained when the music goes uptown? When the artists leave the country, when poverty becomes an abstraction in a forgotten past, when the stars live in mansions and drive Cadillacs and belong to the country club – when they are no longer having the experiences they have always sung about – what will it do to the music? And when it is being packaged on Madison Avenue as "all-American music," will it still be country?

ৡ ৡ ৡ

W. Fitzhugh Brundage

The Southern Past[†]

[T]imeworn controversies still have the capacity to reopen wounds.

[. . .]

The stakes are clear to large numbers of southerners, white and black, who agree about perhaps only one thing: the continuing relevance of history for the contemporary South.

[. . .]

Controversy, of course, is not new. From the first celebrations of Emancipation Day to the present, white and black southerners have labored to advance and enshrine their preferred interpretations of the region's history. Contemporary disputes are continuations of this long-established struggle over the control and meaning of the South's past. Yet significant changes, especially in the relative power of the participants, are evident in present-day contests. Defenders of white southern historical narratives are now challenged by southerners whose competing claims are accorded greater respect than at any time in the region's past. Historical insurgents have political influence and financial resources that command the atten-tion of public officials. As a result, the recalled past that prevails in the South's schools, museums, and civic spaces is under broader revision than at any time

---

[†]W. Fitzhugh Brundage, *The Southern Past: A Clash of Race and Memory* (Cambridge, MA: Harvard University Press, 2008), pp. 272–84, 291, 293, 297–9, 301–3, 305–6, 310–12.

since the Civil War. What once were exclusive and enduring preserves of white memory now increasingly acknowledge a past they had, for so long, both ignored and suppressed.

Desegregation necessarily raised questions about the symbolic content of previously segregated spaces in the South.

[. . .]

When school desegregation finally occurred, it transformed the cultural resources that southerners, both white and black, had fashioned over the previous century.

[. . .]

The unforeseen consequences of merging thousands of schools, tens of thousands of educators, and millions of students were inevitably jarring. Some hardships, however, were the result of conscious design. Once integration became inevitable, white educators and politicians were intent on controlling the process and ensuring that blacks bore the heaviest costs. And, without question, they did.

[. . .]

A 1970 study estimated that integration had resulted in the termination of more than 31,000 black teachers and principals.

[. . .]

Black teachers who weathered the purges that followed integration often faced organized discrimination, especially de facto demotion.

[. . .]

A black teacher whose competence was English, for instance, might be assigned to teach math in an integrated school and then would be dismissed for incompetence in her new subject. And even when qualified black teachers were not fired or driven to retirement, they often were transferred to majority white schools, leaving less competent white teachers to fill their former assignments.

[. . .]

The trauma of integration was compounded by the closing of black schools. As repositories of community lore and pride, black schools were civic spaces whose importance far exceeded their function of teaching children. But with integration, the costly duplication of infrastructure necessitated by segregated school systems became untenable. Because whites were unwilling to integrate into majority black schools, black students typically were transferred to "unitary," majority white schools. The "surplus" schools in black neighborhoods were then closed or converted to administrative facilities. In either case, they no longer served black communities, and their traditions, lore, and spirit expired.

[. . .]

Protests by black students and parents during the early 1970s slowed but could not halt school consolidation. In scattered counties across the South, organized campaigns against school closings and teacher firings demonstrated the depth of black ambivalence toward desegregation.

[. . .]

Desegregation uprooted in particular the tradition of black history in public schools that had been nurtured by Carter Woodson, Luther P. Jackson, and countless other activists since the 1920s. Each time a black history teacher retired rather than accept a demeaning reassignment, and each time a black school closed, traditions and public spaces that had sustained Negro History Week were lost.

[. . .]

Controversies flared, sparking protests, boycotts, and even violence at schools across the region . . . In Portsmouth, Virginia, where black students were already anxious over a proposal to turn a historically black high school into a vocational school, the cancellation of a Black History Week assembly sparked a massive demonstration. After police used dogs and physical force to disperse protesters, the school superintendent suspended more than eight hundred students.

[. . .]

A particular point of friction was the continued use of objectionable textbooks and lesson plans in the South's public schools.

[. . .]

Revision of texts and curricula, nevertheless, was slow to come about. Throughout the 1960s publishers continued to sell to southern schools "segregation" editions – which typically included few pictures of blacks and avoided sensitive topics in southern history – while supplying so-called integrated books elsewhere.

[. . .]

Organized opposition to the texts was a direct outgrowth of black political empowerment. As one critic of the texts pointed out, "There were few public attacks [on] history textbooks so long as the ideals they represented remained dominant." But the destruction of segregation had changed everything; "What used to be good politics has become bad politics."

[. . .]

Another notable transformation in curricula was the introduction of Black History Week ceremonies into the calendars of all schools.

[. . .]

However unfavorably these integrated celebrations may have compared to the ceremonies previously staged by all-black schools, they perpetuated the tradition and familiarized white students with a record of black historical accomplishments.

[. . .]

Opinion polls measured changed attitudes about integrated education among whites; in the early 1960s a large majority of white southerners opposed integrated schools, but by 1970 only 16 percent did. Even the tense controversies over curricula had the salutary effect of hastening negotiation between whites and blacks over the content of their children's education. Blacks may have borne the heaviest costs of school integration, but at least at the end of the 1970s there was cause to hope that the region's schools might become a crucible for racial reconciliation.

[. . .]

Since the 1960s a broad and momentous shift in interpretation has transformed many southern museums, finally loosening the grip of whites on these important repositories of historical memory.

[. . .]

Revision of exhibits that unabashedly defended white supremacy, glorified the Confederacy, or celebrated the antebellum South was probably inevitable after desegregation began. Even so, reinterpretation at most sites came about slowly and unevenly.

[. . .]

Infused with a belief that a museum should be a provocative and "liberating force," the still largely white staffs at a few southern museums began to revise their programs during the late 1970s.

[. . .]

The Museum of the Confederacy in Richmond emerged as another center of revisionist interpretation during the 1970s. Founded in the late nineteenth century as a Confederate reliquary by elite white women, the museum was an unlikely site for new approaches to the history of the antebellum South and the Confederacy. Even so, in 1969 the museum's board signaled its intention to transform the site from a shrine by voting to change the Confederate Museum's name to the Museum of the Confederacy.

[. . .]

In 1978, the appointment as executive director of Edward D. C. "Kip" Campbell, who had earned a Ph.D. in history, accelerated the changes under way at the museum.

[. . .]

[T]he staff began planning more ambitious and innovative exhibitions in the early 1980s, culminating in "Before Freedom Came," which opened in 1991, and "A Woman's War," which debuted in 1996. That one of the first comprehensive American exhibits devoted to slavery, complete with leg irons and an 1863 photograph of the whip-scarred back of a slave, was staged next door to the White House of the Confederacy, where Jefferson Davis had lived during the Civil War, surprised many observers and garnered national acclaim. The exhibit underscored not only that slavery was "a key aspect of secession, the creation of the Confederacy and the Civil War," but also that the museum was committed to a far broader and more inclusive mission than its founders could have imagined or would have condoned.

[. . .]

[M]useums devoted to African American history were slow to emerge.

[. . .]

Not surprisingly, the [civil rights] movement became the focus for the museums. These museums, including the National Civil Rights Museum in Memphis (1991), the Birmingham Civil Rights Institute (1992), the National Voting Rights Museum in Selma (1992), the Ralph Mark Gilbert Civil Rights Museum in Savannah (1996), and the Albany (Georgia) Civil Rights Museum (1998), were self-conscious efforts to institutionalize the links that both social historians and movement activists saw among historical awareness, black identity, and social change in the South.

Without the consolidation of black political power in many southern cities, the proliferation of new museums devoted to black history would have been unlikely. In Memphis, the city's powerful black political leadership, which had emerged during the 1970s, provided crucial allies for the Memphis activists who bought the decrepit Lorraine Motel, the site of Martin Luther King Jr.'s assassination, at a bankruptcy auction in 1982.

[. . .]

Beyond using new exhibit techniques to engage the largest possible audience, the civil rights museums explicitly promoted historical awareness as an agent of social change. In the eyes of their founders, the civil rights museums are continuations of the movement for racial justice. The Martin Luther King Jr. Center for Nonviolent Social Change in Atlanta, founded by King's widow in 1968, was an archetype for this fusion of shrine, interpretative site, and laboratory of social change. The overt insistence on the continuing relevance of the history presented in these museums may be explained partially by their comparatively contemporary subject matter. Exhibits that draw connections between the events of the 1960s and present-day America hardly seemed forced. Yet the civil rights museums go further and attempt to inspire visitors to activism. A panel in the final exhibit space at the Memphis museum proclaims, "We must remember our past and learn from it . . . The struggle will continue, with determination and courage." Outreach programs offered by the museum aim to "teach people their role and their responsibility today."

[. . .]

This reformist orientation extends to the museums' relationship to their immediate urban surroundings. Advocates for the museums predicted that they would stimulate tourism, which in turn would resuscitate the decayed black neighborhoods in which they were located.

[. . .]

These sometimes rosy predictions may have been intended to convince skeptical taxpayers of the worthiness of public subsidies for the museums. But also at work was the belief that an awareness of black history was a prerequisite for any campaign to address the contemporary needs and concerns of African Americans.

[. . .]

For white politicians eager to put the tumult and recriminations of the civil rights struggle behind them, the promotion of "heritage" tourism was of a piece with their efforts to publicize the "New" Sunbelt South. They pointed to the commercialization of black history as a gesture of reconciliation and progress.

[. . .]

Unable to boast any nationally known tourist destinations, Alabama's promoters instead elevated "the darker side of Alabama's past" as one of the state's most marketable assets. Notorious sites in the civil rights struggle, such as the Edmund Pettus Bridge in Selma and the Sixteenth Street Baptist Church in Birmingham, now were officially promoted as tourist destinations.

[. . .]

Tourism promoters elsewhere were slow to follow Alabama's lead. But by the 1990s they could no longer afford to ignore black tourism. Survey data, which revealed that blacks spend more money than other tourists, caught the eye of public officials eager to use tourism to revitalize depressed communities across the South's hinterland.

[. . .]

Beyond profits, boosters promise that black heritage tourism will hasten racial reconciliation.

[. . .]

In the words of a tour guide at a faux plantation home in Greenville, Mississippi . . . [h]eritage tourism has a crucial role to play in a region haunted by its past. "Some parts of it [our history] we're not so proud of, but come see it and let's understand it. And let's hold hands and move on."

ৡ ৡ ৡ

Raymond A. Mohl

Globalization, Latinization, and the *Nuevo* New South[†]

Dixie is experiencing a dramatic demographic, economic, and cultural transformation. These transformations have resulted from two patterns of powerful change

[†]Raymond A. Mohl, "Globalization, Latinization, and the *Nuevo* New South," in Pippa Holloway, ed., *Other Souths: Diversity & Difference in the U.S. South, Reconstruction to Present* (Athens and London: University of Georgia Press, 2008), pp. 409–18, 420–4, 426–30.

that are connected and that have coincided in the state of Alabama and in the South generally. Major shifts in the global economy have produced new forms of both deindustrialization and economic investment. New free trade policies such as the 1994 North American Free Trade Agreement (NAFTA) have encouraged the migration of capital and labor. A restructuring of regional, national, and global economies has undermined older forms of production in the South, such as in agriculture, steel, textiles, and apparel. At the same time, new economic investment has poured into the region as American and foreign capital seeks cheap labor, new markets, and government incentives. The region's new economy features foreign-owned auto plants in Tennessee, Kentucky, Alabama, Mississippi, and South Carolina; high-tech research and manufacturing in Atlanta, Austin, Huntsville, and North Carolina's Research Triangle Park; biomedical research in Birmingham and other major medical centers; and the new food processing plants for poultry, hogs, and seafood that have sprung up all over the rural South. In the past decade, about half of all poultry processing has come to be concentrated in four low-wage, antiunion southern states – Alabama, Arkansas, Georgia, and North Carolina. In addition, rapid population growth in southern states and Sun Belt cities has created an immense service economy and a consequent demand for low-wage labor.

Global economic change has also created new transnational labor migration patterns.

[. . .]

Economic crisis in Mexico in the early 1980s brought to power a new government that promoted free market economic policies. This new economic program encouraged global trade and investment in Mexico, especially American trade and investment, but it did little to improve the economic situation of most Mexicans. These changes coincided with new American immigration policy, primarily the 1986 Immigration Reform and Control Act (IRCA), which beefed up border controls and imposed tough new sanctions on employers who willfully hired undocumented immigrants. Because of worsening economic conditions in Mexico and despite the new American immigration law, Mexicans continued to seek work and higher wages in the United States. However, as sociologist Douglas S. Massey and colleagues have noted, the new border controls eventually "diverted the migratory flows away from traditional points of destination," such as California, thus transforming Mexican immigration "from a regional into a national phenomenon." The same forces encouraged undocumented workers to stay longer, or even permanently, to avoid the now more difficult border crossings that had been more easily managed in earlier years.

IRCA influenced labor migration flows in other ways, as well. Under pressure from big agricultural interests and proimmigrant groups, Congress added an amnesty provision to IRCA, legalizing 2.3 million Mexicans who could document at least five years of work and residence in the United States. Those amnestied subsequently had full labor rights and the freedom to move within the country in search of better opportunities. They also gained the right to bring family members from Mexico, potentially as many as 9.2 million additional Mexican migrants. In addition, IRCA policies eventually encouraged amnestied Mexicans and their families to seek citizenship – an outcome speeded by Mexican legislation in the late 1990s permitting dual U.S.–Mexican citizenship. IRCA's amnesty provisions suggested the contradictions in American immigration policy, seeking to curb illegal Mexican migration while simultaneously granting permanent residency to millions. The surge of Hispanic migration to the South coincided with the new immigration provisions introduced by IRCA, as both illegal and amnestied Mexicans found new labor markets in the Southeast.

[. . .]

Taken together, the globalization of markets and capital *and* new American immigration policy diversified the migratory flows of Mexican labor. Within a few years of passage of IRCA, for example, hiring of legal and illegal Hispanic workers had become "a cornerstone of changing labor relations" in southern poultry processing plants. Hispanic labor flows to the South intensified in the wake of NAFTA, which failed to produce promised wage increases in Mexico and fostered further immigration

[. . .]

New immigration has fueled the South's changing economy, but it has had other consequences, too. Black and white once defined the racial landscape of the American South, but multicultural and multiethnic rather than biracial now describe society in many southern places. As one Alabama editorialist noted in 2000, "Life in the South used to be defined in shades of black and white. But a growing wave of Hispanic immigrants is adding brown to that color scheme."

[. . .]

The seemingly permanent Hispanic influx to the South, a *Washington Post* reporter suggested in 2000, has been "changing forever the old idea of what a southerner is."

[. . .]

In the 1990s, new and different migration streams deposited Latin newcomers all over the southern United States. Texas and Florida continued to attract Hispanics in substantial numbers, but in virtually *every* other southern state the Hispanic growth rate surpassed the national growth rate in Hispanic population by three, four, five or six times.

[. . .]

During the 1990s, for example, the Hispanic population surged nationally by a hefty 61.2 percent, rising from 22.4 million in 1990 to 35.3 million in 2000.

[. . .]

[R]ecent Latino migration to the South has been even more dramatic. The most startling example is that of North Carolina, where the census recorded a sizzling 394 percent growth rate for Hispanics in the 1990s. The decennial growth rate was similarly very high in other southern states: 337 percent in Arkansas, 300 percent in Georgia, 278 percent in Tennessee, 212 percent in South Carolina, 208 percent in Alabama, and by lesser but still substantial amounts in other southern states. Aside from Texas and Florida, the Hispanic population in southern states in 2000 ranged from a low of 39,500 in Mississippi to a high of 435,000 in Georgia. Virginia, with almost 330,000 Hispanics, and North Carolina, with 379,000, also ranked high on the list. Overall, the 2000 census revealed a decennial increase of almost 4.6 million Hispanics in the South, bringing the total Hispanic population of twelve southern states to a little over 11 million.

[. . .]

Many recent Hispanic migrants to the South have settled in small towns and rural areas for agricultural and poultry work. But large numbers of newcomers have chosen urban destinations as well. Metro Atlanta, with 269,000 Hispanics in 2000, provides the most startling example of this pattern of urban migration.

[. . .]

The 2000 census also provided a better sense of Hispanic diversity in the South. The census broke down the Hispanic population into four major categories: Mexican, Puerto Rican, Cuban, and "Other Hispanic or Latino[.]"

[. . .]

[W]ith the exception of Texas and Arkansas, where the proportions of Mexicans surpass 70 percent of all Hispanics, in no southern state do Mexicans exceed about two-thirds of all Hispanics, and in some states the Mexican proportion is quite low: 30 percent in Louisiana, 22.4 percent in Virginia, and 13.6 percent in Florida.

[. . .]

Census statistics reveal only part of the Hispanic migration story, however. Actual Hispanic population counts are much higher, perhaps as much as twice as high in many southern cities, counties, and states, according to local sources.

[. . .]

The Census Bureau, in fact, has routinely undercounted minorities, including new immigrants, many of whom are undocumented and thus avoid any contact with government agencies.

[. . .]

As with other immigrants in past eras, the initial Hispanic newcomers were primarily young, single men who shared cramped housing, worked in teams or crews, and sent earnings to families back home.

[. . .]

Through a familiar process of chain migration, homeland relatives, neighbors, and friends joined compadres.

[. . .]

Mexicans, especially, returned home often, eventually bringing wives, children, and even aging parents to the United States. They began putting down more permanent roots, sending children to American schools, and buying homes and property.

[. . .]

Hispanics in the rural and urban South have become an important component in the region's low-wage, low-skill economy, especially in manufacturing, construction, agriculture, and food processing. They work mostly for minimal pay, often under difficult and dangerous working conditions, especially in poultry and meat processing plants.

[. . .]

Given these circumstances, labor union organizers have targeted new Hispanic immigrants in an effort to revive union activism in the traditionally antiunion South.

[. . .]

Union organizers in the Hispanic South have not had much success. At the Smithfield plant in Tar Heel, organizers from the United Food and Commercial Workers Union recruited Hispanic workers during a collective bargaining election in 1997. Fearing that unionization would bring unwanted attention to their illegal immigration status, most Hispanics voted against the idea, and the union went down in defeat by a two-to-one vote.

[. . .]

Black spokespersons and some scholars have argued that Hispanics have displaced black workers and kept wages low for all workers. As early as 1979, *Ebony* magazine complained that undocumented Mexican immigrants in southern agricultural states such as Florida and North Carolina posed "a big threat to black workers." In many southern places, Hispanics now fill the jobs that used to be held by blacks. Employers' seeming preference for Hispanic workers, often praised as being more compliant and having a strong work ethic, has rankled black communities across the South. Similarly, in many parts of the urban South, Hispanics have been settling in traditionally black neighborhoods where rents seem more reasonable. Not surprisingly, black resentment about job competition and unwelcome neighbors has surfaced in the urban and rural South.

[. . .]

Many immigration scholars, however, reject the wage-competition argument. They contend that the new Latino immigrants are filling jobs that no one else wants. Job turnover in the fields and in food processing plants has been extremely high, they contend, as much as 100 percent a year in some industries. Hispanics, they say, are filling "replacement" jobs abandoned by black workers who have rejected low pay and excessively demanding work.

[. . .]

Whatever the reality, blacks and Hispanics have been at odds over jobs, neighborhoods, and cultural differences for almost a decade. In some places, emerging hostility has led to open conflict and black-on-Hispanic violence. In other places, civic leaders, union organizers, and advocacy groups have sought to mediate emerging ethnic and racial conflicts. In North Carolina, groups such as Black Workers for Justice and the Latino Workers Association created an African-American/Latino Alliance to find common ground among blacks and Hispanics.

[. . .]

Nevertheless, as a consequence of recent Hispanic migration, new patterns of racial and ethnic conflict linger unresolved throughout the South.

[. . .]

Not surprisingly, given their often tenuous immigration status, low incomes, language difficulties, and cultural differences, Hispanics in the South have experienced adjustment problems. However, churches, schools, libraries, and public agencies have responded in positive ways to the new immigrants. The Catholic Church and numerous Protestant denominations have embraced the newcomers, offering Spanish-language religious services, English classes, employment assistance, and varied social services. Migrant Head Start programs in many southern communities provide educational and nutritional benefits to the children of migrant farmworkers. Public schools in small towns and large cities are struggling to provide ESL classes to a growing number of Latino children. Public health agencies are confronting serious problems in serving a new population without proper immunizations and mostly without health insurance. Medical providers, police, and emergency management personnel are getting training in Spanish. The League of United Latin American Citizens now has state directors in several southern states. Various public and private nonprofit groups have also organized to serve and advocate for new Latino southerners[.]

[. . .]

While many agencies and groups have responded positively to the South's Hispanic newcomers, a more hostile response has also become evident in some places.

[. . .]

Anti-immigrant hostility . . . flared up in nearby Cullman, Alabama. Almost 99 percent white, Cullman County had fewer than one thousand Hispanics in 1999, according to U.S. Census estimates. That was too many for some people. In January 1998, after an immigration protest meeting, three men were arrested for burning the Mexican flag, as well as flags of the United Nations and the Communist party.

[. . .]

The new American nativism has not deterred Hispanics from seeking a new and better life in the American South. Like other immigrants to the United States in earlier times, they have found strength in their communal activities and cultural heritage. They have quickly created a vibrant cultural life based on homeland foodways, kinship activities, and musical traditions – a cultural life centered not just in the home but in hundreds of restaurants, grocery stores, music and dance clubs, and in traditional holiday festivals. Mexican national holidays and important religious events become occasions to celebrate ethnic culture. Customary religious practice, such as universal veneration of the Mexican national patron saint, the Virgin of Guadalupe, has sustained cultural persistence.

[. . .]

The South's growing Hispanic population has important political implications.

[. . .]

The 2002 election provided a preview of that future, as three Hispanic candidates – two Democrats and one Republican – were elected to the Georgia legislature from metro Atlanta districts. Equally important, both parties scrambled for votes among Georgia's Hispanics, who are considered liberal on social issues but conservative on economic matters.

[. . .]

[T]he recent success of Hispanic candidates in Georgia signals the arrival of a new political force in the South – one that will only strengthen over time as the citizenship process inevitably produces more Hispanic voters.

[. . .]

COPYRIGHT ACKNOWLEDGMENTS